Basic Police Powers
ARREST AND SEARCH PROCEDURES

FOURTH EDITION

Gino Arcaro

emond

Toronto, Canada
2009

Emond Montgomery Publications Limited
60 Shaftesbury Avenue
Toronto ON M4T 1A3
http://www.emond.ca/highered

Printed in Canada.
Reprinted December 2016.

We acknowledge the financial support of the Government of Canada.
Nous reconnaissons l'appui financier du gouvernement du Canada.   Canadä

Acquisitions and developmental editor: Tammy Scherer
Editorial assistant: Nick Raymond
Supervising editor: Jim Lyons
Copy editor: Jamie Bush
Production editor and proofreader: Debbie Gervais
Text designer: Tara Wells
Indexer: Paula Pike
Cover designer: John Vegter

Library and Archives Canada Cataloguing in Publication

Arcaro, Gino, 1957-
    Basic police powers : arrest and search procedures / Gino Arcaro. — 4th ed.

Includes index.
ISBN 978-1-55239-288-1

    1. Police—Canada.   2. Criminal procedure—Canada.   I. Title.
HV7936.R53A73 2008   345.71'052   C2008-904662-5

Contents

CHAPTER 8   Location of Arrest: Feeney Warrants

CHAPTER 9 Making the Arrest: Use of Force and Preventing Charter Violations

CHAPTER 10 Use of Force: Sections 25–43 Criminal Code

Chapter 11 Release Provisions: Post-Custody Detention

CHAPTER 12   Release Provisions

CHAPTER 13   Charging an Offender and Use of Discretion

CHAPTER 14   Search and Seizure, Part 1: The Decision-Making Model

Chapter 15   Search and Seizure, Part 2: Consent

CHAPTER 16   Search and Seizure, Part 3: Search Warrants

Preface

THE 10 PERCENT DOCTRINE

The good news: this is an era of unprecedented police hiring. The bad news: there will likely be unprecedented numbers of applicants.

There are more police jobs available than ever before, but the competition will be tough. Research shows that approximately 10 percent of police applicants are successful. That amounts to a lot of jobs, but it also means that 90 percent of applicants are unsuccessful.

THE MYTH

Contrary to popular belief, no one is born to be a police officer.

But don't take that to mean that anyone can be a police officer. Many individuals can become police officers, through training and application. But not everyone can.

Police officers are developed, through proper mentoring. Here's the key point: Mentoring is a two-way street, between a mentor and a protegé. It is a special type of coaching. Mentoring may come from one person or from several people, as well as from the young officer's experiences; experience is a mentor.

The protegé has to play his or her part in being committed and making the right decisions. These decisions, in order of priority, are as follows.

1. *Make the right character decisions.* There are a number of competencies essential to your getting hired. None are more important than "good character." If you want to be hired as a police officer, you have to meet the legislative standard of strong moral character. You are not expected to achieve sainthood. But you *are* expected to demonstrate good character. Anyone can achieve this—it's shown through your decisions. Life is about choices. Having a good character is not a static condition. Character never stops developing. It can change at any moment during a lifetime.

   The police will not hire any person with a criminal record. They will not hire any one with habits that suggest bad character. They don't have to, because there are enough suitable candidates who have good character—people who abstain from alcohol abuse, drug abuse, gambling, and general irresponsibility.

2. *Develop the right attitude.* I conducted informal research in 2000 among recruiters from eight large police organizations. I asked them what was their number one reason for excluding applicants from the constable selection process. The number one reason was *arrogance.* That's not surprising, since arrogance in a candidate immediately turns off all police officers involved in the candidate interview or background investigation processes.

   Be humble. Humility is essential.

3. *Mens sana in corpore sano.* This Latin quotation means "a sound mind in a sound body."

There are four types of fitness that you have to show in order to get hired as a police officer: physical, intellectual, emotional, and psychological. Each of these is achieved through deliberate "reps." You have to practise; they don't just happen.

Real front-line policing involves potential violence. Policing always has and always will demand a high level of athleticism. You owe it to the profession. You owe it to the public. You owe it to your platoon and to the officers who need your back-up help. So get to the gym. Do manual labour. Run, lift, eat right. And once you are hired, you have no choice but to keep yourself in peak physical shape.

"Over 80" has a negative connotation in the context of drinking and driving, but it is a positive goal academically. Any police officer in training can achieve an academic goal of over 80 percent—no exceptions.

Get involved in life—that's the only way to get life experience. Get off the couch, and get away from the keyboard. Technology is great, but human interaction is the only way to gain true life experience.

Get a job. Play sports. Join a team. Join a group. Do as much community service as possible until you find some type of volunteer work that you can commit to on a long-term basis. Putting time into volunteer community service is essential to getting hired in policing. Why? It helps develop all essential police competencies. It develops *maturity* in a person—a key to getting hired. Maturity is a fundamental requirement for being selected as a constable. Community service is valuable *because the best way to improve yourself is to improve someone else.* Improving others is the best way to develop the 16 dimensions of maturation. Coach kids. Teach someone something. Share your expertise. You develop as a person by developing others.

Set big goals. Achieve big goals. Stretch yourself and extend your limits. You have to keep growing. Progress, or regress!

Each one of you controls your own destiny. There is no easy road. No one will hand it you. If you want it badly enough, you will work hard and succeed in getting hired.

VOLUME + SIMPLICITY + REALITY

The purpose of this book is to teach you, in the simplest language possible, how to effectively apply as many police authorities as possible.

Canadian laws are extensive and incredibly complex. Your education in this area will never end. You will learn from experienced community college teachers, from police college teachers, from coach officers, from veteran officers, and from practical experience (both your successes and your mistakes). Every novice officer makes mistakes. It's crucial to learn from every mistake and not get dejected when you make them. Mistakes are part of the growing and learning process.

THE PROFESSION

"Being a police officer is a privilege, not a right."

My boss at 33 Division, Niagara Regional Police, said this to me during one of the many occasions when I was hollered at for messing up one thing or another. In his song "Badlands" Bruce Springsteen (The Boss) is paying tribute to those who pay their dues in the anonymity and obscurity and daily struggle of front-line work. He reminds us that such work advances us and serves us well. He cautions impatient and power-hungry individuals to *learn* from and enjoy the tribulations of front-line work rather than resent it.

My boss was paying tribute to the uniform patrol branch, the front line of policing. He was reminding me to pay my dues before getting ambitious about becoming a detective; to *learn* from and enjoy the struggles of front-line police work.

Both bosses made sense—the front line is a place for learning.

Policing is arguably the most misunderstood of jobs, especially by those who aspire to work in it. A variety of factors blur and conceal the *realities* of policing and the hiring process. A healthy grasp of reality is vital for successful police work. Ignoring reality invites failure. So I offer the following *Immutable Realities of Policing* to those who are in or will be entering the police selection process:

1. "Situations which appear quite innocent, with no hostile demonstration by the person being arrested, can explode into violence, leaving the arresting officer *dead* or injured"—Alberta Court of Appeal, *R. v. Lerke* (1986). This is the most accurate, concise description of police reality that I have ever read. Policing is one of the few jobs where being murdered is an occupational hazard. It's a risky business, one that has to be taken seriously. It's not for the faint of heart. Unfortunately, this fact is inexplicitly lost on potential police recruits. The following two examples illustrate this:

    a. During mock interviews, students are asked, "What's the worst consequence that can happen in policing?" Their answers are commonly "losing a court case," "getting sued," or "getting fired." I have never heard the correct answer—"getting killed."

    b. While being interviewed by a radio talk show host about the recent murders of three police officers, I was asked if a problem existed. In response to my comments, a caller stated that she did not see a problem because it was "only three deaths." She said, "This is not like the United States." Shocking perception!

2. Policing should not be seen as an alternative to the academic challenges prerequisite to other careers. A parent recently told me that his son "screwed up" in high school and that he thought policing would therefore be a good career choice. The word "vocation" is derived from the Latin word *voca*, meaning "voice" or "calling." There should be a better reason to want to be a police officer than the misguided notion that academic success is not required.

3. You will not immediately get hired as a detective, undercover officer, SWAT team member, or chief of police. Everyone hired by a police organization is assigned to the uniform patrol branch. Everyone—no exceptions. Patrol officers represent the front line. That's where you learn real policing.

However, I have never heard any prospective candidate say, "I want to be a patrol officer." Everyone wants to be a specialist or a high-ranking officer, and they ask how the patrol branch can be avoided or bypassed. It can't. Getting promoted to a specialist branch or higher rank requires years of patrol experience in which you prove yourself by consistent performance. Goals will remain unrealized dreams without solid performance as a patrol officer.

4. The world distinguishes winners from losers. There is competition in real life. First, there is competition to get hired by a police force; they don't draft people the way the military does. Then, there is competition for advancement after being hired. Sometimes in the real world you won't get what you want the first time or even the second time. Sometimes it may take years. So don't despair if you don't get hired the first time. View it as an opportunity to get better. How you handle adversity and setbacks reveals who you really are.

5. Wearing a uniform will not make you special. A uniform cannot instill courage, intelligence, or morals. If you *need* to wear a uniform to feel bigger or more complete, do whatever it takes to rid yourself of that need. A police uniform is not intended to fill psychological voids and emptiness.

6. You will not save the world. Instead, you will solve problems—some minor, some major.

7. If your parents, teachers, or college coordinators scare you, wait until you meet *real* bad guys. Criminals will not care about your feelings, comfort, or self-esteem. They will not try to make your life easy. Some will be nasty— they may insult you, threaten to kill you and your family, and some may be violent toward you. The worst part is that there is no one to complain to if these things happen.

8. Your days as a front-line officer won't be stress-free. You will be sent to a bar fight or a domestic dispute where you will be required to think quickly, under pressure. You can't ask bad guys for more time to think about the matter when you are trying to figure out if you can arrest or search them. You can't ask to write a "make-up" case if you lose your court case. And you won't be given satisfaction surveys to express frustration about how much stress the bad guys are causing you.

9. Police forces are paramilitary organizations. A rookie's greeting an administrator with a "What's up?" or a "Hey, how's it going?" is not considered appropriate, and will not be tolerated. You'll have to get used to not being on a first-name basis with your bosses.

10. A strong bench press is not enough to succeed in policing. It helps, but there are countless other traits and skills needed.

11. You won't have summers off, you might have to work on Christmas day, you will have to work the midnight shift, you might have to spend all day in court without sleep after a midnight shift, and you won't make $100,000 per year or be given a company car.

12. People with a gun fixation are not normal. Firearms training is essential only because it may save you from being murdered. Don't get excited simply by carrying a gun. Get excited about being an expert in self-defence.

13. Although there are traditional courses called "Police Powers," this does not mean that they will give you special "powers." Laws of arrest and of search and seizure are the focus of these courses. These are *not* powers—they are *solutions* to problems.

14. Television and movies are not real life. Movies like *Lethal Weapon* should never be confused with reality or seen as a substitute for a training curriculum. Movies are not training videos. You can't chase cars at breakneck speed; you can't fire rounds of bullets wildly while chasing people on crowded streets; and you can't create bloodbaths.

15. You can't change your past. The police prefer to hire people who have no criminal tendencies. They prefer people with a proven ability to understand right from wrong, with some semblance of moral standards. They prefer to exclude substance abusers. The term "background check" understates the significance of the task. It should be named "a police investigation of your past behaviour." Before you think about trying to hide your past, think about this—the police are trained to figure out who committed a murder, robbery, or other crime. So they will not have trouble finding out if a police candidate is a substance abuser.

16. Be humble. As I have mentioned, one of the leading factors cited by recruiters as a reason for not hiring candidates is arrogance.

17. Do not do community service simply as a resumé builder. Police organizations value *sincere* volunteer work because such work significantly matures a candidate.

18. Find a mentor. A mentor is not necessarily a friend or cheerleader who simply accepts your weaknesses. A mentor imparts wisdom, develops strengths, and helps eliminate your weaknesses. A mentor is a valuable gift.

19. My boss was right—being hired as a police officer is a privilege, not a right.

NEW TO THE FOURTH EDITION

The fourth edition of *Basic Police Powers: Arrest and Search Procedures* contains a number of new and enhanced features:

▸ New easy to understand, reality-based decision-making models guide students through the basic police powers of arrest, search and seizure, and release used by front-line officers.

▸ An increased number of current, landmark case law decisions affecting front-line police procedures are outlined and explained.

▸ Chapters have been reorganized and restructured to better suit course structure.

▸ A new chapter on Feeney warrants has been included.

▸ Two new application chapters provide full-length tests for powers of arrest and release.

▸ Problem-Solving Case Study scenarios and Test Yourself questions have been revised and expanded.

▸ A comprehensive glossary emphasizes key terms.

- ▸ An accompanying website (**www.emp.ca.arcaro/policepowers4e**) provides exclusive online case law analyses and frequently asked questions, continually updated by the author.
- ▸ An Instructor's Guide and Test Bank are available for instructors.

About the Author

Gino Arcaro (BSc, MEd) is a professor and coordinator of the Police Foundations and Law and Security Administration programs at Niagara College in Welland, Ontario.

His unique 33-year professional career has included duties in policing in addition to those of a college program coordinator and professor, published writer, football coach, and strength training coach.

WORK EXPERIENCE

- 15 years police officer
    - nine years uniform branch
    - SWAT team
    - six years detective
- 18 years college professor
- 10 years college program coordinator
- 37 seasons football coach
- 37 years strength training
    - 23 years strength coaching
- textbook author
    - six published policing textbooks (18 editions; 2 adopted by the military police)
    - two football coaching books
- interrogation case law author for *Reid and Associates* (website)
- former journal article author for *The Canadian Journal of Police and Security Services*
- former *Blue Line Magazine* case law writer

EDUCATION

- PhD—completed one-half of dissertation in police interrogation
- MEd—organizational leadership
- BSc—criminal justice
- Ontario Police College
    - recruit diploma
    - criminal investigation diploma
- Centre for Forensic Sciences
    - homicide/forensic science certificate

VOLUNTEER COMMUNITY SERVICE

- ▸ a Level 3 NCCP coach, Gino has coached football at five different levels; his offense and defense systems have been published
- ▸ head coach of the Niagara X-Men tackle football team that competes against American NCAA Division 3 JV teams
- ▸ founder of the Niagara Colts Football Club Inc., a non-profit organization, to help Canadian student athletes get football scholarships to continue their post-secondary playing careers

CHAPTER 1

Powers of Custody: The Rapid Decision-Making Model

LEARNING OUTCOMES

The student will learn

- How to apply s. 495 *Criminal Code* (C.C.)

- How to apply investigative detention laws in accordance with *R. v. Mann* (2004)

- How to use a rapid decision-making (RDM) model to solve realistic front-line investigations that involve police officers' powers of arrest and detention

THE GOAL OF CHAPTER 1

Sections 495 and 31 C.C. may be the most important provisions for front-line policing. They establish the "powers of arrest without a warrant" authorities for police officers. These authorities provide the necessary *balance* between preventing false arrests and preventing offences. The front-line policing goal is to prevent the arrests of innocent persons while maintaining public safety. Taking custody of a person may be the most important decision a front-line police officer has to make. Removing a person's freedom is a very serious act in a democratic society.

Memorizing and recalling ss. 495 and 31 C.C. *are not enough.* Doing so will not help you apply the powers of arrest in real front-line policing. Police officers must do more than simply regurgitate information during an investigation; they must make rapid decisions. All policing involves decision-making. There are two types of decision-making, slow and fast. For obvious reasons, the first type is far more challenging; it involves limited time, limited information, and increased risk. The purpose of this chapter is to explain the five-step rapid decision-making (RDM) model, a model that will enable you to decide whether to arrest without a warrant. It is a unique model that takes full account of the front-line police officer's thought processes and circumstances. When a police officer arrives at a call in progress, there is no time for consulting or researching, and no time, in most cases, to review statutes and case law. Within seconds you have to process a great deal of information and decide if it is appropriate to arrest without a warrant. This is when the RDM model is required. Following the model and expertly applying it have to become second nature to you. The RDM model (see Figure 1.1) is the most important feature of this chapter. It will be referred to throughout the book.

Figure 1.1   RDM Model

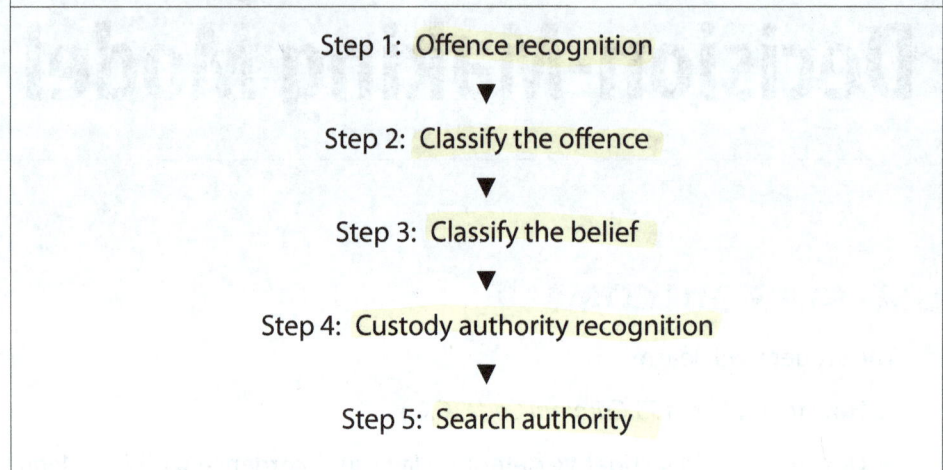

Step 1: Offence recognition

▼

Step 2: Classify the offence

▼

Step 3: Classify the belief

▼

Step 4: Custody authority recognition

▼

Step 5: Search authority

THE "POLICE POWERS OF ARREST" TRANSFORMATION

Historically, learning about "police powers of arrest" has been one of the most important parts of a police officer's education. The passing mark for the Powers of Arrest course at Ontario Police College, in 1976, was 90 percent. Our instructor told us that we would pass the course with a grade of 90 percent, but that being wrong 10 percent of the time in the real world of policing would be very problematic. He urged us to set a goal much higher than 90 percent and not simply to memorize the powers of arrest but to learn how to apply them.

The phrase "powers of arrest" used to be connected exclusively to ss. 495 and 31 C.C. However, a transformation has occurred with the emergence of **investigative detention** laws that, despite their complexities, provide significant investigative benefits to the police. Before these laws were introduced, **arrest** was the only type of custody; grounds for beliefs were either "reasonable and probable grounds" (R&PG) or "mere suspicion." The phrase *reasonable and probable grounds* has since been condensed to *reasonable grounds*. Several case law decisions confirm that R&PG and *reasonable grounds* are the same thing. The term *reasonable grounds* will be used exclusively throughout this book.

The phrase "mere suspicion" still exists. The phrase "reasonable suspicion to detain" has been added in connection with investigative detention. There is a fine line separating "mere suspicion" from "reasonable suspicion to detain." The difference between the two consists in the number of justifiable circumstances and the police officer's level of certainty. As you will learn, **mere suspicion** is a "hunch" based on intuition and experience. **Reasonable suspicion to detain** involves a greater degree of certainty, based on knowledge of specific concrete circumstances connecting a suspect to a specific offence. The important point is that both are suspicions, and that both involve a lower degree of certainty than *reasonable grounds*.

Consequently, a peace officer's authority to arrest is but one authority in the larger scope of "custody" authorities. The term "peace officer" includes various occupations including policing. For simplicity, the term "police officer" will be used throughout this book.

Custody Decision-Making

Custody is defined as any extent of physical or psychological restraint of an individual without his or her consent.[1] There has to be a legal justification for taking even momentary custody of a person. This is the most important principle this chapter teaches. Taking custody of a person must always be justified with concrete reasons that constitute a legal authority. In other words, the custody must be authorized by a legal rule. You cannot arbitrarily take custody of a person.

Applying custody authorities requires decision-making and problem-solving as well as knowledge. Problem-solving is the essence of policing. Every decision about whether to arrest or detain a person will require you to apply a specific five-step process: the RDM model. The first part of this process requires a specific type of analytical thinking called "offence recognition." **Offence recognition** involves analyzing evidence (reported information, your own observations, or physical evidence) and determining whether an offence has occurred. Offence recognition requires you to process a large quantity of information and answer two questions:

1. Did an offence occur?
2. If so, what offence?

Once recognized, the offence has to be classified as either *summary conviction*, *dual procedure*, or *indictable*. Next, you have to classify the *level of belief*. A **belief** is defined as a level of certainty concerning a specific person's connection to a specific offence. There are different levels of certainty, each giving rise to a different level of belief. *Strong certainty* constitutes reasonable grounds. *Weak certainty* constitutes mere suspicion.

After the level of belief has been classified, the next step is to consider the offence and the belief level in relation to ss. 495 and 31 C.C., and the provisions concerning investigative detention. In other words, if you have reasonable grounds, can you arrest without a warrant; if you have *weak certainty*, can you detain for identification purposes. If you decide to take custody, your final decision, step #5 in the RDM, concerns your authority to search the person and the surrounding place without a warrant.

Concept of Custody

One of the objectives of a democratic society is a balance between an individual's right to freedom and society's need for protection from crime. The police are given authority to remove freedom. Proper use of this authority provides the sought-for balance; misuse does not. In other words, the police authority to remove freedom can be either a valuable protection or a danger to the community, depending on how it is used.[2]

To prevent the abuse of this authority, we rely on the combined effect of two factors: limitations and accountability. In other words, the police authority to remove an individual's liberty is *limited* to specific circumstances; and police are *accountable*—they must justify the use of this authority.

There are various levels of custody, differentiated according to duration, nature, and the specific investigative techniques used. There are three ways of taking custody of a person, each based on a different category of authority:

1. Arrest *with* a warrant
2. Arrest *without* a warrant
3. Detention

Arrest with a warrant is based on *judicial authorization* to take custody. Obtaining this authority requires a particular sequence of actions and events. The police must first apply for and justify the need for the warrant. Then a Justice decides about the application. In other words, the final decision to take custody is made by a Justice, not by the police. This authority must underlie any warrant for any classification of criminal offence: summary conviction, dual procedure, or indictable.

In the case of **arrest without a warrant**, police take custody *without judicial authorization.* Here the police make the final decision, not a Justice; however, justification is still needed. The *Criminal Code* restricts the use of this authority to a narrow range of offences and circumstances, and it identifies two groups of people permitted to exercise it:

1. Peace officers, defined in s. 2 C.C. This group includes police officers and members of several other professions, including border protection officers and correctional services officers.
2. "Anyone," referring to *citizens.* Sections 494 and 30 C.C. authorize citizens to make arrests under certain circumstances. The word *citizen* is not used, however. "Anyone" is the legal term used in place of *citizens.*

Detention refers to a shorter duration of custody exercised without judicial authorization. It is specifically intended for investigative purposes in limited circumstances. Investigative detention laws are not found in the *Criminal Code.* They are authorized by common-law and case law precedents.[3]

EVIDENCE, BELIEF, AND CUSTODY— THE RELATIONSHIP

Custody has a complex relationship with two other concepts—*evidence* and *belief.* Before you can learn to apply custody authorities, you must understand the concept of custody in relation to the following principles:

1. The amount of evidence determines the level of belief. Evidence has two sources:
    a. human observation, and
    b. physical items.

    The information you receive from witnesses and from your own observations constitutes evidence. The volume of evidence differs to some extent in every investigation, and it forms the basis of a specific level of belief, which you must identify.

2. There are five levels of belief:
   a. arbitrary
   b. mere suspicion
   c. reasonable suspicion to detain
   d. reasonable grounds
   e. find committing

3. *Arbitrary* means there is no justification whatsoever for a belief. It means no belief.

4. *Mere suspicion* is intuition based on experience. It refers to a weak amount of certainty.

5. Both *arbitrary* and *mere suspicion* fall under the category of "hunch." A *hunch* does not justify an arrest; it justifies a brief detention for identification purposes only.

6. *Reasonable suspicion to detain* is a level of belief based on limited concrete evidence that connects a suspect to a specific offence. It justifies "investigative detention."

7. *Reasonable grounds* is a level of belief based on strong certainty, and under s. 495 C.C. it justifies an arrest without a warrant, under certain circumstances.

8. *Find committing* is a level of belief based on the highest degree of certainty, the police officer (or citizen) having witnessed the offence.

9. The stronger the belief, the longer the custody authorized. In other words, the strength of the police officer's certainty about a person's connection to an offence determines the permitted duration of that person's custody.

10. This progressive scale of belief levels—from arbitrary to find committing— illustrates the relationship between the three key elements of police investigations: evidence, belief, and custody (EBC). This continuum (see Figure 1.2) represents what you are going to learn to apply. It may seem complicated, but every successful police officer has learned to apply it.

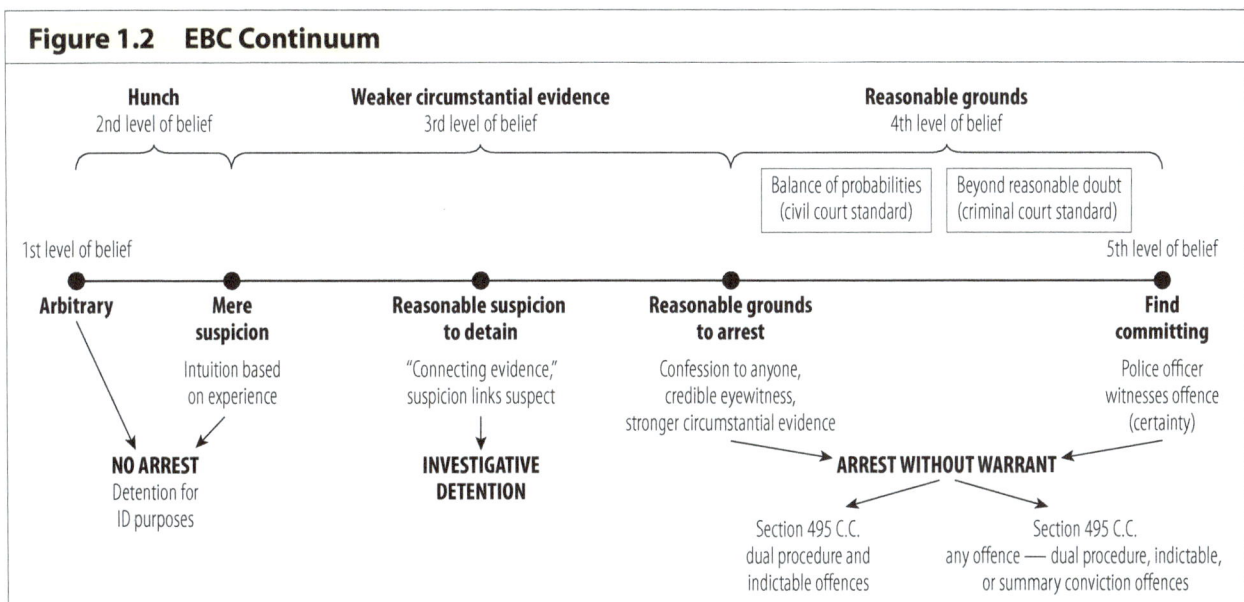

Figure 1.2   EBC Continuum

	Hunch 2nd level of belief	**Weaker circumstantial evidence** 3rd level of belief		**Reasonable grounds** 4th level of belief	
				Balance of probabilities (civil court standard)	Beyond reasonable doubt (criminal court standard)
1st level of belief					5th level of belief
Arbitrary	**Mere suspicion**	**Reasonable suspicion to detain**	**Reasonable grounds to arrest**		**Find committing**
	Intuition based on experience	"Connecting evidence," suspicion links suspect	Confession to anyone, credible eyewitness, stronger circumstantial evidence		Police officer witnesses offence (certainty)
NO ARREST Detention for ID purposes		**INVESTIGATIVE DETENTION**		**ARREST WITHOUT WARRANT**	
			Section 495 C.C. dual procedure and indictable offences	Section 495 C.C. any offence — dual procedure, indictable, or summary conviction offences	

THE RAPID DECISION-MAKING MODEL

Review the RDM model from the beginning of the chapter (Figure 1.1). Table 1.1 explains the individual steps in the RDM model.

Table 1.1   Components of the RDM Model

Step	Investigative Question	Goal
1. Offence recognition	What offence specifically occurred?	Analyze the circumstances (that is, the evidence). Identify whether a criminal offence was committed, and, if so, which one specifically (for example, break, enter, and theft—dwelling-house).
2. Classify the offence	What is the classification of the offence?	Classify the specific criminal offence as summary conviction, dual procedure, or indictable.
3. Classify the belief	What type of belief do I have connecting the person to the offence?	Determine the strength of connection between the suspect and the crime. Determine the degree of certainty and classify the belief as either ▸ found committing, ▸ reasonable grounds, ▸ reasonable suspicion to detain, ▸ mere suspicion, or ▸ no belief (arbitrary).
4. Custody authority recognition	Can I take custody by arresting without a warrant, or detaining for investigative purposes?	Apply two authorities: 1. Section 495 C. C. ("Peace Officers' Powers of Arrest without Warrant") or s. 31 C.C., or 2. "Investigative detention" authority
5. Search?	Can I search the person and/or place, and for what items?	Apply relevant authority: 1. "Search Incident to Arrest" laws 2. "Search Incident to Investigative Detention" laws

APPLYING THE RDM MODEL

Step 1: Offence Recognition

Offence recognition refers to the skill of analyzing circumstances and evidence to determine

1. whether a criminal offence occurred, and, if so,
2. which one(s) specifically.

The first step in mastering this skill is knowing the *facts-in-issue* that constitute an offence. Through study, you will learn the facts-in-issue of various criminal offences, but simple memorization of these facts won't help you at the scene of a crime in progress. Instead, you have to process reported circumstances and your own observations and find a match. This means match an offence to the circumstances. It is a different skill from just memorizing and recalling the facts-in-issue.

For example, you arrive at a domestic to find Claire (40) and Doug (30). Claire is bleeding from the mouth. She points to Doug and says, "He punched me in the mouth for no reason." Doug responds, "Sorry, I lost my temper." After processing all of the information from the different sources (the reported circumstances as well as your own observations), you easily recognize that the offence of "assault" or "assault causing bodily harm" has occurred.

Rule: If no offence is recognized (that is, if no offence occurred), you have no authority to detain or arrest. If an offence is recognized, you should proceed to the next step: classify the offence.

Step 2: Classify the Offence

This skill refers to accurately classifying the offence as "summary conviction," "indictable," or "dual procedure" (hybrid). *Summary conviction* is a category of minor crimes. *Indictable* is a category of major crimes. *Dual procedure* is a category of offences that can be either; dual procedure offences are temporarily classified as *indictable* until a Crown attorney decides on the final classification at an accused person's "first appearance." For the purposes of the police officer trying to decide about custody, dual procedure offences are temporarily classified as *indictable*.[4] Chapter 2 includes lists of summary conviction, indictable, and dual procedure offences.

Step 3: Classify the Belief

A belief is an opinion or conclusion about a specific person's connection to a specific offence. You classify a belief according to its level of strength, based on the degree of certainty underlying it. Table 1.2 summarizes the relationship between belief strength and degree of certainty. Chapter 3 defines each level of belief in detail.

Table 1.2   Belief Strength and Degree of Certainty

Belief strength and degree of certainty ⟶

Belief	No belief (arbitrary)	Mere suspicion	Reasonable suspicion to detain (formerly articulable cause)	Reasonable grounds to arrest	Find committing (police officer)
Degree of Certainty	0%	Minimal • Hunch only • No concrete connection to crime	• Some concrete connection to the crime	Less than 100%	100%
Degree of Doubt	100%	• Considerable doubt • More than reasonable doubt	More than reasonable doubt	Less than reasonable doubt	0%

⟵ Degree of doubt

After completing Step 3 of the RDM model, you have

▸ recognized the offence,
▸ classified the offence, and
▸ classified your belief.

The next step concerns the decision whether to take custody.

Step 4: Custody Authority Recognition

One of the most common and important decisions in front-line policing is deciding whether an arrest or detention can be lawfully made. The right decision will prevent three undesirable consequences:

1. civil liability for a false arrest,
2. criminal liability for unintentional, unlawful arrest or detention, and
3. exclusion of seized evidence during a trial.

The goal at this stage is to determine whether you can arrest without a warrant or detain for investigative purposes. Making the right decision requires that you understand five concepts:

1. definitions of arrest, detention, and voluntary accompaniment,
2. police powers of arrest without a warrant: s. 495 C.C.
3. breach of the peace s. 31 C.C.
4. citizens' powers of arrest: ss. 494 and 30 C.C, and
5. investigative detention authority: *R. v. Mann* (2004) S.C.C.

Chapter 4 explains these five concepts in detail.

Step 5: Search Authority

A search has two goals:

1. protection of oneself and members of the public (the primary goal), and
2. finding evidence that proves the commission of an offence (the secondary goal).

Weapons are the focus of the primary goal; evidence is the focus of the secondary one. Discovering a weapon accomplishes both the primary and the secondary goals. Weapon seizure constitutes self-protection, and it also constitutes evidence for a change related to weapons possession. A full search involves both of these goals; a partial search involves only the primary goal (search for weapons).

There are only two potential targets of a search: a person and a place. A police officer cannot search either of them arbitrarily. A specific lawful authority must allow the search. There are three categories of such authorities:

1. search warrant,
2. search without a warrant, and
3. consent search.

The admissibility of seized evidence is governed by s. 24(2) Charter.

There are many search and seizure authorities, but only two that pertain specifically to custody and that authorize a search without a warrant and without consent:

1. *Search incident to arrest.* This common-law authority automatically permits the police to search a person and his or her surroundings after a full arrest has been made, under ss. 495 or 31 C.C. or any other statute that authorizes arrest without a warrant. In other words, the following simple rule always applies: *If you make a lawful arrest, you can automatically search the arrested person for weapons and for any evidence of any offence.* You do not have to form a separate set of reasonable grounds concerning the person's possession of other items.

2. *Search incident to investigative detention.* This case law authority authorizes a partial search, called a "protective pat down" search. The primary goal of the search is to find weapons. This search is automatic when reasonable suspicion exists for detaining a person.

Chapter 5 explains both of these search authorities in detail.

SUMMARY

This chapter introduced the RDM model. It is the first of six chapters devoted to this topic. Chapters 2–6 will teach you how to apply the model in reality. These chapters will be organized as follows:

- ▶ Chapter 2 will discuss the classification of offences.
- ▶ Chapter 3 will discuss the definition of beliefs: find committing, reasonable grounds, reasonable suspicion to detain, and mere suspicion.
- ▶ Chapter 4 will discuss custody authorities: Ss. 495 and 31 C.C., and authorities governing investigative detention.
- ▶ Chapter 5 will discuss search authorities: search incident to arrest, and search incident to investigative detention.
- ▶ Chapter 6 contains an extensive collection of scenarios, or "how-to-apply" cases.

The accompanying website, **www.emp.ca/arcaro/policepowers4E**, is a major part of this book. It includes ongoing case law analysis for every topic relevant to the RDM model. This is a unique feature that makes this a textbook with unlimited uses.

ENDNOTES

1. *R. v. Mann*, [2004] 3 S.C.R. 59, 2004 CanLII 52.
2. *R. v. Storrey*, [1990] 1 S.C.R. 241, 1990 CanLII 125.
3. Supra note 1.
4. Section 31, *Interpretation Act*, R.S.C. 1985, c. I-21.

CHAPTER 2
Classify the Offence

LEARNING OUTCOMES

The student will learn

- The meaning of "classification of offences"

- How to classify a criminal offence as summary conviction, indictable, or dual procedure

- How the classification of the offence determines the time limit on laying a charge and the maximum penalty attached to the offence

- How a dual procedure offence comes to be permanently classified

INTRODUCTION

Classifying the offence is the second step of the RDM model. After recognizing the offence by name, you immediately have to classify it either as *summary conviction*, *indictable*, or *dual procedure*.

A **criminal offence** is one that violates a federal statute. The majority of criminal offences are defined by the *Criminal Code*. They vary in their severity.

Criminal offences are classified according to their severity. The phrase **classification of offences** refers to the process by which an offence is recognized as either summary conviction, indictable, or dual procedure. The classification of the offence determines what authorities—arrest and release authorities, for example—apply to it. It also determines the time limit on laying the charge and the maximum penalty incurred by the offence.

OFFENCE CLASSIFICATIONS

Two classifications of criminal offences exist in Canada:

1. summary conviction, and
2. indictable

Summary conviction offences are minor criminal offences, while **indictable offences** are major criminal offences. How an offence is classified determines

▸ whether an arrest without warrant may be made,

▸ the terms of the arrested person's release,

▸ the time limit on charging an offender,

▸ the method of trial,

▸ the maximum penalty attacked to the offence, and

▸ the appeal procedures.

The *Criminal Code* does not list offences by classification. Instead, the classification of a specific criminal offence is stated in the relevant section of the statute explaining the punishment for that offence. For example, to determine the classification of "Theft over $5,000.00," refer to s. 334(a) C.C., which states that a person who commits theft of property with a value exceeding $5,000.00 is guilty of an indictable offence and is liable to imprisonment for a term not exceeding 10 years. Another example is the offence of "Cause a disturbance." According to s. 175(1) C.C., a person who commits this offence is guilty of an offence punishable on summary conviction. In addition to indictable and summary conviction, there is a third list of offences called *dual procedure*, or *hybrid*. Both terms are used in law enforcement and have the same meaning. **Dual procedure**, or **hybrid**, **offences** are offences that are classified as *indictable* temporarily, from the time of the offence until the accused's first appearance, at which point they are permanently classified by the Crown attorney. The key point here is that dual procedure offences are temporarily classified as indictable for the purpose of applying arrest authorities—in other words, throughout the police investigation.

Summary Conviction Offences

Summary conviction offences are minor criminal offences. Summary conviction trial procedures are explained in Part XXVII of the *Criminal Code*, ss. 785–840. These offences are tried in provincial court, by a judge without a jury.

The time limit on charging a person for a summary conviction offence is six months. If an "Information" has not been laid within that time, the offender cannot be charged.[1] With some exceptions, the maximum penalty for summary conviction offences is a $2,000.00 fine, six months in jail, or both.[2] When an accused is convicted of a summary conviction offence that has a maximum penalty, the trial judge has no authority to impose a greater penalty.

Table 2.1 lists the nine most common summary conviction offences.

Table 2.1 Common Summary Conviction Offences	
Personating peace officer	s. 130
Indecent act	s. 173(1)
Causing disturbance, indecent exhibition, loitering, etc.	s. 175(1)
Trespassing at night	s. 177
Fraudulently obtaining food, beverage, or accommodation	s. 364
Indecent telephone calls	s. 372(2)
Harassing telephone calls	s. 372(3)
Fraud in relation to fares, etc.	s. 393(1)
Injuring or endangering cattle and other animals	s. 445

Indictable Offences

Indictable offences are major criminal offences. The trial procedures outlined in the *Criminal Code* for indictable offences differ from those outlined for summary conviction offences.

There is no time limit on charging a person who commits an indictable offence. An information may be sworn at any time after the offence date. Sections 7 and 11(b) of the *Canadian Charter of Rights and Freedoms* do provide protection against unreasonable delays in prosecution, but a person who commits an indictable offence is never immune from prosecution. Indictable offences differ in this way from summary conviction offences, for which there is a six-month time limit.

No general maximum penalty exists for indictable offences; penalties may be either 2, 5, 10, or 14 years in duration, or the penalty may be life imprisonment. The maximum penalty is mentioned in the relevant section of the *Criminal Code* that designates the offence. Table 2.2 contains some common indictable offences.

Table 2.2 Common Indictable Offences	
First-degree murder	s. 235(1)
Second-degree murder	s. 235(1)
Infanticide	s. 233
Manslaughter	s. 234
Causing death by criminal negligence	s. 220
Attempt to commit murder	s. 239
Kidnapping	s. 279
Aggravated assault	s. 268
Sexual assault	s. 271
Sexual assault with a weapon	s. 272
Aggravated sexual assault	s. 273
Forcible confinement	s. 279(2)
Robbery	s. 343
Causing bodily harm by criminal negligence	s. 221
Overcoming resistance to commission of offence	s. 246
Weapons trafficking	s. 99(1)
Possession for purpose of weapons trafficking	s. 100(1)
Importing or exporting weapons knowing it is unauthorized	s. 103(1)
Possession of firearm knowing its possession is unauthorized	s. 92(1)
Using firearm in commission of offence	s. 85
Causing bodily harm with intent—firearm	s. 244
Causing bodily harm with intent—air gun or pistol	s. 244.1
Arson—disregard for human life	s. 433
Arson—damage to property	s. 434
Arson—own property	s. 434.1
Arson—for fraudulent purposes	s. 435
Arson by negligence	s. 436
Impaired driving causing death	s. 255(3)
Impaired driving causing bodily harm	s. 255(2)
Dangerous operation [of motor vehicles] causing death	s. 249(4)
Possession of property obtained by crime and valued over $5,000.00	s. 355(a)

(The table is continued on the next page.)

Table 2.2   (Continued)

Fraud over $5,000.00	s. 380(1)(a)
Dangerous operation [of motor vehicles] causing bodily harm	s. 249(3)
Theft over $5,000.00	s. 334(a)
Breaking and entering with intent (house)	s. 348(1)(a)
Breaking and entering and committing an indictable offence (house)	s. 348(1)(b)
False pretence enabling theft over $5,000.00	s. 362(2)(a)
Disguise with intent [to commit an indictable offence]	s. 351(2)
Extortion	s. 346
Obstruct justice	s. 139
Perjury	s. 131

Dual Procedure Offences

The term *dual procedure* refers to offences that can be either summary conviction or indictable; it is not a separate classification. What this means is that dual procedure offences, unlike summary conviction or indictable ones, do not have a fixed or permanent *initial* classification. Dual procedure offences are *temporarily* classified as indictable, retaining this temporary classification until the accused person's first appearance, at which point the Crown attorney decides whether the offence will be finally defined as indictable or summary conviction.

The terms "dual procedure" and "hybrid" are slang terms, used within the criminal justice system but not in the *Criminal Code* or in other federal statutes. Instead, a provision will typically say that an offence is either indictable or punishable on summary conviction. For example, "assault" is a dual procedure offence found in s. 266 C.C. Instead of using the phrase "dual procedure," the section states the following: "Every one who commits an assault is guilty of (a) an indictable offence and is liable to imprisonment for a term not exceeding five years; *or* (b) an offence punishable on summary conviction"[3] [italics added].

STAGES OF DUAL PROCEDURE CLASSIFICATION

A dual procedure offence is temporarily classified as indictable until the accused's first appearance in court.[4] In other words, dual procedure offences may eventually be designated as summary conviction, but they must be classified as indictable during the first five stages of an investigation and prosecution so that the police can correctly apply basic police procedures. These five stages are as follows:

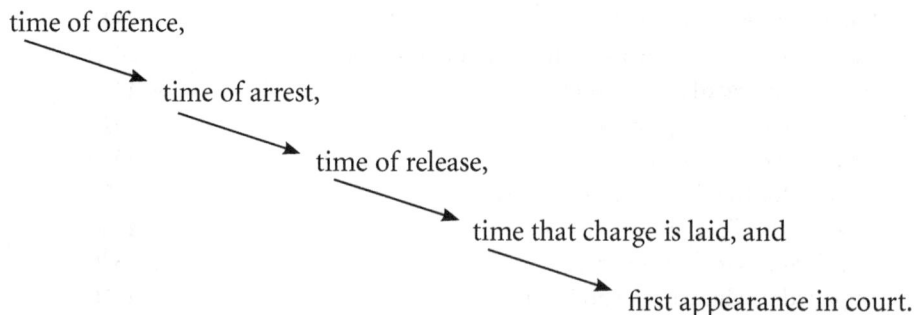

time of offence,

          time of arrest,

                    time of release,

                              time that charge is laid, and

                                      first appearance in court.

The first four stages occur before the first court appearance. The authority for classifying dual procedure offences as indictable during the first stages of an investigation is s. 34(1)(a) *Interpretation Act*. There are no exceptions to this rule.

Therefore, all dual procedure offences are considered to be indictable at the time of arrest. This is advantageous for police officers because it expands the number of offences that do not require the officer to "find committing" in order to arrest without a warrant.

At the accused's first appearance in court, the Crown attorney decides upon the final classification of a dual procedure offence. There is no trial at the first appearance; it is simply an opportunity for the accused person to enter a plea of guilty or not guilty. The trial is scheduled for a future date. Table 2.3 lists some common dual procedure offences.

Table 2.3   Common Dual Procedure Offences

Sexual assault	s. 271
Assault with a weapon or causing bodily harm	s. 267
Assaulting a peace officer	s. 270
Assault	s. 266
Criminal harassment	s. 264
Dangerous operation of motor vehicles, vessels and aircraft	s. 249(1)(a)
Operation of motor vehicle while impaired	s. 253(b)
Theft under $5,000.00	s. 334
Possession of property valued under $5,000.00 obtained by crime	s. 355(b)
Fraud under $5,000.00	s. 380(1)(b)
False pretences enabling theft under $5,000.00	s. 362(2)(b)
Mischief over $5,000.00	s. 430(3)
Mischief under $5,000.00	s. 430(4)
Breaking and entering with intent (place other than dwelling-house)	s. 348(1)(e)
Uttering threats to cause death or bodily harm	s. 264.1(1)(a)
Uttering threats to cause damage to property	s. 264.1(1)(b)
Resisting arrest	s. 270
Uttering threats to kill or injure animal	s. 264.1(1)(c)
Possession of prohibited or restricted firearm with ammunition	s. 95(1)
Possession of weapon obtained by commission of offence	s. 96(1)
Making automatic firearm	s. 102(1)
Pointing a firearm	s. 87(1)
Careless use of firearm	s. 86(1)
Carrying concealed weapon	s. 90(1)
Unauthorized possession of firearm in motor vehicle	s. 94(1)
Unauthorized possession of firearm	s. 91(1)
Possession of firearm at unauthorized place	s. 93(1)
False statement concerning firearm loss, theft, or destruction	s. 107(1)
Tampering with serial number on firearm	s. 108(1)
Transferring firearm without authority	s. 101(1)
Losing or finding firearm—fail to report	s. 105(1)
Destroying firearm—fail to report	s. 106(1)
Possession of weapon for dangerous purpose	s. 88(1)
Forgery	s. 366
Uttering forged document	s. 368(1)
Failure to comply with probation order	s. 733.1
Unauthorized importing or exporting of firearm	s. 104(1)
Public mischief	s. 140
Failure to appear	s. 502
Failure to stop at scene of accident	s. 252

SELECTING THE FINAL CLASSIFICATION

Once charged with a dual procedure offence, the offender appears in court and the Crown attorney decides on the final classification of the offence, either indictable or summary conviction. This whole process involves the following steps:

1. The accused person is "arraigned," which means that the information is read to the accused person in open court.
2. The judge asks the Crown attorney, "How do you wish to proceed?" The formal translation of this question is, "What method of trial do you wish to select?" Informally, it simply means, "How do you wish to classify the offence?" The process of selecting the method of trial must not be confused with the process of "election"—the accused's deciding on the level of court where the trial will be held.
3. The Crown attorney selects the method of trial; in other words, the Crown attorney classifies the offence as summary conviction or as indictable. The Crown attorney's decision is final. Neither the accused person nor the judge participates in this decision, and the decision cannot be appealed or reversed. The authority for this is found not in the *Criminal Code* but in case law.[5]

If the Crown attorney classifies the offence as summary conviction and the accused pleads not guilty, the trial must be held in provincial court. If the Crown attorney classifies the offence as indictable, the accused will generally have an election, or choice, regarding the level of court for the trial and whether it will be a jury trial.[6]

Accused Person's Election

An **election** is the choice an accused person has regarding the level of court where the trial will be conducted and, consequently, whether or not there will be a jury.[7] The accused has three choices:

1. Superior court, judge, and jury (preliminary hearing required);
2. Superior court, judge alone (preliminary hearing required); or
3. Provincial court, judge alone (no preliminary hearing required).

The following seven rules are relevant to an accused person's election.

1. Criminal trials may be conducted in either
   - a superior court of criminal jurisdiction (for example, general division court), or
   - a provincial court.[8]
2. A jury trial may occur only in superior court, not in provincial court.[9] Therefore, a superior court trial may be tried by a judge alone or with a jury.
3. A preliminary hearing is required before a trial occurs in superior court. No preliminary hearing precedes provincial court trials.[10]
4. All summary conviction trials must be held in provincial court.[11]
5. Superior court has absolute jurisdiction over s. 469 C.C. offences. Section 469 C.C. lists specific indictable offences, such as murder and treason, that must be tried in a superior court composed of a judge and jury.[12] However,

a superior court judge alone, without a jury, may try a s. 469 C.C. offence if both the accused person and the attorney general consent.[13]

6. Provincial court has absolute jurisdiction over s. 553 C.C. offences. These include dual procedure offences that must be tried in provincial court regardless of whether the Crown attorney classifies the offence as indictable or as summary conviction. Examples of s. 553 C.C. offences are the five "under $5,000.00" offences (theft, fraud, false pretences, mischief, and possession of property obtained by crime) and the offence of failing to comply with a probation order.

7. Dual procedure offences that the Crown attorney decides to classify as indictable (except s. 553 C.C. offences) and indictable offences that are not s. 469 C.C. offences are referred to as "election indictable offences." Examples of purely indictable offences that are election indictable are attempted murder, robbery, and "Theft over $5,000.00." An accused person charged with these offences is afforded an election, which means that he or she may choose one of the three levels of trial.

Table 2.4   Offences That Allow or Prohibit an Election

No Election	Election
Purely summary conviction offences (provincial court)	Majority of purely indictable offences
Dual procedure offences selected as summary conviction (provincial court)	Dual procedure offences selected as indictable
Section 553 C.C. offences selected as either indictable or summary conviction (provincial court)	
Section 469 C.C. offences (superior court)	

Table 2.4 compares offences in terms of whether an election is allowed or prohibited.

SUMMARY

After an offence is recognized and classified, the rapid decision-making model moves to Step 3—classifying the belief. The next chapter defines the relevant "beliefs" and explains the procedures.

ENDNOTES

1. Section 786(2) C.C.
2. Section 787(1) C.C.
3. Section 266 C.C.
4. *Interpretation Act*, R.S.C. 1985, c. I-21, s. 34(1)(a), and *R. v. Mitchell*, 1997 CanLII 6321 (Ont. C.A.).

5. *R. v. West* (1915), 25 C.C.C. 145 (S.C. App. Div.).
6. Section 536(1) C.C.
7. Ibid.
8. Section 2 C.C.
9. Section 536(1) C.C.
10. Ibid.
11. Sections 785 and 798 C.C.
12. Sections 469 and 471 C.C.
13. Section 473(1) C.C.

CHAPTER 3
Classify the Belief

LEARNING OUTCOMES

The student will learn

- How to define the different levels of beliefs: find committing, reasonable grounds, reasonable suspicion to detain, mere suspicion, hunch, arbitrary

- How to analyze a set of circumstances and recognize which level of belief is appropriate

INTRODUCTION

The third step of the RDM model is classifying the belief. After you have recognized and classified the offence itself, you have to analyze the circumstances and determine the strength of your belief concerning a specific person's connection to a specific offence. The strength of your belief determines the extent of your arrest/detention authority.

FIND COMMITTING

Find committing simply refers to you (the officer) being an eyewitness to an offence. This act of observation represents the highest degree of certainty. Officer eyewitness belief represents the *strongest belief* that connects a person to an offence. You actually see the offence—you do not have to rely on anyone else telling you about it. Nothing gets lost in translation.

The primary element of eyewitness belief is *maintaining sight* of the offender throughout the entire offence until apprehension, which eliminates the need for memory recall and the adverse effects of memory decay. Continuous and uninterrupted sight removes reliance on other people to form a belief.

"Find committing" is not defined in the *Criminal Code*. It is defined in a series of case law decisions, most recently, *R. v. Abel & Corbett* (2008).[1] The definition has two parts because it covers two possible scenarios: in the first, the offender remains at the scene; in the second, the offender leaves the scene.

1. *The offender remains at the scene.* In this case, *find committing* means seeing an offender actually commit an offence.[2] *Find committing* requires that the police officer witness the offence in its entirety,[3] including

   ▸ all the elements that constitute the offence, referred to as the "facts-in-issue," and
   ▸ the person who committed the entire offence.

2. *The offender flees from the scene. Find committing*, in this case, is also defined as seeing an offender actually commit an offence; however, the phrase, "and pursuing him or her *immediately* and *continuously* until apprehension" is also included in the definition. This supplementary phrase should be understood as follows:

   ▸ "Immediately" means *immediately after an offender has been seen committing an offence.* It does not mean immediately after the offence has been discovered or immediately after the commission of the offence (without having seen the offender).[4]
   ▸ "Continuously" means *without a break.*[5] It means never losing sight of the offender from the time of the offence to the time of apprehension. The pursuit and apprehension must form a single transaction.[6] The concept of "never losing sight" causes some controversy, but no amount of time lapse is permitted during a pursuit. Consequently, if the pursuer loses sight of an offender and regains sight at any time later, the pursuer is no longer *found committing*. Instead, the pursuer has *reasonable grounds* for believing that the offender committed the offence.[7] The reason for the "no loss of sight" requirement is the possibility of inaccurate memory regarding facial recognition of the offender.

KEY POINTS

Following are some key points about *find committing*:

▸ Seeing a partial offence or merely being told about an offence does not qualify as *find committing*.[8]
▸ In some cases, *find committing* includes "apparently find committing." This means that the arresting officer either believes the person "at that very moment and at that very place is engaged in criminal activity" or believes he or she "has detected a crime in progress."[9] This definition is based on an extensive "find committing" case law literature review found in *R. v. Abel & Corbett* (2008). This case is important because it deals with a common situation: finding a person who may possess an illegal item either on his person or at another location within his control. The lengthy case law literature review and the circumstances of the case are included on the website that accompanies this book (**www.emp.ca/arcaro/policepowers4E**).

REASONABLE GROUNDS (TO ARREST)

Formerly known as "reasonable and probable grounds" (R&PG), **reasonable grounds** to arrest is used in s. 495 C.C. But the actual phrase "reasonable grounds" is not defined in any Canadian statute. It is defined in case law as "a set of facts or circumstances which would cause a person of ordinary and prudent judgment to believe beyond a mere suspicion."[10] This definition obviously lacks concreteness. Its openness to interpretation represents both an advantage and a disadvantage for police officers. The key point here is that the definition does not explain what specific evidence constitutes the belief level known as "reasonable grounds" or how to form it. Interpretation of the definition reveals the following:

- "A set of facts or circumstances" refers to evidence.
- "A person of ordinary and prudent judgment" refers to the average person in the community who is "dispassionate and fully apprised of the circumstances of the case," with "discretion grounded in long-term community values."[11] This person does not have to be a legal scholar or any other expert. A key element in this phrase is the notion of being fully informed of all the available circumstances. This obligates the police to use the total evidence available, not partial evidence, and to justify themselves. *It clearly imposes an obligation to state the reasons for the belief.*
- "To believe beyond a mere suspicion" defines *reasonable grounds* as a stronger belief than *mere suspicion.* "Beyond mere suspicion" serves as a condensed definition and requires that *reasonable grounds* must exceed an unsubstantiated baseless hunch or intuitive opinion.

A belief based on reasonable grounds has four major elements:

1. The officer is not an eyewitness.
2. Complete certainty, beyond all doubt, is *not* required.
3. The evidence for the belief does not have to constitute a *prima facie* case but it usually exceeds reasonable doubt.
4. The concrete evidence leads to only one logical conclusion.

Three categories of evidence constitute reasonable grounds:

1. confessions, by the offender to anyone (police or citizen);
2. at least one credible eyewitness statement (written or verbal); and
3. circumstantial evidence that leads to *only one logical conclusion* (that is, that a specific person committed the offence).

These categories of evidence can emerge from two sources:

1. another person, or
2. you (the police officer).

When another person is the source, the police officer's skill in evaluating credibility becomes a factor. For example, when a woman reports to you that a suspect told her that he committed an offence, you must evaluate the woman's credibility.

When you yourself are the source of the evidence, the degree of certainty obviously increases. For example, when an offender confesses to you, your level of certainty is almost the same as for *find committing.* The only doubt you might have about such a direct confession is the rare possibility of its being false. But false confession is a more significant concern at the trial stage. During an investigation, a reasonable person may logically assume that no rational (and innocent) person would falsely and voluntarily confess to a crime.

A belief based on circumstantial evidence comes from observing the physical circumstances of an offence and/or a person's actions in relation to an offence, actions that neither represent an eyewitness account nor constitute a confession. The source of such observation may be a witness, the officer, or both. If the evidence produced by this observation leads you to logically conclude that only one person can be connected to the offence, then reasonable grounds exists. If *multiple logical conclusions are possible*, reasonable grounds do not exist; only a belief amounting to suspicion exists.

The following five rules will help you decide whether reasonable grounds exist:

1. Reasonable grounds constitutes a justified opinion. It is a logical conclusion based on concrete evidence.
2. Reasonable grounds is a "bona fide belief in a serious possibility based on credible evidence."[12] This definition puts the onus on police to evaluate witness credibility, when practicable to do so. In other words, where reasonable grounds is concerned, there are two beliefs that need justification: the overall belief in the possibility itself and the belief in the witness's credibility. Police must be able to explain why a witness was believed or assumed to be very credible. Time permitting, the procedure of evaluating a witness's credibility is crucial.
3. Reasonable grounds requires less evidence than two standards of belief that prevail in court:

    a. the civil court standard of "balance of probabilities," and
    b. the criminal court standard of "beyond a reasonable doubt."[13]

    This lower requirement is an investigative benefit for police. A reasonable grounds belief is less strong than a *prima facie* case belief. In other words, the evidence for reasonable grounds does not have to be as strong as the *prima facie* evidence needed to convict.[14]
4. Reasonable grounds is a "strong reason" to believe, or a strong probability predicated on credible evidence.[15]
5. "Reasonable grounds to arrest" and "reasonable and probable grounds" are based on exactly the same level of belief.[16]

Countless case law decisions include point-of-reference cases to help front-line police officers recognize what circumstances constitute reasonable grounds. At the end of this chapter, a brief case law review of *R. v. Mann* (2004)[17] explains the landmark case relating to reasonable grounds. This S.C.C. decision includes a point-of-reference summary of circumstances that is the standard for comparison. The website that accompanies this book includes an ongoing "reasonable grounds" case law section.

REASONABLE SUSPICION TO DETAIN

There are two levels of belief whose definitions include the word *suspicion*—"reasonable suspicion to detain," and "mere suspicion." The first one is a stronger suspicion than the second. The major difference between the two is that **reasonable suspicion to detain** is based on concrete circumstantial evidence concerning a crime in progress, evidence that connects a specific person to the crime. *Mere suspicion* is associated with an offence that is not in progress. It is based on logical but unsubstantiated theories: theories that are supported only by very weak circumstantial evidence.

The level of belief we now call *reasonable suspicion to detain* used to be called "articulable cause." A landmark S.C.C. case, *R. v. Mann* (2004),[18] renamed it "reasonable suspicion to detain" and named the corresponding form of custody "investigative detention." Countless derivative case law decisions have emerged and will continue to emerge, each providing a valuable point of reference for the front-line officer. The website that accompanies this book has a section devoted entirely to investigative detention.

History

In 1993, a case law decision confirmed that the level of belief we now know as *reasonable suspicion to detain* existed in case law. Until then, however, it had rarely, if ever been named. From 1993 to the present, *reasonable suspicion* (or *reasonable grounds) to detain* has evolved into a significant investigative tool and has undergone three name changes.

Beginning with the Ontario Court of Appeal in *R. v. Simpson* (1993),[19] and progressing to the Supreme Court of Canada's landmark decision in *R. v. Mann* (2004),[20] a series of decisions confirmed that a level of belief exists between "reasonable grounds to arrest" and "mere suspicion." The key point here is that the belief is defined as a *suspicion*. It is stronger than "mere suspicion" and weaker than "reasonable grounds to arrest." It is a suspicion.

Originally called "articulable cause," *reasonable suspicion to detain* has been twice renamed, a process that has caused needless confusion, according to two Supreme Court judges in *R. v. Mann*. The Supreme Court of Canada (S.C.C.), in *R. v. Jacques* (1996),[21] renamed the belief "reasonable grounds to suspect" and stated that it was equivalent to "articulable cause." Then, in *R. v. Mann* (2004),[22] the majority of the S.C.C. again renamed the belief, changing it to "reasonable grounds to detain." Their rationale was that "articulable cause" is an American term.

Despite the name change, the definition of this level of belief has remained the same; it is "a constellation of objectively discernable facts which give the detaining officer reasonable cause to suspect that the detainee is criminally implicated in the activity under investigation."[23]

"Reasonable suspicion (or grounds) to detain" requires discernible evidence (concrete circumstances) that logically connects a person to an offence. This connection, however, is but one of many possible conclusions the evidence may point to. Others may exist. "Reasonable grounds to detain" is also defined as a belief beyond a **hunch**, which is defined as "a baseless opinion premised on intuition gained by experience."[24] *Reasonable grounds to detain* is a belief of minimal certainty that involves considerable doubt. Such a belief is still a suspicion, stronger than *mere suspicion* but weaker than *reasonable grounds to arrest*. It does not authorize an arrest under s. 495 C.C.

There are now two levels of suspicion in Canadian law: the first is *reasonable grounds to detain*, the second is *mere suspicion*. The potential confusion of this added level of suspicion was criticized by the dissenting judges of the S.C.C. in *R. v. Mann*.[25] The S.C.C. minority feared that including the phrase "reasonable grounds" in *reasonable grounds to detain* might lead to a wrong conclusion—that it is equivalent to "reasonable grounds to arrest." Their point was that the phrase *reasonable grounds* has "traditionally" been associated with the level of belief needed to make an arrest under s. 495 C.C.

The *R. v. Mann* case is discussed at length in Chapter 4, under "Investigative Detention." However, the following list of concrete circumstantial evidence shows briefly what constituted reasonable suspicion to detain in *R. v. Mann*. This list is a standard point of reference for police officers.

▸ Radio broadcast telling police officers about a break and enter in progress, and giving a description and possible name of one suspect.
▸ While en route, two to three blocks from the crime scene, the officers saw a man walking casually on the sidewalk. He matched the broadcast description "to a tee." The problem was that there was no witness who could positively identify the person who committed the break and enter.
▸ The officers stopped the pedestrian and asked him to identify himself. The man complied and gave his name and date of birth (D.O.B.).

These circumstances did not constitute reasonable grounds, but did constitute reasonable suspicion to detain.

MERE SUSPICION

This is the *weaker* of the two levels of suspicion. **Mere suspicion** is defined as

▸ a hunch, meaning an opinion or theory based on intuition and experience only,[26] or
▸ unsubstantiated speculation, conjecture, rumour, or gossip.

The difference between *mere suspicion* and *reasonable grounds to detain* is the presence or absence of concrete evidence implicating a person in a crime. The following is realistic example of what kind of evidence constitutes mere suspicion.

You are investigating a break and enter (B&E) that took place five days ago, at a house. Using your experience and intuition, you develop a theory. This theory involves four possible suspects, all linked to the crime by their familiarity with the house—prior familiarity and familiarity through planning. The theory is based on your sense of their motive and opportunity. All four suspects had knowledge of the complainant and the place, but there is no concrete evidence connecting any of the suspects to the specific offence. In other words, there has been no confession made to anyone; there is not one credible eye-witness; and there is no circumstantial evidence that leads to only one logical conclusion about a specific person's connection to this specific offence. This theory is good investigative work, but it is very weak circumstantial evidence. This hunch constitutes *mere suspicion*.

Key Points

Following are some key points about *mere suspicion*:

▸ It is possible for circumstantial evidence to constitute reasonable grounds, but only if it is strong enough to encourage only one logical conclusion.

▸ Weak circumstantial evidence refers to circumstantial evidence that permits multiple conclusions. Such evidence is the basis of *mere suspicion*.

▸ The difference between *reasonable suspicion to detain* and *mere suspicion* is the strength of the suspicion, determined by the number of concrete circumstances the police officer has as evidence.

ARBITRARY—NO BELIEF

Arbitrary means you have no justifiable reason at all to connect a person to an offence. It signifies no belief. The difference between "mere suspicion" and "no belief" is that, in the latter case, there is no evidence that an actual offence has taken place. *No belief* is the level of belief that prevails, for example, during proactive patrol. The following describes such a condition:

> It is 3:00 a.m. and you are on patrol, not investigating any specific offence. You see a 30-year-old pedestrian in a subdivision. You think this is suspicious, suspect that he may be involved in some crime, and decide to stop and ask him his name.

Although your belief resembles "mere suspicion," choosing to stop the man qualifies as an arbitrary decision, based on "no belief"; there is no crime being investigated. In this situation, you can ask the man to identify himself but he is under no legal compulsion to answer you.

SUMMARY

After completing Step 3 of the RDM model, you have accomplished the following:

▸ You have recognized the offence.
▸ You have classified the offence.
▸ You have classified your belief.

The next chapter teaches you how to apply ss. 495 and 31 C.C. and to use investigative detention. In other words, it teaches how to move from Steps 1–3 to Step 4 of the RDM model.

ENDNOTES

1. *R. v. Abel & Corbett*, 2008 BCCA 54.
2. R.E. Salhany, *Canadian Criminal Procedure*, 5th ed (Aurora, ON: Canada Law Book, 1989), 44.
3. *R. v. Dean* (1965), 3 C.C.C. 228 (Ont. C.A.).
4. Supra note 2, at A3.
5. E. Ehrlich et al., *Oxford American Dictionary* (New York: Oxford University Press, 1980), 138.
6. *Frey v. Fedoruk et al.* (1950), 3 D.L.R. 527, as in *R. v. Dean*, supra note 3.
7. Classes on arrest procedure. Aylmer, ON: Ontario Police College, 1977 and 1986.
8. Ibid.

9. Supra note 1.
10. *Hicks v. Faulkner*, [1882] 8 Q.B.D. 167, at 171 and 172 (D.C.).
11. *R. v. Collins* (1987), 33 C.C.C. (3d) 1 (S.C.C.).
12. *Chiau v. Canada (Minister of Citizenship and Immigration) (T.D.)*, [1998] 2 F.C. 642, 1998 CanLII 9042.
13. Ibid.
14. *R. v. Storrey* (1990), 53 C.C.C. (3d) 316 (S.C.C.).
15. *Hunter et al. v. Southam Inc.* (1984), 14 C.C.C. (3d) 97 (S.C.C.).
16. Ibid., and *Barron v. Canada*, [1993] 1 S.C.R. 416.
17. *R. v. Mann*, [2004] 3 S.C.R. 59.
18. Ibid.
19. *R. v. Simpson* (1993), 79 C.C.C. (3d) 482 (Ont. C.A.).
20. Supra note 17.
21. *R. v. Jacques*, [1996] 3 S.C.R. 312.
22. Supra note 17.
23. Ibid.
24. Ibid.
25. Ibid.
26. Ibid.

CHAPTER 4
Custody Authority Recognition

LEARNING OUTCOMES

The student will learn

- How to define *arrest*
- How to define *detention*
- How to define *voluntary accompaniment/consent*
- How to apply ss. 495 and 31 of the *Criminal Code*
- How to apply investigative detention

INTRODUCTION

The most important step of the RDM model is Step 4, which helps you answer the fundamental question, "Can I arrest or detain?" Steps 1–3 help you with the individual decisions that lead up to the crucial question of whether to take custody. In other words, Step 4 is the most important step of the entire model—it's the *goal* of the RDM model.

There are two stages to Step 4. First you have to learn the definitions of *arrest*, *detention*, and *consent*. The second phase is learning how to apply ss. 495 and 31 C.C. and how to use investigative detention.

DEFINITIONS OF ARREST AND DETENTION

Oddly, the words "arrest" and "detention" are not defined in any Canadian federal statute. They are defined in case law. **Arrest** is defined as

- ▶ formal actual restraint on a person's liberty, without that person's consent, or
- ▶ formal physical custody of a person with the intent to detain.[1]

Detention is defined as

- ▶ deprivation of liberty by physical constraint,
- ▶ the assuming of control over the movement of a person by demand or direction of a police officer, or

▸ a psychological compulsion existing within a person in the form of a perception that his or her freedom has been removed.[2]

The common denominator of both *arrest* and *detention* is that both involve taking **custody**—that is, removing an individual's freedom by physical or psychological restraint.[3] The differences between arrest and detention are that

▸ an arrest involves a longer, more deliberate form of custody than detention does, and
▸ there are two levels of detention:

    1. **Investigative detention** is a brief removal of freedom for investigative purposes, involving significant psychological restraint, without consent, and without actually making an arrest.
    2. A **brief detention** is a non-investigative detention for the specific purposes of identification.[4]

The differences between these two types of detention are purpose, duration, and extent of restraint. Not every detention falls within the scope of the *Canadian Charter of Rights and Freedoms* (the Charter). A brief detention that involves insignificant, or minimal, psychological or physical restraint does not fall within the scope of ss. 9 and 10 of the Charter. In other words, when a suspect is stopped purely for the purpose of requesting identification, or "brief interview," the person is detained only in the sense of being delayed or kept waiting, and the provisions of the Charter do not apply. The Charter does apply if the duration of the detention is longer and its purpose moves away from "the mere request of ID or brief interview."[5]

Key Points

Following are some key points regarding arrest:

▸ An arrest can be made with or without using the phrase, "You are under arrest."
▸ Saying the actual words "You are under arrest" is not mandatory, but words communicating that concept should be used.[6]
▸ There are two elements in an arrest:

    1. the officer's intention to detain, and
    2. physical custody.

In other words, an arrest is formal. The accused person definitely knows the officer's intention.

Following are some key points regarding detention:

▸ A detention can occur with or without the officer's intention to detain. In other words, the key element defining detention is what the detained person believes. If the suspect believes, even incorrectly, that he or she cannot leave a certain place, a detention has occurred.
▸ One of the elements of detention is whether or not the officer would have allowed the suspect to leave if he or she decided to walk away.

VOLUNTARY ACCOMPANIMENT/CONSENT

Voluntary accompaniment is the same as *consent*. It does not constitute custody; it is the opposite of custody. The distinguishing element of voluntary accompaniment is *choice*. A person in custody has no choice but to remain with the police, whereas a person who voluntarily accompanies the police has chosen to do so.

Consent offers police a valuable investigative tool, one that is used commonly in front-line policing. How to obtain consent is important. However, the terms "voluntary accompaniment" and "valid consent" are not defined in the *Criminal Code*. In other words, the Code outlines no procedure for obtaining valid consent. The definition of **consent** and the guidelines for obtaining it are found in case law. The primary requirement for valid consent is that the suspect be made aware of five things:

1. The specific act that the officer intends to conduct. Tell the person the *purpose* of your request that he or she accompany you (for example, questioning).
2. The possible consequences of the person's accompanying you. Caution the person that

    ‣ charges may result, and
    ‣ any statement he or she makes may later be used in court.

3. Consent may be refused. Inform the person that

    ‣ no obligation exists to give consent, and
    ‣ no consequences exist for refusing to give it. In other words, he or she cannot be charged or arrested for refusing to give consent.

4. Consent may be revoked at any time. Inform the person that even if he does give consent, he can withdraw it at any time.
5. The person may leave at any time. Emphasize that he or she has a choice to stay or leave at any time.

Key Points

Following are some key points regarding consent:

‣ Record conversations verbatim in your notebook.
‣ During testimony, provide the verbatim conversation. Do not paraphrase. In other words, do not say, "He consented to accompany me." Use direct quotes.

PROVING VOLUNTARY ACCOMPANIMENT

Proving voluntary accompaniment involves a simple three-stage question/comment sequence, as in the following example:

1. "Will you come with me (or will you meet me at the police station) for questioning about a robbery?"
2. "You don't have to. The choice is yours."
3. "If you do, you are free to leave at any time during the questioning."

It must be emphasized that you follow this procedure only when no lawful authority exists to arrest the person. Voluntary accompaniment is an investigative procedure that is an alternative to arrest.

ARREST WITHOUT WARRANT—CRIMINAL CODE POLICE OFFICERS' AUTHORITIES

The *Criminal Code* gives the police a total of five "arrest without a warrant" authorities. Four are found in s. 495(1) C.C. and the fifth in s. 31 C.C.

Police officers arrest offenders without a warrant more often than with a warrant. Section 495(1) C.C. may be the most important and most used provision in front-line policing. It establishes four lawful *arrest without a warrant* authorities:

1. find committing a criminal offence,[7]
2. reasonable grounds that an indictable offence has been committed,[8]
3. reasonable grounds that an indictable offence is about to occur,[9] and
4. reasonable grounds that a valid warrant exists in the territorial jurisdiction in which the accused person is found.[10]

In any of these four situations an officer is not required to obtain judicial authorization to arrest.[11] In other words, the officer becomes the decision-maker, not the Justice. These authorities apply to both adult and young offenders.

Find Committing a Criminal Offence

The simplest arrest authority under s. 495 C.C. is "find committing a criminal offence." It authorizes a police officer to make an arrest when he or she is an eyewitness to any classification of offence, anywhere. It is the cornerstone of proactive policing.

KEY POINTS

Following are some key points about *find committing*:

- ▸ It provides the strongest belief—the highest level of certainty (defined in Chapter 3).
- ▸ "Any classification" refers to all offences—summary conviction, dual procedure, or indictable.
- ▸ "Anywhere" refers to any dwelling-house or public place.

In other words, this arrest authority removes offence classification and geographic limitations.

The police are not usually eyewitnesses to crimes, however. Consequently, s. 495 C.C. also provides other arrest authorities, for situations where the police are not eyewitnesses.

Reasonable Grounds That an Indictable Offence Has Been Committed

This authority is the cornerstone of reactive policing—that is to say, when a crime has occurred and the police are not eyewitnesses. This authority is composed of three elements:

1. reasonable grounds that
2. an indictable offence
3. has been committed

REASONABLE GROUNDS

Reasonable grounds is defined in case law as "a set of facts or circumstances which would cause a person of ordinary and prudent judgment to believe beyond a mere suspicion."[12] This authority affords police an investigative benefit by permitting them to form a belief without witnessing an offence. It significantly expands the number of situations where an arrest may be made. The problem with this authority is that the abstract language defining it does not provide you with concrete guidelines. The definition does not specify the amount or type of evidence needed to constitute a *reasonable grounds* belief.

"A set of facts or circumstances" refers to evidence, both admissible and inadmissible.[13] This definition benefits a police investigation; it means that generally inadmissible evidence, such as hearsay, bad character, and legally married spouse statements, may be permitted to contribute to *reasonable grounds* development. This belief may be based on a single type of evidence or on a combination of types (for example, physical items and observations). The amount of evidence needed for *reasonable grounds* exceeds what is needed for *mere suspicion* (that is, intuition, speculation, or conjecture based on unsubstantiated rumour or gossip). However, "beyond mere suspicion" does not mean 100 percent certainty. You do not need absolute certainty, or belief beyond all doubt. What you need for reasonable grounds is *strong certainty*.

R. v. Storrey (1990),[14] a Supreme Court of Canada decision, is considered to be an important case with respect to explaining reasonable grounds. And yet it does not answer the most important question for front-line policing: *What is the minimum amount of evidence that constitutes reasonable grounds?* No statutory or case law answers this question. Despite being limited in this respect, *R. v. Storrey* establishes four major guidelines in connection with reasonable grounds:

1. *The two-pronged test.* The subjective and objective tests are the measure a Justice will use to determine if the officer's belief met the proper standard of reasonable grounds. In ordinary language, the two-pronged test means the following:

   ▸ It is not enough for the police officer alone to believe reasonable grounds existed.
   ▸ The officer must be able to convince a second person—namely, the trial judge who represents a reasonable person standing in the shoes of the arresting officer—that reasonable grounds existed.

   The subjective test refers to the officer's personal belief. The objective test is an independent assessment of the officer's opinion. Essentially, a judge conducts the objective test to evaluate whether the officer's belief was correct. The purpose of the objective test is evaluation—to determine whether "a reasonable person placed in the position of the officer" would conclude that reasonable grounds actually existed. Passing the objective test requires convincing the judge by justifying the belief in the form of *concrete evidence*. The objective test represents accountability—it is a safeguard.

2. *The minimum-standard benefit.* The police are not required to establish a *prima facie* case before making an arrest. Claiming reasonable grounds

does not require you to prove guilt beyond reasonable doubt. In other words, the benchmark for reasonable grounds is below that for a *prima facie* case. This is an investigative benefit for police.

3. *Totality of circumstances.* The police officer must take into account and consider all available information when seeking to establish reasonable grounds. In other words, an officer cannot be selective and consider only some of the available information. For example, if multiple witnesses to an event are available, the officer cannot base his or her belief only on the witnesses who provide positive information; information from other sources cannot be disregarded without justifiable reasons.

4. *Credibility evaluation.* Evaluating the credibility of a witness is a significant skill and a difficult one to develop. Every witness's credibility must be evaluated. A police officer cannot believe or disbelieve a witness arbitrarily, without justification. Of course, an officer is allowed not to believe a witness if concrete reasons justify disbelief. A companion textbook to this one, *Criminal Investigation: Forming Reasonable Grounds*, devotes an entire chapter to the topic of witness evaluation.)

The most important consideration for police officers is how to determine *what specifically constitutes reasonable grounds*. Although *R. v. Storrey* does not offer concrete guidelines, it does indicate that three specific types of evidence constitute reasonable grounds:

1. a confession by an offender to any person,
2. one credible eyewitness, or
3. circumstantial evidence leading to one logical conclusion.

A **confession** is a verbal or written inculpatory statement made by an offender to either a police officer or a citizen. The confession represents the best type of reasonable grounds.

An **eyewitness** is a person who saw the entire offence and is capable of recognizing the offender's face. At least *one credible eyewitness* is sufficient to form reasonable grounds. No law obliges police to obtain corroboration when at least one credible eyewitness exists. Forming reasonable grounds may be either a simple task accomplished in seconds or a complex task requiring a substantial amount of time. Every investigation involves a unique set of circumstances. The reality is that front-line officers encounter situations every day where immediate decisions are needed. An example of such a situation is a domestic complaint where the victim and offender are both present.

Domestic disputes are commonly hostile, stressful situations that pose significant danger to the officer and the participants. It is not uncommon for novice officers to question the credibility or reliability of brief information reported by the victim. For example, the victim often makes a simple statement such as "he hit me," which motivates a tirade by the offender. The uncorroborated, unsupported verbal statement made by the complainant in situations like this constitutes reasonable grounds. The offence of "Assault" does not require corroboration to convict. If investigation reveals that the victim intentionally lied, the victim could be charged with public mischief. Any other evidence, such as visible injuries, simply solidifies the forming of reasonable grounds.

In *R. v. Godoy* (1999),[15] the Supreme Court of Canada ruled that a woman's oral claim that her husband hit her, combined with the officer's observation of her swollen eye, constituted reasonable grounds to arrest the husband. This decision-making process only took the officer a few seconds. This case is significant for showing that quick decisions based on minimal evidence are justified in potentially dangerous situations.

Circumstantial evidence refers to items, observations, or a combination of both. It does not include a confession or an eyewitness account. There are countless varieties of circumstantial evidence. Some lead to multiple *logical conclusions*, others to only one conclusion. In the latter case, circumstantial evidence forms reasonable grounds; in the former, it does not. The key concept is logic, an issue decided during the objective test.

INDICTABLE OFFENCE

This arrest authority governs purely indictable offences and dual procedure offences. Summary conviction offences are not governed by this authority.

HAS BEEN COMMITTED

The phrase "has been" means that *an offence has to have occurred*, and that it has to have occurred *in the past*. Speculating that an offence may have occurred or might occur does not constitute reasonable grounds for believing that an indictable offence has been committed. There is no time limit on making an arrest on reasonable grounds that an indictable offence has been committed.

Knowing when not to arrest is as important as knowing when to arrest. An officer cannot arrest without a warrant under the following circumstances:

- There are reasonable grounds that a *summary conviction* offence has been committed. (An officer can arrest for a summary conviction offence only if he *finds committing*.)
- There is *mere suspicion* that a criminal offence has been committed. Arrest for any classification of offence is not authorized if only mere suspicion exists. The evidence must form a belief that exceeds mere suspicion.

Anonymous Information—Credibility

Anonymous information is common. However, such information is problematic for an officer trying to establish reasonable grounds, because it is difficult to determine whether such witnesses are credible.

Informants are an integral part of police investigations. Informants are witnesses whom the police do not subpoena to court, in order to maintain confidentiality. In some cases, the officer knows the informant by name. In other cases, the informant is anonymous and is unknown to the officer. The following case, *R. v. Bennett*,[16] is enormously significant. It illustrates the relationship between reasonable grounds and anonymous informants.

CASE LAW

R. v. Bennett (1996)

- **Issue:** Anonymous informant

- **Offences:** "Possession of narcotics" and "Obstruct police"

- **Circumstances:** A police officer received the following information from a female citizen who refused to identify herself or her address, or to explain her motive for reporting the information. The citizen reported that a woman was selling crack in the entrance hall of an apartment complex. She provided a detailed description of the suspect and the address of the complex. The informant also reported that the suspect had a key case containing crack in her pocket. The officer evaluated the informant's credibility on the basis of: (a) the precision of the information, and (b) his own prior knowledge that drug trafficking was common at that apartment complex.

  The officer went to the address and saw a woman outside the building who matched the description of the suspect, exactly. The officer arrested the woman for the dual procedure offence of "possession of narcotics" *before* searching her. When the officer prepared to search her, the woman removed a key case from her pocket, held it in her hand, and appeared intent on disposing of it. The officer asked her for the key case, and she gave it to him. A quantity of crack was found inside. The officer later charged the woman with "possession of narcotics" and "obstruct police" for attempting to hide the key case.

- **Trial:** The accused was found guilty of "Possession of narcotics." She was also convicted of "Obstruct police," but the judge ordered a stay of proceedings in the case of this latter conviction, in keeping with the principle that prevents multiple convictions.

- **Appeal:** The accused appealed her conviction for "Possession of narcotics" to the Quebec Court of Appeal. The appeal was dismissed, and the conviction was upheld. The seized narcotics were ruled to be admissible under s. 24(2) Charter even though the arrest was ruled to be unlawful because the circumstances did not constitute reasonable grounds.

  The following reasons were given in the judgment. The informant's refusal to identify herself justified the need for additional investigation. In this case, the anonymous informant's report constituted mere suspicion only. An anonymous "tip" does not constitute reasonable grounds for a belief. The officer must also be satisfied with the reliability of the information, which must be assessed on the basis of the total circumstances. In this case, the officer had no means of verifying the credibility of the informant or of the information.

  The following points are crucial in this case:

  ▸ The officer made the arrest on the basis of the similarity between the informant's description of the suspect and the appearance of the woman he saw at the apartment building. Confirming the identity of the suspect was not the issue; it was the suspect's involvement in drug trafficking that needed confirmation and supporting evidence.

(continued)

- ▸ The unlawful arrest constituted a s. 9 Charter violation. Subsequently, the admissibility of the seized narcotics needed to be determined pursuant to s. 24(2) Charter.
- ▸ However, the narcotics were admissible because their admission would not bring the administration of justice into disrepute. The admission of the evidence was allowed because the Charter violation was *minor*. The Justice emphasized the minor nature of the Charter violation by saying, "I find it difficult to imagine a more minor infringement of a right." The court also rationalized that, although the arrest was unlawful, "the officer could have believed that he was justified in placing her under arrest." The narcotics were physical evidence that existed before the Charter violation occurred.

COMMENTARY

This case illustrates very well the complexity of case law decisions. Specifically, it shows the relationship among minor Charter violations, the seizure of physical items, and how s. 24(2) Charter applies.

The informant's refusal to identify herself created an *investigative bind*. The officer obviously could not evaluate the credibility of an unknown person, and he could not simply ignore the information.

The inability to evaluate the informant's credibility put the officer at a disadvantage that produced a Charter violation. However, the severity of this violation was minor. This connects the situation to the governing principle of s. 24(2) Charter: Which factor will affect the criminal justice system's reputation more, the Charter violation or the admission of the drugs?

This is a point-of-reference case that sheds light on the investigative bind caused by anonymous informants, when the police officer has no way to evaluate or confirm the informant's credibility.

Reasonable Grounds That an Indictable Offence Is About to Occur

This proactive authority authorizes arrest to prevent certain offences. The three component parts of this authority are:

1. reasonable grounds that
2. an indictable offence
3. is about to occur

REASONABLE GROUNDS

One credible eyewitness, a confession to anyone, or circumstantial evidence is sufficient to justify a reasonable belief that an indictable offence is about to occur.

INDICTABLE OFFENCE

This authority covers purely indictable and dual procedure offences. Inexplicably, it does not apply to summary conviction offences. As a result, summary conviction offences cannot be prevented.

ABOUT TO OCCUR

The term **about to occur** is not defined in the *Criminal Code.* It means that an offence has not been committed but a strong probability exists that it may be committed in the near future. The person who is about to commit an indictable offence cannot be charged with the substantive offence, but other offences may well have been committed in the circumstances leading up to the probable offence, and the person can be charged with those.

This authority allows a police officer to *prevent* the commission of an indictable or dual procedure offence when strong certainty exists that the offence will happen. There is no equivalent authority allowing officers to prevent, by means of arrest, a summary conviction offence from occurring. Officers may prevent summary conviction offences only by alternate means, such as by using their communication skills.

Section 503(4) C.C. governs the length of detention and the release procedures for an arrest made under the authority of *reasonable grounds for believing that an indictable offence is about to occur.* The arrested person must be released, unconditionally, as soon as practicable after the officer is satisfied that the continued detention of the arrested person is no longer necessary to prevent the commission of an indictable offence (by the arrested person).

Reasonable Grounds That a Valid Warrant Exists in the Territorial Jurisdiction in Which the Accused Person Is Found

This complex arrest authority applies after an *arrest warrant* has been issued. It authorizes the officer to arrest *without having possession of the original warrant.* The three elements that compose this authority are:

1. reasonable grounds that
2. a valid warrant exists
3. in the territorial jurisdiction in which the accused is found.[17]

Section 29(1) C.C. is the reason that this authority is listed in the "arrest without warrant" section. This provision imposes two obligations on officers executing an arrest warrant: possession and production. The arresting officer must have possession of the original warrant and must produce it for the accused upon request.[18] But here is the problem: in reality, patrol officers generally do not have possession of original arrest warrants while on patrol. The original warrant is usually stored in the central records department at the police station. Section 495(1)(c) C.C. is the solution to the impractical requirement of s. 29(1) C.C. Essentially, s. 495(1)(c) C.C. creates an exception to the s. 29(1) C.C. requirement. In other words, the officer can make an arrest without actually possessing the warrant when he or she has reasonable grounds to believe that the original warrant was issued and is in central records.

REASONABLE GROUNDS

A Canadian Police Information Centre (CPIC) message stating that a person is "wanted" constitutes reasonable grounds for believing that a warrant exists.

VALID WARRANT EXISTS

An arrest warrant must be signed by a **Justice**, defined as a Justice of the Peace or a provincial court judge.[19] A justice usually has authority throughout his or her province. In most cases, then, an arrest warrant signed by a Justice in a particular city is valid throughout that province. For example, an arrest warrant signed by a Justice in Toronto is valid anywhere in Ontario. The CPIC message will state the city where the arrest warrant was signed.

IN THE TERRITORIAL JURISDICTION IN WHICH THE PERSON IS FOUND

This refers to the legal authority or power of a court to conduct the proceeding in a particular city or region[20] where the officer has found the suspect. A CPIC message regarding arrest warrants usually includes the following information, in the following format: Wanted—(offence)—(city where warrant was signed and issued). A typical CPIC message might be as follows:

Wanted—"Theft over $5,000.00"—Calgary.

"Wanted" constitutes reasonable grounds to believe two facts: the warrant exists, and the person named on it committed the offence. The name of the city where the warrant was issued informs the officer that the warrant is valid anywhere in the relevant province (for example, Alberta). Finding the suspect anywhere in that province, a police officer may arrest him or her without actually possessing the warrant at the time of the arrest.

If the warrant is out-of-province and the offence is dual procedure or indictable, an arrest may be lawfully made under the "reasonable grounds that an indictable offence has been committed" authority.

ARREST PROHIBITED

The provisions of s. 495(2) C.C. have a threefold purpose:

1. to explain why an arrest is necessary,
2. to impose limitations on taking custody of persons in every arrestable situation, and
3. to create release provisions, specifically, the first level of release.

Section 495(2) C.C. stipulates the following

▸ When you use the authority of s. 495(1) C.C. to arrest someone for a summary conviction or dual procedure offence, you cannot bring that person to the police station for no reason. You have to justify it by means of four considerations collectively known as RICE—Repetition (of the offence), Identity (of the accused), Court (likelihood of appearing for), and Evidence (protection/seizure of). These four considerations address two risks: (1) potential threat to public safety and (2) the suspect's failing to appear in court.

▸ When a summary conviction or dual procedure offence occurred in the past, and you know that there is no longer a public safety risk or a risk of the suspect's failing to appear in court, you must issue a summons instead of arresting the person.

In other words, when s. 495(1) C.C. is used to arrest for a summary conviction or dual procedure offence, you have to justify why you arrested the person instead of giving him or her a summons.

According to s. 495(2) C.C., an officer is prohibited from arresting without a warrant, even if s. 495(1) C.C. applies, if the following two circumstances exist:

1. The offence is (a) summary conviction or (b) dual procedure or (c) s. 553 C.C. indictable, and
2. An arrest is not necessary in the "public interest," meaning that
   a. there are no *reasonable grounds* for believing that the offender will repeat the offence,
   b. the *identity* of the offender is known,
   c. there are no reasonable grounds for believing that the offender will fail to appear in *court*, and
   d. no *evidence* needs to be secured or preserved.

These four considerations are commonly referred to as RICE. When RICE is fulfilled, an arrest is prohibited if the offence is summary conviction, dual procedure, or s. 553 C.C. indictable. In this case, an officer may charge the offender only by laying an Information and compelling the offender to appear in court by serving either

- an appearance notice,[21] or
- a summons.[22]

Key Points

Following are some key points concerning the prohibitions on arrest created by s. 495(2) C.C.:

1. This prohibition does not apply
   - when the offence is a "straight" indictable one not listed in s. 553 C.C., or
   - when reasonable grounds exist for believing that the offender is a public safety risk or a risk for not appearing in court.
2. Every time you make an arrest under s. 495(1) C.C., justify two things:
   - The appropriate authority (that is, reasonable grounds or find committing) plus the relevant offence, and
   - Grounds for believing that the suspect poses a risk to public safety or that there is a risk of his or her failing to appear in court.

BREACH OF THE PEACE (S. 31(1) C.C.)

A fifth legal authority for arresting without a warrant is established in s. 31(1) C.C. This authority applies to "Breach of the peace," which resembles "Cause a disturbance" with two differences. *Breach of the peace* is not an actual offence. The authority to arrest is a solution to a common problem. *Cause a disturbance*, on the other hand, is a summary conviction offence. Breach of the peace can occur anywhere, including inside a dwelling-house. Cause a disturbance can only occur in a public place.

In the case of breach of the peace, a police officer can arrest without a warrant if the following two conditions exist:

1. The officer has personally witnessed the **breach of the peace**, which is defined as "the violation of the peace, quiet, and security to which one is legally entitled."[23]
2. After personally witnessing the breach of the peace, the officer may arrest anyone who

    ▸ is found committing the breach of the peace,
    ▸ is about to join in the breach of the peace, or
    ▸ is about to renew the breach of the peace.[24]

The starting point for this authority is that the officer must first witness the breach of the peace. Once this occurs, the officer may prevent other persons from joining in or renewing it.

Breach of the peace is not an offence—neither summary conviction, dual procedures, or indictable. Arresting a person for breach of the peace is merely "problem-solving procedure." Persons arrested for breach of the peace will not be charged. An Information cannot be sworn because no offence is involved. The arrested person will simply be released unconditionally, meaning without charges, when peace has been restored and it appears that the person is no longer likely to repeat the breach (that is, when the RICE is fulfilled).

Key Points

Following are some key points concerning breach of the peace arrest:

▸ In the case of public place disturbances, the officer can use discretion in choosing whether to arrest and charge for "Cause a disturbance" or merely to arrest for "Breach of the peace."
▸ In the case of dwelling-house disturbances, only "Breach of the peace" applies.

CITIZENS' POWERS OF ARREST

Citizens have the authority to make an arrest, but the police must be called directly. A citizen has no authority to release an arrested person without calling the police.[25] Because police officers are commonly called upon to take custody of a person arrested by a citizen, officers must be aware of citizens' powers to arrest without warrant. The police have to understand when they can and when they cannot continue this type of detention.

Citizens have four powers of arrest—three are described in s. 495 C.C. and one in s. 30 C.C. The word "citizen" is slang; it is not used in the section. The terms "any one" and "every one" include "citizen." Citizens' arrest authorities are more restrictive than police officers' powers of arrest. Section 494 C.C. applies to both adult and young offenders.

The term **citizen**, not defined in the *Criminal Code*, refers to anyone who is not a peace officer. The term *citizen* applies to ordinary people and to

- security guards,
- private investigators,
- any member of private policing,
- municipal bylaw officers,
- auxiliary members of a police service,[26] and
- hotel security (bouncers).

Section 494 C.C. authorizes citizens to use their powers of arrest under the following circumstances:

1. A citizen finds committing an indictable offence.[27]
2. An owner or person in lawful possession of property, or a person authorized by the owner, finds committing a criminal offence on or in relation to that property.[28]
3. A citizen sees a person believed to be escaping from and freshly pursued by persons who have lawful authority to arrest, and believed to have committed a criminal offence.[29]

Find Committing an Indictable Offence

This authority allows a citizen to arrest an offender who has committed an indictable or dual procedure offence if the citizen sees the entire offence occur and apprehends the offender immediately, or if the citizen sees the entire offence occur and pursues the offender without losing sight of the offender until apprehension occurs. A citizens' arrest cannot be made merely on the basis of a person's having reasonable grounds for believing that an offence has occurred; that is, without the citizen actually witnessing the entire offence.

The citizen involved in an arrest (see below) may or may not be a property owner. The arrest may occur anywhere: in a public place or in a private dwelling-house. Summary conviction offences are not covered by this authority.

Property Owner Finds Committing

This authority is restricted to a specific type of citizen and to a specific geographic location. The specific type of citizen includes the following:

- An owner: the person who actually owns the property.
- A person in lawful possession: not the owner, but a person who has possession and control of the property with the owner's lawful consent.
- A person authorized by the owner: a person who has control of the premises and can regulate the access of other persons to the property (for example, an employee at a business).

Property includes houses, buildings, and motor vehicles. The location is restricted to "on or in relation to" that property. Offences committed outside the owner's property are not covered by this authority. This authority applies to any criminal offence. Summary conviction offences are included *only for this authority*. An arrest may be made only in the case of *finds committing*, not on *reasonable grounds*. A citizen cannot arrest if he or she did not witness the offence being committed.

Escaping Custody

Because the circumstances to which this authority applies rarely occur, you must use caution when using it. The section refers to a citizen's belief based on reasonable grounds, but this does not mean that a citizen may arrest exclusively on the reasonable grounds belief that an offence has occurred.

This authority essentially permits a citizen, without having seen an offence occur, to help another person apprehend a fleeing offender. Seeing one person pursuing another, the citizen may arrest the fleeing offender only if the citizen reasonably believes that

- the pursuer has lawful authority to arrest, and
- the fleeing person has committed a criminal offence.

Citizens have no lawful authority to arrest in the following circumstances:

- They have reasonable grounds for believing that an indictable, dual procedure, or summary conviction offence has occurred.
- They have reasonable grounds for believing that a person is about to commit an indictable, dual procedure, or summary conviction offence.
- A non-owner finds a summary conviction offence being committed on public property.

Breach of the Peace

Section 30 C.C. establishes an additional authority for citizens' arrest. A citizen may arrest a person who commits "Breach of the peace." The rules of this authority for citizens are the same as those for police officers and are detailed in s. 31 C.C. Although the citizens' and police authorities are found in different sections of the *Criminal Code*, "Breach of the peace" is not a criminal offence in either section, and arresting a person for it is simply a problem-solving procedure.

The following conditions must exist for citizens to arrest under the authority governing "Breach of the peace":

1. a breach of the peace has been witnessed; and
2. the person arrested is
   - anyone committing a breach of the peace,
   - anyone about to join in the existing breach of the peace, or
   - anyone about to renew the breach of the peace; and
3. the arrest is made for the purpose of preventing the continuance or renewal of the breach of the peace.[30]

CITIZENS' DUTY AFTER AN ARREST

Section 494(3) C.C. makes it mandatory for a citizen who makes an arrest to "deliver" the arrested person "forthwith" to a peace officer.[31] "Forthwith" is defined as "immediately" or "as soon as practicable."[32] The significance of this provision is threefold:

1. A citizen has no discretion to release an arrested person without notifying and giving custody of the arrested person to an officer.
2. A citizen's failure to deliver an arrested person to a police officer may constitute the offence of "Obstructing justice."[33] This offence may be committed in a variety of ways. For example, a citizen might intentionally not report an offence to the police, thereby allowing an offender to go undetected and escape prosecution.[34]
3. If a citizen arrests an offender but does not wish to have the offender charged, the citizen must call the police, and the officer will decide upon the appropriate course of action. The officer will decide which method of release will be used.

An officer who receives custody of a person arrested by a citizen must interview the citizen and analyze the circumstances of the arrest to determine whether the officer has lawful authority to continue the detention.

ADDITIONAL CASE LAW

There are countless point-of-reference case law decisions that can help front-line police officers determine what constitutes reasonable grounds to make an arrest. The website that accompanies this text (**www.emp.ca/arcaro/policepowers4E**) includes an extensive, ongoing case law review that practically applies relevant case law decisions.

The *Criminal Code* explains only when you *can* arrest; it does not specify when you *cannot* arrest. Table 4.1 lists when police officers and citizens may and may not arrest.

INVESTIGATIVE DETENTION

A series of case law decisions from 1993 to the present have recognized another belief and another type of custody called **investigative detention.**

Investigative detention derives from a common-law authority. In 1993 this authority was called "articulable cause." The transformational case of *R. v. Mann* (2004) was the occasion of its being renamed. Countless derivative cases have and will continue to emerge from *R. v. Mann.* The accompanying website, **www.emp.ca/arcaro/policepowers4E** includes extensive on-going case law review in connection with *R. v. Mann.*

Definition

Investigative detention is defined as the *brief* removal of an individual's freedom for investigative purposes, involving significant psychological restraint, without

Table 4.1 Police/Citizen Arrest Authorities

A **police officer may arrest** when:

1. he or she directly witnesses (that is, *finds committing*)
   ‣ an indictable offence,
   ‣ a dual procedure offence, or
   ‣ a summary conviction offence.

2. there is reasonable grounds that
   ‣ an indictable offence, or
   ‣ a dual procedure offence is about to occur.

3. there is reasonable grounds that a valid warrant exists in the territorial jurisdiction where the accused is found.

4. he or she directly witnesses (*finds committing*)
   ‣ a breach of peace.

A **citizen may arrest** when:

1. he or she directly witnesses (*finds committing*)
   ‣ an indictable offence, or
   ‣ a dual procedure offence.

2. there is reasonable grounds that a person, escaping from and being pursued by a person who may lawfully arrest, has committed
   ‣ an indictable offence,
   ‣ a dual procedure offence, or
   ‣ a summary conviction offence.

3. the citizen is the property owner, or person authorized by property owner, who finds committing on or in relation to that property,
   ‣ an indictable offence,
   ‣ a dual procedure offence, or
   ‣ a summary conviction offence.

4. finds committing
   ‣ a breach of the peace.

A **police officer may not arrest** when:

1. there is reasonable grounds that
   ‣ a summary conviction offence has occurred.

2. there is reasonable grounds that
   ‣ a summary conviction offence is about to occur.

3. there is mere suspicion that
   ‣ an indictable offence,
   ‣ a dual procedure offence, or
   ‣ a summary conviction offence has occurred or is about to occur.

4. there is a warrant not valid in the territorial jurisdiction where the accused person is found.

5. there is reasonable grounds that
   ‣ a breach of the peace has been committed.

A **citizen may not arrest** when:

1. there is reasonable grounds that
   ‣ an indictable offence,
   ‣ a dual procedure offence, or
   ‣ a summary conviction offence has occurred.

2. there is reasonable grounds that
   ‣ an indictable offence,
   ‣ a dual procedure offence, or
   ‣ a summary conviction offence is about to occur.

3. there is reasonable grounds that
   ‣ a breach of the peace has been committed.

4. a non-owner finds committing
   ‣ a summary conviction offence.

that individuals consent but with no arrest made. A police officer may make an investigative detention if there are "reasonable grounds to suspect" that a person has committed any criminal offence.[35]

After an officer makes an investigative detention, the detained person may be searched if reasonable grounds exist that any person's safety is at risk.[36]

The type of detention authorized is a "limited investigative detention," an abstract term that restricts the duration and subsequent investigative procedures. The duration of the detention must be "brief." There is no specific time frame prescribed, but only two investigative procedures are permitted:

1. a protective "pat-down" search of the detained person, and
2. a brief questioning of the detained person, who is under no obligation to answer any questions by the police.

History: The Four Concepts

Understanding investigative detention is simple if you understand its four core concepts:

1. the case law recognition of the legitimacy of risk to police safety,
2. the common-law definition of the general scope of police officers' duties,
3. the history of *articulable cause*—police authority to detain, and
4. the decision in *R. v. Mann*.

LEGITIMACY OF RISK

> Police officers are at high risk every day. They never know when a routine, mundane situation will explode into violence.
>
> —Manitoba Court of Appeal, *R. v. Willis* (2003)[37]

> Judges cannot be blind to the deaths and injuries suffered by police officers on duty as guns and knives become more common. Situations which appear quite innocent, with no hostile demonstration by the person being arrested, can explode into violence leaving the arresting officer dead or injured. It is difficult to second-guess any police officer who ensures that a person is not armed when he/she perceives danger as he/she makes an arrest or escorts a prisoner.
>
> —Alberta Court of Appeal, *R. v. Lerke* (1986)[38]

The above quotations are not merely illustrative; they are enormously significant. They are two of several case law statements that have provided police with *investigative benefits*. They are *legal acknowledgments* of four concepts that are vital to the application of investigative detention laws. These four concepts can be understood as follows:

1. *Reality.* Potential violence toward the police is not a theoretical concept—it is a reality. The above quotations legally acknowledge that front-line police officers' lives are frequently at serious risk.
2. *Priority.* They also legally acknowledge that officer safety and self-protection take priority over all other investigative objectives. In other words, they formally legitimize the notion that considerations of officer safety supersedes goals of seizing evidence.
3. *Expect the unexpected—expect the worst.* These quotations from case law legally acknowledge the reasonableness of such expectations—of believing that the *worst* consequence is a possibility for a police officer even in seemingly harmless situations. They also formally legitimize the primary aim of *eliminating the worst possible consequence.*
4. *Credibility.* These quotations legally justify your detaining and searching a suspect near a crime scene, shortly after a "crime in progress," for weapons (not for evidence relating to an offence). These and similar quotations in

case law are important tools for police. Theoretically, one of their effects should be to neutralize suspicions that your primary intention in detaining a person was to fish for evidence. Thanks to these quotations, no one will question your claim that visual observation alone could not ensure that a suspect was unarmed.

These four concepts provide a crucial investigative *benefit* because they offer police **legal justification** for reasonably believing that a suspect near an "offence in progress" crime scene may be *armed*, may become *violent*, and may pose a *risk* to the investigating officer. Such official validation can be a vital element in proving the necessity of an "investigative detention." For police officers, always accountable for their decisions, to justify an action is to give *concrete reasons* for forming a belief and executing an investigative procedure.

These two case law decisions should constantly be referred to in prosecutions; they support the reasonableness of addressing these risks in *every* situation.

COMMON-LAW POLICE OFFICERS' DUTIES

Prior to 2004 and the legal recognition of investigative detention, a police officer's duties, as defined by common law, made up an obvious list, with no particular significance to police investigations. Today the composition of this list has crucial significance to prosecutions involving an investigative detention. The scope of duties includes three goals:

1. the preservation of peace,
2. the prevention of crime, and
3. the protection of life and property.

This three-part definition of the general scope of police duties has become the first of two standards used for determining whether an investigative detention was valid. In each investigative detention prosecution, the onus is on the Crown to prove that the detention fell within the general scope of police duties. This obliges police officers to explain at a trial what duty they were fulfilling by means of the detention—a simple but inescapable obligation.

Having proved that the investigative detention fell within the scope of the police officer's duties, the Crown must show by a second standard that investigative detention was valid. The Crown must prove that the officer's conduct in using investgative detention involved a justifiable use of the powers associated with his or her duty as a police officer.[39] In other words, the Crown must prove the officer had the "reasonable grounds to suspect" belief prior to imposing the investigative detention.

HISTORY OF ARTICULABLE CAUSE—POLICE AUTHORITY TO DETAIN

As stated previously, the term *investigative detention* emerged from a series of case law decisions. Only the name of the procedure was new, not the definitions and concepts composing it. In other words, the concept of investigative detention was reshaped and reformed—but not created—by *R. v. Mann*. The history of this concept, is vital to understanding investigative detention. The following is a summary of this history.

The term "articulable cause" is not found or defined in any Canadian statute. It was defined by the Ontario Court of Appeal (Ont. C.A.) in *R. v. Simpson* (1993), then adopted by the Supreme Court of Canada in *R. v. Mann* (2004), where the phrase "articulable cause" was changed to "reasonable grounds to suspect." The definition for both "articulable cause" and "reasonable grounds to suspect" is "a constellation of objectively discernible facts which give the detaining officer reasonable cause to suspect that the detainee is criminally implicated in the activity under investigation."[40]

In other words, the officer's suspicion is based on more than a "hunch" (that is, it is based on more than just intuition informed by experience).

THE TRANSFORMATIONAL CASE: R. v. MANN (2004)

Potential violence toward the police is the *reality* of a "crime in progress" investigation. Anyone who has actually responded to a crime in progress is aware of two goals, which are as follows, in order of importance:

1. Protect yourself and the public from death or injury.
2. Form reasonable grounds to believe a specific person or persons committed the offence.

The officer trying to achieve these goals faces two challenging problems:

1. The sequence of events: achieving the first goal (of protecting yourself and the public) is dependent on achieving the second goal (forming reasonable grounds).
2. Two limitations: time and information. In reality, time constraints restrict the amount of information police can obtain as well as their ability to evaluate credibility or corroborate it. These goals and limitations have to be weighed against the need to avoid wrongful arrests and searches of innocent people.

Self-protection as a justification for investigative detention needs to be understood in relation to three levels of belief:

1. *No Belief*: no concrete evidence connects a person to a crime.
2. *Mere Suspicion*: circumstantial evidence, leading to more than one logical conclusion, connects a person to a crime.
3. *Reasonable Grounds* (formerly "reasonable and probable grounds"): concrete evidence leads to a single logical conclusion that a specific person(s) has committed an indictable offence.

Clearly established investigative procedures are set out for the first and the third levels of belief. *No belief* authorizes no detention and no search without arrest. *Reasonable grounds* authorizes an arrest and an automatic search for both weapons and evidence.

The Supreme Court of Canada, in *R. v. Mann* (2004), created guidelines for the second stage.

CASE LAW

R. v. Mann (2004)

- **Issue:** Do police have authority to detain a suspect for investigative purposes based on mere suspicion only?

- **Circumstances:** Two officers responded to a break and enter in progress shortly before midnight. A description and possible name of one suspect was conveyed to the officers. While responding, the officers saw a potential suspect. The following events occurred.

  A man was casually walking on a sidewalk two to three blocks from the crime scene. He matched the broadcast description "to the tee," but there was no further evidence of his being the suspect, such as facial recognition by a witness.

  The officers stopped the pedestrian but did not arrest him; they asked him to identify himself. He complied by orally giving his name and date of birth. The name differed from the name broadcast with the suspect's description.

  The search continued. Small plastic baggies, two Valium pills, and an ID card confirming that the suspect had given his real name were found in a pocket.

  The suspect was arrested and charged for possession for the purpose of trafficking, under s. 5(2) of the *Controlled Drugs and Substances Act*.

- **Trial:** The accused was acquitted. The defence conceded that the police had lawful authority to detain for investigative purposes, based on the fact that the broadcast description matched the accused's appearance "to the tee." The trial judge ruled that the pat-down search was justified for security reasons, but also ruled that the circumstances did not justify the officers' reaching into the accused's pocket to determine what the soft object was. The evidence was excluded under s. 24(2) Charter, on the grounds that its admission would interfere with trial fairness.

  The prosecution appealed.

- **Manitoba Court of Appeal:** The acquittal was set aside and a new trial was ordered. The Manitoba Court of Appeal (Man. C.A.) ruled that both the detention and search for weapons were authorized by law. The search sanctioned by detention is restricted to weapons, but the search of the suspect's pocket was judged to be reasonable, based on the officer's right to execute a protective search.

  Searching the interior of a pocket for concealed weapons is not unreasonable if the search is conducted in good faith, according to the Man. C.A. This court was "wary of placing too rigid a constraint on officers' abilities to ensure a safe environment," and affirmed that the police should be allowed "some latitude" in conducting a good faith search for weapons.

  Accordingly, given the "unquestioned" good faith of the officers in searching the suspect's pocket, their actions were judged not to have contravened s. 8 Charter.

  This decision was appealed to the Supreme Court of Canada (S.C.C.), with interveners that included the Criminal Lawyers' Association (Ontario), the Canadian Civil Liberties Association, the Attorney General of Ontario, and the Canadian Association of Chiefs of Police.

(continued)

■ **S.C.C.:** The appeal was allowed and the acquittal restored. The marijuana seizure constituted a s. 8 Charter violation. The evidence was excluded under s. 24(2) Charter. The reasons were as follows:

1. There is no general police power to detain for investigative purposes. In other words, the S.C.C. did not recognize an automatic, all-encompassing investigative detention power that may be applied in any circumstance. The S.C.C. called on Parliament to decide whether this authority should become a statutory law.

   Although there is no *general* police power to detain, there is *limited* police power to detain for investigation. Investigative detentions should be limited to situations where the police have "reasonable grounds to *suspect*" that a person "is connected to a particular crime."

2. The phrase "reasonable grounds to suspect" should not be confused with "reasonable grounds to arrest," as used in s. 495 C.C. (formerly called "reasonable and probable grounds"). "Reasonable grounds to suspect" means a belief based on mere suspicion, but justified by meaningful, relevant evidence that exceeds a "hunch." *Mere suspicion* must be explained by citing the circumstances that caused the reasonable belief that the suspect was "connected" to the crime.

   In functional terms, having "reasonable grounds to suspect" means that you have *reasonable suspicion*, justified by circumstances, that a specific person was connected to a crime. This authority is intended to deny the police what the S.C.C. called "carte blanche" power to detain anyone at any time. Essentially, the phrase *reasonable grounds to suspect* simply ensures that police are accountable for their investigative detentions. The S.C.C. reminded us of the following: "Police powers and police duties are not necessarily correlative. While the police have a common-law duty to investigate crime, they are not empowered to undertake any and all action in the exercise of that duty."

3. The limited investigative detention authority held by police, based on "reasonable grounds to suspect," is equivalent to "articulable cause" but has been renamed "reasonable grounds to detain" or *reasonable suspicion to detain*.

   "Articulable cause" is an American phrase that has been defined and used in several Canadian lower court case law decisions. Essentially, it means the same as *mere suspicion* and authorizes temporary detention for investigative purposes. The S.C.C. stated that it preferred the wording "reasonable grounds to detain" over "articulable cause" because it is consistent with Canadian criminal law language.

4. An investigative detention does not in itself authorize a search of the detained person. Such a search is authorized only if officers believe on reasonable grounds that their own safety, or the safety of others, is at risk. In other words, the search has to seem rationally necessary, based on the collective circumstances. Conversely, a search is unjustified where a "vague or non-existent concern for safety" or "hunches or mere intuition" exist.

   The common-law "search incident to arrest" needs to be distinguished from search following an investigative detention. After an arrest is made, common law authorizes an *automatic* search of the person for *weapons* and *evidence*. The S.C.C. confirmed this authority in

(continued)

R. v. Golden (2001). But during an investigative detention a search is *not* automatic and a search for *evidence* is not authorized. A search during an investigative detention brings two obligations for police officers:

a. They must justify the search by citing the concrete circumstances that made them suspect a risk to themselves or to the public. In other words, officers must explain why they believed there was a risk. This requirement prevents searches based on abstract explanations.

b. They need to demonstrate that they have not used investigative detention merely to circumvent existing restrictions on searching places and persons.

The S.C.C. stated that the search incident to arrest has to be distinguished from the search incident to investigative detention in order to ensure that an investigative detention "does not give license to officers to reap the seeds of a warrantless search without the need to effect a lawful arrest based on reasonable and probable grounds, nor does it erode the obligation to obtain search warrants where possible."

5. A justified investigative detention search authorizes a "protective patdown search" of the detained person. This means that
    ▸ weapons must be the target of the search;
    ▸ evidence cannot be the target of the search; and
    ▸ the method of the search cannot exceed "pat-down."

6. The duration of an investigative detention must be "brief." This abstract time limit necessitates precise notes and testimony to explain the following:
    ▸ the precise duration of the actual detention, and
    ▸ the specific activity that occurred during it.

7. An investigative detention does not impose an obligation on the detained person to answer questions by the police. This rule has always existed. It changes nothing.

Applying Mann/Investigative Detention

2:00 a.m.: While you are on patrol, you receive the following radio broadcast: "Break and enter in progress, Denison and Smith Electronic Store, 836 Crighton Street."

2:01 a.m.: While you are en route, a second radio broadcast is received: "Anonymous caller reports that a person ran from the store. The suspect is male, white, about 25 to 30 years, wearing a dark jacket and blue jeans. Last seen on foot, running east on Crighton Street. The suspect's name may be Jack Umbriago."

2:04 a.m.: While en route, driving west on Crighton Street, three blocks from the crime scene, you see a man walking casually on the sidewalk. He is alone. The pedestrian is male, white, about 25 to 30 years old, wearing a dark jacket, hooded sweatshirt, the hood over his head, and blue jeans. As you slow down, you observe his face but do not recognize him from any past occurrences.

At this moment, you have to make several decisions:

▸ Can you arrest the pedestrian right now without a warrant?
▸ Can you detain the pedestrian for "investigative" purposes?
▸ Can you search the pedestrian without a warrant and without his consent?
▸ Do you have to leave the pedestrian alone and let him continue on his way?

These circumstances reflect those in *R. v. Mann* (2004), the landmark case that created the "guiding principles" of investigative detention and search.

Mann Guiding Principles

Following is a summary of the guiding principles of *R. v. Mann*:

1. The term "detention" has many definitions and interpretations. Every person stopped by the police for the purpose of identification or interview is "detained" in the literal sense, since the person is "delayed or kept waiting." But this does not mean (for the purpose of Charter analysis) that every police stop constitutes a *detention*. Is every person stopped by the police for whatever length of time *detained*? "Yes." Does it constitute a *detention* in each case? "No." It depends on the extent of the "physical or psychological restraint." "Being detained" and undergoing a "detention" are two different concepts. Being detained happens every time the police stop someone, regardless of the outcome. A detention occurs only when "significant physical or psychological restraint occurs." There are absolutely no guidelines regarding what "significant" means.

2. There is a common-law authority allowing police to detain for investigative purposes. It is not automatic. This authority is derived from a number of case law decisions made over the past decade.

3. There is no "general" investigative detention authority. This means that investigative detention cannot occur without justification. In other words, it cannot occur automatically, on the basis of mere suspicion.

4. Police have a "limited" power to detain for investigative purposes; it is called investigative detention. Investigative detentions are restricted to situations where the police have "reasonable grounds to suspect" that a person is connected to a specific crime. *Reasonable grounds to suspect* has the same meaning as *articulable cause*. To simplify, *reasonable grounds to suspect* is also called *reasonable suspicion*.

5. *Reasonable grounds to suspect* (or *reasonable suspicion*) is a *belief* based on evidence that forms a "clear nexus," or connection, between a specific person and a recent or current offence; or an indication that the specific person is "implicated in criminal activity." This belief requires less evidence than is needed for *reasonable grounds to arrest* but more than is needed for *mere suspicion*, which is defined as a "hunch based on intuition gained by experience." In other words, reasonable *grounds to suspect* is an additional level of belief that falls between *mere suspicion* and *reasonable grounds to arrest*.

6. "Reasonable grounds to detain" has been expanded to cover "a foreseeable future offence" in addition to recent or ongoing criminal offences.[41]

7. "Reasonable grounds to suspect" requires justification—that is, reasons based on circumstantial evidence. Conversely, an unjustified detention, one that cannot be supported with concrete reasons, is an "arbitrary detention," which constitutes a Charter violation.

8. There is no particular list of the kinds of evidence that will justify investigative detention in every case. In other words, there is no list conveniently outlining the justification needed for every investigative detention. This concept was intentionally left indefinite so that each investigative detention could be judged on a case-by-case basis. A two-pronged test determines whether an investigative detention is lawful. The first test is to decide whether the detention falls within the general scope of police duties as defined by statute or common law, including the duties to protect life and property, to prevent crime, and to preserve the peace. The Crown has the onus to prove that the detention fulfilled one of these three duties.

   Afterwards, the Crown moves to the second test, which decides whether a detention involved an unjustifiable use of the powers invested in police in accordance with their official duties. Whether the detention passes this second test depends on the Crown's ability to prove sufficient justification for the detention. Justification requires concrete evidence that there were reasonable grounds for suspecting the detained person of being linked to a specific current or foreseeable future offence.

9. The police do not have "carte blanche" authority to detain. Investigative detention is never authorized by mere suspicion.

10. A justified investigative detention authorizes a *partial search*. A *full search* aims to uncover both weapons and evidence of an offence. A partial search targets weapons alone, with the purpose of self-protection. A justified investigative detention authorizes only a protective "pat-down" search of the detained person. There are three facets to this rule:

    a. Weapons must be the target of the search.
    b. Evidence related to a crime cannot be the target of the search.
    c. The method cannot exceed "pat-down."

    A protective pat-down search is not automatically permitted. The police must first prove reasonable necessity, which means they have a belief based on reasonable grounds that the officer's safety or the safety of others is at risk.

11. Unlike search incident to arrest, a search incident to investigative detention is never automatic. Some concrete evidence must prove that a search was needed for protection.

12. The duration of an investigative detention must be "brief." This abstract time limit requires precise notes and testimony to explain

    ▸ the duration of the actual detention, and
    ▸ the activity that occurred during it.

13. An investigative detention does not impose an obligation on the detained person to answer any questions asked by the police, including questions about identity.

The power of investigative detention confers on police today the benefit of *self-protection*. *R. v. Mann* permits police to detain and search a suspect when reasonable grounds to arrest do not exist. But they cannot do so automatically; there must be reasonable grounds, based on concrete evidence, to suspect that there is a connection between the person and a crime (past, present, or future) and, second, that the person poses a risk to the officer's safety.

SUMMARY

In the absence of a belief or a hunch, detention should not occur. Intuition alone is insufficient. Consent or voluntary accompaniment is the only solution, in this case.

Reasonable suspicion permits investigative detention. You justify the detention by establishing

> ▸ that there is a connection between the person and the crime, based on concrete evidence or circumstances;
> ▸ that the person poses a risk to police and/or the public, in which case a "pat-down" search exclusively for weapons is justified.

Having reasonable grounds (formerly reasonable and probable grounds) for believing that a person has committed an indictable offence means that an arrest and an automatic search for weapons and evidence are authorized.

PROBLEM-SOLVING CASE STUDIES

You are a police officer in each case. Each offender is an adult, unless otherwise indicated.

Problem 1

You are dispatched to a disturbance at a bar. Upon arrival, you see Eddie causing a disturbance inside. Can you arrest without a warrant?

_____

_____

Problem 2

You are dispatched to a domestic dispute at a house. Upon arrival, you see Ward assault June inside the house. Can you arrest Ward without a warrant?

_____

Problem 3

You see Wally steal a $20,000.00 car and you pursue him continuously until he stops. Can you arrest him without a warrant?

_____

_____

_____

Problem 4

June reports to you today that Ward assaulted her three days ago. Can you arrest Ward today without a warrant?

_____

_____

_____

_____

_____

Problem 5

You are questioning Wally, with his consent, about a robbery that occurred eight months ago. Wally confesses to you. Can you arrest him without a warrant?

_____

_____

_____

Problem 6

You see Ralph (16) steal a $20,000.00 car. You pursue him, but lose sight of him. You see him 24 hours later. He is walking on a sidewalk and you recognize him. Can you arrest Ralph without a warrant?

_____

_____

_____

_____

_____

Problem 7

Wally reports the following to you right now: He met Eddie at a bar last night at 11:00 p.m. Eddie confessed to him that he committed "Break, enter and theft" at a house situated at 10 King St., seven days ago. Can you arrest Eddie without a warrant?

_____

_____

_____

_____

_____

Problem 8

June reports to you right now that she saw Eddie commit an "Indecent act" on King St. one hour ago. Can you arrest Eddie without a warrant?

_____

_____

_____

_____

_____

_____

Problem 9

June reported to you yesterday at 5:00 p.m. that she received three obscene phone calls between 1:00 and 4:00 p.m. You develop a suspicion that Eddie, a next-door neighbour, committed the offences. The suspicion is based merely on unsubstantiated speculation. You interrogate Eddie today, with his consent. He confesses that he committed the offences. Can you arrest Eddie without a warrant?

_____

_____

_____

Problem 10

You are investigating an "Attempted murder" that occurred five days ago. Ward is the victim. You form a suspicion that Eddie may be the offender, based merely on unsubstantiated speculation. Can you arrest Eddie for suspicion of "Attempted murder" or for the purpose of questioning him in order to form reasonable grounds?

_____

_____

_____

_____

_____

_____

Problem 11

You see an intoxicated person walking toward his car. He insists that he is driving home. Can you arrest him?

_____

_____

_____

Problem 12

You arrive at a dispute between two people. One person becomes hostile and indicates, by means of words and/or conduct, that he may assault the other person. Can you arrest him?

_____

_____

_____

Note: If no offence actually occurs, and an officer arrests a person to prevent an offence from being committed, the arrested person may be detained only until the reasonable grounds no longer exist. The arrested person must be released when the detention is no longer needed to prevent the commission of the indictable offence.[42] For example, in Problem 11, reasonable grounds no longer exist when the intoxicated person becomes sober. At this time, the arrested person must be released unconditionally, meaning that no charge will be laid.

This particular arrest-without-warrant authority does not frequently apply because many "about to commit" circumstances also constitute actual offences. For example, in Problem 11, if the intoxicated person is standing near the driver's door while holding the car keys, he may be charged with "Care or control of a motor vehicle while impaired," which is a dual procedure offence. Although the intoxicated person is about to commit "Impaired driving," he has already committed "Care or control while impaired."

In Problem 12, if the person makes a threatening act or gesture, the offence of "Assault" has been committed.[43] Also, if the person makes a verbal statement threatening to cause bodily harm, the offence of "Uttering threats" has been committed.[44]

Other circumstances pose problems to police officers requiring a decision about whether to arrest a person before the actual offence occurs. The following problem illustrates this.

Problem 13

Eddie tells Wally that he intends to commit robbery at a specific store, or commit a break and enter at a specific place. Wally reports this to you. What are your alternatives?

_____

_____

_____

_____

_____

_____

Problem 14

You stop Wally in St. Catharines, Ontario. A CPIC check reveals the following message: Wanted—"Robbery"—Toronto. Can you arrest him without having possession of the warrant?

_____

_____

_____

Problem 15

You stop Eddie in Calgary, Alberta. A CPIC check reveals the following message: Wanted—"Assault"—Edmonton. Can you arrest him without having possession of the warrant?

_____

_____

_____

_____

Problem 16

You stop Wally in Edmonton, Alberta. A CPIC check reveals the following message: Wanted—"Trespass by night"—Calgary. Can you arrest him without having possession of the warrant?

_____

_____

Problem 17

You stop June in Halifax, Nova Scotia. A CPIC check reveals the following message: Wanted—"Assault"—Montreal. Can you arrest her?

_____

_____

Problem 18

You stop Eddie in Regina, Saskatchewan. A CPIC check reveals the following message: Wanted—"Indecent act"—Montreal. Can you arrest him?

_____

_____

Problem 19

Five days ago, June reported a "Mischief under $5,000.00" to you. Today, you form reasonable grounds that Eddie committed the offence. You also determine the following during the investigation:

- ▸ Eddie's correct identity is known.
- ▸ All necessary evidence is secured, and no other evidence needs to be preserved.
- ▸ No reasonable grounds exist that indicate that he will repeat this offence or any other offence.
- ▸ No reasonable grounds exist indicating that he will fail to appear in court.

Can you arrest Eddie without a warrant, and, if not, what can you do?

_____

_____

_____

_____

_____

Problem 20

You form reasonable grounds today that Eddie committed "Assault" five days ago. How will you determine whether to arrest him without a warrant?

_____

_____

_____

_____

Problem 21

You attend at a dwelling-house regarding a domestic. Two occupants, Ward and June, are present. Ward is drunk. You see him screaming and shouting at June, preventing her from enjoying the peace, quiet, and security to which she is entitled. No assault or threats have been committed by Ward. What can you do in this case?

_____

_____

_____

Problem 22

Ward is a security guard working in a department store. He sees Eddie commit "Theft under $5,000.00" by stealing an item. Eddie leaves the store without paying for the item. Ward follows Eddie, never loses sight of him, and approaches Eddie in the parking lot. Can Ward arrest Eddie without a warrant?

_____

_____

_____

Problem 23

Wally is assaulted by Eddie. The assault occurs on the sidewalk of Rice Rd. Can Wally arrest Eddie?

Problem 24

Ward is walking his dog on the sidewalk of King St. He sees Eddie on the roadway of King St. committing "Cause a disturbance." Can Ward arrest Eddie?

Problem 25

Ward is a bouncer at a privately owned bar. He sees Eddie, a customer inside the bar, commit "Cause a disturbance." Can Ward arrest Eddie?

Problem 26

Eddie is drunk and driving on Lincoln St. He stops at Wally's house and, after Wally enters the front seat of the car, Eddie drives away from the house. Wally then realizes that Eddie is intoxicated while he is driving. Can Wally arrest Eddie?

Problem 27

Ward is driving his car on Barton St. and stops for a red light. He sees Eddie, a pedestrian, walk toward his (Ward's) car then smash the passenger window. Can Ward arrest Eddie?

Problem 28

June owns a house on Parkdale Avenue. She is home alone at 11:00 p.m. She sees Eddie commit "Trespass by night" in her backyard. Can June arrest Eddie?

Problem 29

June is a private investigator, working in a department store. She is investigating a "Theft over $5,000.00" incident that occurred seven days ago. She interrogates Eddie, an employee, right now with Eddie's consent. Eddie confesses that he committed the offence. Can June arrest Eddie?

_____

_____

_____

Problem 30

June is a security guard at a community college. Clarence reports to her right now that he saw a man commit "Mischief under $5,000.00," 15 minutes ago, by breaking a glass door in the college. The offender left the scene immediately. Clarence recognizes Eddie as being the man who broke the window and informs June.

a. Can June arrest Eddie?

_____

_____

_____

_____

b. Can Clarence arrest Eddie?

_____

_____

_____

c. June and Clarence call the police. Cst. Friendly arrives. Clarence reports his observation. Can Cst. Friendly find Eddie and arrest him without a warrant?

_____

_____

Problem 31

Ward is at his house right now. He hears a news broadcast that Eddie is wanted for "Robbery." Eddie arrives at Ward's house 15 minutes later to visit. Can Ward arrest Eddie?

_____

_____

_____

Problem 32

June is a security guard at a community college. Clarence reports the following to her right now. Eddie told Clarence one hour ago that he intended to steal a college van that is currently parked near the main building. Eddie is in a class right now. Can June arrest Eddie to prevent the offence of "theft over $5,000.00"?

_____

_____

_____

ENDNOTES

1. *R. v. Whitfield* (1969), 1 C.C.C. 129 (S.C.C.); *R. v. Latimer* (1997), 112 C.C.C. (3d) 193 (S.C.C.).
2. *R. v. Therens* (1985), 18 C.C.C. (3d) 481 (S.C.C.).
3. *R. v. Mann*, [2004] 3 S.C.R. 59, 2004 SCC 52.
4. Ibid.
5. Ibid. and supra note 2.
6. Supra note 1.
7. Section 495(1)(b) C.C.
8. Section 495(1)(c) C.C.
9. Section 495(a) C.C.
10. Section 495(1)(c) C.C.
11. Section 495(a) C.C.
12. *Hicks v. Faulkner* (1878), 8 Q.B.D. 167, at 171, 172 (D.C.).
13. *R. v. Debot* (1989), 30 C.C.C. (3d) 193 (S.C.C.).
14. *R. v. Storrey* (1990), 53 C.C.C. (3d) 316 (S.C.C.).
15. *R. v. Godoy* (1999), 131 C.C.C. (3d) 129 (S.C.C.).
16. *R. v. Bennett* (1996), 108 C.C.C. (3d) 175 (Que. C.A.).
17. Section 495(1)(c) C.C.
18. Section 29(1) C.C.
19. Section 2 C.C.
20. D.A. Dukelow and B. Nuse, *Pocket Dictionary of Canadian Law* (Toronto: Carswell, 1991).
21. Section 496 C.C.
22. Section 504 C.C.
23. Supra note 20, at 57.
24. Section 31(1) C.C.
25. Section 494(3) C.C.
26. *Police Services Act*, R.S.O. 1990, c. P.15, s. 2.
27. Section 494(1)(a) C.C.
28. Section 494(2) C.C.
29. Section 494(1)(b) C.C.
30. Section 30 C.C.
31. Section 494(3) C.C.
32. *R. v. Grant* (1991), 67 C.C.C. (3d) 268 (S.C.C.); *R. v. Cunningham and Ritchie* (1979), 49 C.C.C. (2d) 390 (Man. Co. Ct.).

33. Section 139(2) C.C.

34. *R. v. Wijesinha* (1995), 100 C.C.C. (3d) 410 (S.C.C.); *R. v. Whalen* (1974), 17 C.C.C. (2d) 217 (Ont. Co. Ct.); and *R. v. Spezzano* (1977), 34 C.C.C. (2d) 87 (Ont. C.A.).

35. *R. v. Mann*, supra note 3.

36. Ibid.

37. *R. v. Willis* (2003), 174 C.C.C. (3d) 406.

38. *R. v. Lerke* (1986), 24 C.C.C. (3d) 129 (Alta. C.A.).

39. *R. v. Mann*, supra note 3.

40. *R. v. Simpson* (1993), 12 O.R. (3d) 182 (C.A.).

41. *R. v. Cooper* (2005), 195 C.C.C. (3d) 162 (N.S.C.A.).

42. Section 503(4) C.C.

43. Section 265(1)(b) C.C.

44. Section 264.1(1)(a) C.C.

CHAPTER 5

Search Authority

LEARNING OUTCOMES

The student will learn

- The definition of a common-law search incident to arrest

- The definition of a common-law search incident to investigative detention

- The definition of a consent search

- How to recognize the two common-law searches

- How to apply both common-law search authorities

INTRODUCTION

The final step in the RDM model is deciding what can be searched after an arrest or a detention. A search has two primary goals: (1) protection and (2) investigation. In other words, the primary objective is to disarm a suspect; the secondary objective is to seize any item that is evidence of any offence.

The search authorities in Canadian law fall into three categories:

1. consent,
2. search with a warrant, and
3 search without a warrant

There are two common-law search authorities permitting a search without a warrant and without consent after an arrest or a detention. The third way for police to be allowed to search is by consent. This chapter explains these three search authorities.

SEARCH INCIDENT TO ARREST

Search incident to arrest is defined as "the search of the person and the immediate surroundings after an arrest." This means that a search incident to arrest can be directed at the following: (1) the arrested person; (2) the place where the arrest occurs, which is termed the arrested person's *immediate surroundings*. The latter is a concrete definition. You define *immediate surroundings* according to what is reasonable in the situation.

The phrase "incident to" means "naturally connected with." This search authority licenses a search that is continuous with and forms a part of the arrest. Even though the arrest and the search are two separate acts, they work in conjunction. The lawful arrest initiates the search.

There are three reasons that this common-law authority allows an automatic full search of a lawfully arrested person. Such a search is needed

1. to prevent injury,
2. to secure evidence, and
3. to prevent escape.

These three reasons also define the types of items that can be seized: items that could be used to inflict injury; items that may serve as evidence; and items the suspect might use to escape. These items can be simply categorized as weapons and evidence.

The search incident to arrest is automatic, which means you only have to prove that the arrest was lawful; you do not have to have separate reasonable grounds for believing that the arrested person possesses weapons.

The Supreme Court of Canada (S.C.C.) has confirmed this authority in a series of case law decisions. The only limits that have been imposed on this search authority are the following:

‣ the arrest must be lawful,
‣ the search must be conducted "incident to" the lawful arrest, and
‣ the manner of the search must be reasonable.[1]

Key Points

Following are some key points regarding the objectives of a *search incident to arrest*:

‣ *Evidence*. This refers to any physical item that proves the commission of any offence. This means that an item may be seized from an arrested person if it directly proves the offence for which he was arrested, or any unrelated offence. For example, if you lawfully arrest a person for impaired driving, you may automatically search the person. If you find a stolen credit card, you can seize it, even though the credit card does not prove the offence of impaired driving. The evidence may be searched for on the person (in clothes, attachments to clothes, and items being held); or inside or beneath clothing (such a search is not limited to a "pat-down" search).
‣ *Items capable of causing injury to any person, including the accused*. This category includes any item that can be used as a weapon to harm anyone, *including the arrested person*. Any clothing, jewellery, or other items in pockets except for personal money may be seized from the accused before he or she enters a police jail cell in order to prevent injury or suicide. Belts, shoelaces, jewellery, and lighters should always be seized and kept in a property locker while the accused is in a police jail cell. The accused is

usually allowed to wear his or her own clothing. Clothing should be seized only when some evidence indicates or suggests that the accused is suicidal. All efforts must be made to *prevent a suicide while an accused is in police custody.*

▸ *Any item that can facilitate escape.* These items are essentially the same as weapons.[2]

A search incident to arrest is not limited to only one search at the scene of the arrest. The person can be searched before entering the cruiser and again at the police station before entering the cells.

The only item that cannot be seized without consent is money that is not evidence and is lawfully owned by the accused.[3] Usually, an officer asks the accused to consent to the money being kept in a police property locker for safekeeping while the accused is in the police cells. Consent is commonly given.

Items seized by the police that are evidence of any offence may be detained until court proceedings conclude. Items seized that are not evidence and are not illegal but are taken to prevent injury or escape, must be returned to the accused at the time of his or her release from custody.

Regarding the S.C.C.'s prescription that the manner of the search must be *reasonable*, the court explained this rule as follows:

▸ This search authority does not impose upon police a positive duty to search. In other words, officers have the discretion not to search an arrested person when they are satisfied that such a search is unnecessary.

▸ The focus of the search must be weapons and evidence. The search cannot be used to "intimidate, ridicule, or pressure" the arrested person, to obtain a confession.

▸ The search cannot be conducted in an "abusive fashion," which is defined as using unjustified physical or psychological constraint.[4]

The authority to search after an arrest is not found in any Canadian statute. It is a common-law authority that originated in 1853 English law. Canadian courts recognized this common-law authority in 1895. The S.C.C., in *Cloutier v. Langlois* (1990), reiterated support for the lawfulness of the search of an arrested person. This common-law authority is formally called a "search incident of arrest."

It is difficult to imagine how a police officer could be positively satisfied beyond all doubt that an arrested person is unarmed without searching the person. Any arrest poses a potential risk to the arresting officer. Any officer who has routinely arrested persons has learned through experience that no arrested person may be assumed to be unarmed or incapable of using violence.

Immediate Surroundings

Arrests occur in a wide range of *places*, including dwelling-houses, businesses, cars, parking lots, and streets. The place of the arrest is a target of the police officer's search that is separate from the search of the person. Significant evidence of an offence can be transferred from the person to the place where the arrest occurs.[5] The best way to search for and seize evidence at the place of arrest is to obtain a search warrant. However, the common-law authority for search incident to arrest extends to a *place* called the "immediate surroundings," which can be searched without a warrant. This place is not concretely defined. It is abstractly defined as the proximity of the arrest. No warrant or consent is required to search the immediate surroundings.[6] Countless case law decisions create valuable points of references for police officers. The accompanying website (**www.emp.ca/arcaro/policepowers4E**) has an extensive and expanding list of case law decisions that help define "place."

The crucial question concerns the specific dimensions of the "immediate surroundings" that police officers can search without a warrant. The size of the area searched is determined by what is *reasonable* according to s. 8 Charter. In other words, the search incident to arrest works in conjunction with s. 8 Charter. A search of the place that exceeds reasonableness may result in exclusion of the evidence found, under s. 24(2) Charter. In other words, items seized during a search incident to arrest are not automatically admissible if the search constitutes a Charter violation.

Appeal courts in Ontario and British Columbia have liberally defined *immediate surroundings* as including the following areas, when the accused is arrested in a vehicle:

- the interior of a vehicle (Ontario C.A. and B.C.C.A.),[7]
- the trunk of a vehicle (B.C.C.A.),[8] and
- the inside of a vehicle door, after the police remove a door panel (B.C.C.A.).[9]

Other case law decisions have established guidelines regarding *immediate surroundings* for places other than vehicles. As a general rule, the "entirety of what may reasonably be considered the surroundings" constitutes the *place* that can be searched without a warrant.[10] This suggests that if a person is arrested inside a place, the entire room may be searched, but it does not imply that the entire house or premises may be searched. The key is justification. Justification will prove reasonableness. Justification has to be determined by your primary goal. If the goal was to protect life, the warrantless search of the immediate surroundings will likely be considered reasonable. In other words, the *immediate surroundings* search is justified so long as a risk to life exists—yours or anyone else's. However, once the risk is removed and your intention is to search for evidence, apply for a warrant. When a risk no longer exists, there is time to get a warrant. Obtaining a warrant should never be considered an inconvenience. It is a necessity. Searches conducted without a warrant are justifiable exceptions only when the circumstances make it impracticable to obtain a search warrant.

The key to *reasonableness* is striking a balance between self-protection for police and privacy protection for the person arrested.

Time Limit: Delay Between Arrest and Search

The circumstances of every arrest are unique. There are many tasks that have to be completed. Consequently, time may elapse between the arrest and the search of the person and the surrounding area. The question of delayed search is addressed in the landmark S.C.C. decision in *R. v. Caslake* (1998).[11] The *Caslake* decision addressed two questions:

1. whether the common-law search authority extends to vehicles, and
2. the validity of an "inventory search" of a car conducted six hours after the arrest.

CASE LAW

R. v. Caslake (1998)

- **Issues:**

  1. Does the common-law search-incident-to-arrest authority apply to vehicles?
  2. Is an "inventory search" of a car conducted six hours after the arrest reasonably considered part of a search incident to arrest?

- **Offences:** "Possession of marijuana for the purpose of trafficking" and "Possession of cocaine."

- **Circumstances:** A Natural Resources officer saw a car parked by the side of a highway and stopped to investigate. The officer saw the accused standing in tall grass, about 40 feet from the roadway. The officer questioned the accused, who stated that he was relieving himself. They returned to their respective vehicles, and the accused drove away.

  The officer then returned to the area where the accused had been standing. A garbage bag containing about nine pounds of marijuana wrapped in cellophane was found and seized. The officer returned to his vehicle, contacted the RCMP, pursued the accused, stopped him, and arrested him.

  An RCMP officer arrived at the scene and took custody of the accused, transporting him to an RCMP detachment. The accused's vehicle was towed to a garage. Approximately six hours after the arrest, the RCMP officer went to the garage, unlocked the accused's vehicle, and searched it without a warrant and without consent. According to the officer's testimony, the search was conducted pursuant to RCMP policy requiring that inventory be taken of the condition and contents of a vehicle seized during an investigation. The officer testified that this was the sole reason for the search. The search resulted in the seizure of two packages containing 0.25 g of cocaine each, and $1,400 in a case.

- **Trial:** The accused was convicted. His appeals were based on the grounds that the search violated s. 8 Charter and that the evidence should be excluded under s. 24(2) Charter. The accused argued that the six-hour delay between the arrest and the search disqualified the search from being "incident to" the arrest. Appeals to the Manitoba Court of the Queen's Bench and to the Manitoba Court of Appeal were both dismissed because no substantial wrong or miscarriage of justice was perceived to have occurred.

- **Supreme Court of Canada:** The Supreme Court of Canada dismissed the accused's appeal. The court was unanimous in deciding to admit the seized evidence.

  However, the reasons given by the majority differed from the minority. The majority ruled that a s. 8 Charter violation occurred but admitted the evidence under s. 24(2) Charter. The minority ruled that no Charter violation had occurred.

- **Majority Reasons:** The three main purposes of a search incident to arrest are

  - ensuring the safety of the police and the public,
  - preventing destruction of evidence, and
  - discovering evidence that can be used at the accused's trial.

(continued)

A search conducted after an arrest must be "truly incident" to the arrest, meaning that the police must be attempting to achieve a valid purpose relating to the arrest.

Ordinarily, the accused has the onus of proving that a Charter violation has been committed. The exception is cases involving a warrantless search, which are unreasonable unless the Crown proves otherwise. In other words, the Crown has the onus of proving that a warrantless search was reasonable. In order to be reasonable, a search must be authorized by a statute or common law. If a search is not authorized by law, it could be defined as a theft or a trespass.

There are three ways that the Crown may fail to prove that a search was authorized by law:

1. No statute or common law actually authorized the search.
2. The search was authorized by law but was not executed in accordance with the procedures stipulated by that law.
3. The search exceeded the scope of the search authority, relating to factors such as the place, the items seized, and the time of the search.

In the case of *R. v. Caslake*, the Crown relied on the common-law search-incident-to-arrest authority to prove reasonableness. No readily ascertainable limits exist relating to the scope of this search authority because it is a common-law power. Consequently, the courts are responsible for establishing procedural boundaries that may limit the authority.

The scope of the search-incident-to-arrest authority extends to both persons and places, including vehicles. The Supreme Court of Canada, in this decision, stated that this power to search may be applied to an automobile if it constitutes the accused's immediate surroundings, because no "heightened expectation of privacy" exists to prohibit the search. However, some limits are imposed relating to vehicle searches incident to arrest. The reasonableness of a vehicle search incident to arrest will depend on certain factors, including

- the basis for the search,
- the location of the vehicle in relation to the location of the accused's arrest, and
- other relevant circumstances, such as "temporal" factors—that is, how much time elapsed before the search was conducted.

No procedural guideline exists for determining what specific amount of time defines the search of a vehicle as "incidental to" an arrest. Time limits do exist and are derived from the same principles that are used to determine whether a search of a vehicle incident to an arrest is reasonable. A substantial delay between arrest and vehicle search will not automatically make the search unreasonable. A reasonable explanation may justify a substantial delay.

In this case, the six-hour delay itself was not the problem. The problem was that the officer's stated reasons for searching the car—that is, to conduct an "inventory search"—caused the search to fall outside the scope of the common-law authority. An inventory search does not serve a "valid objective in pursuit of the ends of criminal justice." The inventory search in this case constituted a s. 8 Charter violation.

Despite this Charter violation, the evidence was admitted under s. 24(2) Charter because the trial was fair, the Charter violation was not serious, and the

(continued)

exclusion of evidence would have had a "detrimental impact" on the administration of justice.

The Supreme Court of Canada minority ruled that no s. 8 Charter violation occurred for the following reasons:

1. A search incident to arrest extends to an accused's automobile as part of the accused's immediate surroundings.
2. The inventory search was justified because its purpose was related to the lawful arrest and impounding of the vehicle, and was "incidental to" the arrest.

In summary, the following rules apply to the common-law search-incident-to-arrest authority:

1. No specific time is prescribed for the interval between arrest and search.
2. A substantial delay between arrest and search will not automatically make the search unreasonable. A substantial delay may be considered a reasonable delay. In this case, the six-hour delay itself was not the problem.
3. The common-law search-incident-to-arrest authority extends to both persons and places, including vehicles.
4. The reasonableness of a vehicle search depends on
   ▸ the basis for the search,
   ▸ the location of the vehicle in relation to the arrest, and
   ▸ other relevant circumstances, such as the time interval between arrest and search.

Arrest Outside a Dwelling-House

In some cases, a person is arrested outside a house but in close proximity to it. The question is whether the house may be searched without a warrant as a search incident to arrest.

In *R. v. Golub* (1997),[12] an accused person was arrested outside his house, about 4.5 metres (14 feet) from the door. The police had reasonable grounds for believing that a firearm was in the house and suspected that someone else may have been in the house. Officers entered without a warrant, searched the entire house for other persons, and seized a loaded rifle. In that case, the Ontario Court of Appeal ruled that the search was a justified search incident to arrest.

The court created the following procedural guidelines about warrantless entry and search of a house when an arrest is made outside the house but in close proximity to it

▸ A search is justified when "exceptional circumstances" exist.
▸ "Exceptional circumstances" are defined as situations "where the law enforcement interest is so compelling that it overrides the individual's right to privacy within the home."
▸ The risk of physical harm to persons at an arrest scene constitutes exceptional circumstances that justify a warrantless entry and search of the house.

CASE LAW

R. v. Golub (1997)

■ **Issues:**

1. Was the arrest lawful? Did the information obtained by the police constitute reasonable grounds for believing that the accused committed an indictable offence? What impact does a witness's failure to remember at the trial have on reasonable grounds?
2. Did the warrantless search of the house qualify as a "search incident to arrest"?
3. Was a "Feeney" warrant required to enter and search the house?
4. Did the circumstances constitute a "public safety" risk, thus justifying a warrantless search for firearms?

■ **Offences:** The accused was charged with multiple offences. All but one involved the possession of a sawed-off, .22-calibre, semi-automatic rifle.

■ **Circumstances:** The accused person and his friend were in a bar at 10:30 p.m. The manager of the bar refused to serve the accused any more drinks. The accused and his friend left, and visited various bars. The accused became upset and angry. He told his friend he was having trouble with his ex-wife. He also struck his friend. The accused twice threatened to "get even" with the staff at the bar that had refused to serve him, and showed the friend an 18-inch rifle, which was concealed beneath his jacket.

The friend called the police and reported the following information to the officers:

- ▸ The accused caused a disturbance at the bar.
- ▸ The accused showed him the gun at another bar.
- ▸ The gun was described to the police as an "Uzi sub-machine gun," loaded with five clips.
- ▸ The accused was upset and agitated.
- ▸ The accused threatened to "get even" with the staff at the bar.

■ An investigation resulted. The police found the basement apartment rented by the accused. Initial attempts to gain entry were unsuccessful.

The Emergency Task Force (ETF) was contacted. The apartment building was evacuated at 7:00 a.m. The officer-in-charge phoned the apartment at 7:28 a.m. and spoke to the accused. The officer instructed the accused to come out the apartment door with nothing in his hands and to follow instructions from officers at the door.

At 7:35 a.m., the accused opened the door and had nothing in his hands. He was told to leave the door open, but instead he closed the door and locked it. The accused was formally arrested about 4.5 metres outside the apartment door. The accused was asked if anyone else was in the apartment. He shrugged and said, "I don't think so." The officer-in-charge formed the belief that other occupants could be in the apartment and ordered the ETF to enter the apartment and search it. This order was made within seconds of the arrest. A key was used to enter. Four officers entered. The officer-in-charge testified at the trial that the intention of the search was to look for persons, not evidence, and that "public safety" was definitely a concern. The ETF team was not looking for the gun upon

(continued)

entry, but if it was found, they were to secure it, continue the search, and turn over the scene and firearm to the investigating officers. The ETF officer-in-charge never thought about obtaining a search warrant.

One of the searching officers testified that he was instructed to look methodically in "every room, every crevice" for other persons. The officers subsequently searched every conceivable place in the apartment where a person could hide. A .22-calibre, sawed-off, semi-automatic rifle was found under a mattress in a bedroom. The 15-round magazine was fully loaded. Two clear boxes, each containing 100 rounds of .22-calibre, hollow-point ammunition, were beside the gun. Fifteen rounds were missing from one box. The search continued. No persons were found.

At the completion of the search, the investigating officers entered the apartment and seized the weapon and ammunition. They also searched the apartment without a warrant under the authority of s. 103(2) C.C., then in force but since replaced with s. 117.04(2) C.C. Consequently, two separate warrantless searches occurred.

■ **Trial:** The rifle was excluded under s. 24(2) Charter, and seizure was ruled to be a s. 8 Charter violation since its admission would bring the administration of justice into disrepute. The accused was acquitted.

■ **Appeal:** The Crown appealed the acquittal to the Ontario Court of Appeal. The appeal was allowed, and a new trial was ordered.

COMMENTARY

■ **Issue 1:** The police relied solely on the eyewitness information provided by the accused's friend. The trial judge ruled that this information did constitute reasonable grounds to arrest. However, the accused raised a unique issue for appeal that would have significantly affected arrest without warrant procedures. The accused's appeal argument was that evidence from one unconfirmed eyewitness, without corroboration (supporting evidence), was insufficient to form a basis for reasonable grounds to make an arrest. The argument was based on the standards applicable to obtaining a search warrant, which stipulate that the information of an untested informant requires supporting evidence to confirm it.

■ The Ontario Court of Appeal rejected this argument, ruling that the information of one eyewitness is sufficient to form reasonable grounds to make an arrest without warrant. No corroboration is required to confirm the information of one eyewitness. The following reasons were given:

1. The dynamics of an arrest situation are very different from those relating to a search warrant application.
2. An officer's decision to arrest must often be made in "volatile and rapidly changing situations."
3. The decision to arrest is based on available information, which is often less than complete or exact.
4. The law does not expect a police officer, when deciding if reasonable grounds exist, to make the same inquiry as a Justice is required to make when examining a search warrant application.

The court stated that the information from the accused's friend constituted reasonable grounds because the officers had a first-hand opportunity to evaluate his credibility and had no reason to ignore the information. Additionally, the

(continued)

court noted that not only were the police justified in acting on the information, "they would have been derelict in their duty had they not acted on it." Finally, the court answered the question, "What impact does a witness's failure to remember at the trial have on reasonable grounds?" At the trial, in this case, the witness (the accused's friend) testified that he had been too drunk on the night of the offence to remember the events. The Ontario Court of Appeal ruled that this testimony was not relevant to the existence of reasonable grounds for the arrest. No evidence presented at the trial suggested that the witness's condition at the time of the police interview should have discredited his information. The following significant rule was made by the court: "A failed memory several months after the events, even if legitimate, does not imply that information provided at the relevant time was unreliable."

■ **Issue 2:** The search of the immediate surroundings of a place where a person is arrested is authorized by common law and case law. The arrest in this case was made outside the accused's house, about 4.5 metres from his door. The entire house was searched without a warrant after the arrest. The issue on appeal was, "Was the warrantless search of the house a search incident to a lawful arrest?"

The Ontario Court of Appeal ruled that the search was incident to the arrest and did constitute a reasonable search. No Charter violation was ruled to have occurred. The following reasons were given, which provide useful procedural guidelines:

1. The search of a house as an incident to an arrest is generally prohibited, but it is authorized when "exceptional circumstances" exist.
2. "Exceptional circumstances" are defined as situations where the law enforcement interest is so compelling that it overrides the individual's right to privacy within the home.
3. The following elements constitute exceptional circumstances:
   ‣ the need to secure the arrested person,
   ‣ the need to protect persons at the arrest scene, and
   ‣ the need to preserve evidence.
4. The police interest in protecting the safety of people at the scene of an arrest is the most compelling concern at an arrest scene and one that must be addressed immediately.
5. The police cannot be asked to place themselves in potentially dangerous situations in order to make an arrest. If the police cannot protect themselves and others, they will avoid making arrests, thereby compromising law enforcement.
6. The risk of physical harm to persons at an arrest scene constitutes exceptional circumstances, which justify a warrantless entry and search of the house.
7. A reasonable suspicion that "someone is on the other side of a closed door with a loaded sub-machine gun, or that someone is lying injured on the other side of that door, creates a legitimate cause for concern, justifying entry and search of the apartment for persons."

■ **Issue 3:** The arrest occurred outside the accused's home. Therefore, the Feeney warrant and procedure were inapplicable to the accused's arrest. Since no other person was found in the house, the court did not consider the Feeney case or the relevant legislation. However, it is presumed that these circumstances constituted

(continued)

exigent circumstances pursuant to s. 529.3(2) C.C. that would have justified a warrantless search of a dwelling-house for a person as an exception to the Feeney warrant requirement.

■ **Issue 4:** A public safety risk combined with exigent circumstances justifies a warrantless search of a house for firearms under s. 117.04(2) C.C. The suspicion of the ETF's officer-in-charge that someone else was in the apartment was sufficient to justify a warrantless earch.

The sufficient suspicion was based on

- ▸ the witness's information,
- ▸ the accused's failure to leave the apartment door open when asked to do so, and
- ▸ the reasonable belief that there was a loaded, dangerous firearm inside the apartment.

ADDITIONAL CASE LAW

The *Golub* case is one of countless cases. Refer to the accompanying website (**www.emp.ca/arcaro/policepowers4E**) for more relevant case law decisions.

Summary

Never forget the primary purpose of the search incident to arrest: self-protection. An immediate search of the person should be conducted after any arrest, regardless of how minor the offence may be, to prevent any possibility of harm being done to you. Regarding the immediate area, always remember the following quotation from the Alberta Court of Appeal, in *R. v. Lerke* (1986):

> The reluctance of Canadian courts to invalidate searches after arrest is understandable. Judges cannot be blind to the deaths and injuries suffered by police officers on duty as guns and knives become more common. Situations which appear quite innocent, with no hostile demonstration by the person being arrested, can explode into violence leaving the arresting officer dead or injured. It is difficult to second-guess any police officer who ensures that a person is not armed when he perceives danger as he makes an arrest or escorts a prisoner.[13]

SEARCH INCIDENT TO INVESTIGATIVE DETENTION

This search authority accompanies investigative detention. Unlike a search incident to arrest, a **search incident to investigative detention** is not automatic and it does not authorize a search for evidence. It authorizes a partial search, and only if a specified standard of belief is proved. After an investigative detention is lawfully imposed, an officer may search the person without consent, but only if the officer has reasonable grounds for believing that his or her own safety or the safety of others is at risk. In other words, a reasonable necessity has to be proved. For the search to be justified, a concrete list of circumstances must support the officer's belief that a risk exists.

A justified investigative detention search authorizes a partial search only—that is, a "protective pat-down" search, which must meet the following criteria:

1. The primary aim must be seizure of weapons.
2. The gathering of evidence cannot be the goal of the search.
3. The method of the search cannot exceed "pat-down."

In summary, the search incident to investigative detention must meet two successive standards of two beliefs. First, the officer must have reasonable grounds to suspect in order to justify the detention itself. Second, to justify the search, there must be reasonable grounds for believing that a risk exists.

ADDITIONAL CASE LAW

The website that accompanies this text (**www.emp.ca/arcaro/policepowers4E**) is a particularly valuable tool for this topic. The principle of search incident to investigative detention is in an evolutionary stage. The website offers extensive coverage of ongoing developments in case law so that front-line officers can research point-of-reference circumstances.

CONSENT SEARCH

When only a *hunch* or *no belief* exists, the consent of the person is the only means available of conducting a legal search of a person or place. **Consent** is defined in case law as a person's "voluntary and informed decision" to allow the police to search or question."[14]

There are two key elements to this definition:

1. Consent is an *informed decision*. The person making the decision must be sufficiently informed of facts and must have adequate knowledge of exactly what has been decided.
2. The decision must be voluntarily made. No person is obliged to give consent to the police for a warrantless search. Every person has the right to refuse consent.

Section 8 Charter Waiver

Valid consent to search or seize constitutes a waiver of the s. 8 Charter right. Waiving a Charter right means surrendering it or giving it up. If the consent given is valid, the search or seizure will be reasonable and no s. 8 Charter violation will have occurred. The seized item will be admissible.

Conversely, if valid consent is not obtained, and the police search for or seize evidence, a s. 8 Charter violation will have occurred. Evidence obtained by means of invalid consent may be deemed inadmissible, but *not automatically*. If a physical item is seized after a search and seizure based on invalid consent, it will usually be admissible according to the Supreme Court of Canada guideline established in the *Collins* case.

Obtain Consent: Procedure

Neither the *Criminal Code* nor the Charter provides precise guidelines for obtaining valid consent. Two case law decisions establish procedures that guide obtaining valid consent:

1. *R. v. Wills* (1992) Ontario Court of Appeal[15]
2. *R. v. Borden* (1994) Supreme Court of Canada[16]

ONTARIO COURT OF APPEAL GUIDELINES

The *R. v. Wills* case is a significant one insofar as it establishes seven conditions needed for consent to be valid. The prosecution must be able to prove that each of these seven conditions existed. However, the court did not provide specific guidelines as to how to achieve these conditions. The following is a list of the conditions necessary for valid consent, established by the Ontario Court of Appeal, along with suggested procedures for achieving each condition:

1. *Consent must be expressed or implied.* The meaning of the accused's consent must be unequivocal; the words must clearly and unmistakably state that consent is being given. No ambiguity is permitted. If the accused's statement is vague, no valid consent will exist.

   Consent from an adult offender may be obtained orally or in writing. Consent in writing means a written consent form, or a statement signed by the consenting person. Written consent brings the benefit of proving that valid consent was given. Oral consent refers to a spoken expression of consent, which should be recorded verbatim by the officer in a notebook.

   Consent from a young offender should be obtained in writing. Written consent is a statement transcribed either on a statement document or in an officer's notebook. The content should convey that the seven conditions required for valid consent exist, and it should be written in the first person format, as if by the consenting person. For example: "I, Robert Johnson, consent … ." The consenting person then signs the statement.

   Procedure: Record *verbatim* all conversation with the accused. In other words, record direct, word-for-word quotations from the accused, including all questions, comments, and responses pertaining to consent. When testifying in court, convey the conversation verbatim. Do not paraphrase the accused's words either when you are recording them or when you are testifying. **Paraphrasing** means condensing or summarizing the accused's verbatim response into a general statement such as "the accused consented." Whether the accused actually consented is a conclusion for the judge, not you, to make. A paraphrase is vague and does not prove unmistakable consent.

   Obtain written consent from a young offender by drafting a consent statement in your notebook or on a statement form. Obtain the young offender's signature. This procedure may be used for adults, but verbal consent from adults is also sufficient.

2. *Consent must be voluntary.* "Voluntary" means free from coercion, oppression, inducement, or any other external pressure on the accused to give consent. **Inducements** are defined as threats or promises. The accused

must be made fully aware of the consent process and not influenced by any threats or promises. *Voluntariness is proven by an absence of inducements.* Again, recording and testifying about verbatim conversation is essential to prove the absence of inducements.

Procedure: Inform the accused that there is no obligation to consent and that the decision to consent is a purely personal choice. Avoid using any words that constitute or imply any of the following:

- threats of violence, or of being arrested or charged if consent is denied;
- favourable promises related to the arrest, charge, and release of the accused.

In speaking to the suspect about consent, emphasize that "the choice is yours." Ask the accused if this is understood and record the response verbatim so that you can later prove that the decision about consent was exclusively the accused's. Again, avoid paraphrases such as "the accused voluntarily consented" or "I did not threaten or make promises to the accused." These are unconvincing during testimony.

3. *The accused must be aware of the specific act to be conducted.* The accused must have specific knowledge of what procedure the officer intends to undertake. The exact nature of the search and seizure procedure needs to be understood by the accused before he or she gives consent.

Procedure: Inform the accused of the following:

- that a search and/or seizure is being requested;
- what the specific target of the search (person or place) is;
- what specific evidence is being sought, if that is known;
- what offence is being investigated.

Providing the accused with as much information as possible ensures that the consent will be valid and may also convince the accused to cooperate and surrender the property voluntarily before a search is conducted.

4. *The accused must be aware of the potential consequences of giving consent.* The accused must have knowledge of the possible consequences of the search and seizure—namely, the possibility of prosecution and the admissibility of the evidence seized.

Procedure: Inform the accused of the following:

- that charges may be laid;
- what is the specific offence that the accused may be charged with, if this is known;
- that the evidence seized may be used at a trial.

5. *The accused must have knowledge that consent may be refused.* No law exists in Canada that compels or obliges a person to consent to a search or seizure. Refusal to consent is not an offence; a person cannot be charged or arrested for refusing to give it. The accused must understand that it is purely his or her choice whether to consent to a search or to withhold consent.

Procedure: Inform the accused, "You don't have to consent. You may refuse to give consent. The choice is yours. If you refuse, you cannot be charged for refusing."

6. *The accused must have knowledge that consent may be revoked at any time after consent is initially given.* A person who consents to a search may change his or her mind; the consent is not irrevocable. By removing consent the person may stop the search at any time. The accused must be informed of this option and the prosecution will be required to prove the accused's knowledge of it.

   Procedure: Inform the accused, "If you consent to this search, you can revoke consent at any time you choose and stop the search."

7. *You must prove the accused gave consent and did not then revoke consent at any time during the search.* The prosecution has the onus of proving that the accused said or did nothing during the search that directly indicated or indirectly implied an intent to choose to terminate the search. This condition is proven by the absence of any statement or conduct, made between the time that consent was given and the time that any seizure was made, to the effect that the accused wished to terminate the search.

   Procedure: Proving that the accused never chose to revoke consent requires more than a simple paraphrase, such as "The accused did not revoke consent at any time during the search." Avoid stating a conclusion— that is for the judge alone to make. Instead, record all conversation verbatim, between the time consent was given and the time the seizure was made. Note even the time periods when the accused was silent. Record the location and conduct of the accused during the search.

   When testifying, report the entire conversation, the periods of silence, and all relevant observations. Valid consent will be demonstrated by the absence from your testimony of any statement from the accused to the effect that he or she wished to revoke consent.

SUPREME COURT OF CANADA GUIDELINES

R. v. Borden (1994)[17] provides examples of invalid consent and shows how the court applies s. 24(2) Charter when determining the admissibility of evidence acquired through the accused's consent (for example, blood samples). See the website that accompanies this textbook for the entire case.

Situation

The police arrested an adult already accused of one count of sexual assault; he was being arrested on suspicion of committing a second count of sexual assault. The police sought blood samples from the accused in connection with the second count of sexual assault, for the purpose of DNA comparison. The accused signed a written consent form that simply indicated that he consented to the taking of a blood sample "for the purpose relating to their investigations." The accused was not specifically informed that the blood sample was taken in connection with the second count of sexual assault. After the blood sample was obtained, a positive comparison was made, and the accused was charged with the second count of sexual assault. Was the consent valid?

No. Although the plural "investigations" was deliberately used on the consent form, this form did not specify that the blood sample was to be used for the second count. The second investigation exceeded the exploratory stage. The police were obliged to inform the accused that the blood sample was intended to be used in a different investigation from the one for which he was detained. In other words, the accused was not informed of the main purpose of the blood sample. The taking of blood was a seizure, and the consent was invalid, constituting a s. 8 Charter violation. The Supreme Court of Canada ruled that the admission of the blood sample would bring the administration of justice into disrepute. Consequently, the blood sample was excluded under s. 24(2) Charter.[18]

In the *Borden* case, the Supreme Court considered the *R. v. Wills* ruling made by the Ontario Court of Appeal and established a similar list of requirements for valid consent:

1. The accused must have the choice of deciding whether or not to consent. The decision must be voluntarily made.
2. The accused must be informed of sufficient available information by the police.
3. The accused must know that consent is not required.
4. The accused must know in what specific investigation the police intend to use any product of the seizure.
5. If the police arrest or detain an accused for one offence and ask for consent to seize evidence to use in the investigation of an unrelated offence, the accused must be informed of this fact.
6. The police do not have to ensure that the accused has a detailed comprehension of every possible outcome of giving consent. The accused must understand generally the consequences of giving consent and must know that any item seized by consent may be used for another specific investigation.
7. If the police arrest or detain an accused for one offence and are in only the exploratory stage of investigating another, unrelated offence, they have no obligation to inform the accused that evidence he or she gives by consent, regarding the offence for which he is arrested, may be used in the investigation of another offence. If the investigation is beyond the exploratory stage and the police suspect the accused in the other offence, they must inform the accused that any evidence seized will also be used in the other investigation.

SUMMARY

This chapter explained the final step of the RDM model (see Chapter 1 to review). In the next chapter, you will learn how to apply the RDM model in realistic front-line police scenarios.

ENDNOTES

1. *R. v. Backhouse* (2005), 127 C.R.R. (2d) 1 (Ont. C.A.).
2. *Cloutier v. Langlois* (1990), 53 C.C.C. (3d) 257 (S.C.C.).
3. Ibid.
4. Ibid., at 278.
5. *R. v. Lim (No. 2)* (1990), 1 C.R.R. (2d) 136 (Ont. H.C.J.).
6. *R. v. Caslake* (1998), 121 C.C.C. (3d) 97 (S.C.C.).
7. *R. v. Speid* (1991), 8 C.R.R. (2d) 383 (Ont. C.A.); *R. v. Charlton*, 1992 CanLII 367 (B.C.C.A.).
8. *R. v. Charlton*, ibid.
9. *R. v. Smellie* (1994), 95 C.C.C. (3d) 9 (B.C.C.A.).
10. Ibid.
11. *R. v. Caslake*, supra note 6.
12. *R. v. Golub* (1997), 117 C.C.C. (3d) 193 (Ont. C.A.).
13. *R. v. Lerke* (1986), 24 C.C.C. (3d) 129 (Alta. C.A.).
14. *R. v. Wills* (1992), 70 C.C.C. (3d) 529 (Ont. C.A.).
15. Ibid.
16. *R. v. Borden* (1994), 92 C.C.C. (3d) 404 (S.C.C.).
17. Ibid.
18. Roger E. Salhany, *Canadian Criminal Procedure*, 5th ed. (Aurora, ON: Canada Law Book, 1989), 44.

CHAPTER 6

Applying Powers of Arrest

LEARNING OUTCOMES

The student will learn

- How to apply the RDM model to a number of reality-based scenarios

- How to test his or her knowledge through self-evaluation questions

INTRODUCTION

Scenario-based learning is a potent educational tool. It is the first step in *applied learning*.

Applied learning is the objective in occupational or vocational study. Knowing facts is not enough. The objective is to apply that knowledge in performing a job. Applied learning moves through stages: interpretation, scenario-based application, practical application, and, finally, "deliberate" practice.

Scenario-based application is an intermediate step between interpreting laws and hands-on practical application. Scenarios are simply realistic front-line situations that require decisions. Specifically, the objective of this chapter is to teach the decision-making process by which you answer the question, "Can I arrest without a warrant?"

You have to apply the RDM model to answer that question. The RDM model allows you to simulate exactly front-line police thinking. It promotes the rapid decision making that front-line officers are expected to perform countless times during every patrol.

Scenario-based exercise eventually leads to practical application—role-playing and supervised practical experience. "Deliberate practice" refers to an advanced phase of practical experience, the most challenging phase. In short, the road to becoming a front-line expert is a long one. Front-line officers did not become experts overnight. Their expertise developed.

This chapter includes a number of scenarios that show you how to apply the RDM model, and then it gives you opportunities for self-evaluation.

HOW TO APPLY THE RDM MODEL

Step 1: Offence Recognition

Rule: While reading each case study, learn to recognize the facts-in-issue. For example, a scenario might include the following words and phrases:

- bar
- customer is drunk, fighting, shouting
- other customers present

These facts concerning behaviour and physical locale constitute a "Cause a disturbance" situation. The key to recognizing the facts-in-issue is identifying all information relevant to conduct, place, and intent. In other words, identify the elements of the scenario. After you have done this, you should be able to match each case to definable offences. For more scenarios, see the accompanying website (**www.emp.ca/arcaro/policepowers4E**).

KEY POINT

In reality, police officers learn to blend all the steps of the RDM model in order to understand the larger context of a situation. In other words, you will progress to a stage where you will see the "big picture" of a situation rather than its individual elements. You will be able to recognize situations and make decisions without having to follow a step-by-step sequence.

Step 2: Classify the Offence

After you have recognized an offence, match it by its short-form name to the classification lists that you memorized from Chapter 2.

Step 3: Classify the Belief

This step responds to the question, "How do you know what happened?"

Start with the following question: "Did I witness the occurrence, or not?" If you did witness it, the belief is classified as "find committing." If you did not witness the offence, answer the question, "Do reasonable grounds exist for believing that a certain person committed the offence?" The answer to that question requires answers to the following questions:

- Did the offender confess to anyone (citizen or police)?
- Did at least one credible eyewitness see the offender commit the offence?
- Is there circumstantial evidence strong enough to lead to only one logical conclusion—that a specific offender committed a specific offence?

If the answer to any of the above is *yes*, reasonable grounds exist. If the answer to all three questions is *no*, then the belief is classified as "mere suspicion."

Steps 2 and 3 give you a "*belief + offence classification*" statement. Following is the list of possible "*belief + offence classification*" statements, with bold lettering indicating circumstances where police have powers to arrest without a warrant:

- **found committing + indictable offence**
- **found committing + dual procedure**
- **found committing + summary conviction**
- **found committing + breach of the peace**
- **reasonable grounds + indictable offence has been committed**
- **reasonable grounds + dual procedure offence has been committed**
- reasonable grounds + summary conviction offence has been committed
- mere suspicion + indictable offence has been committed
- mere suspicion + dual procedure offence has been committed
- mere suspicion + summary conviction offence has been committed
- **reasonable grounds + indictable offence is about to occur**
- **reasonable grounds + dual procedure offence is about to occur**
- reasonable grounds + summary conviction offence is about to occur
- **reasonable grounds + valid arrest warrant exists in territorial jurisdiction where person is found (in-province arrest warrant)**
- reasonable grounds + invalid arrest warrant exists in territorial jurisdiction where person is found (out-of-province arrest warrant)

Step 4: Custody Authority Recognition

Answer the following question: "Can you arrest right now without a warrant?"

This is the most important question in the sequence. Answering that question is the goal, and you have to answer it quickly. *Can I arrest without a warrant?*

You answer this question by matching the "belief + offence classification" statement from Steps 2 and 3 to the applicable police powers of arrest.

Step 5: Search Authority

The question you ask yourself here is: "Can I search the person and immediate surrounding without a warrant and without consent?"

Steps 4 and 5 have related answers. If the answer to the Step 4 question is yes, so is the answer to the Step 5 question. If the answer to the Step 4 question is no, so is the answer to the Step 5 question.

SCENARIO-BASED APPLICATIONS

For each case, consider yourself a police officer in your city. Each case includes

- a radio broadcast, time of arrival, and observations; or
- observations made while on patrol.

■ SCENARIO 1

11:00 p.m.: Radio broadcast—"Disturbance, Tombstone Bar, 3227 Brockport Rd."
11:06 p.m.: Time of arrival.

- You enter the bar via the front entrance.
- About 40 people are in the bar.

- ▸ You see the following:
  - – A man about 30 years old is screaming profanities at a woman who appears to be 40 years old.
  - – The man shouts, "Who do you think you're talking to?"
  - – The man is holding a beer bottle; he is uncoordinated, has red, bloodshot eyes, and smells of alcohol.
  - – Customers and employees are obviously alarmed.

Apply the RDM model as follows.

Step 1: Offence Recognition

a. Has an offence occurred? *Yes*

b. Which one? *Cause a Disturbance*

The defintion of the offence matches the facts-in-issue of this situation:

- ▸ bar (public place)
- ▸ screaming profanities + intoxicated (prohibited conduct)
- ▸ 40 people in the bar (complainants)

Step 2: Classify the Offence   *Summary conviction*

Causing a disturbance is on the "summary conviction offences" list, provided in Chapter 2.

Step 3: Classify the Belief   *Find committing*

You are an eyewitness.

Belief + offence classification statement = find committing + summary conviction. This fits s. 495 C.C. The next question will concern whether you may arrest without a warrant.

Step 4: Custody Authority Recognition

Can you arrest the man right now without a warrant?   *Yes*

Reason: Find committing + summary conviction, anywhere = authorized arrest under s. 495 C.C.

Together, the belief and the offence classification statement authorize the police officer's powers to arrest without a warrant. The next question is whether you can search the arrested person and the immediate surrounding area automatically, without a warrant and without his consent.

Step 5: Search

Can you search the man?   *Yes. Such a search is automatic after you make a lawful arrest.*

The answer to the Step 4 question was "yes." This means the answer to the Step 5 question is "yes."

■ SCENARIO 2

1:10 a.m.: Radio broadcast—"Disturbance, Tombstone Bar, 3227 Brockport Rd."
1:16 a.m.: Time of arrival.

- ▸ You enter the bar via the front entrance.
- ▸ About 40 people are in the bar.

- Gloria (48) introduces herself as the manager and reports the following:
    - Ike (38) is a frequent customer.
    - He entered the bar earlier at 11:30 p.m.
    - He drank about six beers.
    - At 1:00 a.m., he walked around the bar, staggering and yelling obscenities at customers.
    - Gloria told him to shut up. Ike yelled rude names at her. Several customers were disturbed and complained to Gloria about Ike's behaviour.
    - Gloria phoned the police. Ike left the bar on foot shortly afterwards, prior to your arrival.
    - Gloria describes Ike as wearing a dark jacket with a red "X" printed on the front.
- You have dealt with Ike before and are familiar with him.
- You return to your cruiser and search the area.
- Three blocks away, you see Ike walking near his house, about to enter by a door.
- You stop and walk to the door. He is now inside the house. You knock on the door. He answers. He politely asks, "How can I help you, officer?"

Step 1: Offence Recognition
    a. Did an offence occur at the bar? *Yes*
    b. What offence was committed in the bar? *Causing a disturbance*

Step 2: Classify the Offence *Summary conviction*

Step 3: Classify the Belief *Reasonable grounds*

Step 4: Custody Authority Recognition
Can you arrest the man right now, without a warrant, for causing a disturbance at the bar? *No*
    Reason: Reasonable grounds + summary conviction = cannot arrest without a warrant. Although you cannot arrest Ike, you may charge him. You can lay an Information any time within six months of the offence. You can charge him because you have reasonable grounds. A summons may be issued to compel him to court.

Step 5: Search
Can you search without a warrant and without consent? *No*

■ SCENARIO 3

1:14 a.m.: Radio broadcast—"Domestic, 3836 Buffalo St."
1:20 a.m.: Time of arrival.

- You are met by Phyllis (37) in her house. She allows you to enter. She is sober. She reports the following:
    - She owns the house.
    - Her boyfriend, Greg (38), is visiting. He is downstairs in the basement, watching television.
    - Greg has been drinking.

- Ten minutes ago, he became upset for no reason and started shouting obscenities at her. During the argument, Greg said to her, "Some day I will beat you until you die."
- No one else was present.

▸ During this interview, you assess Phyllis's credibility as strong; there is no indication that she is lying.

Step 1: Offence Recognition
  a. Did an offence occur?   *Yes*
  b. What offence?   *Uttering threats*

Step 2: Classify the Offence   *Dual procedure*

Step 3: Classify the Belief   *Reasonable grounds*

Step 4: Custody Authority Recognition
Can you arrest right now, without a warrant?   *Yes*
  Reason: Reasonable grounds + dual procedure = may arrest without a warrant.

Step 5: Search
Can you search without a warrant and without consent?   *Yes, after you lawfully arrest.*

■ SCENARIO 4

4:10 p.m.: Radio broadcast—"Attend at Brockport-Mart. Security guard has one person under arrest."
4:18 p.m.: Time of arrival.

▸ You are met by Laura (49). She is a security guard.
▸ Christine (17) is in custody in Laura's office.
▸ Laura reports the following:

- At 3:45 p.m., she saw Christine reach for a $35.00 CD, put it in her purse, walk past the cash register without paying, and leave the store.
- Laura apprehended her 10 metres outside the store without losing sight of her.
- Laura arrested Christine, brought her to the security office, and phoned the police.
- Christine immediately gave the CD to Laura and said, "I'm sorry for stealing this CD."

Step 1: Offence Recognition
  a. Did an offence occur?   *Yes*
  b. What offence?   *Theft under $5,000.00* and *Possession of property obtained by crime under $5,000.00*

Step 2: Classify the Offence   *Dual procedure*

Step 3: Classify the Belief   *Reasonable grounds*

Step 4: Custody Authority Recognition
Can you arrest right now without a warrant?   *Yes*

Reasons: Reasonable grounds + dual procedure = may arrest without a warrant. Section 495 C.C. applies to both young and adult offenders. Furthermore, Laura's citizen's arrest was lawful: she saw a dual procedure offence being committed (that is, *found committing*) while she was a lawful occupant of the store. You have authority to continue the detention.

Step 5: Search

Can you search without a warrant and without consent?   *Yes, after you lawfully arrest.*

■ SCENARIO 5

11:15 p.m.: Claire (44) is at the police station right now. You interview her. She reports the following:

- ▸ She was at her home 30 minutes ago with her husband Doug (46).
- ▸ Doug punched her in the mouth during an argument.
- ▸ Claire is bleeding from the mouth. She agrees to go to the hospital after the interview.
- ▸ Doug was still at home when she left.

Step 1: Offence Recognition
   a. Did an offence occur?   *Yes*
   b. What offence?   *Assault or assault causing bodily harm (if a doctor finds injuries)*

Step 2: Classify the Offence   *Dual procedure (both)*

Step 3: Classify the Belief   *Reasonable grounds*

Step 4: Custody Authority Recognition
Can you arrest right now, without a warrant?   *Yes*
   Reason: Reasonable grounds + dual procedure = may arrest without a warrant.

Step 5: Search

Can you search without a warrant and without consent?   *Yes, after you lawfully arrest.*

■ SCENARIO 6

2:12 a.m. Radio broadcast—"Domestic, 2825 Brooklyn Rd."
2:17 a.m. Time of arrival.

- ▸ A woman allows you to enter the house. After you enter, you see two men, approximately 40 years old, drunk, screaming obscenities at each other.

Step 1: Offence Recognition
   a. Did the offence of causing a disturbance occur?   *No, the occurrence was inside a dwelling-house*
   b. Did a breach of the peace occur?   *Yes*

Step 2: Classify Breach of the Peace   *No classification*

Step 3: Classify the Belief   *Find committing*

Step 4: Custody Authority Recognition

Can you arrest right now, without a warrant?   *Yes*

   Reason: Find committing + breach of the peace = may arrest both men without a warrant.

Step 5: Search

Can you search without a warrant and without consent?   *Yes, after you lawfully arrest.*

■ SCENARIO 7

5:45 p.m.: Radio broadcast—"Unknown problem, Badland's Fast Food Restaurant, 5045 Halton Road."

5:53 p.m.: Time of arrival.

- ▸ Ellen (23) is an employee.
- ▸ She reports the following:
    - − At 5:40 p.m., she was working at the drive-thru window.
    - − A blue car stopped.
    - − Francis, approximately 50 years old, was the driver. He was alone in the car.
    - − Ellen knows his full name because he is a frequent customer. She has been familiar with him for over a year and can facially recognize him easily.
    - − Francis exposed himself to Ellen. She screamed. He drove away without saying anything.
    - − She observed the licence plate number of his car and recorded it as "2214 HEC," Ontario plate.
- ▸ A CPIC check reveals Francis's address

6:27 p.m.: You attend at Francis's house. A man opens the door. You ask him to identify himself. He identifies himself as Francis (with the same last name as the suspect).

Step 1: Offence Recognition

   a. Did an offence occur?   *Yes*

   b. What offence?   *Indecent act*

Step 2: Classify the Offence   *Summary conviction*

Step 3: Classify the Belief   *Reasonable grounds*

Step 4: Custody Authority Recognition

Can you arrest right now, without a warrant?   *No*

   Reason: Reasonable grounds + summary conviction = cannot arrest without a warrant. Although you cannot arrest Francis, you may charge him. You can lay an Information at any time within six months of the offence. You can charge him because you have reasonable grounds. A summons may be issued to compel him to court.

Step 5: Search

Can you search without a warrant and without consent?   *No*

The objective in each of the following scenarios is to be able to answer a single question at the end of each case—the question addressed by Step 4 of the RDM model: "Can you arrest right now without a warrant?" The process of answering *yes* or *no* reflects the decision making you will have to perform repeatedly in front-line policing. Explain your answer with reference to the RDM model. This explanation will be your justification for the decision.

Note: All witnesses in the scenarios have strong credibility.

■ SCENARIO 8

2:44 p.m.: Radio broadcast—"Attend at the north parking lot of Jake High School, 5000 King St., regarding belated theft. Meet Andrew (Heath)."

2:51 p.m.: Time of arrival.

▸ Andrew reports the following to you while seated in your cruiser:

– He has known Amelia Jones for three years.

– Two hours ago, he was in the high school cafeteria sitting with Amelia.

– Amelia told him that the previous week she stole $150.00 cash and a blue purse from the open locker of Sarah, a fellow student.

– She showed Andrew the purse and the cash.

▸ You assess Andrew as having strong credibility.

▸ Andrew gives you Amelia's address and various locations where she may be.

Question: When you find Amelia today, can you arrest her without a warrant?

■ SCENARIO 9

7:30 p.m.: Radio broadcast—"Belated break and enter, house situated at 3001 Hec St."

7:37 p.m.: Time of arrival.

▸ You are met by the complainant, Angela (41), who reports the following:

– There are four people in her family.

– Everyone was gone today between 9:00 a.m. and 7:00 p.m.

– When she returned at 7:00 p.m., she found the back door forced open, and her DVD player and TV had been stolen ($1,000.00 value).

– Nothing else was touched, and the suspect(s) was/were gone.

▸ At the conclusion of the report, you remember that Virgil (28) lives nearby. He has a criminal record for two daytime B&Es committed in 2003 and 2005. He is a drug abuser and he is probably broke.

Question: Can you arrest Virgil today without a warrant?

■ SCENARIO 10

9:37 p.m.: Radio broadcast—"Non-payment of gas, Badland's Gas Station, 4 Creighton St."

9:49 p.m.: Time of arrival.

▸ Suspect gone on arrival (GOA).

▸ An employee, Lisa (40), reports the following:
  – A man pumped $30.00 worth of gas into his car. He drove away without paying.
  – License plate and description are provided by Lisa.
▸ 10:16 p.m.: You attend at the suspect's house, question him, and he confesses.

Question: Can you arrest this man right now, without a warrant?

■ SCENARIO 11

10:17 p.m.: Radio broadcast—"Obscene phone call, 18 Elm St."
10:26 p.m.: Time of arrival.

▸ Complainant is Sheila (41). She reports the following:
  – At 10:03 p.m. she answered the phone. A male voice said a very sexually explicit comment to her, breathed heavily, and hung up.
  – No other calls were received.
  – She positively recognized the voice as being that of a co-worker, Drew Fuccillo (36). She has worked with him for seven years and is very familiar with him.
▸ 10:47 p.m.: You attend at Drew's house. He identifies himself as Drew Fuccillo (36).

Question: Can you arrest Drew right now?

■ SCENARIO 12

9:08 p.m.: Radio broadcast—"Customer dispute, Highlands Restaurant, 32 Benoit St."
9:17 p.m.: Time of arrival.

▸ You are met by the manager, Maria (41), who reports the following:
  – Bill (58) is a regular customer. He entered the restaurant at 8:00 p.m. He consumed 20 chicken wings and 3 beers.
  – At 9:00 p.m., he was given the bill. The amount was $19.50.
  – Bill ran out of the restaurant and did not pay.
▸ 9:36 p.m.: You attend at Bill's house. He confesses.

Question: Can you arrest Bill right now?

■ SCENARIO 13

2:35 p.m.: Radio broadcast—"Customer dispute. Meet taxi driver in front of 88 Swart Street."
2:43 p.m.: Time of arrival.
▸ George (46), a taxi driver, meets you in front of a house. He is alone. He reports the following:
  – He drove a customer 15 km to this house and arrived at 2:33 p.m. The cost for the ride was $17.50.

- George asked the customer for payment. The customer said, "Screw you," and ran into the house.
- The suspect is described as male, white, 38 years old, 6'3" tall, 210 lbs, brown hair.

▸ 2:47 p.m.: You knock on the door. A man answers. He looks similar to the man described by George. This man gives you a $20 bill and says, "Here, I'll pay it."

Question: Can you arrest the suspect right now?

■ SCENARIO 14

Denise (47) is the manager of Freeman Electronics, 2825 Sleightholme Street. She attends at the police station, right now, and reports that a customer purchased a $1,200.00 TV six days ago. He paid by cheque and took the TV. Yesterday, the cheque was returned to the store marked NSF. You present her with a photo lineup. She positively identifies Damian (36) as the suspect.

Question: Can you arrest Damian today without a warrant?

■ SCENARIO 15

7:15 p.m.: Radio broadcast—"Home owner receiving harassing phone calls."
7:23 p.m.: Time of arrival.

▸ Glenda (41) lives alone. She reports the following:

- She received seven hang-up calls during the past seven days.
- The caller never spoke during any of the calls.
- She suspects an ex-boyfriend, Mark (43), and questioned him today at 6:00 p.m.
- Mark told Glenda he made all seven calls and told her that he "hates her guts."

▸ Glenda reports the confession to you. She informs you that Mark is harmless, she has no fear of him, and that he is not a potential risk.

Question: Can you arrest Mark today without a warrant?

■ SCENARIO 16

2:28 a.m.: You are driving on King Street.

▸ You see a parked car in the parking lot of a bar.
▸ A middle-aged man is staggering from the bar to the parked car.
▸ You stop your car and walk over to him; you can smell alcohol on his breath.
▸ He is holding keys, and unlocks the driver's door.
▸ He is in an advanced state of intoxication, and calls you a "pig."
▸ You are alone without any backup.

Question: Can you arrest the man while he is standing outside the car?

■ SCENARIO 17

7:37 p.m.: Radio broadcast—"Decomposed body in a field across from Last Chance
        Bar, 2825 Wildcat St."
7:48 p.m.: Time of arrival.

- ▸ Decomposed body found.
- ▸ You question the residents on Wildcat Street near the bar.
- ▸ You interview Nelly (40) at 8:30 p.m. She informs you of the following:
    - – She was speaking in person to her sister, Kate (43), seven days ago.
    - – Kate told her that she killed her husband, Theodore, last month by
      cutting his throat, then dumped his body in the field across from the
      bar.
    - – Kate had been planning to kill Theodore since last January (according
      to Nelly).
- ▸ Two weeks later, forensic testing reveals that the dead person is Theodore
  (45), Kate's husband.

Question: Can you arrest Kate right now, without a warrant?

■ SCENARIO 18

10:47 p.m.: Radio broadcast—"Disturbance, Brockport Bar, 88 Swart Street."
10:50 p.m.: Time of arrival.

- ▸ Mary (40), the bartender, witnessed the disturbance. She said it was caused
  by a man she could not identify. The man left before your arrival.
- ▸ She also informs you of the following:
    - – She was speaking with Boris (33) yesterday at 9:00 p.m. in a bar.
    - – She has known him for six years.
    - – They went to Mary's apartment, where they drank and injected drugs
      together for a few hours.
    - – Boris told Mary that he punched an elderly woman on Niagara St.
      last Saturday at 6:00 p.m. The woman fell to the ground. He looked
      through her purse. Nothing was in it. He left the purse and ran off.

Question: Can you arrest Boris right now, without a warrant?

■ SCENARIO 19

2:55 a.m.: You stop a blue car on Barton St.

- ▸ The driver is Howard Joy, DOB Dec. 16, 1970.
- ▸ A CPIC check reveals the following message: "10-63 (wanted) assault
  causing bodily harm—(a city in the same province that you've stopped
  him)."

Question: Can you arrest Howard right now?

FURTHER SELF-EVALUATION SCENARIOS

Additional self-evaluation scenarios can be found online at **www.emp.ca/arcaro/policepowers4E**, the website that accompanies this textbook.

SUMMARY

In each of the preceding reality-based scenarios, you were to determine whether an arrest was possible. There are two types of arrest: with and without warrant. The next chapter will discuss how to obtain and execute a warrant when you have no authority to arrest without warrant.

APPENDIX: ANSWERS TO SELF-EVALUATION SCENARIOS

■ SCENARIO 8

Yes

Reason: Reasonable grounds + dual procedure (theft under $5,000.00).

■ SCENARIO 9

No

Reason: Mere suspicion + indictable offence (break, enter, and theft—dwelling-house).

■ SCENARIO 10

Yes

Reason: Reasonable grounds + dual procedure offence = temporarily classified as indictable (theft under $5,000.00).

■ SCENARIO 11

No

Reason: Reasonable grounds + summary conviction offence (obscene phone call); you may lay an Information and compel Drew to court by summons.

■ SCENARIO 12

No

Reason: Reasonable grounds + summary conviction offence (food fraud). For an arrest you would have to have found the suspect committing the offence. The confession and the eyewitness observation constitute reasonable grounds only.

■ SCENARIO 13

No

Reason: Reasonable grounds + summary conviction offence (transportation fraud). For an arrest you would have to have found the suspect committing the offence. You may lay an Information within six months and compel the suspect to court by means of a summons.

■ SCENARIO 14

Yes

Reason: Reasonable grounds + dual procedure = temporarily classified as indictable (fraud under $5,000.00); no time limit on arresting and charging the suspect.

■ SCENARIO 15

No

Reason: Reasonable grounds + summary conviction (harassing phone calls); no threats were made (this would not qualify as criminal harassment because Glenda does not fear Mark).

■ SCENARIO 16

Yes

Reason: Two authorities:
1. Find committing + dual procedure = temporarily classified as indictable (actual care or control while impaired).
2. Reasonable grounds + dual procedure = temporarily classified as indictable (about to occur—impaired driving).

■ SCENARIO 17

Yes

Reason: Reasonable grounds + indictable offence (murder); no time limit.

■ SCENARIO 18

Yes

Reason: Reasonable grounds + indictable offence (robbery); no time limit.

■ SCENARIO 19

Yes

Reason: Two authorities:
1. Reasonable grounds + valid arrest warrant existing in the territorial jurisdiction that you found Howard in (in-province arrest warrant).
2. Reasonable grounds + dual procedure—temporarily treated as indictable (assault causing bodily harm).

CHAPTER 7

Arrest with Warrant

LEARNING OUTCOMES

The student will learn

- How to identify the elements of an arrest warrant

- How to obtain an arrest warrant

- How to execute an arrest warrant

INTRODUCTION

Criminal law is complicated because its components don't work in isolation. Laws interact. This chapter exemplifies this principle. Arrest warrants interact with warrant-less arrest (Chapter 4) and with release provisions (Chapters 11, and 12). In other words, this chapter teaches about arrest warrants and *introduces* release provisions.

Arrest warrants are covered by complex legislation, including ss. 498–514 C.C. The goal of this chapter is to simplify the subject for practical use in reality front-line policing situations.

ARREST WARRANT: INTRODUCTORY CONCEPTS

There are seven introductory concepts that will help you understand the subject of arrest warrants.

1. The first concept is that there are two categories of arrest authorities:
    a. arrest without warrant, and
    b. arrest with warrant.

    Arrest without warrant means arrest without judicial authorization—in other words, an arrest without the authorization of a provincial court judge or Justice of the Peace (JP). An **arrest with a warrant** is an arrest with judicial authorization, meaning that a Justice has formally authorized the arrest, with a warrant. A *Justice* is defined as a JP or a provincial court judge. When an arrest is made without a warrant, *you* are the decision-maker. When an arrest warrant is issued, the justice is the decision-maker; he or she decides that the arrest is justified and authorizes it.

2. There is only one type of *Criminal Code* arrest warrant: "Form 7—Warrant for Arrest."[1] There are two streams leading to it:

  a. arrest warrant in the first instance,[2] and
  b. bench warrant.[3]

Figure 7.1 illustrates the two streams to Form 7 (an arrest warrant). Stream 1 applies to an arrest warrant in the first instance. Stream 2 applies to a bench warrant.

Figure 7.1   Two Streams Leading to an Arrest Warrant

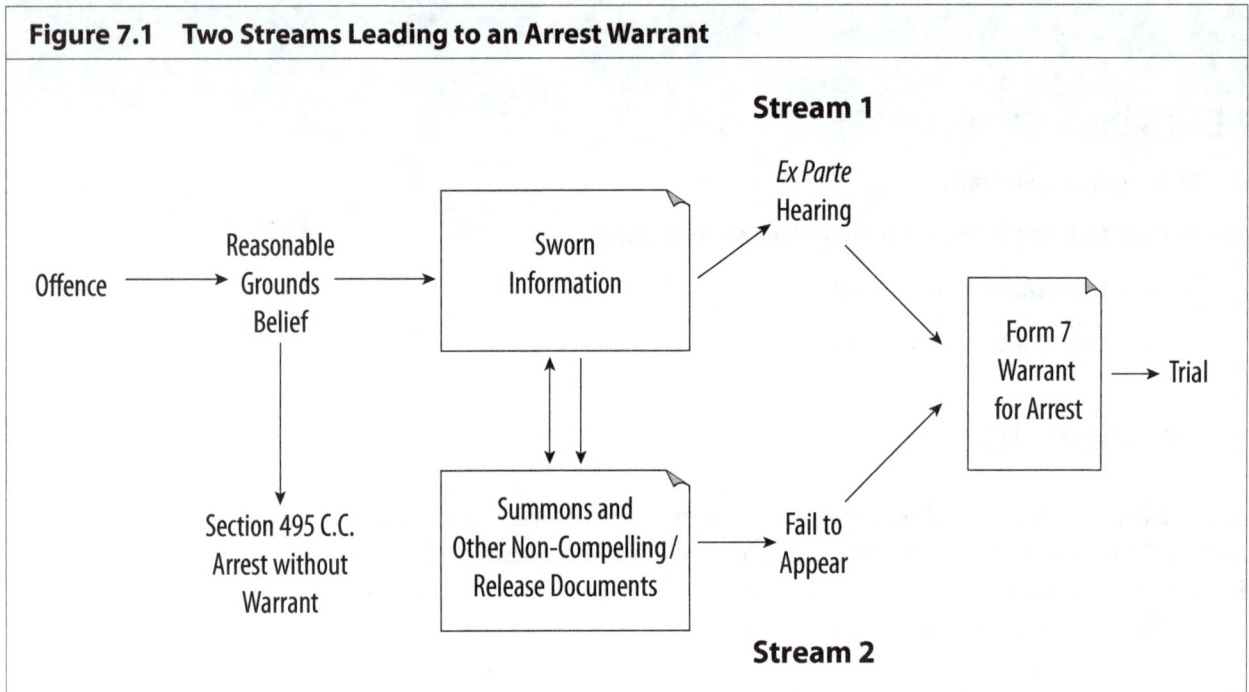

3. An *arrest warrant in the first instance* is issued for an offender who has committed an indictable, dual procedure, or summary conviction offence. A *bench warrant* is issued for a person who fails to appear in court.

4. An *arrest warrant in the first instance* is not automatically issued or granted to police on request. An application and a hearing are compulsory. Without them, it is impossible to get a warrant. These requirements apply to warrants for both adult and young offenders.

5. No arrest warrant in the first instance can be issued until an *Information is laid*—in other words, until the offender is charged. If no Information is laid, no arrest warrant in the first instance can be issued.

6. An arrest warrant in the first instance may be issued for any classification of offence—that is, for summary conviction, dual procedure, or indictable offences.

7. The following is the important concept—an arrest warrant in the first instance communicates to police officers throughout the country the existence of reasonable grounds for arresting someone. When the police choose to arrest without a warrant, a limited number of officers know that the offender is "wanted." For practical purposes, "wanted" means that

reasonable grounds exist for believing that the offender committed an offence.

In arrest-without-warrant cases, the only officers who know about the existence of reasonable grounds are those few officers whom the primary investigator informs. This makes it possible for a patrol officer to stop a wanted offender and not know that he is wanted. Essentially, an arrest warrant *broadcasts nationally* that an offender is wanted. By performing a simple computer check, every police officer in Canada will discover the offender is wanted.

ARREST WARRANT GLOSSARY

The following terms are relevant to arrest warrants.

arrest warrant—Form 7; judicial authorization to arrest

bench warrant—an arrest warrant issued to replace a non-custodial compelling document; sequentially speaking, it is the second compelling document issued

"case made out for compelling an accused"—a phrase in s. 504 C.C. referring to the court's conclusion, after an *ex parte* hearing, that reasonable grounds exist for believing that the named offender committed the named offence

charge—occurs when a Justice signs an Information; initiates "proceedings"

commencement of proceedings—synonymous with the laying of a charge

compelling document—a *Criminal Code* document that compels an accused person to appear in court

custodial compelling document—a "compelling document" that authorizes arrest/custody (for example, Form 7—Warrant for Arrest)

ex parte hearing—a hearing conducted by a Justice, after an Information is received, for the purpose of determining whether there are reasonable grounds for believing that the person named on the Information committed the named offence

fail to appear (FTA) in court—the dual procedure offence of ignoring any compelling document

fail to appear (FTA) photographs or fingerprints—the dual procedure offence of ignoring a compelling document's instructions regarding photographs or fingerprints

in the first instance—firstly; first in the sequence of documents

Information—a formal allegation; Form 2

judicial authorization—authority granted by a Justice as defined in s. 2 C.C.

laying an Information—the three-part process of (1) *completing* Form 2, (2) *bringing* it to a Justice, and (3) *swearing* under oath that the contents are not fabricated; the act of formally laying a charge against someone

necessary in public interest—the existence of any public interest needs (PIN); a prerequisite and justification for an arrest warrant

non-custodial compelling document—any one of six "compelling documents" that does not authorize arrest/custody

Part XVI—a group of provisions, encompassing s. 493 to s. 529.5 of the *Criminal Code*, entitled "compelling appearance of an accused before a Justice and interim release"

pathways to the proceedings—the non-custodial pathway and the two custodial pathways with judicial authorization

proceedings—the period of time that starts with the charge and ends with the conclusion of the trial

public interest needs (PIN)—reasonable grounds for believing that any one of the following circumstances exists: (1) repetition/continuation of any offence, (2) identity of the accused needs to be established, or (3) outstanding physical evidence relevant to the investigation/offence has not been seized

receiving an Information—the *acceptance* by a Justice of an Information, for the purpose of reviewing it during formal hearing

release document—the same thing as a "compelling document"

RICE—repetition, identity, court, outstanding evidence

section 495 C.C.—a peace officer's powers of arrest without warrant

section 504 C.C.—a dual-purpose provision that authorizes laying an Information for indictable offences and mandating that an Information be received by a Justice

section 507 C.C.—the triple-purpose provision that (1) mandates an *ex parte* hearing, (2) determines whether "case is made out for compelling an accused," and (3) determines whether the means of compelling the court appearance will be a summons or an arrest warrant in the first instance; a provision that establishes two custodial "pathways to the proceedings"

section 509 C.C.—the provision authorizing the issuance of a summons

section 514 C.C.—the provision that authorizes an arrest with a warrant; referred to as "execution of warrant," it represents judicial authorization to arrest

section 788(1) C.C.—the same as s. 504 C.C., in relation to summary conviction offences

sections 496–501 C.C.—provisions authorizing non-custodial compelling documents

summons—Form 6; a non-custodial compelling document issued after an Information is signed by a Justice, when an *ex parte* hearing reveals no evidence of PIN

warrant in the first instance—an arrest warrant that is the first compelling document issued for an offender

THE CONCEPT OF PROCEEDINGS

Arrest warrants are part of the concept of "proceedings." Arrest warrant procedures make more sense when we see how they fit into that context.

Proceedings are the central focus of the Canadian justice system. Also called a *process*, the term *proceedings* is defined as a series of formal steps that lead to a prosecution.[4] Proceedings are a continuum that starts with a charge and ends with the court's verdict. There are two types of proceedings: (1) criminal; and (2) civil. There are two types of criminal proceedings: (1) indictable; and (2) summary conviction. Part XVI C.C. governs indictable proceedings (ss. 493–529.5). Part XXVII C.C. governs summary conviction proceedings.

The three basic parts of a criminal proceeding are the making of a formal allegation, the accused person's answer or response to the charge, and the prosecution's attempt to prove the charge (*he or she who asserts must prove*).

"Commencement of proceedings" refers to the starting point. This occurs when a person is "charged with an offence"—that is, when an Information is laid alleging an offence.[5]

Charging a person starts with the "laying" of an Information, sometimes referred to as the *application* for the charge. This stage involves a three-step process:

1. completing Form 2,
2. bringing it to a justice, and
3. swearing under oath that the contents are not fabricated.

After the Information is laid, the Justice "receives" it, meaning that he or she accepts it for review. The Justice cannot refuse to accept the Information for review. He or she has no mandatory obligation to sign it, but has a mandatory obligation to receive it and decide whether to sign it.

After the Justice receives the Information, an "*ex parte* hearing" is held in which the person making the allegation must prove a reasonable grounds belief. If such a belief is successfully proved, the Justice signs the Information, which signifies two things:

1. the accused is formally charged, and
2. the proceeding is commenced.[6]

The "pre-Information stage" represents the "pre-Information *investigation*," not the total investigation period. The commission of an offence starts an investigation. Laying an Information is the by-product of an investigation but does not conclude it. An investigation may resume after the Information is sworn and may continue until the end of the proceedings. The "pre-Information investigation" is not part of the proceedings. It is a decision-making process, unpredictable in duration, that *precedes* the proceedings.

Proceedings Continuum

The proceedings are divided into two stages: (1) pre-trial proceedings; and (2) trial proceedings. The duration of both is unpredictable. A guilty plea reduces the trial proceedings stage significantly.

The Information (Form 2) alone does not compel the accused person to appear in court. Its sole purpose is to initiate proceedings by formally alleging an offence. A document must always accompany the Information. The purpose of the second document is to *compel* the accused person's court appearance. The compelling documents include five non-custodial documents and one custodial document. The only custodial compelling document is an arrest warrant.

Non-custodial documents include the following:

- summons,
- appearance notice,
- promise to appear,
- recognizance,
- undertaking.

There are three means of compelling an accused person to appear in court. The first is the basic, fundamental non-custodial path. The second is a custodial path with a warrant. The third is a custodial path without a warrant. See Figure 7.2.

1. *Basic, non-custodial path*: This represents the fundamental, ordinary kind of proceedings, involving no custody and no arrest. It follows the ss. 504 → 507 → 509 path:

    - An offence is committed, investigated, and a reasonable grounds belief is formed.
    - An Information is laid (504).
    - A hearing is held (507). If the offender poses no risk of repeating an offence or failing to appear, a *summons* is laid. The summons is served (509), compelling the offender to appear in court. No arrest or custody is needed.

2. *Custodial path with a warrant*: This is the same as the basic, non-custodial path, with one exception—the offender poses a risk of committing a repeat offence or failing to appear in court. The risk changes the summons to an arrest warrant. The path follows ss. 504 → 507 → 514:

    - An offence is committed, investigated, and a reasonable grounds belief is formed.

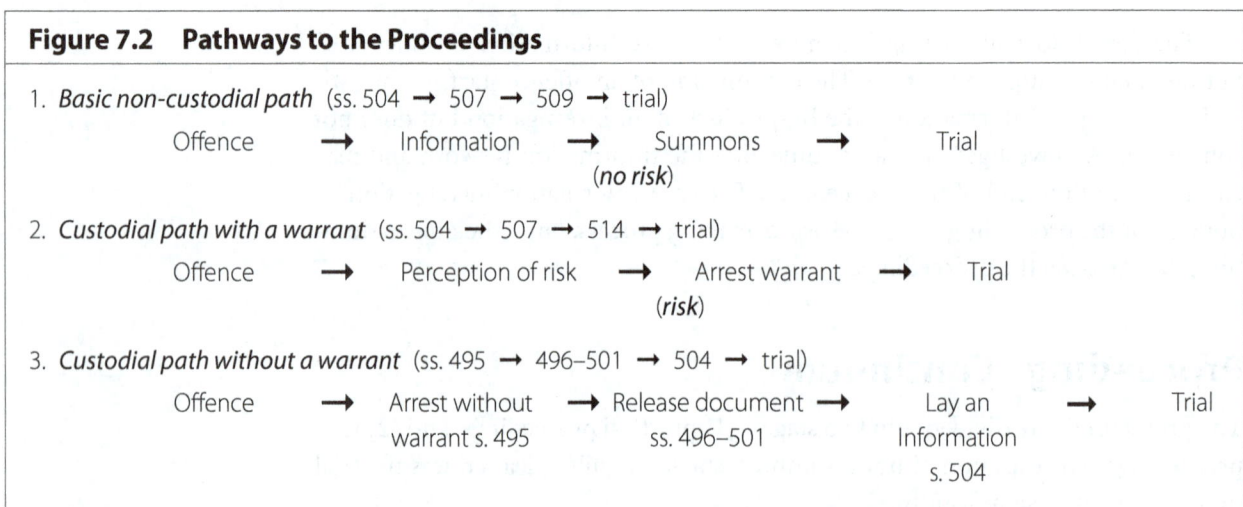

Figure 7.2   Pathways to the Proceedings

1. *Basic non-custodial path* (ss. 504 → 507 → 509 → trial)

    Offence → Information → Summons → Trial
    (*no risk*)

2. *Custodial path with a warrant* (ss. 504 → 507 → 514 → trial)

    Offence → Perception of risk → Arrest warrant → Trial
    (*risk*)

3. *Custodial path without a warrant* (ss. 495 → 496–501 → 504 → trial)

    Offence → Arrest without warrant s. 495 → Release document ss. 496–501 → Lay an Information s. 504 → Trial

- An Information is laid (504).
- A hearing is held (507). Risk is proved, arrest warrant issued.
- Arrest warrant executed (514).

3. *Custodial path without a warrant*: This path *reverses* the direction of the second path—the police have no time to obtain an arrest warrant or summons. This reversal permits an arrest without a warrant to be made *before* an Information is laid. After the arrest, a compelling document is issued. Following the issuance of this document, an Information is laid.

The only difference between the two custodial paths is the Information–arrest sequence. In path 2 (with a warrant), the Information precedes the arrest. In path 3 (without a warrant), the sequence is reversed—the Information follows the arrest. Otherwise, there is no difference between arrest with a warrant and arrest without a warrant with respect to proceedings. Despite the different sequence of steps, both paths involve two documents—an Information and a compelling document—that are issued within a relatively narrow timeframe. The different order of the documents' issuance has no effect on the proceedings.

Arrests and compelling/release documents are "not investigatory instruments, but vehicles to court."[7] They are not part of the actual investigation. They are products of the investigation. In some cases, the arrest or summons occurs after the investigation concludes. But often an investigation continues after an arrest or summons has occurred. Taking custody and issuing release documents are not investigative procedures. They are intended to achieve the goals and objectives of the proceedings.

THE CONCEPT OF JUDICIAL AUTHORIZATION

Taking custody of an offender is not an investigative procedure; it is the *result* of such a procedure, and it is intended to ensure two things:

1. the offender's court appearance, and
2. public safety.

Custody is included in two of the three "proceedings pathways" as an alternative to a summons. A number of custody authorities are available to the police. These authorities are defined as "circumstances constituting legal permission to arrest that emerges from a source of law," and they fall into one of two categories depending on whether the actual decision to arrest was made by a Justice or by the police:

1. with a warrant (judicial authorization)—s. 514 C.C., or
2. without a warrant (without judicial authorization)—s. 495 C.C.

"Warrant" is synonymous with the phrase "judicial authorization";[8] it is the formal permission to arrest granted by a Justice in response to a justified police application. An arrest with a warrant has judicial authorization—a Justice has made the decision. Conversely, an arrest without a warrant is an arrest without judicial authorization—the arresting officer is the decision-maker.

From a police perspective, both methods have benefits and disadvantages. Warrantless arrest is faster because no documentation has to precede it. The limitation of this method is that only a restricted number of police officers will know the offender is wanted. In other words, few officers will have the required belief, based on reasonable grounds, that the offender has committed an indictable offence and needs to be arrested. An arrest with a warrant is more time consuming because the warrant must be applied for. But once the warrant is granted, a nationwide network of police officers across Canada will know, or will be informed electronically within seconds, that an offender is wanted. An arrest warrant is a means of communicating nationwide that reasonable grounds exist for arresting someone.

Extend the Belief

An arrest warrant is the outcome of a decision-making process and is a solution to a problem. The following are two case studies that will test your problem-solving skills.

■ REALITY CASE STUDY 1

11:15 a.m.: Alarm—bank, downtown/urban location.
11:21 a.m.: Arrival—suspects GOA.
Preliminary investigation reveals the following:

- ▸ Three men armed with shotguns entered the bank at 11:10 a.m.
- ▸ They pointed the weapons at bank employees and demanded money.
- ▸ The offenders were given $22,500.00.
- ▸ They left the bank prior to police arrival.
- ▸ No direction or means of travel observed.
- ▸ Forensic analysis of the crime scene commences.

12:16 p.m.: Report of a car fire on a rural street, approximately 25 km from the crime scene.
12:28 p.m.: Arrival—fire department present.

- ▸ No one else is present.
- ▸ CPIC check on the plate reveals that the car was reported stolen at 10:39 a.m. this morning from a street situated 0.5 km from the bank.

5:17 p.m.: Claire (38) contacts you. You interview her. She provides you with a written statement reporting that her boyfriend Doug (42) arrived home today at 3:30 p.m. He told her he committed the robbery. He had a canvas bag with a substantial amount of cash in it.
7:23 p.m.: A forensics officer informs you that fingerprints found on a counter in the bank and on the door of the stolen car were positively identified as Doug's fingerprints.

In reality, reasonable grounds exist to believe that Doug committed the robbery. Although authority to arrest without a warrant exists under s. 495 C.C., Doug may or may not be found quickly. If he cannot be found quickly, the obvious goal is to inform as many officers as possible, in the widest geographical area, that there are reasonable grounds for believing he committed the offence—this will prevent Doug from repeating this or any other offence and from failing to appear in court.

You have a decision to make. Two alternatives exist for arresting Doug:

1. section 495 C.C., arrest without a warrant, or
2. obtain an arrest warrant.

Which is your choice and why?

_____

_____

_____

■ REALITY CASE STUDY 2

Five complaints concerning an indecent act have been lodged within the past 10 days, and you are investigating them. Based on the evidence, you develop a belief (mere suspicion) that Bill (52) is the offender. Bill has a criminal record that includes a sexual assault conviction five years ago. After obtaining a mugshot from central records, you compose a photo lineup, and present it separately to each complainant. All five complainants positively identify Bill.

Reasonable grounds exists to believe that Bill committed all five offences. However, the offences are classified as summary conviction. Consequently, no authority exists under s. 495 C.C. to arrest Bill without a warrant.

You lack the authority to arrest him without a warrant, but Bill is an obvious risk to be a repeat offender. You may charge him by laying five Informations. After the Informations are sworn, either one of these documents may be issued: (1) a summons; or (2) an arrest warrant.

What procedure is required to obtain an arrest warrant?

_____

_____

_____

What factors determine whether a summons or an arrest warrant is issued?

_____

_____

_____

DEFINITION OF AN ARREST WARRANT

The objective of the arrest warrant procedure is to apply and prove the need for, and thereby receive, a *document* called an arrest warrant. In other words, this document is the final outcome and the goal of the procedure.

An arrest warrant is defined in s. 493 C.C. as a "Form 7 document." Form 7 is illustrated in s. 849 C.C. The document is formally entitled "Warrant for Arrest."

A Form 7 warrant for arrest is a written order that contains comprehensive instructions concerning nine matters, or elements of information:

1. who can arrest,
2. who will be arrested,

3. who authorized the arrest,

4. the reason for the arrest,

5. the reason for the issuance of the warrant,

6. the type of custody prescribed for the accused,

7. the absence of a discretionary element (the officer must arrest—no discretion),

8. when to arrest, and

9. details about the accused's post-custody appearance.

The following are these nine elements of information in greater detail:

1. *Who can arrest.* Arrest warrants are directed to peace officers in the territorial jurisdiction named on the warrant. Conversely, arrest warrants are not directed to the following:

   ▸ peace officers outside the territorial jurisdiction, or
   ▸ citizens.

2. *Who will be arrested.* Only one accused person can be identified on an arrest warrant. Two rules emerge from this point:

   a. The *name* of *one* specific offender must be included on the warrant. If the accused person's name is unknown, a description of the accused may be included instead of a name. This is an unlikely exception to the general rule that a name be included. Although the language in s. 511(1)(a) C.C. allows the possibility that a description may need to replace a name, this is rarely necessary. It is also impracticable, for two reasons: first, the description has to be so specific that only one person can be positively identified; second, an offender must be charged before an arrest warrant can be issued. Laying an Information requires that you have reasonable grounds for believing that a specific person committed an offence. All of this is difficult to accomplish without a name.

   b. In cases involving multiple offenders, more than one offender cannot be named on one arrest warrant. Each offender must be identified on a separate warrant.

3. *Who authorized the arrest.* The signature of a Justice, defined in s. 2 C.C., is needed. The signature does not merely represent judicial authorization; most Justices have jurisdiction across their respective provinces. Consequently, the arrest warrant is valid province-wide but not Canada-wide.

4. *The reason for the arrest.* An offence must be "set out briefly." A formal, lengthy wording is not required; the short-form name of the offence is sufficient.

5. *Reason for issuance.* The legal justification for the issuance of the warrant must be included. Nine possible reasons exist:

   a. There are reasonable grounds to believe that it is necessary in the public interest to issue this warrant for the arrest of the accused.[9]

   b. The accused failed to attend court in accordance with the summons served on him.[10]

   c. An appearance notice *or* a promise to appear *or* a recognizance entered into before an officer-in-charge was confirmed and the accused failed to attend court in accordance therewith.[11]

   d. It appears that a summons cannot be served because the accused is evading service.[12]

e. The accused was ordered to be present at the hearing of an application for a review of an order made by a Justice and did not attend the hearing.[13]

f. There are reasonable grounds to believe that the accused has contravened or is about to contravene the promise to appear *or* undertaking *or* recognizance on which he was released.[14]

g. There are reasonable grounds to believe that the accused has since his release from custody on a promise to appear *or* an undertaking *or* a recognizance committed an indictable offence.[15]

h. The accused was required by an appearance notice or a promise to appear or a recognizance entered into before an officer in charge or a summons to attend at a time and place stated therein for the purposes of the *Identification of Criminals Act* and did not appear at that time and place.[16]

i. An indictment has been found against the accused and the accused has not appeared or remained in attendance before the court for his trial.[17]

Points a–i (reasons for issuing a warrant) fall into two streams. The first point constitutes an "arrest warrant in the first instance." Points b–i are categorized as "bench warrants."

The last four "elements of information (points f–i)" on the arrest warrant interact; they are linked by a phrase that emerges from the combined effect of ss. 511(1)(c) and 849 C.C.: "command/order forthwith to arrest the accused and bring him to a Justice." Four instructional elements are implicit in this phrase:

6. *Type of custody.* An "arrest," by definition, is authorized; a "detention" is not.

7. *No discretion.* The words "command/order" impose a mandatory obligation to arrest. The element of discretion is removed.

8. *When to arrest/to bring to a Justice.* The position of the word "forthwith" imposes a time frame for both the arrest and the appearance before a Justice. Both tasks have to be accomplished "forthwith," defined in case law as "without unjustified delay."[18]

9. *Post-custody appearance.* After the arrest, the accused must be brought to a Justice with jurisdiction for a bail hearing. This appearance determines release or pre-trial detention.

In summary, these nine elements constitute a sequence that starts and ends with appearances before a Justice. A Justice authorizes the arrest in response to a formal request and a "return" to the Justice, once the suspect is apprehended, is required.

PURPOSE OF AN ARREST WARRANT

The purpose of a Form 7 warrant for arrest is to compel an accused to appear in court. The court appearance is the primary aim. The arrest represents the *means* of compelling the court appearance. Laying an Information sets in motion a process called a "proceeding." The formal allegation triggers the need for a response. The accused person must respond to the formal allegation by appearing in court. The

Information initiates the *need* for the accused's response, but that particular document does not legally compel the accused to appear in court.

The means of compelling an accused person to court is governed by Part XVII C.C., entitled "Compelling Appearance of Accused before a Justice and Interim Release." A *compelling document* is the means of compelling an accused's appearance before a Justice. There are two types of compelling documents: (1) custodial (a Form 7 warrant for arrest); and (2) non-custodial (summons, appearance notice, promise to appear, undertaking, and recognizance).

The arrest warrant procedure is outlined in Part XVI C.C. but not in its entirety. No part of the *Criminal Code* is exclusively devoted to or entitled "arrest warrants."

ONE WARRANT—TWO STREAMS

There is a common misconception that there are two types of *Criminal Code* arrest warrants. There is only one type: a Form 7 warrant for arrest. But there are two streams leading to it. They are the following:

1. arrest warrant in the first instance, and
2. bench warrant.

The two streams names are informal terms, not used in Part XVI C.C. The term "bench warrant" is only used in s. 597 C.C. (Part XX), referring to a Form 7 warrant issued when, for example, an accused fails to appear after an indictment has been preferred against the accused.

A warrant in the first instance and a bench warrant share the same outcome (Form 7), but differ in issuance sequence. A warrant in the first instance is the first compelling document, and it is issued as a companion document to a sworn Information. A bench warrant is the second compelling document and it is issued after an initial non-custodial release/compelling document has been ignored—for example, after an accused has failed to appear in court. A bench warrant replaces the first compelling document.

Characteristics of the Two Streams

A Form 7 warrant for arrest is the end result of both an arrest warrant in the first instance and a bench warrant. It is one of seven compelling documents and it is the only *custodial* document. The other six are *non-custodial* compelling documents. They are as follows:

1. summons,
2. appearance notice,
3. promise to appear,
4. officer-in-charge (OIC) recognizance,
5. Justice's recognizance, and
6. Justice's undertaking.

Primary Objective

All seven compelling documents have the primary goal of ensuring the accused's court appearance, or, in other words, of preventing his or her failure to appear in court. Of the seven compelling documents, the arrest warrant is the only custodial one—the only one that authorizes arrest/custody. The other six are non-custodial compelling/release documents. They are dual-purpose documents. They compel a court appearance while exempting a person from custody.

Secondary Objective

The Form 7 arrest warrant has the secondary objective of preventing public safety risks, which are formally called "public interest needs (PIN)."[19] Specifically, these needs are as follows:

- the need to establish the offender's identity;
- the need to prevent the continuation or repetition of *any* offence, not just the offence for which the offender was arrested; and
- the need to seize outstanding physical evidence relating to the offence being investigated.

If there are reasonable grounds for believing that any one of these needs exists, then arrest/custody is justified because it is "necessary in the public interest." Conversely, if none of these needs exists, arrest/custody is not "necessary in the public interest."

A judgment that custody is "necessary in the public interest" is the prerequisite and justification for an arrest warrant.

A compelling document is a companion document to a sworn Information. Although they are linked, each of these documents has a distinct purpose. The Information formally alleges an offence and charges the offender; the compelling document forces him or her to appear in court.

FIRST STREAM

Custodial and Non-Custodial Pathways

See Figure 7.2. Together, ss. 504 and 507 C.C. form the two pathways to the proceedings for indictable offences (s. 788 C.C. represents the same pathways for summary conviction offences. From another perspective, these sections govern "how to obtain a summons" and how to obtain "an arrest warrant in the first instance."

PATHWAY 1: BASIC NON-CUSTODIAL PATH

This pathway involves using the "Information–summons" base formula for *no-risk* offenders. It is the easiest and most fundamental way to charge a no-risk offender and compel him or her to appear in court. The 504/507 concept is simply the following: If, once you can prove reasonable grounds in relation to any class of offence (and you have chosen not to arrest the person), you lay an Information but introduce no evidence that an arrest is "necessary in the public interest," the Justice *must* issue a summons. No discretion is allowed the Justice in this regard. A sworn Information, in the absence of evidence that arrest is "necessary in the public interest," means the *mandatory* issuance of a summons. Under these circumstances the offender is deemed to pose no risk of failing to appear in court and no risk to public safety. A summons is the non-custodial compelling document.

PATHWAY 2: CUSTODIAL PATH WITH A WARRANT

If evidence exists that an arrest is "necessary in the public interest," the Justice issues a Form 7 warrant for arrest *instead of a summons*. This second pathway is called "warrant in the first instance" and is sometimes referred to as "the custodial path with authorization."

The phrase "in the first instance" means "firstly."[20] It refers to the sequence of documents. An arrest warrant *in the first instance* is the *first compelling document issued to accompany a sworn Information*.

PATHWAY 3: CUSTODIAL PATHWAY WITHOUT A WARRANT

This pathway begins with the arrest. Figure 7.3 outlines the procedure for arrest warrants in the first instance.

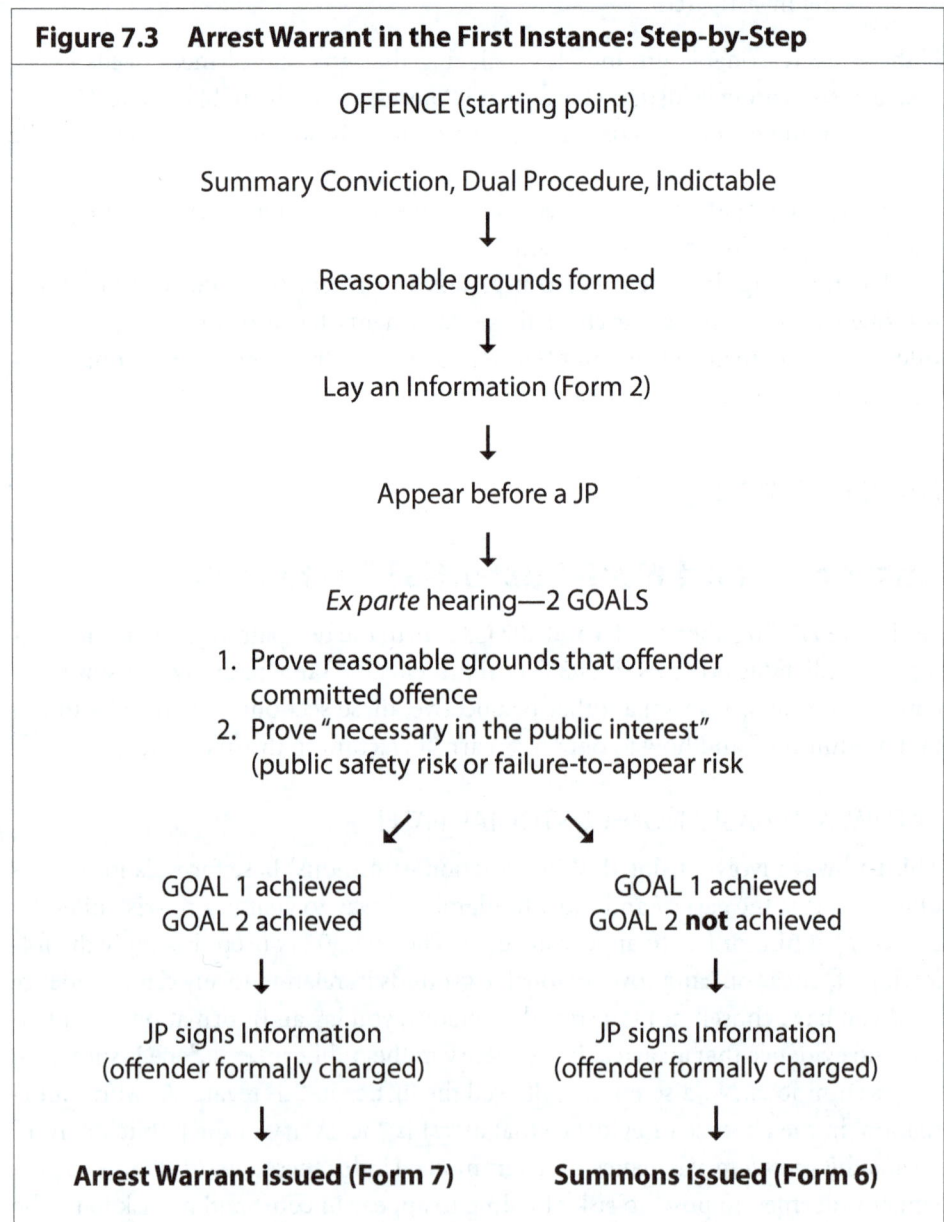

Figure 7.3   Arrest Warrant in the First Instance: Step-by-Step

OFFENCE (starting point)

Summary Conviction, Dual Procedure, Indictable

↓

Reasonable grounds formed

↓

Lay an Information (Form 2)

↓

Appear before a JP

↓

Ex parte hearing—2 GOALS

1. Prove reasonable grounds that offender committed offence
2. Prove "necessary in the public interest" (public safety risk or failure-to-appear risk

↙   ↘

| GOAL 1 achieved | GOAL 1 achieved |
| GOAL 2 achieved | GOAL 2 **not** achieved |

↓   ↓

| JP signs Information | JP signs Information |
| (offender formally charged) | (offender formally charged) |

↓   ↓

| **Arrest Warrant issued (Form 7)** | **Summons issued (Form 6)** |

SECOND STREAM

Bench Warrant

The second stream leading to a Form 7 arrest warrant is called the "bench warrant" method. *Bench warrant* is an informal term not used in the *Criminal Code*. It is most commonly used as solution to the *risk* and the *actuality* of the suspect failing to appear in court.

A bench warrant is not issued directly in response to a sworn Information. A *replacement document*, it takes the place of the non-custodial compelling document that was issued in response to the sworn Information alleging the original offence.

Essentially, a bench warrant is the *second* compelling document—the second attempt to compel the accused to appear in court for the purpose of answering the original charge.

A bench warrant may be issued by a Justice in four situations:

1. The accused fails to appear in court.[21]
2. Arrest is deemed "necessary in the public interest"—a risk of the accused's repeating the offence or failing to appear in court emerges *after* a non-custodial compelling document has been issued and served but *before* the scheduled court appearance.[22]
3. The accused is intentionally evading the service of a summons.[23]
4. The accused fails to appear for fingerprinting and photographs.[24]

A bench warrant may replace a non-custodial document at three possible junctures:

1. after the summons has been served and the accused has actually failed to appear;
2. after the summons has been served but the accused has not yet failed to appear; and
3. after the summons has been issued but not yet served.

Fail to Appear in Court

The procedure followed when a defendant fails to appear in court is governed by three provisions—ss. 512(2), 524(1), and 145(2)–(5) C.C. Formally, this bench warrant is called a "warrant in default of appearance."[25] An accused's failure to appear in court poses two separate problems:

1. a failure to answer to the original offence, and
2. the commission of a second offence (failure to appear in court is a separate dual procedure offence).

This failure to appear disrupts the original path by which the accused would come to appear in court (initiated by the laying of an Information and the serving of a non-custodial compelling document) and—if a separate charge of failure to appear is laid—marks the beginning of the second stream.

A bench warrant is intended to solve the first problem directly, but it also indirectly solves the second problem. The primary aim of the bench warrant is to compel the accused to appear in court to answer the original charge. It replaces the original non-custodial release document. In other words, an Information does not have to be sworn before the bench warrant is issued because the sworn Information already exists.

After the bench warrant is issued to ensure the accused will now appear in court, an Information may be laid to charge the accused with having previously failed to appear. The bench warrant facilitates the court appearance in connection with the second offence. Therefore, the bench warrant serves a dual purpose.

The bench warrant is not automatically issued. The Crown prosecutor must apply for it and justify its need. The judge has the discretion to issue it or deny it. The judge does not have a mandatory obligation to issue it.

SEQUENCE

Following is what happens when a suspect fails to appear in court:

1. *Charged and compelled.* The sequence starts with an Information being sworn and a release /compelling document being issued and lawfully served.
2. *The accused fails to appear.* On the scheduled court date at the allotted place, the accused is called to answer to the charge. Failure to respond constitutes non-appearance.
3. *The Crown* orally *applies for a bench warrant.* No document is needed. An Information does not have to be laid first.
4. *The Crown has the onus of proving that the release/compelling document was lawfully issued and served.*
5. *Judge's decision.* The judge may either grant or deny the request for a bench warrant. If granted, the bench warrant is issued on Form 7, to signify a second compelling document, replacing the first.

Necessary in the Public Interest

Sections 512(1) and 524(1) C.C. provide solutions to the problem that arises when a public safety or fail-to-appear (FTA) risk develops *after* a release document has been issued and served. If there are reasonable grounds for believing that an arrest is *necessary in the public interest,* a police officer may appear before a Justice, apply for cancellation of the first release document (to be replaced by a bench warrant), and present evidence in support of his belief at an *ex parte* hearing. In this case the bench warrant serves as a second, or replacement, document, aimed at preventing a public safety or FTA risk.

SEQUENCE

Following is the procedure an officer follows to obtain a bench warrant:

1. *Charge and compel.* The sequence starts with an Information being sworn and a release/compelling document being issued and lawfully served.

2. *Obtain evidence.* At some point between the service of the summons and the scheduled court appearance, there emerges evidence, sufficient to support a belief based on reasonable grounds, that the accused

    a. has committed an indictable offence; or

    b. is about to commit an indictable offence; or

    c. is about to or intends to fail to appear.

3. *Officer appears before a Justice* anywhere except open court.
4. *Orally applies to have the release document replaced with a bench warrant.*
5. *Ex parte hearing begins.*
6. *The officer making the application has the onus of proving that an arrest is "necessary in the public interest."*
7. *Justice's decision.* The Justice may grant or deny the application for a bench warrant. If granted, the first release document is cancelled and replaced with a Form 7 arrest warrant. If denied, the first document remains in force.

Evading Service

Section 512(2)(c) C.C. addresses the problem that arises when an accused evades the service of a summons. This provision authorizes the replacement of a summons after it is issued but before service. "Evading" means *intentional* avoidance. It does not mean that efforts to serve the summons have simply been unsuccessful. The evading service procedure is designed to address a deliberate evasion. It cannot be used simply for the police officer's convenience. There must be evidence of intentional avoidance by the accused.

The intent to evade the service of a summons is proved the same way that *mens rea* is proved in any other case—by confession or by circumstantial evidence. The latter includes evidence of a *sufficient number of attempts by law enforcement officers to serve the summons.* The problem is that the *Criminal Code* does not specify what constitutes "sufficient," nor does it concretely define the term "evading service."

The amount of evidence needed and the standard of belief required to demonstrate evasion both depend on the abstract word "appears." The evidence must make it apparent that a summons cannot be served because of the accused's apparent intentional evasion.

SEQUENCE

Following is the order in which events occur when an accused is evading the service of a summons.

1. *Charge and compel by summons.* The sequence starts with a sworn Information and a summons being issued.
2. *Officer makes attempts to serve the summons.*
3. *Officer records the precise details surrounding each failed attempt.*
4. *Officer obtains any relevant witness statements pertaining to the accused's intent to evade.*
5. *Officer appears before a Justice* anywhere except in open court.

6. *Officer orally applies for cancellation of the summons and replacement by a Form 7 arrest warrant.*
7. *Ex parte hearing begins.*
8. *Justice's decision.*

Failure to Appear for Fingerprints and Photographs

Release documents may require the accused to appear at a specific time and place, for the purpose of fingerprinting and photographing, in accordance with the *Identification Act.* Failure to appear for this is a single act that constitutes two offences. First, it signifies non-compliance with a release order. Second, it constitutes a separate dual procedure offence.

Sections 502 and 510 C.C. allow the release document to be cancelled and replaced by a bench warrant, without another Information being laid. The accused's non-appearance for fingerprinting and photographs is sufficient grounds to trigger this process. An Information may be laid *after* the issuance of the bench warrant, to charge the accused with the additional "fail to appear" offence.

SEQUENCE

Following is the order of events when an accused fails to appear for fingerprints and photographs:

1. *Charge and compel.* The release order must specify a date, time, and place when the accused should appear, in accordance with the *Identification of Criminals Act,* for the purposes of fingerprinting and photographs.
2. *Accused fails to appear on the scheduled date at the allotted place.*
3. *Officer appears before a Justice anywhere except open court.*
4. *Officer applies for cancellation and replacement.*
5. *Ex parte hearing.*
6. *Justice's decision.*
7. *Bench warrant issued.*
8. *Officer lays an Information charging accused with "Fail to appear."*

SECTION 788 C.C.

This provision governs the issuance of an arrest warrant in the first instance for a *summary conviction* offence.

One of the six non-custodial compelling documents is issued either

▸ to release a person after an arrest without warrant has been made pursuant to s. 495 C.C.; or
▸ in accordance with the basic procedure "Information–summons."

Applying the Three Pathways

CIB: CRIME–INVESTIGATION–BELIEF

This sequence represents the pre-Information/investigation stage. It precedes all three pathways to the proceedings. The belief (reasonable grounds) is the starting point for all three pathways—summons, arrest warrant in the first instance, and s. 495 C.C. arrest without warrant. (See Figure 7.2.)

Once the belief is formed, you must choose a pathway to the proceedings. Which pathway you choose is dictated by the objectives of public safety and of ensuring the accused appears in court. If the offence is minor and RICE is fulfilled (see Chapter 11), path 1 (summons) may be chosen to achieve the goal. If the offence is major and RICE is not fulfilled, paths 2 and 3 (arrest without warrant) will be chosen to achieve the goals. The only issue for the investigator is deciding how strong his or her belief is and how much time is available.

Procedure

The following is the step-by-step procedure for the *application* and issuance of an arrest warrant in the first instance. It is derived from four *Criminal Code* provisions (504, 507, 788, 795). This procedure is the same for all classification of offences.

1. *Offence recognition.* After the investigation starts, analyze the accumulated evidence, prove that a criminal offence has occurred, and identify a specific offence or offences.
2. *Form reasonable grounds—connect suspect to offence.* This is the first of two beliefs that need to be established. Obtain sufficient evidence so that you have a belief based on reasonable grounds that a specific person is connected to the offence.
3. *Form reasonable grounds—"necessary in the public interest."* This is the second belief that needs to be established. Prove the existence of PIN. There must be evidence amounting to reasonable grounds for believing that an offender may fail to appear in court or may commit a repeat offence.

    You prove that an arrest is "necessary in the public interest" (PIN) through reference to the offender's past, present, and the circumstances surrounding the specific offence. You use such information to demonstrate that the offender's future behaviour poses a risk.

    The following are specific guidelines:

    a. *The risk of the offender's failing to appear.* There are two ways to prove this. The first is by demonstrating any past failure on the part of the accused to comply with court proceeding documents (regardless of whether those failures resulted in charges or convictions). The second way is by means of circumstantial evidence. A workable formula for this combines two factors—*severity of offence* plus the *absence of community-binding elements* in the life of the accused (factors tying him or her to the community). The goal is to demonstrate that the severity of the offence, in combination with a lack of community-binding elements, make the suspect a risk for leaving the jurisdiction and avoiding prosecution. Community-binding elements include family, assets, and income.

    b. *Risk to public safety.* You prove this by citing patterns and trends from the offender's past, including the following:

        ▸ number of charges (with or without conviction),
        ▸ past criminal record,

- criminal conduct solved without charges,
- history of violence,
- substance addiction,
- animosity or threats to victim or witnesses,
- no source of income,
- mental problems, and
- any other evidence of bad character and the potential for criminal behaviour.

4. *Complete an Information.* Prior to appearing before a JP, privately compose an Information, and make sure you do this without assistance from the JP. Any assistance from a JP constitutes a Charter violation. Completing the Information serves the dual purpose of applying for the charge and the warrant.

5. *Appear before a JP.* There are two ways to make an appearance before a JP:

   a. in person,[26] or
   b. "by any means of telecommunication that produces a writing."[27]

   A personal appearance occurs anywhere except open court.

6. *Oath.* Swear that the contents of the Information are not fabricated and sign it.[28]

7. *Ex parte hearing.* The offender cannot be present at this hearing.[29] No exceptions to this rule exist. The offender will not even be notified. Generally, two people are present—the investigating officer and the Justice—and the hearing is brief and informal. In most cases, the officer reads relevant statements or reports.

   This hearing has two goals and is divided into two stages. The first goal is to demonstrate there are reasonable grounds for believing that the named offender committed the alleged offence. The second goal is to prove that the accused's arrest is "necessary in the public interest."[30]

   The following rules apply to the *ex parte* hearing:

   a. The evidence must be introduced orally, not in writing.[31]
   b. Hearsay evidence is allowed.[32]
   c. Witnesses do not have to appear and testify. Although their attendance and testimony are not compulsory, the JP has the discretion to require witnesses to be called.[33]
   d. All witness evidence must be sworn, under oath.[34]

8. *JP's decision.* The JP has a mandatory obligation to analyze the evidence and make certain decisions.

   First, the JP decides whether to sign the Information and thereby formalize the allegation. If the investigating officer proves reasonable grounds, the JP signs it. If not, the JP will not sign it, ending the procedure.

   If the JP signs the Information, he or she must issue a second document compelling the accused to appear in court. The JP's only two means of accomplishing this are (1) issuing a summons; or (2) issuing an arrest warrant.[35] If the evidence does not prove an arrest "necessary in the public interest," the summons becomes the compulsory method.[36]

   If the evidence constitutes "necessary in the public interest," an arrest warrant in the first instance is issued.[37]

REPLACING A SUMMONS WITH A WARRANT

In some cases, no evidence of there being a risk to public safety or a risk of the accused's failing to appear will be clear at the time of an *ex parte* hearing, but will emerge subsequently. Section 512(1)(b) C.C. provides an investigative solution to this problem by allowing an arrest warrant to replace the summons.

The procedure is simple and follows the principles governing the issuance of an arrest warrant in the first instance:

1. First, a summons is issued at the conclusion of an *ex parte* hearing because there is no evidence that an arrest is in the public interest.
2. At any time after the summons is issued, whether before or after it is served, evidence emerges of either a public safety or a fail-to-appear risk.
3. The investigating officer appears for a second time before a JP. No document has to be completed.
4. Another *ex parte* hearing begins. The officer gives sworn oral testimony that an arrest is now in the public interest.
5. The JP analyzes the evidence and makes a decision. If PIN is proved, a Form 7 arrest warrant is issued to replace the summons. If no risk is proved, the summons remains in force.

The following principles apply to this "summons replacement" provision:

▸ The issuance of a summons at the conclusion of the initial *ex parte* hearing does not represent a final decision. It is a temporary decision based on existing evidence.

▸ After a summons is issued, there is no limitation on the number of *ex parte* hearings that may be conducted if new evidence emerges of an arrest being "necessary in the public interest."

▸ A summons may be replaced with a warrant at any time before or after the summons is served.

▸ Theoretically, this provision *binds* the accused's behaviour after a summons is issued. Section 512(1)(b) C.C. essentially prohibits the accused from evading a court appearance or becoming a risk to public safety, *after* the issuance of a summons.

▸ Conversely, s. 512(1)(b) C.C. imposes an obligation on police to investigate any circumstances relating to "necessary in the public interest" *after* the issuance of a summons. In other words, the investigation does not end until the suspect's court appearance.

▸ A summons is not the only compelling document that may be replaced. An appearance notice, promise to appear, or an OIC recognizance may also be replaced by means of an arrest warrant if evidence of an arrest being "necessary in the public interest" emerges after those documents are issued.[38]

Multiple Offenders

In cases where more than one person commits an offence, separate determinations about arrest must be made for each individual. A collective treatment of the offenders cannot occur for two reasons. First, s. 507(1)(b) C.C. refers to "the accused" in the singular, not the plural. Secondly, although the *ex parte* evidence concerning the offenders may be similar, their personal histories and current circumstances will not be identical.

Young Offenders

The procedures described above apply to both adult and young offenders.

■ CASE STUDY

1:30 a.m.: While on patrol, you see a blue car with plate 362NCK. You stop it on Crighton Street. The driver is the lone occupant; he identifies himself as Jack Umbriaggo, DOB July 4, 1976. A CPIC check reveals that Jack is wanted (10-63) on an arrest warrant for robbery, issued in the *same* city in which you are patrolling.

Question 1: Is the warrant valid at the location where you are stopped with Jack?

Answer: Yes, the Justice who signed the warrant has jurisdiction throughout the province. The warrant is valid anywhere in that province.

Question 2: What is the classification of this offence?

Answer: Indictable.

Question 3: Can you arrest Jack?

Answer: Yes.

CONTENTS OF ARREST WARRANT

The information printed on a Form 7 arrest warrant is strictly governed by s. 511 C.C. The contents include three mandatory elements and one discretionary element. The goal of the contents is to inform the *police* who to arrest and why.

The three mandatory elements are as follows:

1. the accused's identity,
2. the offence, and
3. custody instructions.

1. *Accused's identity.* An arrest warrant must be concerned with *one* specific person who can be positively identified by the police. More than one offender cannot be named on one arrest warrant. The rule is one accused per arrest warrant. The reason for this is that the circumstances justifying an arrest warrant are unique to each offender. In cases involving more than one offender, a separate *ex parte* hearing is required for each offender.

   The accused's name or description is included on the arrest warrant. In theory, it is possible for a warrant to be issued without the accused's name if the physical description is so precise and unique that only one person may be identified. In practice, a description alone is unlikely to suffice.

2. *Offence.* This represents the *reason* for the arrest. There are two possible ways to describe an offence on a warrant:

   a. formal wording, and
   b. short-form name of offence.

   Section 511(1)(b) C.C. stipulates that the offence must be "set out *briefly*." This phrase encourages the use of the informal, short-form name (for example, break, enter, and theft). The formal wording is not essential.

3. *Custody instructions.* This final element communicates *who* is authorized to arrest, *when* the arrest has to be made, and *where* to bring the accused.

> *Who*: The arrest warrant authorizes only the *peace officers* in the territorial jurisdiction to make the arrest. Citizens have no authority to execute an arrest warrant.
>
> *When*: The arrest must occur "forthwith," defined in case law as "without unjustified delay." No "return day" is printed on the warrant, meaning that no time limit restricts the execution of the warrant. Arrest warrants remain in force until they are executed or until the Crown attorney withdraws the Information. The withdrawing of an Information negates the accompanying compelling document.[39]
>
> *Where*: After the accused is arrested, he or she must be brought before a Justice in the jurisdiction where the warrant was issued, for a bail hearing.

Section 511(1)(c) C.C. prohibits the police from releasing a person arrested with a warrant—only a Justice may release in this case. There is one exception to this release prohibition. The Justice who issues an arrest warrant for any offence other than a s. 469 C.C. offence may authorize the officer-in-charge (OIC) to release the accused. The Justice does this by "endorsing" the warrant on Form 29.

By *endorsing* the warrant, the Justice has authorized the addition of the s. 499 C.C. release provisions, known as Level 2 release. Level 2 allows the OIC to release. Therefore, an *endorsed* arrest warrant gives the police two release options—Level 3 bail hearing (see Chapter 11) and Level 2.

Discretionary element. This element allows for a temporary suspension of the custody instructions. Section 511(3) C.C. gives a Justice the "discretion to postpone execution" by specifying a period of time in which the accused may voluntarily appear before a judge or Justice in response to the charge. If the allotted period is specified on the warrant, execution of the warrant by the police is prohibited during this time. If an accused voluntarily appears in response to any warrant, the voluntary appearance constitutes execution of the warrant.[40]

Jurisdiction

Arrest warrants are valid anywhere in the province where the warrant is signed. Most Justices have provincial jurisdiction, which means that whatever document they sign becomes valid province-wide.

Two rules emerge from the concept of jurisdiction:

1. An arrest warrant is not valid only in the city in which it is issued. It is valid province-wide.
2. An arrest warrant is not valid nation-wide. An arrest warrant is not valid outside the province in which it is issued.

Radius

Radius is defined as the maximum geographical distance that the Crown attorney will pay for the police to travel in returning an offender arrested with a warrant. Not all offenders are arrested in the city where the arrest warrant is issued. Post-offence travel by the offender creates the problems of cost and jurisdiction. The cost of travelling to return an offender is paid by the Crown's office in the city where the warrant was issued. Consequently, a radius is attached to every arrest warrant, informing the police how far the Crown will authorize travel costs incurred in returning an arrested person. Three examples of radius are the following: (1) Canada-wide, (2) province-wide, and (3) 200 km.

The radius prescribed does not correspond to jurisdiction. For example, a "Canada-wide" warrant does not mean the arrest warrant is valid nationwide. It means the Crown will pay the travel costs police incur in returning an accused from anywhere in Canada.

Belief Extension

The issuance of an arrest warrant constitutes a *reasonable grounds belief* that the person named on the warrant committed the specified offence. This belief is based on the sworn Information that preceded the arrest warrant.

Consequently, when a person is stopped and a CPIC check reveals that there is a warrant for the person's arrest, the officer has to reach two conclusions:

1. If the offender is found in the province where the warrant was issued, the warrant is valid. If the offender is found outside the province, the warrant is invalid.
2. Regardless of where the offender is found, reasonable grounds exist for believing that the offender committed the offence.

Again, the existence of the arrest warrant justifies the existence of the reasonable grounds belief.

SECTION 29(1) C.C.

Section 29(1) C.C. imposes two mandatory obligations on the police when they are executing an arrest warrant: *possession* and *production* (upon request). The police must *possess* the original arrest warrant in order to execute it. If the offender requests to read or view the warrant, the police are obliged to *produce* it.

Possession of the warrant by police is mandatory. Production is conditional upon request. There is no requirement to show the offender a copy of the arrest warrant if he or she does not request it. However, one significant problem exists in connection with these requirements. In most cases, the police do not have original warrants in the cruiser while on patrol. The original warrants are usually stored in the police central records department. Consequently, when a wanted person is stopped, the police usually do not possess the warrant. The solution to this logistical problem is found in s. 495(1)(c) C.C.

SECTION 495(1)(c) C.C.

This provision creates an exception to the s. 29(1) C.C. rule. When a wanted person is apprehended in the province where the arrest warrant was issued, the police may arrest without actual possession of the warrant if the officer has reasonable grounds to believe that a valid warrant exists within that province. The reasonable grounds usually take the form of a CPIC message stating the offender is wanted because of a warrant.

If the offence specified on the warrant is classified as indictable or dual procedure, a second authority—arrest without warrant—exists. The officer can arrest because he or she has reasonable grounds to believe that the offender has committed an indictable offence. Section 495(1)(a) C.C. provides this second authority.

For example, you are on patrol in Oakville. You stop a driver. A CPIC check reveals the driver is "10-63, Hamilton, Robbery." You do not have the original arrest warrant. But under s. 495 C.C. you have two authorities to arrest without having possession of the original warrant:

1. reasonable grounds for believing that a valid warrant exists in the place where you found the offender, and
2. reasonable grounds for believing the offender has committed an indictable offence.

After transporting the accused to the police station, you fulfill the requirements of s. 29(1) C.C. by taking possession of the original arrest warrant, bringing it to the accused in the cells, and producing it for the accused upon request.

SECTION 528 C.C.—"ENDORSEMENT"

Section 29(1) C.C. explains *how* to execute an arrest warrant. Section 514 C.C. explains *where* it can be executed—that is, in the same province only (within the territorial jurisdiction of the issuing Justice). A problem arises when post-offence travel carries an offender outside the province in which the arrest warrant was issued.

This problem is solved by s. 528 C.C., in conjunction with ss. 495(1)(a) C.C. and 503(3) C.C. This provision authorizes the temporary validity of an arrest warrant in another province (another jurisdiction). An "endorsement" is defined as the authority to execute an arrest warrant beyond the boundaries stipulated by s. 514 C.C. In other words, an arrest warrant becomes temporarily valid outside its provincial jurisdiction. Form 28 (s. 849 C.C.) is used to endorse a warrant.

This endorsement is not automatically issued. It must be applied for, and the authenticity of the issuing Justice's signature must be proved by one of two means:

1. verbal testimony under oath, or
2. an affidavit.

This evidence must be presented to a Justice in the jurisdiction in which the offender is found. The arrest is authorized if the offence is dual procedure or indictable. But the actual source of the authorization is not the warrant directly. Authorization comes from having reasonable grounds to believe that the accused committed an indictable offence.

The offender is brought to a Justice in the jurisdiction where the arrest was made, and detained until the original warrant is transported from the issuing province. Section 503(3) C.C. authorizes a six-day detention to allow the police from the issuing province to travel there and execute the original warrant. The six-day detention is not automatic. You must prove the reasonable grounds belief that justified the arrest.

Upon arrival in the jurisdiction where the arrest was made, the officers from the issuing province appear before a Justice with the original warrant and apply for the Form 28 endorsement by proving, through verbal testimony under oath or through an affidavit, the authenticity of the issuing Justice's signature. Once the authenticity of this signature is proved, the endorsement is issued, establishing the temporary validity of the out-of-province warrant. The warrant is executed and the accused is returned to the original jurisdiction.

For example, you are on patrol in Hamilton. You stop a driver. A CPIC check reveals he is wanted ("10-63, Attempted Murder, Vancouver, Canada-wide"). The warrant is not valid in Hamilton. It is valid in British Columbia only. The BC Crown has authorized Canada-wide travel cost. You may arrest the person on the authority of s. 495(1)(a) C.C. (reasonable grounds to believe he has committed an indictable offence). The arrest is not authorized by s. 514 C.C. (execution of the arrest warrant) or s. 495(1)(c) C.C. (reasonable grounds to believe that a valid warrant exists).

You are authorized to bring the accused before a Justice in Hamilton. You have the onus of proving the reasonable grounds belief that justified the arrest. You are successful, and a six-day detention order is issued. The BC police travel to Hamilton with the original arrest warrant and evidence. To authenticate the BC Justice's signature upon arrival in Hamilton, the BC police appear before a Hamilton Justice and apply for a Form 28 endorsement. The authenticity of the signature is proved and the endorsement is granted, making the BC arrest warrant temporarily valid in Hamilton.

The BC police execute the endorsed arrest warrant in accordance with s. 29(1) C.C. and return the offender to Vancouver.

Figure 7.4 describes in-province and out-of-province pathways to the execution of a warrant.

Time Limit

The *Criminal Code* prescribes no time limit on the validity of an arrest warrant. It is valid, or remains in force, until the arrest warrant is executed—that is, until the warrant is carried out and the accused is arrested.[41]

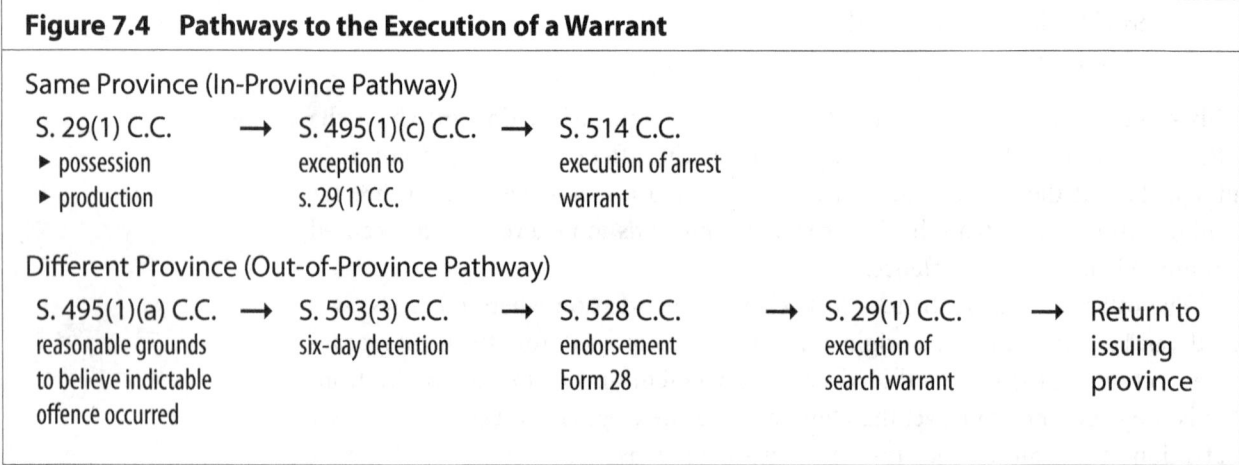

Figure 7.4   Pathways to the Execution of a Warrant

Same Province (In-Province Pathway)

S. 29(1) C.C.	→	S. 495(1)(c) C.C.	→	S. 514 C.C.
▸ possession ▸ production		exception to s. 29(1) C.C.		execution of arrest warrant

Different Province (Out-of-Province Pathway)

S. 495(1)(a) C.C.	→	S. 503(3) C.C.	→	S. 528 C.C.	→	S. 29(1) C.C.	→	Return to
reasonable grounds to believe indictable offence occurred		six-day detention		endorsement Form 28		execution of search warrant		issuing province

The time limit on the validity of an arrest warrant is controlled by the Crown attorney. An Information, once signed by a Justice, is "owned" by the Crown attorney, who may withdraw it at any time before the trial. If the Crown attorney decides not to prosecute the offender and withdraws the Information, the arrest warrant becomes invalid. In other words, an arrest warrant is valid until it is executed or until the Crown attorney withdraws the Information.

EXECUTION OF AN ARREST WARRANT

"Executing" a warrant means to carry it out or complete the task it requires. The following rules apply.

1. A warrant may be executed anywhere.
2. A warrant may be executed at any time, on any day, including a holiday.[42]
3. The officer who executes the warrant has a duty under s. 29(1) C.C. to have possession of the warrant, when feasible, and to produce it when requested to do so.[43]

An officer will usually have possession of the warrant when he or she intends to execute it at a specific time and place. However, it is common for an officer to stop persons and conduct routine CPIC checks. Sometimes such a routine check reveals that a warrant exists for the person's arrest, a warrant that the officer obviously does not possess. Section 495(1)(c) C.C. creates a temporary exception to s. 29(1) C.C. by allowing an officer to arrest without actually possessing the warrant. If the officer arrests the accused without possessing the warrant, the warrant must be retrieved from central records and produced for the accused while he or she is at the police station. Although, strictly speaking, producing the warrant is necessary only when the accused requests it, in practice, all accused persons should be shown the warrant to prevent accidental violations of s. 29(1) C.C. Production of the warrant entails reading its contents to the accused, which informs him or her of the reason for the arrest, a statutory requirement. The warrant is considered to have been fully executed when it has been produced for the accused.

A copy of the warrant does not have to be given to the accused. In fact, this is something that should never be done, since the copy could be unlawfully used on some future occasion.

After Execution

After an accused person is arrested with a warrant, he or she must be brought to a Justice for a bail hearing. The reason for this is that the arresting officer or the OIC of the police station has no authority to release the accused. An exception exists to the rule, however. A Justice may make an endorsement on a warrant that permits release if the offence is not a s. 469 C.C. indictable offence, such as murder. This endorsement allows the OIC to release the accused if certain release provisions are fulfilled (see Chapter 11). This may eliminate the need to bring the accused before a Justice for a bail hearing.[44]

EXECUTING IN-PROVINCE AND OUT-OF-PROVINCE WARRANTS

Police officers commonly find persons in one city who are wanted in another. The cities may be in the same province or in different provinces. The officer must determine where the arrest warrant was issued to determine what procedure to use. Different procedures are used for in-province and out-of-province arrest warrants because a warrant is valid throughout the province where the Justice who issued it has jurisdiction. This jurisdiction usually includes the entire province. But the warrant is not valid outside that province.

Before learning the procedures for executing warrants, the following general rules must be understood:

1. An arrest warrant signed by a Justice is valid only in the province where the Justice has jurisdiction. For example, an arrest warrant signed by a Justice in Toronto is usually valid anywhere in Ontario but not elsewhere.

2. An arrest warrant signed in a particular province is invalid in all other provinces. For example, an arrest warrant signed by a Justice in Toronto is invalid in all provinces other than Ontario.

3. An out-of-province arrest warrant requires the endorsement (signature) of a Justice who has jurisdiction where the arrest is made. For example, if a police officer in Vancouver arrests an accused person for whom there is an arrest warrant signed by a Justice in Ontario, the arrest warrant must be endorsed by a Justice who has jurisdiction in British Columbia.[45]

4. A CPIC message stating that there is a warrant for a certain person's arrest represents reasonable grounds for believing that a warrant exists and that the person committed the offence for which the arrest warrant was issued. For example, a police officer in Vancouver stops a person in that city. A CPIC message reveals that the person is wanted for "Robbery" in Toronto. Reasonable grounds exist for believing that the person committed the indictable offence of "Robbery," and the officer may arrest without the warrant. The warrant is invalid in Vancouver in any case, though an endorsement by a Vancouver Justice will make it valid.

5. Arrest warrants have a specified *radius*—that is, the maximum distance, authorized by a Crown attorney, that custodial authorities may travel in transporting the prisoner back to the location where the offence was committed. The radius does not correspond to the area where the warrant is valid. Typical examples of radius include the following:

   ▸ *Specific number of kilometres.* A CPIC message may state, for example: "Wanted—'Theft under $5,000.00'—Toronto, radius 200 km." In this case, the Crown attorney has authorized transportation and return of the accused only if he or she is arrested within a 200 km radius of Toronto. However, the warrant is valid anywhere in Ontario. The radius does not define the scope of the warrant's validity. The 200 km radius informs the arresting officer that transportation and return of the accused will not be authorized if the arrest is made beyond the 200 km radius. The Crown attorney usually decides on the specific number of kilometres.

▸ *Province-wide.* This radius informs an officer that the Crown attorney has authorized the transportation of the accused person from any area of arrest within the province.

▸ *Canada-wide.* This radius informs an officer that the Crown attorney has authorized transportation and return of the accused from anywhere in Canada. However, a Canada-wide radius does not extend the area of the warrant's validity; the warrant remains valid only in the province where the Justice signed it. If the arrest is made in Canada but outside the province where it was signed, the warrant requires an endorsement by a Justice where the arrest is made.

6. A trial must be held in the city/jurisdiction where the offence occurred.

In-Province Warrant

Officers who find a person in one city and learn that the person is wanted in another city in the same province may arrest the person regardless of whether the offence is summary conviction, dual procedure, or indictable. The reason for this is that the arrest warrant is valid throughout the province where the Justice signed it, if the Justice has provincial jurisdiction.

For example, a police officer in Toronto stops a person, and a CPIC check reveals that the person is wanted for "Robbery" in Hamilton. To determine whether an arrest is justified, the officer needs to analyze the CPIC information. "Wanted" means that reasonable grounds exist for believing that a warrant exists and that the accused committed the offence stated in the message. "Robbery" is classified as an indictable offence. The Hamilton police service notifies the officer that the warrant is valid where he or she has stopped the accused, in this case Toronto. The officer may arrest the person in this case and justify the arrest with either of the two following authorities:

1. the warrant is valid in Toronto, or
2. reasonable grounds exist for believing that the person has committed an indictable offence.

Consider another example. A police officer in Windsor, Ontario, stops a person, and a CPIC message states that he or she is wanted for an "Indecent act" in Toronto. Performing an "Indecent act" is classified as a summary conviction offence. "Wanted" means that reasonable grounds exist for believing that a warrant exists and that the person committed the offence. "Toronto" informs the officer that the warrant is valid in Windsor. The officer may arrest the person without having possession of the warrant because reasonable grounds exist for believing that a valid warrant exists in the territorial jurisdiction where the accused person is found. This particular example often causes confusion because most people focus only on the fact that the offence is classified as summary conviction and that no authority exists to arrest on reasonable grounds in the case of a summary conviction offence. When analyzing a case study, the reader must recognize whether *any* authority exists to arrest, not just one specific authority.

PROCEDURE AFTER ARREST

Both of the above examples illustrate that the procedure for executing warrants must follow some general rules. It needs to be emphasized that an arrest warrant does not have to be endorsed by another Justice anywhere in the province in which it was signed. The procedure for executing an in-province warrant is as follows:

1. The arresting officer transports the accused person to the police station in the city where the arrest is made.
2. The arresting officer notifies the police service holding the warrant that the accused is in custody.
3. The officers from the city where the warrant is held and where it was issued travel to the city where the accused is detained, bringing the original arrest warrant.
4. Upon arrival, the officers holding the original warrant execute it at the police station where the accused is detained. Executing the warrant requires that they possess it and produce it for the accused. The warrant does not have to be endorsed by a Justice in the city where the accused person is detained because it is valid throughout the province.
5. The accused is then transported to the city where the warrant was issued. Then he or she is, usually, brought to a Justice for a bail hearing. Other possible release procedures may apply, which will be explained in Chapter 11. The trial will be conducted in the city/jurisdiction where the offence occurred.

Out-of-Province Warrant

The procedures for executing out-of-province arrest warrants depend on the classification of the offence for which the accused person is wanted. Determining whether an out-of-province arrest warrant authorizes a particular arrest depends on whether the CPIC message states that the accused is

- wanted for a summary conviction offence; or
- wanted for an indictable or dual procedure offence.

WANTED FOR A SUMMARY CONVICTION OFFENCE

If a police officer stops a person, and a CPIC message states that there is an out-of-province warrant for that person's arrest for a summary conviction offence, no arrest may be made for the following reasons:

- The warrant is not valid in the province where the officer stopped the person.
- A police officer cannot arrest for a summary conviction offence on the basis of reasonable grounds alone.
- The officer did not find the offence being committed.

Although no arrest may be made in this situation, the warrant remains in effect. The accused may be arrested in the future in the province where the warrant is valid.

WANTED FOR AN INDICTABLE OR DUAL PROCEDURE OFFENCE

A warrant for an indictable or dual procedure offence is not valid outside the province where it was issued. However, this type of warrant permits the police to arrest by means of another authority. An out-of-province warrant for indictable or dual procedure offences represents reasonable grounds for believing that the accused committed the offence, and the arrest is authorized on that basis. Once arrested, the accused is brought to the police station in the city where the arrest occurred. He or she must ultimately be returned to the city or jurisdiction where the offence occurred, to appear in court.

Before this can be accomplished, though, the warrant must be made valid in the province where the accused is detained. This requires officers from the province where the warrant was issued to travel with the original warrant to the province where the accused is detained. The warrant is then brought to a Justice where the accused is detained. The Justice endorses the warrant by signing it, which signifies two things: (1) it makes the warrant valid in the province where the accused is detained, so that it can be executed; and (2) it temporarily makes the out-of-province officers peace officers in the province where the accused is detained. Otherwise, the out-of-province officers are citizens in the province where the accused is detained. The procedure used to execute an out-of-province warrant is illustrated in the following example.

CASE STUDY

You stop John in Toronto. A CPIC message reveals the following about John: "Wanted—'Attempted murder'—Calgary, radius Canada-wide." What procedure will you follow to execute this out-of-province warrant?

STEP 1

The Calgary warrant is invalid in Toronto. However, you have reasonable grounds to believe that John committed the indictable offence of "Attempted murder." Therefore, you may arrest John without a warrant.

STEP 2

John is transported to a Toronto police station and detained there. You notify the Calgary police service of the arrest. Calgary officers will come to Toronto to pick up John. The Toronto police cannot transport John to Calgary.

STEP 3

John must be brought before a Justice in Toronto without unreasonable delay, within 24 hours after the arrest.[46] If a Justice is not available within 24 hours, John must be brought before a Justice as soon as possible. The only purpose in bringing John before a Justice is to prove the reasonable grounds for making the arrest.[47]

STEP 4

When John is before a Toronto Justice, you must prove that reasonable grounds exist for believing that John committed the alleged offence.[48] Reasonable grounds may be proven by submitting to the justice a copy of the CPIC message or a copy of the Information and the warrant from Calgary. Testimony from any conversation you have had with Calgary officers may be used as supporting evidence. If you fail to prove there are reasonable grounds for believing that John committed the offence, he must be released.[49]

STEP 5

If you successfully prove reasonable grounds, John may be detained in Toronto for a period of up to six days. The Calgary police must attend Toronto within six days, to execute their warrant and return John to Calgary.[50] Additionally, the

(continued)

Calgary police may bring an affidavit that proves the signature of the Calgary Justice who signed the warrant.[51]

Note: If the Calgary police fail to execute the warrant within six days, John must be released.[52] However, John remains charged, and the warrant will remain valid in Calgary. If John is released after six days, reasonable grounds will still exist for believing that he committed an indictable offence. Nothing prevents another arrest. Upon arrest, you must repeat the procedure by bringing John before a Justice and obtaining another detention order of up to six days.

STEP 6

Upon arrival in Toronto, the Calgary officers must appear before a Toronto Justice and present the arrest warrant. The Calgary officers must prove the signature of the Calgary Justice by

- an affidavit of the signature of the Calgary Justice; or
- sworn evidence under oath by the Calgary officer, if the officer can testify that he or she knows the signature is valid.[53]

STEP 7

The Toronto Justice endorses the Calgary warrant. The endorsement signifies two things:

1. The Calgary officers are authorized to act as peace officers in Toronto for the purpose of executing the warrant.
2. The warrant becomes valid in Toronto. It may be executed in Toronto, and John may be returned to Calgary.[54]

STEP 8

The Calgary officers return John to Calgary and bring him before a Calgary Justice.[55] The trial will be conducted in Calgary; it may not be conducted in Toronto.

Summary

The following is a summary of the responsibilities of the officers involved in the execution of an out-of-province arrest warrant. Two officers are involved:

1. the arresting officer, who is outside the province where the warrant was issued; and
2. the executing officer, who is from the province and jurisdiction where the warrant was issued.

ARRESTING OFFICER'S RESPONSIBILITIES

The arresting officer

1. ensures that the CPIC message states that the accused is wanted for an indictable or dual procedure offence (do not arrest if it is for a summary conviction);
2. transports the accused to the police station in the city where the arrest was made;
3. brings the accused before a Justice within 24 hours of making the arrest, or as soon as practicable; and
4. proves to the Justice that reasonable grounds exist for believing the accused committed the offence.

EXECUTING OFFICER'S RESPONSIBILITIES

The executing officer

1. obtains an affidavit to verify the signature of the Justice who issued the warrant;
2. within six days of the arrest, brings the arrest warrant and affidavit to a Justice in the place where the accused is detained;
3. attends before a Justice where the accused is detained;
4. verifies the signature on the arrest warrant by means of the affidavit or, alternatively, swears under oath to prove that the Justice signed the warrant;
5. takes custody of the accused once the Justice endorses the warrant;
6. returns the accused to the city where the offence occurred and the warrant was issued; and
7. brings the accused to a Justice within 24 hours or as soon as practicable.

OVERVIEW OF TRIAL PATHWAYS

Figure 7.5 represents the four "proceedings pathways"—that is, the four routes to a trial. They are as follows:

- Path 1: Summons
- Path 2: Arrest warrant in the first instance (this could lead to trial or to non-custodial compelling document [NCD])
- Path 3: Warrantless arrest + non-custodial document
- Path 4: Bench warrant

Figure 7.5   Trial Pathways

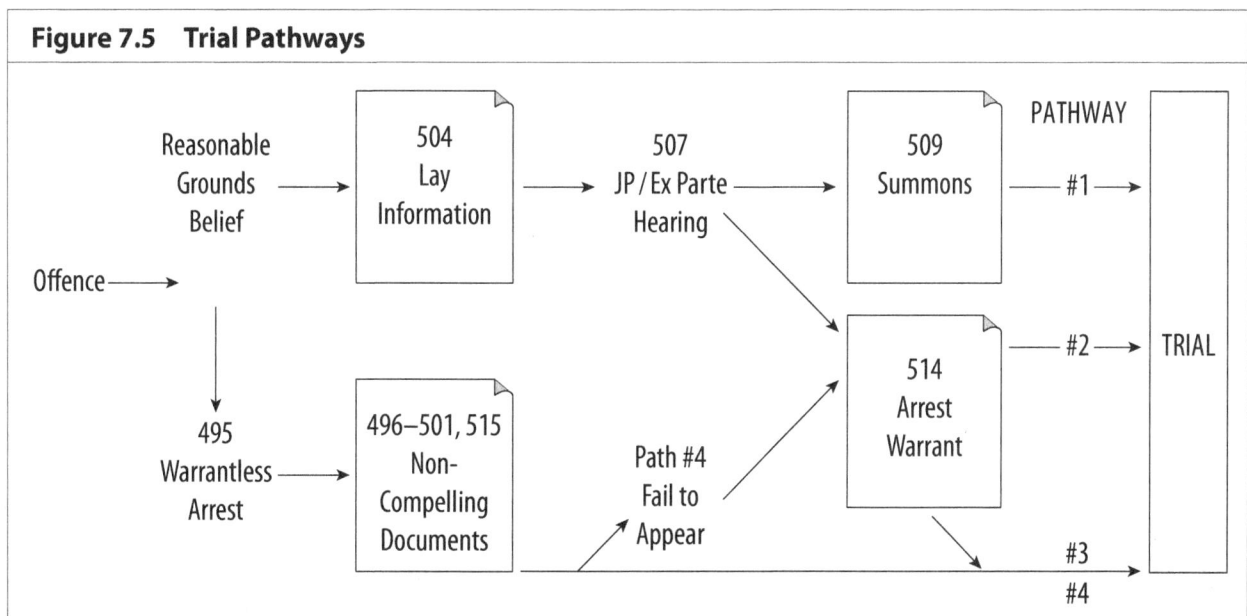

SUMMARY

The next chapter deals with "Feeney warrants." This topic is specific to situations dealing with exigent circumstances in relation to both a dwelling-house and a public place.

SELF-EVALUATION SCENARIO

The following is a single scenario with 25 questions that reflect reality decision making. The accompanying website **www.emp.ca/arcaro/policepowers4E** will include additional self-evaluation scenarios.

■ SCENARIO

You are a police officer in Toronto in this case. You are in the middle of an investigation pertaining to two offences:

1. a violent robbery that occurred four days ago;
2. a B & E and violent assault that occurred six days ago.

You have mere suspicion that Bill (30) committed both offences. Today (45 minutes ago), you interviewed Justin (26). Justin gave you a written witness statement reporting that Bill confessed to him that he (Bill) committed both offences. Answer the following questions.

1. Do you have the authority to arrest Bill right now without a warrant, under s. 495 C.C.?

   a. Yes
   b. No

2. Which of the following is true about an arrest warrant in the first instance?

   a. It is possible to obtain one in this case.
   b. You must obtain one in this case; it's the only way to arrest him.
   c. It is impossible to obtain one in this case.

3. What is the reason for your answer to question 2?

   a. An arrest warrant in the first instance is possible when a reasonable grounds belief exists for any classification of offence.
   b. You cannot get an arrest warrant unless corroboration exists.
   c. Both a and b.
   d. None of the above.

4. You decide to obtain an arrest warrant in the first instance. What is the reason for your decision?

   a. You wish to broadcast nationally that reasonable grounds exist for believing that Bill has committed an indictable offence.
   b. *R. v. Mann* makes it mandatory that you get the warrant.
   c. *R. v. Andrusyk* makes it mandatory that you get the warrant.
   d. Together, *R. v. Pooler* and *R. v. Tripp* create the decision-making guidelines, which indicate that you should get the warrant.

5. This case is very urgent. Can you *automatically* get an arrest warrant without an application?

   a. Yes
   b. No

6. What is the emergency alternative to an arrest warrant?

    a. The *R. v. Andrusyk* "warrant."

    b. The *R. v. Pooler* "warrant."

    c. Feeney warrants.

    d. Section 495 C.C.—go arrest him without a warrant.

    e. None of the above.

7. You decide to get an arrest warrant in the first instance. Is it mandatory to apply?

    a. No

    b. Yes

    c. It's discretionary; it's your choice.

8. What is the application for an arrest in the first instance called?

    a. "Application for Arrest Warrant"

    b. "*Ex parte*" application

    c. An "Information"

    d. All of the above are applications

    e. None of the above

9. Who has the onus of writing or filling out the Information?

    a. JP

    b. Judge

    c. Crown

    d. You

    e. None of the above

10. Where do you bring this document, and to whom?

    a. To the Crown in "open court"

    b. To a JP anywhere except "open court"

    c. To an "*ex parte* Marshall" in "*Ipso Facto*" court

    d. All of the above

    e. None of the above

11. During the application process, question 10 asks about, who is present?

    a. Crown, accused, you, JP

    b. "De facto" judge, accused, prosecutor, witness (Justin)

    c. You and the JP

    d. All of the above

    e. None of the above

12. The JP hands you a Bible and asks you to swear under oath, *before* the testimony actually starts. What is the purpose of this?

    a. The JP is in effect asking, "Have you fabricated anything on the Information?" or "Is all the content true on the Information?"

    b. The JP is asking you if you want to bypass the *ex parte* hearing.

    c. The JP is asking you if you want the warrant to have a "Canada-wide" radius.

    d. All of the above are being asked.

    e. None of the above.

13. The hearing starts. What is the name of the hearing?

    a. Bail hearing
    b. Preliminary hearing
    c. *Ex parte* hearing
    d. All of the above
    e. None of the above

14. Are you under oath when you testify?

    a. Yes
    b. No

15. If you intentionally lie during your testimony, can you be charged with perjury?

    a. Yes
    b. No; perjury applies to trials only, not hearings.

16. May you read all the witness statements yourself or do you have to subpoena the witnesses to testify at this hearing?

    a. You can read the witness statements.
    b. You must subpoena all witnesses.

17. What is the reason for the answer in question 16?

    a. Hearsay is admissible at this hearing.
    b. Hearsay is inadmissible at this hearing.

18. To get the arrest warrant, what do you have to prove? What are your goals?

    a. You have one goal—to prove that Bill is "clinically insane" and cannot stand trial.
    b. You have two goals—to prove there are reasonable grounds for believing that he committed the offences and reasonable grounds for believing the warrant is "necessary in the public interest."
    c. You have three goals—demonstrating articulable cause that an investigative detention is needed, mere suspicion that Bill has stolen items, and 100 percent proof that physical evidence is in his house.
    d. None of the above.

19. Which part of the hearing occurs first?

    a. Proving Bill is insane.
    b. Proving there are reasonable grounds to believe he committed the offence.
    c. Proving articulable cause.
    d. None of the above.

20. What is the second part of the hearing?

    a. Proving that physical evidence is in Bill's house.
    b. Proving there are reasonable grounds to believe that Bill is a public safety and/or FTA (failure-to-appear) risk.
    c. Both a and b.
    d. There is no second part.

21. If you succeed only at the first part of the hearing, what happens?

    a. Bill is acquitted.
    b. All of the evidence is excluded.
    c. A summons is issued.
    d. All of the above.
    e. None of the above.

22. To get an arrest warrant, is it mandatory to prove that you tried to find Bill first to arrest him under s. 495 C.C.?

    a. Yes
    b. No

23. If an arrest warrant is issued, what is the time limit on the warrant—that is, for how long will it be valid?

    a. Six days only
    b. Six months only
    c. Two years
    d. None of the above

24. If the arrest warrant is issued with a "Canada-wide" radius, where is it valid?

    a. Niagara region only
    b. Ontario only
    c. Anywhere in Canada
    d. Anywhere in North America—the warrant is valid in the United States and Mexico in accordance with NAFTA.

25. If the arrest warrant is issued "Canada-wide" and a Calgary police officer stops Bill in Calgary and a CPIC check reveals 10-63 (for this warrant), which of the following is true?

    a. The Calgary officer may arrest without possession of the original warrant because reasonable grounds exist for believing that Bill committed an indictable offence.
    b. The Calgary officer may arrest without the warrant because the arrest warrant classifies Bill as a "dangerous offender."
    c. The Calgary officer cannot arrest Bill unless he or she has possession of the original warrant.

PROBLEM-SOLVING CASE STUDIES

You are a police officer in each case. Each offender is an adult, unless otherwise indicated.

Problem 1

Yesterday, you attended at Wally's residence in response to a call. Wally was found unconscious and had suffered serious injuries. The offender had left prior to police arrival. Statements obtained from witnesses who were present and from Wally after he regained consciousness constitute reasonable grounds that Eddie committed "Aggravated assault."

    a. Can you arrest Eddie today, without a warrant?

_____

_____

_____

    b. Is it possible for you to obtain an arrest warrant?

_____

_____

_____

    c. Can an arrest warrant be obtained in this case without first swearing an Information?

_____

_____

    d. You appear before a Justice to swear an Information. What do you have to prove to convince the Justice to sign the Information?

_____

_____

    e. If you successfully prove the reasonable grounds but prove nothing else, will the arrest warrant be automatically issued?

_____

    f. What do you have to prove in order for the Justice to issue an arrest warrant?

_____

    g. Do you have to complete any other document to apply for an arrest warrant?

_____

_____

_____

Problem 2

You form reasonable grounds today that Eddie has committed an "Indecent act" three times during the past week.

    a. Can you arrest without a warrant?

_____

_____

    b. Is it possible to obtain an arrest warrant?

_____

_____

Problem 3

You stop George in Winnipeg. A CPIC message reveals: Wanted—"Indecent act"—Halifax. Can you arrest?

_____

_____

Problem 4

You stop Wally in Calgary. A CPIC check reveals the following: Wanted—"Trespass by night"—Edmonton.

a. Can you arrest?

_____

_____

b. An Edmonton officer travels to Calgary with the warrant to execute it. Does the warrant require an endorsement?

_____

_____

APPENDIX: ANSWERS TO SELF-EVALUATION SCENARIOS

1. A	10. B	19. B
2. A	11. C	20. B
3. A	12. A	21. C
4. A	13. C	22. B
5. B	14. A	23. D
6. D	15. A	24. B
7. B	16. A	25. A
8. C	17. A	
9. D	18. B	

ENDNOTES

1. Section 849 C.C.
2. _R. v. MacPherson_, 1998 CanLII 6710 (B.C.S.C.).
3. Ibid.
4. _R. v. Kalanj_, [1989] 1 S.C.R. 1594.
5. Ibid.
6. Ibid.
7. Ibid.
8. _R. v. Sharpe_, 2002 BCSC 213.
9. Sections 507(4) and 512(1) C.C.

10. Section 512(2) C.C.
11. Section 512(2) C.C.
12. Section 512(2) C.C.
13. Sections 520(5) and 521(5) C.C.
14. Sections 524(1), 525(5), and 679(6) C.C.
15. Sections 524(1), 525(5), and 679(6) C.C.
16. Sections 502 and 510 C.C.
17. Section 579 C.C.
18. *R. v. Grant* (1991), 67 C.C.C. (3d) 268 (S.C.C.).
19. Section 495(2)(d) C.C.
20. *Webster's English Dictionary,* s.v. "firstly."
21. Section 512(2) C.C.
22. Section 512(1) C.C.
23. Section 512(2) C.C.
24. Sections 502 and 510 C.C.
25. Section 512(2) C.C.
26. Section 504 C.C.
27. Section 508.1(1) C.C.
28. Section 504 C.C.
29. Section 507(1)(a) C.C.
30. Section 507(4) C.C.
31. Section 507(1)(a)(i) C.C.
32. Section 507(1)(a)(i) C.C.
33. Section 507(1)(a)(i) C.C.
34. Section 507(3)(a) C.C.
35. Section 507(1)(b) C.C.
36. Section 507(4) C.C.
37. Section 507(4) C.C.
38. Section 512(1)(a) C.C.
39. Section 511(2) C.C.
40. Section 511(4) C.C.
41. Section 511(2) C.C.
42. Section 20 C.C.
43. Section 29(1) C.C.
44. Section 507(6) C.C.
45. Section 528 C.C.
46. Sections 503(3) and 503(1)(a) C.C.
47. Section 503(3) C.C.
48. Section 503(3) C.C.
49. Section 503(3)(a) C.C.
50. Section 503(3)(b) C.C.
51. Section 528(1) C.C.
52. Section 528(1) C.C.
53. Section 528(1)(a) C.C.
54. Section 528(2) C.C.
55. Section 528(2) C.C.

CHAPTER 8
Location of Arrest: Feeney Warrants

LEARNING OUTCOMES

The student will learn

- Where an arrest can be made
- How to make an arrest in a public place
- How to enter a dwelling-house to make an arrest
- How to obtain a Feeney warrant
- How to recognize exigent circumstances
- How to obtain implied or expressed consent to enter a house
- When forcible entry is authorized

> "The *frustration* of the effective enforcement of the criminal law is the hallmark of the exceptional circumstances identified in *Feeney*."
>
> —Ontario Court of Appeal in *R. v. Golub* (1997)[1]

INTRODUCTION

A wanted person is always in a *place*. In other words, the suspect is in some sort of location—for example, in a dwelling-house, in a building other than a dwelling-house, in a motor vehicle, or in a public street. When you have the authority to arrest someone, he cannot be immune from arrest because of the place he is in. In other words, there is a legal authority to enter every *place*. Your job is to match the authority to the circumstances. In some cases you will need a warrant, in some cases you will not. Once again, a rapid decision-making (RDM) model should inform your decision.

The first seven chapters of this text have explained when a warrantless arrest is authorized and when a warrant is required. The next topic of instruction is how to enter the location occupied by the offender.

TWELVE INTRODUCTORY CONCEPTS

Among the laws governing entry into a *place* are "Feeney Warrants." These represent complex legislation. To simplify the topic, we will begin by learning 12 introductory concepts:

1. "The community wants privacy but it also insists on protection. Safety, security, and the suppression of crime are legitimate countervailing concerns. . . . A *balance must* be struck."[2] This case law quotation explains the "investigative paradox." A balance must be struck between protecting the public and protecting privacy in dwelling-houses and other places.

2. *Private residence vs. public place.* There are only two general classifications of places where an arrest can be made:

    a. a dwelling-house, and
    b. a public place.

    A dwelling-house refers to a private residence.[3] A public place, for arrest purposes, refers to any place that is not a private residence.

3. *Sanctity of the home vs. common-law police duties.* The privacy in a dwelling-house is a hallmark of democracy. The law gives this kind of privacy greater protection than it does privacy in a public place, including privately owned businesses. Despite the privacy protection the law gives to the inside of a private residence, the police have a mandatory common-law duty to *protect life* and investigate crime in *any place.*[4] The operative word is "duty." When their common-law duty calls on them to protect life, the police have no discretion about responding or acting on this duty. Failure to act or respond constitutes "neglect of duty," defined as an offence by the provincial statutes that govern policing.[5]

4. *"A man's home is his castle" vs. "No criminal is immune from arrest in any place."*[6] These two longstanding and opposing principles of Canadian law create an investigative challenge for police. The police cannot barge into a house without legal justification; at the some time, a criminal cannot hide anywhere in Canada to escape arrest, including his or her own home. When the police have lawful authority to arrest a person, there is no place where they are *totally* prohibited from entering.

5. *Defence of property vs. prior announcement by police.* Sections 38–42 C.C. create a common-sense authority permitting people to defend their property, forcibly if necessary, against intruders and trespassers. It is a statutory requirement—with exceptions—that police make a proper prior announcement before entering a suspect's home.[7] This requirement poses both a benefit and a risk. The prior announcement informs the occupants that the police are not criminal intruders or trespassers, which cancels the occupant's authority to forcibly defend his or her residence. At the same time, this prior announcement makes the police potential targets of violence. That is to say, alerting occupants of an imminent police presence

eliminates the element of surprise and creates an opportunity for occupants to use violence toward police.

6. There are three ways of being authorized to enter a dwelling-house for the purpose of making an arrest:

    a. the occupant's consent,

    b. a Feeney warrant, and

    c. warrantless entry (justified by exigent circumstances).

7. **Feeney warrant** is an informal term for the two types of warrants that authorize the police to enter a *dwelling-house* for the specific purpose of arresting an offender. Searching for physical evidence is not the primary purpose of a Feeney warrant.

8. The two Feeney warrants are formally designated as follows: (1) included authorization to enter—arrest warrant, s. 529 C.C.; (2) warrant to enter dwelling-house, s. 529.1 C.C.

9. Both Feeney warrants have to be applied for.

10. There is an exception to the Feeney requirement that a warrant authorize police entry into a dwelling-house; it is called **exigent circumstances**—in other words, an emergency. When an emergency exists, a warrantless entry is authorized.

11. Feeney warrants do not apply to places that are not dwelling-houses. This means you cannot obtain a Feeney warrant to enter a non-dwelling-house place.

12. There are only two authorities for entering non-dwelling-house places:

    a. consent, and

    b. warrantless entry.

SIX BASIC CONCEPTS

The decision-making process relating to dwelling-house entry for the purposes of making an arrest involves six basic interrelated concepts:

1. place,
2. entry path,
3. invitation to knock,
4. consent,
5. Feeney laws, and
6. emergencies.

The following summary briefly introduces each concept. All of them are discussed throughout this chapter and illustrated with reference to case law decisions.

1. *Place.* The *location* of an offender or emergency has to be assigned one of *two classifications* in order to fall within the scope of available authorities and strategies:

    a. a dwelling-house, or

    b. a non-dwelling-house.

    The perimeter of a dwelling-house is a place and is classified as a non-dwelling-house.

2. *Entry path.* A house is usually situated on property, called the perimeter. This means that a house involves two places. The concept of "entry path" refers to a sequence of two entries into two places:

    a. perimeter entry, and

    b. house entry.

    Rule: When the police enter a house to make an arrest, they have the *onus* of proving that two entries were lawfully authorized and justified.

3. *Implied invitation to knock.* The concept of perimeter entry is governed by a common-law authority, explained in *R. v. Evans* (1996), known as the "implied invitation to knock."[8] The police authority to enter a house, with or without a warrant, is governed by wide-ranging statutory laws, common law, and case law.

4. *Consent.* The occupant's consent represents the easiest method of achieving entry and justifying it. The police benefit from having two types of consent available to them:

    a. expressed consent, and

    b. implied consent.

5. *Feeney laws.* The term *Feeney* laws refers to the *Criminal Code* provisions that create three authorities by which police may enter a dwelling-house. Two of these authorities involve a warrant and one does not. Feeney laws apply

    a. only to dwelling-houses, not to any other places; and

    b. only when belief amounting to *certainty* exists, not in circumstances of *uncertainty*.

6. *Emergency.* A condition of emergency or urgency creates an exception to the general prohibition against entering a house without a warrant; in other words, exigent circumstances create a warrantless *authority* to enter a house. There are two types of exigent circumstances:

    a. common-law exigent circumstances (CLEC), and

    b. s. 529.3 C.C. exigent circumstances.

REVIEW

Emerging from these six basic concepts are the following:

- two classifications of places,
- two types of entries,
- two types of consent,
- three Feeney authorities to enter a house,
- two types of emergencies,
- two different Feeney warrants, and
- five warrantless entry authorities.

FEENEY DECISION-MAKING MODEL

The necessity of obtaining a warrant to enter a dwelling-house for the purpose of making an arrest is based in case law that provides guidelines for police officers to follow in such cases. A complex decision-making process, based on these guidelines, involves four steps that are interchangeable depending on the circumstances when the police arrive at the "place." Those steps are:

- *Step 1*: Translate information (belief formula);
- *Step 2*: Emergency recognition (presence or absence of exigent circumstances);
- *Step 3*: Consent recognition (presence or absence of valid consent); and
- *Step 4*: Entry authority recognition (solution).

Figure 8.1 demonstrates the decision-making process a police officer must consider when he or she has reasonable grounds that an offender is in a "place." As can be seen, at each stage of the "dwelling-house" side of the chart, an officer must re-evaluate the necessity of obtaining a Feeney warrant to enter. All "concepts"—consent, exigent circumstances, etc.—will be explained throughout the chapter in relation to the landmark case *R. v. Feeney* (1997).

Step 1: Translate Information (Belief Formula)

The goal of this step is to analyze all available information and translate it into a belief that will resemble a formula.

Figure 8.1   Feeney Warrant Decision-Making Model

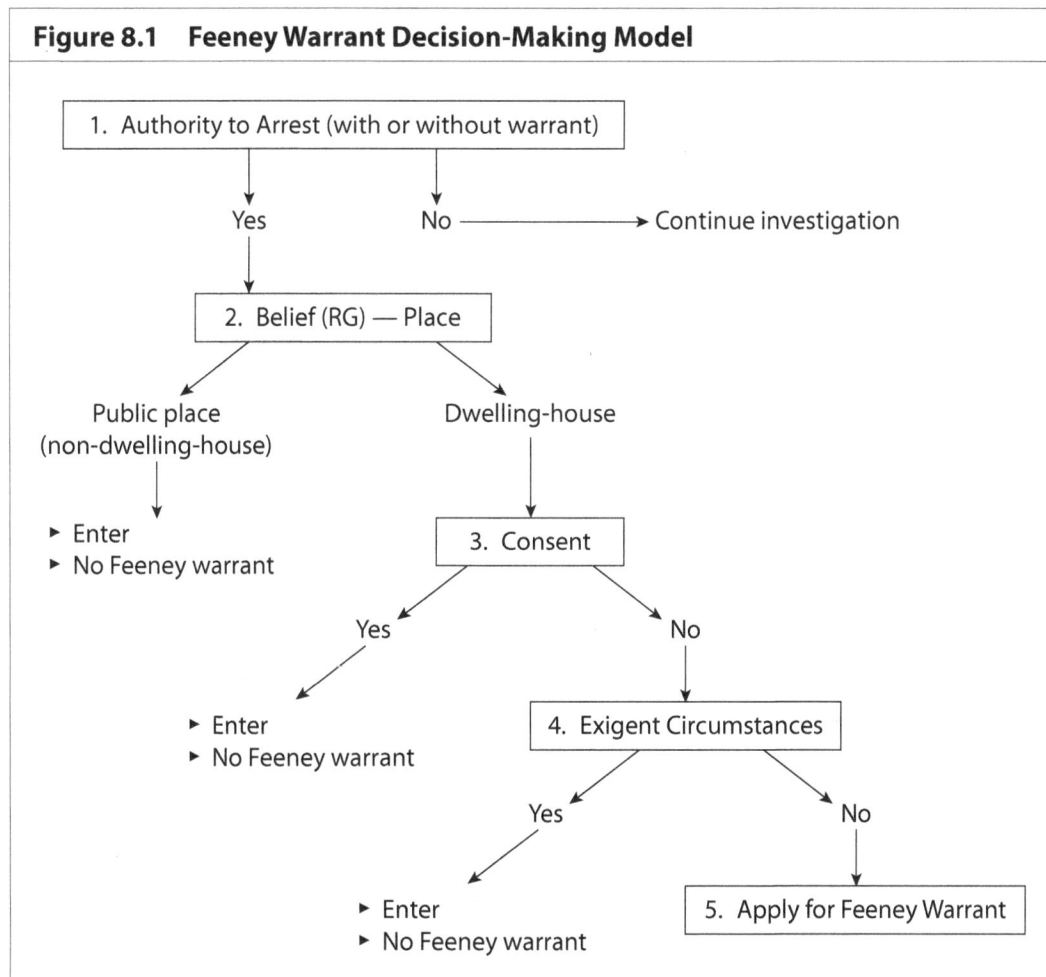

The belief formula is a two-part determination:

Part 1. Do you have lawful authority to arrest?
Part 2. Where is the offender?

The information on which you base this determination emerges from one or a combination of the following three sources:

1. radio broadcast or computer message,
2. personal observations, and
3. witness observations.

Part 1 of the belief formula answers the question, "Is there lawful authority to arrest?" Using the decision-making formula from Chapter 1, determine whether reasonable grounds exist for believing that a person has committed an indictable offence, is about to commit an indictable offence, or that a valid arrest warrant exists.

For simplicity's sake, two short-form Part 1 belief formulas will be used:

1. "RG-IND": this acronym means that lawful authority does exist to arrest (that is, there are **R**easonable **G**rounds for believing that an **IND**ictable offence occurred or is about to occur).
2. "MS-IND": this acronym means that *no* lawful authority exists to arrest (that is, there is **M**ere **S**uspicion of an **IND**ictable offence). This acronym will be used for *any* belief below the "reasonable grounds" standard.

Part 2 of the belief formula answers the question, "Where is the offender?" or "Where did the incident occur?"

One of two possible places is defined:

1. a dwelling-house, or
2. a public place.

A dwelling-house is a private residence as defined in s. 2 C.C. A public place is any place that does not qualify as a private residence, including privately owned businesses. In addition to the place, a *belief of presence* is needed—do reasonable grounds exist for believing that the offender is in the place, or is there mere suspicion in this regard?

This belief formula will be represented with the following codes:

▸ RG in DH (reasonable grounds for believing the offender is in the dwelling-house),
▸ MS in DH (mere suspicion the offender is in the dwelling-house; this code will be used for any belief below the reasonable grounds standard),
▸ RG in PP (reasonable grounds for believing the offender is in the public place), or
▸ MS in PP (mere suspicion the offender is in the public place).

A full belief formula is reached by combining Part 1 and Part 2. The eight possible belief formulas are:

1. RG-IND, RG in DH (Feeney Formula),
2. MS-IND, RG in DH,
3. RG-IND, MS in DH,

4. MS-IND, MS in DH,
5. RG-IND, RG in PP,
6. RG-IND, MS in PP,
7. MS-IND, RG in PP, and
8. MS-IND, MS in PP.

The first belief formula—RG-IND, RG in DH—will be called the "Feeney formula." This means that Feeney warrants apply only when the circumstances have been analyzed and translated into the following belief formula: (1) RG-IND—reasonable grounds exist for believing that a person has committed or is about to commit an indictable offence, or that a valid arrest warrant exists; and (2) RG in DH—reasonable grounds exist for believing that the specific offender is in a specific dwelling-house. The Feeney formula represents "certainty." All other belief formulas represent "uncertainty."

Step 2: Emergency Recognition

The goal here is to identify whether "exigent circumstances" exist. There are two types of exigent circumstances:

1. s. 529.3 C.C. exigent circumstances, and
2. common-law exigent circumstances (CLEC).

Section 529.3 C.C. exigent circumstances create an exception to the Feeney warrant requirement. This exception applies only when the Feeney formula exists: RG-IND, RG in DH. If the Feeney formula applies, s. 529.3 C.C. exigent circumstances authorize warrantless entry when public safety or an investigative need demands it (in other words, when warrantless entry will protect life or prevent the loss of evidence). The nature of the emergency must make it impracticable to obtain a Feeney warrant.

The term **common-law exigent circumstances (CLEC)** refers to a public safety emergency in which there is a risk to any person's life and to which the Feeney formula does not apply.

The conclusion of this step is a conclusion either that exigent circumstances exist or that they do not exist.

Step 3: Consent Recognition

The goal of this step is to identify whether the occupant has given police actual or implied consent to enter a house.

The conclusion reached is either that valid consent has been given or that it has not been given.

Step 4: Entry Authorized Recognition (Solution)

The final step correlates the conclusions reached in Steps 1–3 with all available lawful authorities regarding house entry. A decision whether to enter with or without a Feeney warrant, or not to enter at all, is the outcome.

The possible decisions are as follows:

▸ apply for a Feeney warrant,
▸ warrantless entry, or
▸ no entry—continue investigation or make additional attempt to obtain valid consent.

Table 8.1 outlines the steps in the Feeney decision-making model.

Table 8.1   Feeney Decision-Making Model Summary

Step	Investigative Question	Goal
1. Translate Information	Does lawful authority to arrest exist? Where is the offender (place)?	▸ Analyze the information and form two beliefs about two connections: a. between offender and offence b. between offender and place ▸ Reach a belief formula that includes both.
2. Emergency Recognition	Do exigent circumstances exist?	▸ Analyze the circumstances and identify whether a public safety risk or an investigative risk exists.
3. Consent Recognition	Did an occupant give actual or implied permission to enter the house?	▸ Determine presence or absence of valid consent.
4. Authority Recognition	Does statutory, common law, or case law authorize entry?	▸ Reach a *solution* that identifies whether lawful authority, with or without a warrant, exists to enter.

■ CASE STUDY

1:15 a.m.: Radio broadcast—"Disturbance—Ellen's Bar, 467 Longhorns Street."
1:19 a.m.: Arrival

You are met by Claire, 49 years old. You see a man, Drew (42), lying on the floor bleeding; he is being treated by ambulance attendants. Claire reports that she saw the following:

▸ Her ex-boyfriend, Doug (51) was in the bar for about two hours.
▸ Doug drank heavily and became intoxicated.
▸ Doug started an argument with Drew.
▸ Doug smashed a beer bottle over Drew's head repeatedly.
▸ Doug ran into the men's washroom with the beer bottle.

Claire phoned the police. Doug never left the washroom. You check the washroom door. It is locked. You knock and receive no response.

Questions

1. Do Feeney laws apply?
2. Can you apply for a Feeney warrant to enter to arrest?

Answer

No, to both questions, because Doug is not in a dwelling-house. Although the bar is a privately owned business, it is classified as a public place for Feeney provision purposes. *Warrantless entry is authorized* because it is not possible to obtain a Feeney warrant to enter this place for the purpose of making an arrest.

CONCEPT OF "PLACE"

The following three principles are crucial to an understanding of *place*:

▸ After every crime, the *offender is in a place* regardless of where he or she goes.
▸ Every emergency occurs in a place.
▸ Feeney laws apply only to dwelling-houses and not to any other place.

"Place" refers to location. There are only two classifications of places:

1. a dwelling-house, and
2. a non-dwelling-house.

A dwelling-house is defined as "the whole or any part of a building or structure that is kept or occupied as a permanent or temporary residence, and includes the following:

▸ a building within the cartilage of a dwelling-house that is connected to it by a doorway or by a covered and enclosed passageway, and
▸ a unit that is designed to be mobile and to be used as a permanent or temporary residence and that is being used as such a residence."[9]

The term *dwelling-house* is synonymous with "residence." What defines a place as a dwelling-house is its use as a "permanent or temporary residence." If the place in question is "kept or occupied" as a residence, it is considered to be a dwelling-house. The following are considered dwelling-houses when used as temporary or permanent residences:

▸ house or apartment,
▸ garage attached to a house,
▸ motel room or rented room,
▸ tent, and
▸ mobile unit designed to be used as a permanent or temporary residence, such as a trailer.

The term *non-dwelling-house* is synonymous with both "non-residence" and "public place." It is defined as "any public place that is not a structure, including:

▸ a sidewalk,
▸ a street,
▸ privately or publicly owned field including the *perimeter* of a house, and
▸ any publicly or privately owned building or structure or conveyance that is not kept or occupied as a permanent or temporary residence, including:

  – commercial premises,
  – public sector buildings such as a school or government building,

- motor vehicle or any other conveyance, and
- unattached garage on the perimeter of a dwelling-house."[10]

After committing an offence, the offender will (always) be in a *place*. The *type* of place is significant because Feeney laws apply only to dwelling-houses.

CONCEPT OF "ENTRY PATH"

Rule: When an arrest is made inside a residence, the police generally have the onus of proving that *two entries* were lawfully authorized and justified.

Generally, a residence is a building situated on property called "the perimeter." The **perimeter** is privately owned property surrounding a house. Although it is not a building or a structure, the perimeter qualifies as a "place" separate from the actual house.[11] Perimeter entry is governed by a common-law authority called "implied invitation to knock."

Arresting an offender inside a house requires a *two-part path* composed of *two entries*. The *sequence* consists of an entry onto the perimeter and an entry into the house. The door of the house is the dividing line and mid-point of the sequence. The *first entry* leads to the door. The *second entry* crosses the threshold. "Threshold crossing" is defined in case law as a *limited* entry into a foyer, entryway, or hallway of a house and not beyond that area. It is considered a "benign" act and "common courtesy" extended to all people, including police officers; it has no bearing on a final decision about the lawfulness of a warrantless entry.

The dimensions of threshold crossing are not precisely defined but may be said to extend to a physical point immediately inside the entrance only.[12] Full entry is defined as entry beyond the restricted dimensions of threshold crossing. It means entry into all areas beyond a foyer, entryway, or hallway. Both entries must be justified by a lawful authority.

CONCEPT OF "IMPLIED INVITATION TO KNOCK"

Perimeter entry is needed before a decision can be made regarding the second entry—that is, the house entry. Perimeter entry is composed of three separate acts:

1. walking into the perimeter,
2. approaching a door, and
3. knocking on the door.

The following is the relevant investigative question: Can the police walk onto the perimeter of a house *without a Feeney warrant*, approach a door, and knock on the door before deciding about warrantless entry into the house? Specifically, can the police, without a Feeney warrant, knock on the door of a house to (1) gain consent to enter; or (2) decide if exigent circumstances exist?

The answers are not in any federal statute. Instead, they are found in case law. The leading case is *R. v. Evans* (1996),[13] in which the S.C.C. confirmed the following common-law rule: the *occupier* of a residential dwelling-house is deemed to grant the public *conditional permission* to *approach* a door and *knock*. This rule is entitled "implied invitation to knock." It is not a new law. Common law has long recognized its existence. The components of the rule are as follows:

- A rebuttable presumption exists that all members of the public have an implied licence or consent to enter the perimeter of a house, approach a door, and knock on it.[14] The implied invitation is extended to everyone, police as well as citizens.[15] Implied consent means that the occupant does not have to expressly consent.

- The person giving the implied consent to knock is the occupier.[16] An occupier is not necessarily the owner. "Occupiers" include non-owners who are not guests or visitors.[17] The scope of the implied permission extends only to those who have "legitimate business" in coming onto the property, and the "implied licence ends at the door."[18]

- The "legitimate business" phrase makes the permission conditional. The implied invitation to knock does not mean that all persons, regardless of the purpose of their visit, are invited or welcome to approach the door and knock. For example, the implied invitation does not extend to persons who walk onto the property with criminal intent.[19]

- Consequently, the "implied licence to knock" rule means the owner may have authorized "certain persons" to approach the owner's home "for certain purposes."[20] This restriction limits the "activities" authorized on the occupier's property. The scope of activities authorized by implied invitation to knock depends on the "purpose" of the implied invitation.[21]

- The only legitimate purpose of the implied invitation is to facilitate communication between the public or the police, and the occupant.[22] This phrase is not concretely defined. When the police act in accordance with the legitimate purpose, they are not intruding on or diminishing the privacy of the occupant. They will not be considered trespassers.[23]

- The implied invitation constitutes a waiver of the occupier's expectation of privacy unless the implied invitation is rebutted or negated by a "clear expression of intent" to conduct a purpose other than the facilitation of communication.[24] Consequently, the privacy waiver has terms—the waiver applies only if the visitor's purpose is to facilitate communication. If the purpose is other than this approved intent, "s. 8 Charter comes into play."[25]

- The objective of s. 8 Charter is to preserve citizens' privacy interests. Its goal is to "protect individuals from unjustified state intrusions upon their privacy."[26] Consequently, s. 8 Charter "comes into play" when a citizen's reasonable expectation of privacy is "somehow diminished by an investigatory technique."[27]

- An "investigatory technique" is the same as a "form of examination." The key legal issue is whether an investigatory technique, or form of examination, constitutes a search. Not every investigatory technique constitutes a search that must meet the requirements of s. 8 Charter. The determining factor is how much effect the technique or examination has on the individual's privacy. Does the investigatory technique diminish or intrude upon some reasonable privacy interest?[28] As a rule, an investigatory technique that diminishes or intrudes on a person's privacy constitutes a search. Conversely, if it does not diminish or intrude on a person's privacy, it does not constitute a search.[29]

▸ There is no concrete definition of what specifically constitutes a privacy diminishment or intrusion. However, the S.C.C. has provided the following procedural concepts:

   a. "Privacy" is defined as "the right of the individual to determine for himself when, how, and to what extent he will release personal information about himself."[30]

   b. Although a person may explicitly "invite" another to engage in private conversation, the invitation does not authorize an activity with a different purpose or outside the boundaries of the invitation.[31]

   c. Activity that exceeds the boundaries of the invitation to knock may constitute a "search."[32]

   d. "Securing evidence against the occupant" does exceed the boundaries of an implied invitation to knock and does constitute a search.[33]

   e. *Purpose* is the defining element of the "implied invitation to knock." Consequently, the police officer's *purpose* or *intent* determines whether the investigative activity is authorized by the invitation.

   f. The existence of *implied invitation* gives the police permission "to proceed from the street to the door of a house" for one *specific purpose*—that is, "enabling the police officer to reach a point in relation to the house where he or she can *conveniently* and in a *normal manner* communicate with the occupant. Implied invitation to knock does not extend beyond what is required to permit and achieve the goal of convenient, normal communication with the occupant."[34]

   g. The purpose of securing evidence against the occupant is secondary and is not authorized by the implied invitation to knock. Obtaining evidence constitutes a search. If the intention of the police while approaching the door and knocking is to secure evidence against the occupant, the subsequent investigative procedure(s) will be considered an unreasonable search and a s. 8 Charter violation.

Procedure

The starting point for justifying an entry decision is proving the existence of the following with respect to the implied invitation to knock:

1. that your intention, or purpose, was normal, convenient communication;
2. that your target was the occupant of the house; and
3. that your path was directly from the cruiser onto the perimeter, and then to the final destination.

INTENTION/PURPOSE

This represents the investigative *goal*. Only one goal is permitted—normal, convenient communication. Keep notes that verify with supporting evidence that this was your intention, or purpose. In other words, keep a record of *concrete* circumstances that leave no doubt that your goal was normal, convenient communication. If the goal is to secure evidence, implied invitation to knock is cancelled and no longer applies.

TARGET

The goal must be linked to a person(s) inside the house. The occupant is the target of the communication, a fact that must be conveyed and demonstrated by your notes.

PATH

Every investigation involves a unique set of circumstances between the following two points:

1. *Point of entry onto the perimeter (property of the house).* The specific route must be described and the reason it was chosen must be justified. Such precision is necessary because a wide range of buildings, vehicles, physical items, and people may exist within the perimeter. Observations cannot be avoided. If some of these observations become evidence against the occupant, your presence at a particular location will have to be justified. Only one reason will justify your taking a specific route—that it was needed to achieve the basic goal of *communication.*

2. *The final destination where the communication with the occupant occurred.* Threshold crossing is defined in case law as a *limited* entry into the foyer, entryway, or hallway of a house, and not beyond that area. It is regarded as a "benign act" and "common courtesy" extended to all people, including police officers. Threshold crossing has no bearing or significance when it comes to a final decision about the lawfulness of a warrantless entry. The physical scope of threshold crossing is not concretely defined but is said to extend to a physical point immediately inside the entrance only.[35] Full entry is defined as entry beyond the limited dimensions of a threshold crossing. It includes all areas beyond a foyer, entryway, or hallway.

Once you have proven these three conditions existed—that is, that your primary goal was communication, that the occupant was the "target" of your communication, and that your path was in keeping with your primary goal—you have legally justified your entry onto the property and your presence on the perimeter and at the door. At this point, you and the occupant will have the *communication* that will usher in your next set of decisions about warrantless entry—namely, does the occupant consent to an entry or do exigent circumstances justify it?

THE CONCEPT OF "CONSENT"

The simplest way to enter a house is by consent. The benefits of consent to an investigator are as follows:

▸ It is the quickest and easiest way to enter a house because it requires no documents and no judicial authorization. It requires only a brief oral communication, which you record verbatim in your notes and convey with precision during testimony.
▸ It authorizes entry into *any* type of place.
▸ A reasonable grounds belief is not a prerequisite of obtaining the occupant's consent—*any* belief may precede it (mere suspicion or reasonable grounds).
▸ It constitutes a s. 8 Charter waiver.

The *Criminal Code* does not include a specific provision that authorizes entry by consent, and it does not supply guidelines explaining how to obtain consent. Consensual entry is authorized by common law,[36] but the guidelines concerning it emerge from case law.

Definition of Consent

No Canadian statute defines **consent**. Valid consent is defined in case law as a person's "voluntary and informed decision to permit the intrusion of the investigative process upon his constitutionally protected rights."[37] The key elements of this definition are as follows:

> ▸ Consent is an informed decision. The person making the decision must be sufficiently informed of facts of the situation and must have adequate knowledge of exactly what has been decided.
> ▸ The decision must be voluntarily made. No person is obliged to consent to a warrantless search. Every person may choose to refuse consent.

There are two types of consent:

1. expressed or explicit consent, and
2. implied consent.

EXPRESSED/EXPLICIT CONSENT

This refers to direct, unmistakable permission. It is the ideal type of consent and is the subject of an extensive instructional component that has emerged from two case law decisions: *R. v. Wills* (1992), Ontario Court of Appeal; and *R. v. Borden* (1994), S.C.C.

Seven conditions, articulated by the court and referred to as the "*Wills* instructional component," are required for expressed/explicit consent to exist. They are as follows:

1. Consent must be expressed or implied.
2. Consent must be voluntary.
3. The accused must be aware of the specific act the police intend to conduct.
4. The accused must be aware of the potential consequences of giving consent.
5. The accused must know that consent may be refused.
6. The accused must know that consent may be revoked at any time after it is initially given.
7. If the accused gives consent, he or she must not have revoked consent at any time during the search.[38]

IMPLIED CONSENT

This is an exception to the rigid policy that emerged from *R. v. Wills*. Implied consent refers to permission or invitation that the police infer from the conduct or words of an "active participant," defined as a cooperative occupant.[39]

Circumstantial evidence is sufficient to prove implied consent. The key elements of implied consent are as follows:

1. The circumstances must reasonably support the inference that the occupant is permitting or inviting entry.
2. Conduct alone may constitute implied consent. Words are not mandatory. An example would be an occupant opening the door and "backing away" from the entrance in response to a request to enter.
3. Failure to inform an occupant of the entire *Wills* instructional component does not nullify implied consent. For example, a knock on the door followed by an occupant's response of "come in" constitutes implied consent despite the absence of strict adherence to the *Wills* component.
4. There is a distinction between two concepts:
   a. cooperation, and
   b. compliance.

   Cooperation is conduct that constitutes *voluntary* assistance. *Compliance* involves acquiescence—an induced, involuntary conduct that does not amount to cooperation. Cooperation constitutes implied consent. Compliance does not.

An "active participant" is defined as an occupant who voluntarily cooperates and assists the police, and whose conduct and communication exceed mere compliance or acquiescence. An "active participant" is also defined as an occupant who gives *informed* implied consent. In other words, an active participant has made an informed decision to give implied consent.[40]

Lawful Occupier

The question of "who may give consent to enter a house" was answered by the S.C.C. in *R. v. Edwards* (1996):[41] "a lawful occupier" may give consent. Any of the following kinds of occupants may lawfully give consent or invite the police to enter a place:

- the owner,
- the lawful possessor of the place,
- a person authorized by the owner, and
- a person who has the authority to regulate access to the place. "Regulating access" refers to the authority to permit entry, prohibit entry, or remove persons from the place.[42] As a general rule, guests and visitors are not lawful occupiers. Conversely, a lawful occupier is any occupant who is not a guest or a visitor.

THE CONCEPT OF "FEENEY LAWS"

The majority of this chapter is devoted to six *Criminal Code* provisions informally known as "Feeney" warrants or laws. Most authorities governing police entry into a house for the purpose of arrest emerge from, but are not limited to, these Feeney laws. Additional authorities emerge from common law and case law.

The concept of Feeney warrants is relatively new. In 1997, five majority judges of the S.C.C., in *R. v. Feeney*, ruled that a *general*, but not total, prohibition existed on entering a house without a warrant, for the purpose of making an arrest. In other words, they ruled that the police must first obtain a warrant to enter a dwelling-house in order to arrest an offender inside the dwelling-house.[43] The problem was that no such warrant existed in Canadian law at that time. The *Criminal Code* did not include any laws governing warrants to enter dwelling-houses to carry out an arrest. For obvious reasons, the police could not obtain such warrants.

Parliament responded to the S.C.C. decision by enacting Bill C-16. This *Criminal Code* amendment had a dual purpose: (1) it gave the police the authority to enter dwelling-houses both *with* and *without a warrant*, to carry out an arrest; and (2) it respected individuals' right to privacy in their houses, as guaranteed by the Charter.[44] Parliament's intention was to "strike the balance"[45] between these two imperatives by means of a flexible statutory framework.[46] The legislation was designed to balance the competing interests of privacy and public safety "without jeopardizing the safety of Canadians."[47]

Parliament's goal was not to hinder policing. Instead, Bill C-16 established the authorities by which police could enter houses with or without a warrant to arrest an offender. Specifically, it established two types of warrants, plus an authority for entering a house without a warrant in an emergency. The reason for creating two types of warrants was to *benefit* the police. One warrant requires the police to formally charge an offender before obtaining a warrant to enter. The second type allows the police to obtain a warrant to enter *without first formally charging an offender*.[48]

There are two significant rules restrictions on the Feeney laws:

1. Feeney laws apply only to dwelling-houses, not to any other place that is not a private residence.
2. Feeney warrants apply only when

   a. there are reasonable grounds to believe that an indictable offence was committed by a specific person (RG-IND), and
   b. there are reasonable grounds to believe that the offender is in a specific residence (RG in DH).

Conversely, Feeney laws do not apply when mere suspicion exists relative to either the offence or the place. Nor do they apply in emergencies involving *uncertainty*, such as 911 calls and "unknown problem" calls. Common-law authorities apply in these cases.[49]

Striking the Balance

> The poorest man in his cottage bid defiance to all the forces of the Crown. It may be frail. Its roof may shake. The wind may blow through it. The storm may enter. The rain may enter. But, the King of England cannot enter! All his force dares not cross the threshold of the ruined tenement.[50]

The path to Feeney warrants started in 1793 when William Pitt (the Elder), during a speech before the British Parliament, proclaimed a person's right to privacy in his or her house.[51] Since then, police entry into houses to make arrests has been a controversial, complex issue.

Incredibly, before 1997, no *Criminal Code* or statutory laws governed forcible police entry into houses to arrest offenders. Common law and case law created the rules. Dramatic change came in 1997, when *Criminal Code* amendments were enacted in response to the landmark S.C.C. decision in *Feeney*.[52]

"Feeney" warrants/laws became the informal term given a new group of six *Criminal Code* sections in Part XVI under the title "Powers to Enter Dwelling-houses to Carry Out Arrests." Sections 529 and 529.1–529.5 C.C. created a new decision-making model for police within a legislative system that governs lawful entry into houses to arrest offenders.

The immediate post-*Feeney* era was one of gloom and doom for law enforcement, with a rising number of acquittals in cases where arrests were made in houses following warrantless *entry by consent.* These court decisions set a judicial trend that challenged the simple investigative method of approaching the door of a house, knocking, and obtaining legitimate consent to enter for the routine purpose of arresting offenders inside private houses.[53] Fortunately for law enforcement, a formal shift in the trend of judicial decision making has since restored common sense and balance, returning dramatic investigative benefits to police.

Historical Continuum

Examining the evolution of the principles that have culminated in the Feeney laws will help you to understand these laws. This evolution spans a 400-year history that has had one primary objective—striking a balance between the need for public safety and the need for privacy in a house.

Dwelling-houses are controversial places. Although they are strictly protected by privacy laws, offenders occasionally seek refuge in them to escape arrest.

Six cases form a historical sequence from which emerges the lawful authority to enter a house to make an arrest:

1. *Semayne's Case* (1604),[54]
2. *Eccles v. Bourque* (1974),[55]
3. *R. v. Landry* (1986),[56]
4. *R. v. Macooh* (1993),[57]
5. *R. v. Feeney* (1997),[58] and
6. *R. v. Godoy* (1999).[59]

This continuum takes us from past legal thinking on the subject to the viewpoint now prevalent.

SEMAYNE'S CASE (1604)

This English civil case established three common-law concepts:

1. "every man's house is his castle";
2. "no criminal is immune from arrest in his own home nor in the home of one of his friends"; and
3. law enforcement has authority to forcibly enter a house, upon notice, to arrest an offender.[60]

Semayne's case established the basic principle, still firmly entrenched, that a house is the owner's castle and may be defended against unlawful trespassing. But it also imposed a limitation on this principle—being in the home could not protect an offender from arrest.[61]

ECCLES v. BOURQUE (1974)

The S.C.C. created four investigative rules that apply to s. 495 C.C. procedures:

1. The police have authority to enter a dwelling-house *without a warrant*, for the purpose of executing an arrest warrant, if two conditions exist:

    a. the police have reasonable grounds to believe the offender is inside; and

    b. they make a "proper announcement" before entering.

    The *Criminal Code* at that time did not include a warrant to enter a dwelling-house for the purpose of making an arrest. The S.C.C. recognized common law as the source that authorized entry to arrest. This warrantless house entry could be made without consent to enter and, if necessary, forcibly.

2. "Proper announcement" was defined as communicating three notices:

    a. notice of presence (knock on door or ring bell),

    b. notice of authority (identify as police officer), and

    c. notice of purpose (state reason for entry).

    The concept of "proper announcement" was intended to protect the police by distinguishing them from unlawful trespassers and criminal intruders.

3. At minimum, the police should (a) request admission; and (b) have admission denied.

4. Exigent circumstances constituted an exception to the "proper announcement" rule. "Exigent circumstances" were defined as an urgency created by risk to life or to the destruction of evidence—in other words, a public safety risk or an investigative risk.

R. v. LANDRY (1986)

The *Eccles v. Bourque* rules applied when police had s. 495 C.C. authority to arrest *without* a warrant. This case added one simple rule: the warrantless authority to enter a house was extended to arrest with a warrant—s. 514 C.C.

R. v. MACOOH (1993)

The S.C.C. authorized warrantless entry into a dwelling-house to make an arrest if the police were in "hot pursuit" of the suspect.

Hot pursuit was defined as "continuous pursuit conducted with reasonable diligence, as that pursuit and capture along with commission of the offence may be considered as forming part of a single transaction."

The decisions in *Eccles v. Bourque*, *R. v. Landry*, and *R. v. Macooh* all preceded *R. v. Feeney* (1997). The *Criminal Code* did not provide for a warrant to enter a house to make an arrest until the *Feeney* case precipitated a C.C. amendment.

In other words, before 1997, the police could not obtain a warrant to enter a house to make an arrest even if they wanted; no such warrant existed. All forcible entries into houses to make arrests were authorized without a warrant.

R. v. FEENEY (1997)

Police were investigating the murder of an 85-year-old man who was beaten to death. Investigation led to a suspect, to the suspect's residence (a house trailer), and to a belief that the suspect was in the residence.

The police entered the residence without a warrant to enter, as lawfully permitted at that time. The police could not have obtained a warrant to enter because no such warrant was provided for in Canadian law.

The police found the suspect inside the trailer, arrested him, and seized relevant physical evidence. The S.C.C., in a 5–4 decision, ruled that (1) the police had only mere suspicion, not reasonable grounds; and (2) the warrantless authority to enter houses was unconstitutional. A recommendation was made that Parliament enact legislation to provide for a warrant to enter a house to arrest. Parliament responded by passing Bill C-16 and enacting s. 529(1) and 529(1–5). These provisions created statutory authorities by which police could enter a house with or without a warrant. However, these provisions apply only when lawful authority to arrest exists (that is, reasonable grounds, indictable offence) and reasonable grounds exist for believing that the offender is in a specific dwelling-house.

R. v. GODOY (1999)

This was the first post-Feeney decision relating to the scope of police powers in response to emergency 911 calls or "unknown problem" calls. The uncertainty associated with these calls makes the Feeney authorities inapplicable, with or without a warrant, because these calls involve no reasonable grounds for believing that a person committed an indictable offence or that an offender whose arrest is lawfully authorized is in a specific dwelling-house.

The S.C.C. solved this investigative problem with three rulings:

1. It recognized the existence of common-law exigent circumstances (CLEC).
2. It confirmed that a disconnected 911 call or an unknown problem call are examples of CLEC.
3. It stated that CLEC, including 911 calls, represent an exception to the prior announcement rule.

Case Law

R. v. Feeney (1997)

- **Issue:** Is warrantless entry into a dwelling-house to make an arrest permitted when only mere suspicion exists?

- **Offence:** "Second-degree murder"

- **Circumstances:** The body of an 85-year-old man was found in his home, at 8:20 a.m. He had suffered five blows to the head with an iron bar or similar object. The exact time of death could not be determined. The victim had last been seen alive the previous evening. During the preliminary investigation, police found blood splattered inside the victim's house and a pack of Sportsman cigarettes at the scene. Receiving information about an accident, three officers attended at the scene of a motor vehicle collision about half a kilometre from the victim's house. At the scene, the victim's pickup truck was found in a ditch. A female witness informed officers that the truck was in the ditch at 6:45 a.m. She identified the suspect by given name only and said that a few minutes earlier she had seen him

(continued)

walking along a road near where the victim lived, carrying a bottle of beer or cup of coffee. The suspect's residence was known to be a trailer situated on another person's property. Upon arrival at the property where the suspect lived, a witness informed the police that the suspect returned home at 7:00 a.m. He had been drinking and was currently sleeping in the trailer behind the residence.

The officer-in-charge of the investigation went to the trailer, knocked on the door, and identified himself by saying, "Police." Receiving no answer, the officer entered the trailer, went to the suspect's bed, shook the suspect's leg, and said, "I want to talk to you." The officer asked the suspect to get out of bed and move to the front of the trailer, where the light was better. The officer saw blood splattered all over the front of the suspect, read him the right to counsel, and cautioned him. The officer's reading of the right to counsel did not include reference to a toll-free number. The officer arrested the suspect and asked whether he understood his right to counsel. The suspect did not initially respond. When asked again, the suspect answered, "Of course, do you think I'm illiterate?" Immediately afterward, the officer asked the suspect how he got the blood on him. The suspect answered that he had been hit in the face with a baseball bat the day before. The officer seized a pair of blood-stained shoes, a package of Sportsman cigarettes, and the blood-stained T-shirt worn by the suspect.

At 12:17 p.m., the suspect left a message for a lawyer to call the police station. At 12:33 p.m., a breath sample was taken. The suspect was not informed that he did have a choice about whether to give the breath sample in that situation. The suspect was detained in a cell. At 10:00 p.m., two detectives began interrogating the suspect. The suspect stated, "I should have a lawyer," but the questioning continued. The suspect confessed that he struck the victim and stole the cigarettes, beer, and cash from the victim's house. He put the cash under his mattress in the trailer. A search warrant was obtained to search the suspect's trailer and to seize the money beneath the mattress. A second interrogation occurred at 3:05 a.m. It lasted for 1½ hours. The suspect still had not spoken to a lawyer. Two days after the arrest, the suspect was fingerprinted at 9:25 a.m. and again at 9:54 a.m. The suspect spoke to a lawyer for the first time between the fingerprinting sessions.

- **Trial:** The accused was convicted of second-degree murder after a jury trial in the British Columbia Supreme Court. His appeal to the British Columbia Court of Appeal was unanimously dismissed.

- **Appeal:** The accused appealed to the S.C.C. The majority, in a 5–4 decision, allowed the appeal, ordered a new trial, and recommended C.C. amendments. The specific reasons were as follows:

  ▸ The arrest was unlawful. Reasonable grounds did not exist to believe, before entry and at the time of arrest, that the accused committed the offence. Mere suspicion alone existed.

    There were four elements of the total evidence available to the police at the time of entry and arrest:

    1. The deceased person's truck appeared to have been stolen before it had been involved in the collision.
    2. The accused had been seen walking near the scene of the accident.
    3. A witness assumed that the accused had driven the deceased person's truck because the accused had been involved in a collision at the same location earlier, while driving another vehicle.

(continued)

4. An occupant at the accused's residence told the police that the accused returned home at 7:00 a.m. after drinking all night, and had earlier been involved in a collision, while driving another vehicle, at the site where the victim's vehicle was found.

Subjective grounds did exist because the officer testified in cross-examination that he did not believe he had reasonable grounds to arrest. The four elements of the total evidence did not pass the objective test—objectively considered, reasonable grounds did not exist.

▸ A warrantless forcible entry authorized by common law and case law was no longer lawful in light of the Charter. The sanctity of a dwelling-house demands that forcible entry should only be authorized by judicial authority. The S.C.C. ruled that, to make an arrest, a warrant was needed to enter dwelling-houses without consent. However, no such warrant existed in statutory law. The S.C.C. recommended that Parliament create such a warrant.

▸ All the physical evidence was excluded under s. 24(2) Charter after the S.C.C. ruled that a number of Charter violations occurred. A new trial was ordered.

Realizing that this judgment would need legislative changes, the S.C.C. granted a six-month transition period for enactment.

The four-judge dissenting ruling commended the police for acting quickly to prevent further violence after "a savage, physical beating inflicted on a helpless victim for no apparent reason." They found that the police entry was lawful, the existing laws were lawful, no legislative changes were needed, and reinforced the lawfulness of common law and case law warrantless entry authority, based on the previous S.C.C. fundamental principle that "the criminal is not immune from arrest in his own home nor the home of one of his friends."

The S.C.C. decision ignited considerable debate in the federal House of Commons during Bill C-16 readings. For example, the Honorable J. Ramsay strongly criticized the "horrendous decision," made by five people on the S.C.C.—who are supposed to represent the interests of average Canadians—as failing to strike the balance favoured by the community. He argued that the S.C.C. had incorrectly decided that a suspected murderer's privacy interest outweighed the interest of society's protection. To support his argument, Mr. Ramsay emphasized that all the lower courts and the four S.C.C. judges disagreed with the S.C.C. majority.[62]

BILL C-16: C.C. AMENDMENT— THE NEW "FEENEY" LAWS

Parliament responded to the S.C.C. decision by amending the *Criminal Code* through Bill C-16. It created the following six provisions under the title "Powers to Enter Dwelling-Houses to Carry Out Arrests":

▸ Section 529 C.C.—Including Authorization to Enter in Warrant of Arrest
▸ Section 529.1 C.C.—Warrant to Enter Dwelling-house
▸ Section 529.2 C.C.—Reasonable Terms and Conditions
▸ Section 529.3 C.C.—Authority to Enter Dwelling-house without Warrant
▸ Section 529.4 C.C.—Omitting Announcement before Entry
▸ Section 529.5 C.C.—Telewarrant

This legislative system creates three authorities enabling police to enter houses without consent for the purpose of making arrests: two warrants, and one warrant-less authority.

The availability of two warrants benefits police by enabling them to obtain warrants either before or after formally charging the offender. In other words, police can obtain a warrant to enter a house whether or not an Information has already been laid. The police are not restricted to obtaining a warrant only after the offender is formally charged.

The third authority gives police the authority to enter without a warrant when exigent circumstances exist—in other words, in the case of emergencies and urgencies that afford no time to obtain a warrant before entering. This common-sense benefit reflects the pre-Feeney procedures used by police, based on common law and case law.

Essentially, laws were not replaced—they were expanded. The warrantless entry authority based on common law and case law was not eliminated—it remains. Bill C-16 simply added the requirement that police obtain judicial authorization when exigent circumstances are absent.

Finally, Feeney laws did not change the procedure for making arrests in public places or outside dwelling-houses.

TWO TYPES OF FEENEY WARRANTS

One type of Feeney warrant requires that an Information be laid before the warrant is executed; the other does not. One is used pre-charge and one is used post-charge.

Thus the police have the discretion of obtaining a warrant to enter either before or after charging the offender.

Feeney Warrant 1 is defined as follows:

- Included Authorization to Enter in Warrant to Arrest
- Form 7
- Post-charge warrant to enter

Feeney Warrant 2 is defined as follows:

- Warrant to Enter Dwelling-house
- Form 7.1
- Pre-charge warrant to enter

Both documents share three characteristics:

1. They authorize entry into a dwelling-house.
2. The sole permitted purpose of the entry they authorize is arresting an offender.
3. An application is mandatory in either case.

The purpose of the mandatory application is to transfer the decision-making responsibility from the police to a Justice (defined in s. 2 C.C.). The police apply; a Justice decides to grant or reject. The application is called an "Information to Obtain" (Form 1).

Again, the difference between the two warrants is the sequence in which they are obtained in relation to a formal charge:

▸ Warrant 1 (Included Authorization) is obtained after the offender is charged; the warrant to enter, in this case, is represented by an additional paragraph on the arrest warrant. In other words, a formal charge has to be laid before this arrest warrant may be issued. The offender is charged first and the warrant to enter is issued second.

▸ Warrant 2 (Warrant to Enter) is obtained before a formal charge is laid. This warrant is applied for when s. 495 C.C. (authority to arrest without a warrant) exists. Consequently, the warrant to enter is issued first and the formal charge occurs second.

Table 8.2 summarizes the differences between Warrants 1 and 2.

Table 8.2   Feeney Warrants 1 and 2: Key Points

	Warrant 1	**Warrant 2**
Name	Included Authorization—Arrest Warrant	Warrant to Enter
Application Required?	yes	yes
Form Number	7	7.1
Formal Charge	*before* warrant	*after* warrant
Sequence	▸ formal charge first ▸ warrant to enter second	▸ warrant to enter first ▸ formal charge second

Feeney Warrant 1 Elements

INCLUDED AUTHORIZATION TO ENTER—ARREST WARRANT, SECTION 528 C.C.

By breaking it into its constituent parts we can identify the six key elements of this kind of Feeney warrant:[63]

1. a *warrant to arrest* or apprehend a person, issued by a judge or Justice under the C.C. or any other act of Parliament
2. may authorize a *peace officer*
3. to *enter* a *dwelling-house* described in the warrant
4. for the purpose of arresting or apprehending the person
5. the judge or Justice is satisfied by *information on oath in writing*
6. there are *reasonable grounds* to believe that the person *is* or *will be* present in the dwelling-house

When issued, this type of Feeney warrant cannot automatically be executed. The rule governing execution has four elements:[64]

1. if an arrest warrant with included authorization to enter is granted
2. execution is subject to the condition that
3. the peace officer *may not enter* the dwelling house unless
4. the peace officer has, *immediately* before entering the dwelling-house, reasonable grounds to believe that the person to be arrested or apprehended *is* present in the dwelling-house

Police must lay a formal charge before obtaining this type of Feeney warrant. The process has three stages, involving three documents. The path starts with laying an Information, progresses to the issuance of an arrest warrant, and culminates in an application for warrant 1 (authority to enter included on the arrest warrant).

None of the goals at the three respective stages is automatically fulfilled or granted. Each one requires a hearing at which evidence must be presented to prove certain conditions.

Stage 1: Laying an Information

This Feeney warrant differs from the other in having an additional paragraph of instructions on the traditional document.

An arrest warrant cannot be issued until an Information, or formal charge, is laid. So the starting point here is completing an Information, bringing it to a Justice, and conducting an *ex parte* hearing to prove there are reasonable grounds to believe that the person named on the Information committed the specific offence(s) alleged on it. If unsuccessful, the process ends, and the investigation continues until more evidence is obtained.

If successful, the Justice signs the Information, which signifies that the named person is formally charged. But the arrest warrant is not automatically issued at this stage.

The Information may be laid by anyone—police officer or citizen.

Stage 2: Arrest Warrant

If the Justice signs the Information, he or she next decides whether to issue a summons or an arrest warrant.

The determining factor is whether there is sufficient evidence to prove the arrest is "necessary in the public interest"[65]—that is to say, necessary to public safety or to ensuring the accused appears in court. Then the second stage of the *ex parte* hearing occurs. If "necessary in the public interest" is not proved, the Justice issues a summons instead of an arrest warrant. The process ends. A Feeney warrant cannot be obtained in this case.

If "necessary in the public interest" is proved, an arrest warrant is issued. This document represents judicial authority to arrest the named person, but at this stage it does not authorize entry into a house.

The arrest warrant, at this stage, represents a *potential* Feeney warrant.

Stage 3: Included Authorization (Feeney Warrant)

The final stage is applying for the authority to enter a specific house to make the arrest.

Section 529 C.C. stipulates that an "Information on oath in writing" is required to prove the need for authorization to enter a house. The phrase refers to a C.C. document entitled an "Information to Obtain," a form of application the police must fill out. This application must convince a judge or Justice that reasonable grounds exist to believe that the person named on the arrest warrant is or will be present inside a specific house. An oral application is prohibited.

The written evidence is analyzed by the judge or Justice. If reasonable grounds do not exist for believing the person is in the house, the Feeney warrant will not be issued. In this case, the house cannot be entered without consent. You will need additional evidence to prove reasonable grounds or, alternatively, you will need to arrest the offender elsewhere in public.

If reasonable grounds do exist, the Justice authorizes conditional entry into the specific house by including on the warrant a paragraph of instructions.

A separate warrant to enter is not issued. The arrest warrant becomes a *dual purpose* document. It authorizes: (1) an arrest, and (2) entry into the house.

This warrant (Feeney Warrant 1) is directed to police officers, not citizens. It *does not* authorize a search for evidence—it authorizes *entry* and *arrest* of the named person. Figure 8.2 outlines this three-stage path.

The issuance of an "Included Authorization" Feeney warrant means you have *conditional* authority to enter the house, not automatic authority. Section 529(2) C.C. makes it mandatory for police to *re-evaluate* their reasonable grounds belief that the accused is in the house, and to do so at a specific time—that is, "immediately" before entry. The goal here is to confirm your belief that the accused is *currently* in the house.

The purpose of this provision is to prevent police from entering a house when the basis of their authority for entering no longer exists—that is to say, when they no longer have reasonable grounds to believe the suspect is currently in the house.

Feeney Warrant 2 Elements

WARRANT TO ENTER DWELLING-HOUSE, SECTION 529.1 C.C.

Viewed in sequence, the elements of the second Feeney warrant are as follows:

1. a judge or Justice may issue
2. a warrant in Form 7.1 authorizing a peace officer
3. to enter a dwelling-house described in the warrant
4. for the purpose of arresting or apprehending a person identified or identifiable by the warrant
5. if the judge or Justice is satisfied by Information on oath
6. that there are reasonable grounds to believe that the person *is* or *will be* present in the dwelling-house and
7. grounds exist to arrest the person *without* a *warrant* under

   ▸ section 495(1)(a) C.C.,
   ▸ section 672.91 C.C.,
   ▸ and federal statute, or
   ▸ an arrest warrant exists under any federal statute.[66]

Figure 8.2   "Included Authorization" Three-Stage Path

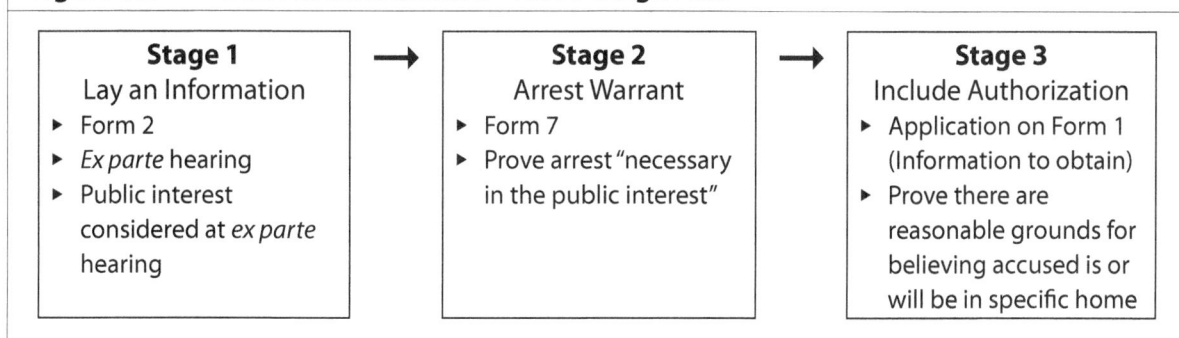

| **Stage 1**
Lay an Information
▸ Form 2
▸ *Ex parte* hearing
▸ Public interest considered at *ex parte* hearing | → | **Stage 2**
Arrest Warrant
▸ Form 7
▸ Prove arrest "necessary in the public interest" | → | **Stage 3**
Include Authorization
▸ Application on Form 1 (Information to obtain)
▸ Prove there are reasonable grounds for believing accused is or will be in specific home |

Three characteristics distinguish this Feeney warrant from the first one:

1. A formal charge does not have to be laid first. A "warrant to enter" may be obtained without laying an Information beforehand.
2. The "warrant to enter" is a separate warrant, Form 7.1. It is a single-purpose document, unlike the dual purpose arrest warrant, which has authorization included.
3. The application may be made orally or in writing, unlike the application for the "included authorization" warrant, which permits a written application only. "Information on oath *in writing*" is used in s. 529 C.C. (included authorization) whereas "in writing" is absent from s. 529.1 C.C. (warrant to enter). The latter requires an "Information on oath," which does not limit the application to writing only.

Obtaining a "warrant to enter" involves a three-stage process:

1. establishing or acquiring lawful authority to arrest,
2. forming reasonable grounds to believe that the offender is or will be in a specific house, and
3. applying for the "warrant to enter."

Stage 1: Establish Lawful Arrest Authority

The starting point in obtaining a warrant to enter is establishing that you have lawful authority to arrest, either with or without an arrest warrant.

To establish that you have lawful authority to arrest without an arrest warrant, you need to do the following:

▸ Form reasonable grounds for believing that a specific person

  – has or is about to commit an indictable offence (s. 495(1)(a) C.C. authority);
  – contravened or willfully failed to comply with a "disposition," defined as an order made by a court or review board, regarding Part XX.1 C.C.—Mental Disorder treatment or detention (s. 672.91 C.C.); or
  – may be arrested or apprehended without an arrest warrant under any federal statute.

▸ Form reasonable grounds for believing that a valid arrest warrant, pursuant to any federal statute, is in force anywhere in Canada.

Stage 2: Form Reasonable Grounds to Believe That Offender Is or Will Be in a Dwelling-House

Acquire evidence that proves beyond mere suspicion that the offender is located inside a specific house.

Stage 3: Apply for and Obtain Warrant to Enter

Although there is no absolute requirement that the "Information on oath" be in writing, your best course of action is to complete an "Information to Obtain" (Form 1), bring it to a judge or Justice, and show him or her the evidence that there are reasonable grounds to believe the offender (1) has committed an indictable offence; and (2) is or will be in a specific house.

Unlike the "Included Authorization" warrant, s. 529.1 C.C. does not require police to re-evaluate and confirm their reasonable grounds belief immediately before entering.

Figure 8.3 outlines the three-stage path to obtaining a warrant to enter.

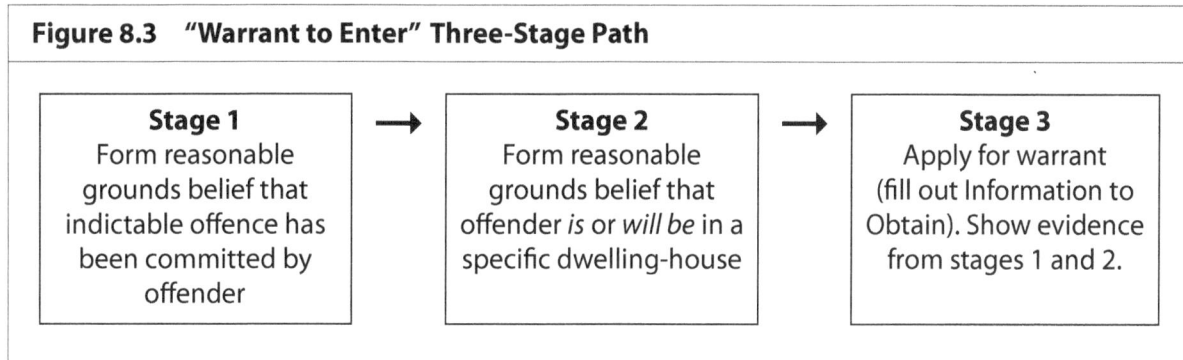

Figure 8.3   "Warrant to Enter" Three-Stage Path

| **Stage 1** Form reasonable grounds belief that indictable offence has been committed by offender | → | **Stage 2** Form reasonable grounds belief that offender *is* or *will be* in a specific dwelling-house | → | **Stage 3** Apply for warrant (fill out Information to Obtain). Show evidence from stages 1 and 2. |

CONTENTS OF FEENEY WARRANTS 1 AND 2

Both Feeney warrants have *mandatory* and *discretionary* instructional content.

Mandatory Content

The *target* of a Feeney warrant is a specific house. The *goal* is to arrest a specific person. Section 529.2 C.C. makes it mandatory that both warrants include specific instructions concerning the identity of the house and *how* to enter it. A Feeney warrant must convey five things:

1. the name of the accused (that is, the person to be arrested);
2. an address or description that specifies the house;
3. the authority to enter the house without consent;
4. the purpose of the entry (that is to arrest the named person); and
5. reasonable terms and conditions, in accordance with s. 529.2 C.C. ("The judge or Justice *shall* include in a warrant under s. 529 or 529.1 *any* terms and conditions that the judge or Justice considers *advisable* to *ensure* that the entry into the dwelling-house is reasonable in the circumstances"[67]).

The judge or Justice has no discretion about whether to include these instructions—he or she "shall" include them.

As regards the fifth instruction, the phrase "any terms and conditions" is wide ranging and non-restrictive; the Justice is not limited to set terms and conditions or to particular words or phrases. These elements may be customized to suit the circumstances.

The only requirement is that the terms and conditions be linked to entry—their goal is to ensure reasonable entry. This basic aim, in combination with the particular circumstances of the situation, will determine the appropriate terms and conditions chosen by the judge or Justice (*not* by the police).

Discretionary Content

The execution of a Feeney warrant requires "prior announcement" before entry. *Prior announcement* involves three steps—that is to say, three separate notifications or instructions to the occupant(s):

1. notice of presence,
2. notice of authority, and
3. notice of purpose.

The prior announcement requirement can benefit the police but it can also put their investigation at risk. It is helpful in that it tells the occupant that the entry is not being committed by a criminal intruder or trespasser. This knowledge may prevent the occupant from responding to an unexpected entry with violent self-defence.

However, the prior announcement also gives occupants time to plan and execute an assault on police or to destroy evidence. The prior announcement can put the police at greater risk of violence than they would be with no prior announcement.

This risk is addressed by s. 529.4(1) C.C., the "omitting announcement before entry" provision that creates a statutory exemption to the prior announcement requirement. It gives the judge or Justice *discretion* to include in the warrant written authorization exempting police from the prior announcement requirement.

The five elements of s. 529.4(1) C.C. are, in order, as follows:

1. a judge or Justice who authorizes an officer to enter a dwelling-house under s. 529 or s. 529.1, or any other judge or Justice
2. may authorize the peace officer to enter the dwelling-house without prior announcement
3. *if* the judge or Justice is satisfied by "Information on oath"
4. that there are reasonable grounds to believe that prior announcement of the entry would
5. expose the peace officer or any other person to imminent bodily harm or death; or result in the imminent loss or imminent destruction of evidence relating to the commission of an indictable offence.

The person who authorizes this exemption may or may not be the same judge or Justice who issues the Feeney warrant. In other words, a Feeney warrant originally issued without the prior announcement exemption may later be supplemented with this exemption, by a different Justice, if evidence comes to light that the accused has weapons or may destroy evidence. This gives police the opportunity to have the exemption authority added without having to find the original judge or Justice. An exemption is not added automatically. Police must apply for one, showing evidence that it is necessary. The application may be oral or written, delivered under oath. An "Information to obtain" is the usual document used.

The onus is on the police to prove there is a need to eliminate the prior announcement requirement from the warrant. Two reasons are seen as justifying the exemption:

1. risk of death or bodily harm, and
2. risk of destruction of evidence.

Police must introduce evidence sufficient for a reasonable grounds belief concerning one or both of these risks. The application may be made concurrently with the actual Feeney warrant hearing or it may be made later, separately, after the warrant is issued.

If an exemption is granted, the authorization for police to enter the house without making a prior announcement is written on the Feeney warrant. However, the exemption is conditional. Entry without prior announcement is not automatic. Re-evaluation and confirmation of the reasonable grounds belief are required immediately before entry.

Re-evaluation/Confirmation

Section 529.4(2) C.C. makes it mandatory for police to re-evaluate, immediately before entering the house, the evidence constituting the belief, and to confirm they still have

- reasonable grounds to *suspect* that prior announcement of the entry would expose the police or another person to imminent bodily harm or death; or
- reasonable grounds to *believe* that prior announcement of the entry would result in imminent loss or destruction of evidence relating to the commission of an indictable offence.

Note that these are two different standards of belief. Confirmation of there being a risk to life must be based on reasonable grounds to *suspect*, whereas confirmation of there being a risk to evidence must be based on reasonable grounds to *believe*.

Procedure: Feeney Warrant 1— Included Authorization

Obtaining an "Included Authorization" Feeney warrant (Feeney Warrant 1) involves a 10-step procedure:

1. Form a reasonable grounds belief that the offender has committed any classification of offence.
2. Form a reasonable grounds belief that the offender is currently in a specific dwelling-house.
3. Complete two documents privately, not in the JP's presence:
   a. an Information to charge the offender, and
   b. an Information to Obtain—this document is Form 1 and is illustrated in s. 841 C.C.

   The *Information to Obtain* is the application to have authority to enter the dwelling-house included on the arrest warrant. This application must include the following:
   - name of the accused,
   - name of the offence,
   - specific address of the house, and
   - reasonable grounds for believing that the accused is currently in the house.

What circumstances constitute reasonable grounds? Refer to the definition of *reasonable grounds*. As we have seen, it does not state what specific circumstances actually constitute reasonable grounds. The definition tells us only that a reasonable grounds belief is one that exceeds mere suspicion. Examples of circumstances that *usually* constitute reasonable grounds include the following:

- a credible eyewitness (citizen or police) who saw the offender inside the house or saw him enter the house;
- the accused's admission that he is in the house—for example, through informing another person by telephone that he is inside the house; and
- circumstantial evidence that exceeds mere suspicion.

The basis of the reasonable grounds belief must be described in writing on the Information to Obtain. The amount of writing this tends to entail usually means that additional pages are required. You entitle these pages "Appendix A." A detailed explanation of how to complete an Information to Obtain is found in Chapter 16.

Only one dwelling-house may be named on the Information to Obtain. The reasonable grounds belief must pertain specifically to the accused's presence in one house. You cannot make one application to search multiple houses, even if the circumstances indicate that the accused may be in one of several houses. In this case, your application will be denied because you obviously only have mere suspicion about the accused's actual whereabouts.

The place named on the Information to obtain must be a dwelling-house (no warrant is needed for places that are not dwelling-houses). Finally, the Information to Obtain must be written without any assistance from the Justice.

4. After completing both documents, you appear before a judge or Justice. A Justice is a provincial court judge or a JP. The appearance is made out of court. The first document you present is the Information to charge the offender. The reason it comes first is that an arrest warrant must exist before you can apply to enter a house. The first step in obtaining an arrest warrant is laying the Information to charge the offender.

5. You try to prove reasonable grounds to believe that the accused committed the offence. This procedure is called an "*ex parte* hearing," which is explained in detail in Chapter 13, Charging an Offender.

6. If reasonable grounds are proven, the Justice signs the Information. The accused is formally charged at this time.

7. The Justice decides what method to use to compel the accused to appear in court. As we have seen, the officer must introduce evidence showing there are reasonable grounds to believe an arrest warrant is necessary in the public interest. If the officer fails to prove this necessity, a summons will be issued not an arrest warrant.

8. After the officer proves that a warrant is necessary in the public interest, the Justice issues an arrest warrant. The Justice, not the officer, completes the warrant.

9. You present the Information to Obtain to the Justice and swear the contents under oath. The JP reads the sworn written contents and decides

whether there are reasonable grounds to believe that the accused is currently in the house.

10. If the JP concludes that reasonable grounds do exist, he or she will include an additional paragraph on the arrest warrant authorizing entry into the specific house. The contents of the authorization are found in s. 841 C.C. on Form 7. A separate document is not issued. If the Justice concludes that reasonable grounds do not exist, the authorization will not be included. Entry into the house will not be authorized unless the accused consents to your entry. The arrest must be made at another location if such consent cannot be obtained.

Procedure: Feeney Warrant 2—Warrant to Enter

Obtaining a Feeney Warrant 2—a warrant to enter—involves the following procedure:

1. Form a reasonable grounds belief that someone has committed an indictable or dual procedure offence and may be arrested without a warrant; or obtain an arrest warrant for any classification of offence.
2. Complete an Information to Obtain as you did for a Feeney Warrant 1 (see Step 3 of the previous section), plus an explanation that proves you have lawful authority to arrest the offender.
3. Appear before a Justice and swear the Information to Obtain under oath. The Justice analyzes the contents and decides whether reasonable grounds exist to believe that the offender is currently in the specifically named dwelling-house and whether lawful authority to arrest is justified.
4. If the Justice concludes that both requirements have been met, he or she will issue a warrant to enter the specifically named dwelling-house, on Form 7.1.

CONCEPT OF "EMERGENCY"

◼ CASE STUDY

1:30 a.m.: While on patrol you receive a radio broadcast stating the following: "911 call, unknown problem, at a house situated at 1084 Niagara Street." No additional information is given.

1:35 a.m.: You arrive at the address. One car is parked in the driveway. One light is on in the house. You knock on the front door. A man in his mid-30s opens the inside door and tells you through the screen door, "There is nothing wrong here." You ask to enter to check. He refuses and closes the door.

Question

At this point, with no additional information, can you enter the house without a warrant or without consent?

Answer

Yes. The police have a common-law authority to forcibly enter a dwelling-house for the purpose of ascertaining the health and safety of a 911 caller. The Feeney provisions under ss. 529.1 and 529.3 C.C. do not apply because the uncertainty of "911" or "unknown problem" calls means that reasonable grounds are lacking for a belief that a specific person committed an indictable offence and is in the house. In short, warrantless entry is justified under common law, but not under s. 529.3 C.C., which creates the "exigent circumstances" exception to the Feeney warrants. And you could not obtain a Feeney warrant even if you wanted to because the preconditions of the warrant are absent.[68]

Regardless of how it is communicated, an emergency call represents the ultimate problem-solving challenge for police because it always involves the elements of *urgency* and *uncertainty*.

An emergency call immediately does three things:

1. It *conveys* a *problem* needing an urgent solution.
2. It *forms a belief* that death or injury may be a consequence.
3. It *restricts the time* and *information* available to police for making a decision.

Typically, emergency calls convey little or no information. The immediate investigative goal for police, on receiving an emergency call, is entry for the purpose of protecting life. The problem is that the *Criminal Code* does not address emergency calls. The C.C. Feeney laws generally do not apply. It is the common-law exigent circumstance (CLEC) rule that applies.

COMMON-LAW EXIGENT CIRCUMSTANCES (CLEC)

Emergency calls activate two legal imperatives for police:

1. warrantless authority to enter, and
2. the police duty to protect life.

CLEC is an abstract concept that lacks concrete guidelines. It is in an evolutionary phase at the moment. Its development may be followed through five case law decisions:

1. *R. v. Golub* (1997)
2. *R. v. Godoy* (1999)
3. *R. v. Nicholls* (1999)
4. *R. v. David* (2002)
5. *R. v. Pillay* (2004)

The following investigative concepts emerged from these five case law decisions:

- 911 unknown problem,
- spark of life,
- realistic leeway, and
- protective sweep.

911 Unknown Problem

911 is the most common type of emergency call. The following are the principles associated with it:

1. An "unknown problem," or "unknown trouble," call is a disconnected 911 call or a case where the caller was unable to convey or was prevented from conveying information.

   According to police policy, unknown problem calls are superseded, in priority, only by "officer needs assistance" calls. All 911 calls are requests for immediate assistance, but unknown problem calls include the "added element of the unknown," which usually necessitates a back-up officer.

2. The purpose of emergency response systems is to provide "effective and immediate" assistance to citizens in need. The 911 system is intended to handle "all manner of crises," including those that involve no criminal conduct whatsoever.

3. When a caller uses the 911 system, he or she initiates both a *request* for "direct and immediate intervention" and the *expectation* that emergency services will "arrive and locate" the caller.

4. A 911 call is a "distress call—a cry for help." It may or may not signal a criminal act. The 911 call immediately engages police officers' common-law duty to "preserve the peace, prevent crime, and protect life and property." This common-law duty is legislated in provincial statutes that govern policing, such as s. 42(3) *Police Services Act* of Ontario.

5. Police officers' duty to protect life is a "general duty," not one limited to protecting the lives of crime victims only. It includes other emergencies, such as medical urgencies.

6. A 911 call automatically creates a reasonable and "imperative" belief that the caller is in distress and needs immediate assistance.

7. A disconnected 911 call or any emergency call conveying an "unknown problem" (in other words, that does not include information to define the problem) strengthens the reasonableness and imperativeness of the belief. The use of "imperative" uniquely removes the police officer's discretion about forming the belief. It imposes an obligation to actually believe. It is one of the few sources of law that directs the police to form a specific conclusion, giving them no choice in the matter.

8. Failure to form this belief and respond accordingly impairs the system's effectiveness, undermines its purpose, and constitutes a neglect of duty.

9. The "pressing nature" of a disconnected 911 call tilts the "public safety needs" versus "privacy right" balance in favour of the public safety needs. The concern that a person's life may be in danger outweighs the concern about occupants' right to privacy in their homes.

10. A disconnected 911 call or emergency call concerning an unknown problem authorizes warrantless entry into a house, with force if necessary, *without consent* and *without* a Feeney warrant.

11. The Feeney provisions of ss. 529 and 529.1 C.C. do not apply. A Feeney warrant cannot be obtained to enter for the purpose of investigating an emergency because *two* reasonable grounds beliefs are needed for that warrant—one, that a specific person committed an indictable offence; and,

two, that the person is currently in the specific house. The uncertainty accompanying emergency calls precludes the use of either Feeney warrant.

12. Nor does the warrantless entry exception for exigent circumstances, justified under s. 529.3 C.C., authorize warrantless entry to investigate emergencies (for the reasons established by rule 11).

13. An occupant's refusal or failure to consent in any manner to police entry does not prevent their warrantless entry. Should an occupant, upon the arrival of police, suggest that no emergency exists or that it is not necessary to question other occupants, and should this occupant refuse or fail to consent to police entry, he or she may be disregarded. Any delay by police in entering is "not only *impractical* but *dangerous*." If the 911 caller is in danger and cannot communicate with the dispatcher or police by answering the door upon police arrival, the caller's "only hope is that the *police physically locate* him or her within the residence and come to the caller's aid."

14. The police *cannot* simply take the word of the person who answers the door and says there is no problem inside. There are two reasons for this rule:

    a. The nature and prevalence of domestic abuse. The "sanctity" of the home is often the crime scene. Privacy is one of the hallmarks of the crime. "Privacy cannot trump the safety of all household members." The 911 system provides a method of responding to crises involving domestic violence.

    b. A "break and enter" may be in progress. The person answering the door may be an occupant forced at gunpoint to say "there is no problem," or he or she may be the intruder.

15. The police do not have to walk away from *no response*. A person inside may have had a heart attack and dialed 911, and then been unable to communicate. It may be the case that no one else is home to answer the door, so it would be unreasonable and illogical for police to leave without entering the house and taking all necessary steps to ensure the safety of a 911 caller.

16. In addition to establishing rules 14 and 15, the court actually made it obligatory for police to investigate further regardless of what the person answering the door says. The court stated that it would be "unthinkable to take the word of whoever answers the door without further investigation." By saying this, the court did not simply mean that police *may* disregard a claim of "no problem"; it imposed on them a mandatory obligation to "investigate further" regardless of what the occupant says. The court's terminology strongly suggests that failure to investigate further constitutes neglect of duty.

Three investigative rules emerge from *R. v. Godoy*:

1. A disconnected 911 call, an unknown problem call, and any emergency call about a problem that is not clearly defined—all of these automatically constitute a reasonable grounds belief and a justification for police to enter a house without a warrant and without consent.

2. The common-law authority gives police the power to enter forcibly, without a warrant,

    a. to determine whether an emergency exists, and

    b. to verify an occupant's claim that there is "no problem" inside.

3. To accomplish these two investigative goals, police are justified in conducting a physical *search* of the inside of the house. In the *Godoy* case, a woman was found lying on the floor, sobbing, with a swollen left eye. She told the police that the man who opened the door had hit her. Her condition together with her statement constituted reasonable grounds to arrest the accused. It follows from this that the *search* may lawfully produce observations and evidence that contribute to a reasonable grounds formulation, so long as the search is conducted for the *purpose* of achieving the two goals in rule 2.

Spark of Life and Realistic Leeway Principles

These two principles, both of which are investigative benefits, emerge from "dead body" cases. "Dead body" calls suggest diminished urgency. At the same time, the "spark of life" principle states that the police must assume that a person who is reported dead by a non-medical reporter may be alive.

The "realistic leeway" principle lowers expectations of police officers in life-and-death decisions. The police are not expected to analyze every probability with absolute precision. Leeway is afforded in life-and-death decision-making, justifying urgent and immediate police response.[69] Refer to *R. v. Pillay* (2004) on the accompanying website, www.emp.ca/arcaro/policepowers4E, for the full decision.

Protective Sweep Principle[70]

This rule authorizes warrantless entry into a house when an arrest is made *outside* a house but in close proximity to it, and evidence suggests that a weapon(s) may be inside the house. Refer to *R. v. Golub* (1997) for a full account.

SECTION 529.3(1) C.C.

Section 529.3(1) C.C. authorizes police to enter a house without a warrant for the purpose of making an arrest if exigent circumstances exist. Such a warrantless entry is justified under the following conditions:

- the police officer has reasonable grounds to believe that the person is present in the dwelling-house;
- the conditions exist for obtaining a s. 529.1 C.C. warrant to enter, or
- exigent circumstances exist that make it impracticable to obtain a warrant.

Exigent circumstances are defined in s. 529.3(2) C.C. as circumstances in which a police officer has reasonable grounds

- to suspect that entry into the dwelling-house is necessary to prevent imminent bodily harm or death to any person; or
- to believe that evidence relating to the commission of an indictable offence is present in the house and that entry into the house is necessary to prevent imminent loss or destruction of the evidence.

In either of these circumstances, an officer must follow the procedural rules established in s. 529.4(3) C.C. regarding the appropriate manner of gaining physical entry. The primary issue is whether a prior announcement is required. Section 529.4(3) C.C. provides for two alternatives. Will a prior announcement decrease the risk to persons and evidence, or increase it?

Comparison of CLEC and Section 529.3 C.C.

Despite the differences in scope of information, CLEC and s. 529.3 C.C. have the same basic goals and the same strategy. The goals are preventing death or injury, and preventing destruction or loss of physical evidence. Warrantless entry into a house is the strategy. See Table 8.3 for a comparision.

Table 8.3   CLEC vs. S. 529.3 C.C. Circumstances

	Common-Law Exigent Circumstances	S. 529.3 C.C. Exigent Circumstances
Belief	‣ uncertainty ‣ limited or no information ‣ distress call	‣ certainty ‣ considerable concrete information ‣ RG-IND plus RG in DH
Goal	Prevent death or injury	Prevent death or injury, and destruction or loss of physical evidence
Strategy	Warrantless entry	Warrantless entry

HOT PURSUIT

The S.C.C., in *R. v. Macooh* (1993),[71] defined **hot pursuit** as the continuous pursuit of an offender, conducted with reasonable diligence, in such a way that the pursuit and capture of the offender, along with the commission of the offence, might be considered part of a single transaction. *Hot pursuit* begins with the commission of any classification of offence. A police officer finds the offence being committed, the offender flees, and the officer pursues continuously until apprehension.

The S.C.C. in *R. v. Feeney*, recognized that exigent circumstances exist when police are in hot pursuit of an offender who enters a house, and that police in this situation are authorized to enter the dwelling-house without a warrant.

911 RADIO BROADCASTS/PROTECTING LIFE

The Feeney provisions are relevant to entering a dwelling-house to arrest an offender. *R. v. Godoy* (1999)[72] was the first post-*Feeney* decision relating to the scope of police powers in response to emergency 911 calls or "unknown problem" calls. The uncertainty associated with these calls makes the Feeney authorities inapplicable, both of them. They do not apply because, in the case of these calls, no reasonable grounds exist for believing that a specific person is in a specific residence (and that he or she has committed an indictable offence for which a lawful authority exists to arrest). The Feeney authorities depend on such a reasonable grounds belief.

The S.C.C. addressed with three rulings the investigative problem posed by emergency calls:

1. It recognized the existence of *common-law exigent circumstances* (CLEC) that authorize the warrantless entry of a house. This authority to enter is not in statute law and is separate from Feeney authorities.
2. A disconnected 911 call or unknown problem call are examples of CLEC. They constitute common-law exigent circumstances and justify *forcible* warrantless entry into a dwelling-house.
3. CLEC, including 911 calls, exempts police from the prior announcement rule.

A useful set of procedural guidelines are found in the following case study, which pertains to disconnected 911 calls, where the protection of life and prevention of death or injury are the primary issues.

Case Law

R. v. Godoy (1997)

In emergency cases where a person requires immediate assistance in a dwelling-house, police officers are reliant upon the content of a radio broadcast to form reasonable grounds and make decisions about entering a house to protect potential victims inside the house. Sufficient information reported by a complainant to the dispatcher facilitates the responding officer's decision. However, in some situations a complainant may only be able to dial 911 without verbally conveying information. Consequently, the responding officer may have only a disconnected 911 telephone call as the basis for making a decision about entering a house. No applicable authority is found in statutory law. No case law decisions are directly related to this issue.

To justify entering the house, officers relied on a combination of the common-law authority to protect life and the principles established by the S.C.C. in *R. v. Landry*. Although this issue appears to be a simple common-sense topic, the Ontario Court of Appeal, in *R. v. Godoy*, made a significant ruling relating to police authority to enter a dwelling-house to investigate the nature of an unknown problem following a disconnected 911 call.

- **Issue:** Does a disconnected 911 call constitute reasonable grounds to enter a dwelling-house without a warrant and without consent, to protect life, prevent death, or prevent serious injury?

- **Offences:** "Assaulting a peace officer with intent to resist arrest" and "Assault"

- **Circumstances:** Officers received a radio broadcast of an "unknown problem" at an apartment, originating from a 911 call that was disconnected before the caller spoke. This type of call is of the highest priority for police, second only to a call concerning an "officer down."

  Four officers went to the apartment. They listened at the door before knocking, and heard nothing. After knocking on the door, officers waited a few minutes. Then the door was partially opened by a person, later identified as the accused, who asked them, "What do you want?" An officer asked, "Something has occurred

(continued)

here. Is everything all right?" The accused responded, "Sure, there is no problem." An officer stated, "Well perhaps there is a problem here, and we'd like to find out for ourselves if there is a problem inside the apartment."

The accused tried to close the door. An officer prevented the closing of the door with his foot and entered, followed by the other officers. One officer heard a woman sobbing. The woman was found in a bedroom. Her left eye was swollen and beginning to close from the swelling. She informed the officer that the accused had hit her. The accused was arrested on the basis of the complainant's information and the officer's observation of the injury. The accused resisted the arrest and a struggle ensued. During the struggle, the accused bent an officer's finger and broke it. The accused was charged with assaulting the woman and assaulting the officer with intent to resist arrest.

- **Trial:** The trial judge acquitted the accused of both charges. The reasons were as follows:

  ▸ The accused testified that the victim had slipped and fallen against some furniture.
  ▸ The officers' entry into the apartment was unauthorized, which rendered all subsequent police action illegal. The trial judge ruled that a mere 911 call and a denial of entry did not constitute reasonable grounds to enter without a warrant, as required by case law. Oddly, the judge stated, "I have no doubt that the police officers in this case were acting in what they thought were the best interests of (the complainant) and the question of what would have been sufficient to allow them to enter is difficult to answer, but based on the facts of this case when the accused denied entry to the police officer, which I find as a fact, the police officers were not acting lawfully at the time of the arrest of the accused and therefore cannot be said to have been in the execution of their duty."

  The Crown appealed this decision to a Summary Conviction Appeal Court.

- **Summary Conviction Appeal Court:** The appeal was allowed. The 911 call and denial to enter did constitute reasonable grounds to enter. The appeal judge stated, "One can only speculate as to what the response would have been had the police taken 'no' for an answer only to have it reported later that a homicide had taken place."

  The accused appealed to the Ontario Court of Appeal.

- **Ontario Court of Appeal:** The court unanimously dismissed the accused's appeal for the following reasons:

  ▸ The police had no intention of arresting anyone when they entered the apartment.
  ▸ The reason they entered was to determine the origin and reason for a properly interpreted distress call.
  ▸ They considered it their duty to respond.

  Section 42(1) of the *Police Services Act* of Ontario explains the duties of a police officer to be

  ▸ preserving the peace,
  ▸ preventing crimes and other offences, and
  ▸ providing assistance and encouragement to other persons in preventing crime and offences.

(continued)

■ As regards assisting crime victims, s. 42(3) states that a police officer has the powers and duties of a constable at common law.

The Supreme Court of Canada, in *Dedman v. The Queen* (1981),[73] stated that "at common law, the principal duties of police officers are the preservation of the peace, the prevention of crime, and the protection of life and property." Based on the Supreme Court of Canada's statement, the Ontario Court of Appeal emphasized that a police officer's duty to protect life is a "general duty."

A disconnected 911 call does not constitute reasonable grounds to believe that an indictable offence has been committed. However, it does constitute reasonable grounds to believe that an emergency exists in the apartment and that the caller is in distress. Although the reason for the call was unknown in the case of *R. v. Godoy*, the police were clearly obliged to investigate further.

Police had no time to obtain a warrant to enter, and in any case no warrant exists for entering under these circumstances.

By making a 911 call, an occupant has asked for help and is asking for direct intervention. A compelling public interest depends on prompt and effective police response to a 911 call. The common law is flexible regarding the possible circumstances. Where human life and safety are at stake, it is in the public interest that the police enter the dwelling-house rather than leave and, quite possibly, find out later that an avoidable death had occurred.

In summary, the court concluded that the forced entry in response to a disconnected 911 call was a justifiable use of police powers. The officers had authority to enter the apartment without a warrant and without consent, and they were lawfully executing their duties at the time the officer was assaulted.

The accused appealed to the S.C.C., which dismissed his appeal and ordered a new trial in provincial court. The S.C.C., in endorsing the Ontario Court of Appeal's conclusion that the officers' warrantless entry into the house, was a justifiable use of police powers, established an authority that allows police officers to enter a dwelling-house to investigate the extent of a 911 call. The S.C.C. gave the following reasons and explanations for their ruling, which constitute procedural guidelines for 911 calls:

1. The police clearly have the authority to investigate 911 calls, which justifies their presence on the person's property outside the house. Whether forcible warrantless entry into the house is justified depends on the circumstances of the 911 call.
2. A disconnected 911 call, or an "unknown problem" call, extends the police duty to ascertain the reason for the call, and constitutes reasonable grounds to believe that "the caller is in some distress and requires immediate assistance." This amounts to exigent circumstances.
3. When the accused told the police that there was "no problem," the police had common-law authority to enter the house to verify that there was in fact no emergency. Accepting the accused's statement that there was "no problem" would have contravened their common-law and statutory duty to protect life and safety.
4. The accused's attempt to close the door on the police provided additional justification for forcible entry without a warrant.
5. The privacy of the accused person at the door is secondary to the interest of any person inside the house.
6. After the police entered the house, hearing the wife's crying justified searching the house for her.

(continued)

7. The Feeney case and relevant *Criminal Code* provisions do not apply to this case because the Feeney procedures apply to entry into a house for the specific purpose of making an arrest.
8. The wife's condition, combined with her statement, constituted reasonable grounds to arrest the accused.

■ **Conclusion:** The following procedural guidelines emerge from this decision:

1. A disconnected 911 call, or a radio broadcast stating "911" or "unknown problem," justifies
   ▸ the presence of police on the property,
   ▸ their warrantless, forcible entry into a house, and
   ▸ a search for injured persons.
2. A person who answers the door and informs the police that there is no problem inside cannot prevent their entry into the house. Taking the person's word in this situation and not entering the house to investigate further would constitute a neglect of duty by police.
3. A disconnected 911 call authorizes police officers' warrantless entry into a house to search for injured persons, who may then provide information that will enable police to form reasonable grounds to make an arrest.
4. A disconnected 911 call allows an officer to form reasonable grounds to believe that the caller is in some distress and requires immediate assistance. This constitutes exigent circumstances, which would justify a forcible, warrantless entry with no prior announcement.

EXECUTING AUTHORITY TO ENTER (WARRANTS 1 AND 2)

Executing an authority means to carry it out. Executing the warrants to enter and executing the authority to enter without a warrant require procedures for the following:

▸ method of entry (that is, whether to use force),
▸ time of execution (that is, when the warrant must be executed),
▸ what documents to bring, and
▸ what "other" items can be seized (seizure of evidence).

Use of Force

The *Criminal Code* sections authorizing powers to enter a dwelling-house do not specify the exact circumstances that justify use of force to enter or the degree of force allowed under justifiable circumstances. The use of force and the degree of force depend on the following factors:

1. The terms and conditions authorized on a warrant.
2. The effect that prior announcement will have on life or on evidence, when a warrantless entry is justified.
3. Sections 25–28 C.C.: These provisions are entitled "Protection of Persons Administering and Enforcing the Law." They offer guidelines and general

principles regarding the use of force and the degree of force that may justifiably be used.

Section 25 C.C. justifies the use of force by a police officer in situations where he or she is authorized by law to do anything in the administration or enforcement of the law—for example, where he or she has case law authorization to enter dwelling-houses, or any other place, without a warrant.

The degree of force that may be used is described in general terms in s. 25(1) and s. 26 C.C. Specific guidelines are not given. Section 25(1) C.C. states that "as much force as is necessary for that purpose" may be used. Section 26 C.C. imposes a limit on the force that may be used, stating that excessive force cannot be used and may result in criminal liability. Determinations about how much force to use should be made "according to the nature and quality of the act."[74] The degree of force that is appropriate varies in each case, and common sense will be a proper guide. The appropriate degree of force is one that accomplishes the basic goal of gaining entry.

Finally, when can force be used, and at what point in the procedure? The S.C.C. in the previously noted case law decisions, did not prescribe a particular waiting period before police may forcibly enter. Force may be used immediately after the occupant denies a request to enter, or after police perceive exigent circumstances to exist and cannot gain entry without force—for example, if the door is locked. Any hesitation may be detrimental to personal safety or to the lives of persons inside the house.

4. Section 8 Charter: The key element of this provision, which governs the entire execution of a warrant, is *reasonableness*. It states that the use and degree of force must be reasonable under the circumstances, though it outlines no specific procedures for achieving this.

Time of Execution

Generally, a Justice writes one date on the warrant, the date of issuance. The authorization to enter is valid for that day. If the authorization is an arrest warrant, the police must re-evaluate, immediately before entry, whether they still have reasonable grounds to believe that the offender is in the house. In other words, the police officer(s) must on two occasions prove that reasonable grounds exist to believe the offender is in the house: when the Information to Obtain is presented to the Justice, and immediately before entry.

A separate warrant to enter a house does not require police to re-evaluate the reasonable grounds belief immediately before entry.

However, the execution of both warrants is governed by s. 8 Charter. The entry must be reasonable, which means that if police, just before entry, no longer believe the offender is in the house, they cannot execute the warrant.

Documents

Section 29(1) C.C. obliges police to "have" the warrant, where it is feasible to do so, and to produce it at the occupant's request during the execution of any warrant. In other words, the officer has two obligations:

1. to possess the warrant, and
2. to produce the warrant, when requested.

Police have no obligation to give the accused or any occupant an original or photo-copy of any document.

Seizure of Evidence

Both types of Feeney warrants, as well as the authority for warrantless entry, author-ize entry into a house and a search only for the purpose of making an arrest. They do not authorize the search for and seizure of physical items that constitute evidence.

However, search and seizure authorities do exist that permit the seizure of evi-dence inside the house:

- ▸ section 489(2) C.C.,
- ▸ plain-view doctrine, and
- ▸ search incident to arrest.

All three search and seizure authorities are explained in Chapter 17. The fol-lowing is a summary of the three authorities:

1. *Section 489(2) C.C.* This provision gives the police authority to seize an item without a warrant if the officer:
   - ▸ is lawfully present in a place with or without a warrant, and
   - ▸ believes on reasonable grounds that the item is evidence of any criminal offence—for example, items that appear to have been obtained by or used in the commission of a criminal offence. The offence may be the one for which the offender is being arrested or any unrelated offence.

   To be lawfully in a place, police must enter a house by either
   - ▸ Feeney warrant,
   - ▸ warrantless authority under s. 529.3 C.C., or
   - ▸ consent.

   Section 489(2) C.C. does not specify by what means the evidence may be found. No reference is made to the process of searching for the item. The absence of any such reference suggests that only items in plain view may be seized.
2. *Plain-view doctrine.* This case law authority authorizes the police to seize any item found in plain view when they are lawfully on any premises, whether by means of a warrant, without a warrant, or by consent. "Plain view" refers to the inadvertent finding of an item. "Inadvertent" means that the item was not deliberately searched for and then found—that is, the police had no prior knowledge that the item was in the place.[75]
3. *Search incident to arrest.* This is a common-law authority that permits the police to automatically search the following:
   - ▸ the arrested person,[76] after the person has been lawfully arrested inside a house or any other place; and
   - ▸ the immediate surroundings.[77]

The arrested person may be searched immediately. This means that a reasonable grounds belief does not have to be formed, prior to the search, that the offender has an item that may be seized. Any item may be seized from the offender that

- ▸ is evidence of any offence, whether or not the offence is related to the one for which the offender has been arrested;
- ▸ may cause injury to any person, including the offender; or
- ▸ may help the offender escape.

Afterward, police may search the "immediate surroundings" of the place of arrest without a search warrant. The *immediate surroundings* include the entire room where the arrest was made. But it does not include the entire house or premises.[78]

TELEWARRANT—SECTION 529.5 C.C.

Section 529.5 C.C., entitled "Telewarrant," is a *solution* to a problem that may arise when police are applying for a Feeney warrant. The following principles are derived from this provision.

1. All Feeney warrants require an application—no exceptions.
2. When *it is practicable* for the officer applying for the Feeney warrant to appear personally before a judge or Justice, the officer must do so.
3. Section 529.5 C.C. *exempts* officers from the personal appearance rule.
4. Section 529.5 C.C. does *not* exempt officers from the application process itself.
5. A personal appearance, during the application process, may be replaced by a telephone call or by "other means of telecommunication." Again, the officer may submit the application by telephone or by other telecommunications means, but is never exempt from submitting it altogether.
6. The only way to avoid applying for a Feeney warrant is by employing the warrantless entry authority, justified by exigent circumstances.
7. The recognized justification for an officer's submitting an application by telephone or by other means rather than in person is that circumstances make a personal appearance *impracticable*.
8. *Impracticable* and *emergency* represent two different concepts. *Impracticable* means that no emergency exists—that is, there is time to obtain a warrant but no reasonable way to personally appear before a judge or Justice (for example, if the officer is in a rural area, distant from the Justice). *Emergency* refers to a public safety risk where there is no time to obtain a warrant, circumstances that eliminate the need for the application.
9. Consequently, an emergency does not justify a telewarrant—it justifies *no* warrant.

In summary, the "telewarrant" provision solves the problem that arises when a police officer has time to obtain a warrant but not enough time to apply for it personally—as when, for instance, excessive distance separates the police officer from the Justice. It does not eliminate the need to apply for the warrant.

Elements

The five elements of the telewarrant provision, organized sequentially, are as follows:

1. if a peace officer believes that it would be *impracticable* in the circumstances
2. *to appear personally* before a judge or Justice
3. to make an *application* for a warrant under s. 529.5 or an authorization under s. 529 or s. 529.4,
4. the warrant or authorization may be issued on an *Information* submitted by *telephone* or other means of telecommunication
5. for that purpose, s. 487.1 applies with any modifications that the circumstances require, to the warrant or authorization

The telewarrant application process involves a three-stage path whereby the police officer meets the requirements of the Feeney warrant, explains why applying for the warrant in person is impracticable, then submits the application in accordance with the procedures explained in s. 487.1 C.C.

Figure 8.4 outlines this three-stage path.

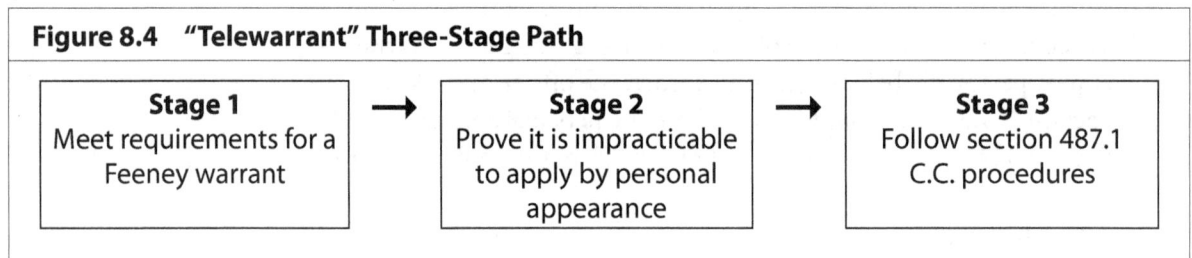

Figure 8.4   "Telewarrant" Three-Stage Path

| **Stage 1**
Meet requirements for a Feeney warrant | → | **Stage 2**
Prove it is impracticable to apply by personal appearance | → | **Stage 3**
Follow section 487.1 C.C. procedures |

Section 487.1 C.C.

Fifteen subsections govern the issuance and execution procedure for telewarrants (see Table 8.4).

Table 8.4   Other Provisions Respecting Search Warrants

Telewarrants	**487.1** (1) Where a peace officer believes that an indictable offence has been committed and that it would be impracticable to appear personally before a Justice to make application for a warrant in accordance with section 256 or 487, the peace officer may submit an Information on oath by telephone or other means of telecommunication to a Justice designated for the purpose by the chief judge of the provincial court having jurisdiction in the matter.
Information submitted by telephone	(2) An Information submitted by telephone or other means of telecommunication, other than a means of telecommunication that produces a writing, shall be on oath and shall be recorded verbatim by the Justice, who shall, as soon as practicable, cause to be filed, with the clerk of the court for the territorial division in which the warrant is intended for execution, the record or a transcription of it, certified by the Justice as to time, date and contents.

Information submitted by other means of telecommunication

(2.1) The Justice who receives an Information submitted by a means of telecommunication that produces a writing shall, as soon as practicable, cause to be filed, with the clerk of the court for the territorial division in which the warrant is intended for execution, the Information certified by the Justice as to time and date of receipt.

Administration of oath

(3) For the purposes of subsection (2), an oath may be administered by telephone or other means of telecommunication.

Alternative to oath

(3.1) A peace officer who uses a means of telecommunication referred to in subsection (2.1) may, instead of swearing an oath, make a statement in writing stating that all matters contained in the Information are true to his or her knowledge and belief and such a statement is deemed to be a statement made under oath.

Contents of Information

(4) An Information submitted by telephone or other means of telecommunication shall include

(*a*) a statement of the circumstances that make it impracticable for the peace officer to appear personally before a Justice;

(*b*) a statement of the indictable offence alleged, the place or premises to be searched and the items alleged to be liable to seizure;

(*c*) a statement of the peace officer's grounds for believing that items liable to seizure in respect of the offence alleged will be found in the place or premises to be searched; and

(*d*) a statement as to any prior application for a warrant under this section or any other search warrant, in respect of the same matter, of which the peace officer has knowledge.

Issuing warrant

(5) A Justice referred to in subsection (1) who is satisfied that an Information submitted by telephone or other means of telecommunication

(*a*) is in respect of an indictable offence and conforms to the requirements of subsection (4),

(*b*) discloses reasonable grounds for dispensing with an Information presented personally and in writing, and

(*c*) discloses reasonable grounds, in accordance with subsection 256(1) or paragraph 487(1)(*a*), (*b*) or (*c*), as the case may be, for the issuance of a warrant in respect of an indictable offence, may issue a warrant to a peace officer conferring the same authority respecting search and seizure as may be conferred by a warrant issued by a Justice before whom the peace officer appears personally pursuant to subsection 256(1) or 487(1), as the case may be, and may require that the warrant be executed within such time period as the Justice may order.

Formalities respecting warrant and facsimiles

(6) Where a Justice issues a warrant by telephone or other means of telecommunication, other than a means of telecommunication that produces a writing,

(*a*) the Justice shall complete and sign the warrant in Form 5.1, noting on its face the time, date and place of issuance;

(*b*) the peace officer, on the direction of the Justice, shall complete, in duplicate, a facsimile of the warrant in Form 5.1, noting on its face the name of the issuing Justice and the time, date and place of issuance; and

(*c*) the Justice shall, as soon as practicable after the warrant has been issued, cause the warrant to be filed with the clerk of the court for the territorial division in which the warrant is intended for execution.

Issuance of warrant where telecommunication produces writing

(6.1) Where a Justice issues a warrant by a means of telecommunication that produces a writing,

(*a*) the Justice shall complete and sign the warrant in Form 5.1, noting on its face the time, date and place of issuance;

(*b*) the Justice shall transmit the warrant by the means of telecommunication to the peace officer who submitted the Information and the copy of the warrant received by the peace officer is deemed to be a facsimile within the meaning of paragraph (6)(*b*);

(*c*) the peace officer shall procure another facsimile of the warrant; and

(*d*) the Justice shall, as soon as practicable after the warrant has been issued, cause the warrant to be filed with the clerk of the court for the territorial division in which the warrant is intended for execution.

Providing facsimile

(7) A peace officer who executes a warrant issued by telephone or other means of telecommunication, other than a warrant issued pursuant to subsection 256(1), shall, before entering the place or premises to be searched or as soon as practicable thereafter, give a facsimile of the warrant to any person present and ostensibly in control of the place or premises.

Affixing facsimile

(8) A peace officer who, in any unoccupied place or premises, executes a warrant issued by telephone or other means of telecommunication, other than a warrant issued pursuant to subsection 256(1), shall, on entering the place or premises or as soon as practicable thereafter, cause a facsimile of the warrant to be suitably affixed in a prominent place within the place or premises.

Report of peace officer

(9) A peace officer to whom a warrant is issued by telephone or other means of telecommunication shall file a written report with the clerk of the court for the territorial division in which the warrant was intended for execution as soon as practicable but within a period not exceeding seven days after the warrant has been executed, which report shall include

(*a*) a statement of the time and date the warrant was executed or, if the warrant was not executed, a statement of the reasons why it was not executed;

(*b*) a statement of the things, if any, that were seized pursuant to the warrant and the location where they are being held; and (*c*) a statement of the things, if any, that were seized in addition to the things mentioned in the warrant and the location where they are being held, together with a statement of the peace officer's grounds for believing that those additional things had been obtained by, or used in, the commission of an offence.

Bringing before Justice

(10) The clerk of the court shall, as soon as practicable, cause the report, together with the Information and the warrant to which it pertains, to be brought before a Justice to be dealt with, in respect of the things seized referred to in the report, in the same manner as if the things were seized pursuant to a warrant issued, on an Information presented personally by a peace officer, by that Justice or another Justice for the same territorial division.

Proof of authorization

(11) In any proceeding in which it is material for a court to be satisfied that a search or seizure was authorized by a warrant issued by telephone or other means of telecommunication, the absence of the Information or warrant, signed by the Justice and carrying on its face a notation of the time, date and place of issuance, is, in the absence of evidence to the contrary, proof that the search or seizure was not authorized by a warrant issued by telephone or other means of telecommunication.

Duplicates and facsimiles acceptable

(12) A duplicate or a facsimile of an Information or a warrant has the same probative force as the original for the purposes of subsection (11).

SUMMARY

Earlier chapters taught *when* an arrest (with or without a warrant) is authorized. This chapter explained arrest, with or without a warrant, in relation to *where* the arrest is made. The place of the arrest is divided into "dwelling-house" and "non-dwelling-house." Feeney warrants apply only to dwelling-houses.

The objective in carrying out the arrest of an offender is to achieve a balance between preventing Charter violations and self-protection. The objective of self-protection is self-explanatory. The goal of preventing Charter violations is to ensure the admissibility of evidence obtained after the arrest. The next chapter explains how to achieve these objectives.

ENDNOTES

1. *R. v. Golub* (1997), 117 C.C.C. (3d) 193, at para. 45 (Ont. C.A.).
2. *R. v. Tessling* (2004), 189 C.C.C. (3d) 129, at para. 18 (S.C.C.).
3. Section 2 C.C.
4. *R. v. Golub*, supra note 1, at paras. 44-45.
5. Ibid.
6. *R. v. Feeney* (1997), 115 C.C.C. (3d) 129 (S.C.C.).
7. Section 529.4 C.C.
8. *R. v. Evans* (1996), 104 C.C.C. (3d) 23 (S.C.C.).
9. Section 2 C.C.

10. Section 348(3) C.C.
11. *R. v. Grant* (1993), 84 C.C.C. (3d) 173 (S.C.C.).
12. *R. v. Guiboche* (2004), 183 C.C.C. (3d) 361 (Man. C.A.).
13. *R. v. Evans*, supra note 8.
14. Ibid.
15. Ibid.
16. Ibid.
17. *R. v. Edwards* (1996), 104 C.C.C. (3d) 136 (S.C.C.).
18. *R. v. Evans*, supra note 8.
19. Ibid.
20. Ibid.
21. Ibid.
22. *R. v. Bushman* (1968), 4 C.R.N.S. (B.C.C.A.), as in *R. v. Evans*, supra note 8.
23. *R. v. Evans*, supra note 8.
24. Ibid.
25. Ibid.
26. *Hunter et al. v. Southam Inc.* (1984), 14 C.C.C. (3d) 97, at 160 (S.C.C.), as in *R. v. Evans*, supra note 8.
27. *R. v. Evans*, supra note 8.
28. Ibid.
29. Ibid.
30. *R. v. Duarte* (1990), 53 C.C.C. (3d) 1 (S.C.C.).
31. *R. v. Evans*, supra note 8.
32. Ibid.
33. Ibid.
34. Ibid.
35. *R. v. Guiboche*, supra note 12.
36. The Law Reform Commission of Canada. Working Paper 30: "Police Powers—Search and Seizure in Criminal Law Enforcement (1983)," at 52, as in *R. v. Mercer* (1992), 70 C.C.C. (3d) 180, at 187 (Ont. C.A.).
37. *R. v. Wills* (1992), 70 C.C.C. (3d) 529 (Ont. C.A.).
38. Ibid.
39. *R. v. Guiboche*, supra note 12.
40. Ibid.
41. *R. v. Edwards*, supra note 17.
42. Ibid.
43. House of Commons, *Debates*, October 31, 1997. http://www.parl.gc.ca/36/1/parlbus/chambus/house/debates/025_1997-10-31/han025_1000.
44. Ibid.
45. *R. v. Tessling*, supra note 2.
46. Ibid.
47. Ibid.
48. Ibid.
49. Ibid.
50. Lord H. Broughman, *Historical Sketches of Statesman Who Flourished in the Time of George III* (1855), vol. 1, at p. 42, as in *R. v. Tessling*, supra note 2.
51. *R. v. Tessling*, supra note 2.
52. *R. v. Feeney*, supra note 6.

53. *R. v. Petri* (2003), 171 C.C.C. (3d) 567 (Man. C.A.).

54. *Semayne's Case* (1558–1774), All E.R. Rep. 63 (1604).

55. *Eccles v. Bourque* (1974), 19 C.C.C. (2d) 129 (S.C.C.).

56. *R. v. Landry* (1986), 25 C.C.C. (3d) 1 (S.C.C.).

57. *R. v. Macooh* (1993), 82 C.C.C. (3d) 481 (S.C.C.).

58. *R. v. Feeney*, supra note 6.

59. *R. v. Godoy* (1999), 131 C.C.C. (3d) 129 (S.C.C.).

60. *R. v. Feeney*, supra note 6.

61. Ibid.

62. House of Commons, *Debates*, October 31, 1997, supra note 43.

63. Section 529(1) C.C.

64. Section 529(2) C.C.

65. Section 507(4) C.C.

66. Section 529(1) C.C.

67. Section 529(2) C.C.

68. *R. v. Godoy*, supra note 59.

69. *R. v. Pillay* (2004), 119 C.R.R. (2d) 346 (Ont. S.C.).

70. *R. v. Golub*, supra note 1.

71. *R. v. Macooh*, supra note 57.

72. *R. v. Godoy*, supra note 59.

73. *Dedman v. The Queen* (1985), 20 C.C.C. (3d) 97 (S.C.C.).

74. Section 25(1) C.C.

75. *R. v. Shea* (1982), 1 C.C.C. (3d) 316 (Ont. H.C.J.).

76. *Cloutier v. Langlois* (1990), 53 C.C.C. (3d) 257 (S.C.C.).

77. *R. v. Smellie* (1994), 95 C.C.C. (3d) 9 (B.C.C.A.).

78. Ibid.

CHAPTER 9

Making the Arrest: Use of Force and Preventing Charter Violations

LEARNING OUTCOMES

The student will learn

- How to interpret use-of-force provisions so as to maximize self-protection during an arrest

- How to interpret s. 24(2) Charter

- How to interpret and apply s. 10(a) Charter—reason for arrest

- How to interpret and apply s. 10(b) Charter—right to counsel

- How to interpret and apply the "caution"

- How to prevent Charter violations during an arrest

COMMENTARY

This chapter starts with a commentary—the most important commentary in this book.

The phrase "you're under arrest" is capable of bringing out the darkest response from the person it is addressed to. The reason is very simple—being arrested is unpleasant for the offender, a negative experience that changes his or her life for the worse. The potential for conflict between police and offender is present during every single arrest. For the arrested person, there is nothing at all positive about this experience. Factor in the arrested person's perception that the arresting officer's attitude is condescending, and you have an explosive situation. People are naturally inclined to fight for their freedom.

There are two well-documented facts about policing: (1) it is one of the most dangerous jobs in the world; and (2) police officers have been killed or injured in the line of duty. There have always been violent offenders who will be violent toward the police, and there always will be.

This chapter covers the topic commonly known as "use of force." However, the actual phrase "use of force" is not used extensively, because it is misleading. It is misleading because it suggests that the use of force is somehow automatically allowed. This is not the case. The phrase "use of force" really represents the following: (1) *justified* use of force, and (2) *protection*. The need to qualify the phrase "use of force" with the words *justified* and *protection* is a very important principle for police officers.

The *Criminal Code* offers no *concrete* guidelines about how to apply the use of force. Instead, it offers only abstract provisions. Use-of-force laws are outlined in the *Criminal Code*'s account of a cluster of offences ranging from ss. 25–33 C.C. These offences go under six different headings, none of which is "use of force." The words *protection* and *defence* occur in some of these headings. There are countless criminal and civil case law decisions that provide valuable point of reference comparisons for police officers learning about the use of force. That is why case law research about this topic is compulsory. The accompanying website, **www.emp.ca/ arcaro/policepowers4E**, includes an extensive and ongoing account of case law research into the use of force.

Always remember how broad the definition of assault is. Whenever you put your hands on someone or communicate a "threatening act or gesture," you have committed the *actus reus* of assault. In other words, the use of force involves the same physical act that is involved in a criminal offense. When you commit the *actus reus* during your tour of duty, the question becomes one of *mens rea* (intent). Did you have lawful justification for using force? If not, you are criminally responsible—you committed a crime. You may be charged, convicted, and go to jail. Conversely, if you did have justification, you had no intention of committing assault, and committed no crime.

Justification is the concept most important to police officers in connection with the use of force. By *justification* we mean an explanation supported with *concrete* reasons. Every act of physical force must be justified regardless of how minimal it is.

Never forget two phrases that are vital to "use of force" provisions: (1) tacit knowledge and (2) deliberate reps. **Tacit knowledge** is the most important of your cognitive goals in front-line policing. It means, in effect, "experience-based expertise." Having tacit knowledge allows you to sort rapidly through extensive information and, judging from your experience, select the best solution to a problem in a specific situation. Tacit knowledge allows you to see the big picture instead of the individual parts. It is the key to making correct "use of force" decisions. *Deliberate reps* is a kind of training that allows you to develop tacit knowledge. It involves the practical application of your policing skills in increasingly challenging situations. Ordinary practice does not make perfect—deliberate practice *strives* to approach it.[1]

The only people qualified to teach "use of force" tactics are certified trainers in the area. As a police officer in training, you will learn the fundamentals from these experts. Take their training seriously.

From the moment you are hired as a police officer, you forfeit discretion about your level of physical fitness. Police officers have to be athletes. *Anima sana in corpore sano* is Latin for "a sound mind and a sound body." Visit **www.emp.ca/fitness** to access a free strength training and conditioning program that accompanies *Fitness* *and Lifestyle Management for Law Enforcement*, 3rd ed., by Nancy Wagner Wisotzki. Peak strength and conditioning need to be life-long goals for police officers.

INTRODUCTION

Front-line policing is dangerous. Making an arrest is not a simple job; it is inherently oriented toward conflict. Some arrested people cooperate, some do not. The actual act of making an arrest requires of police various decisions governed by two general objectives: (1) self-protection, (2) preventing Charter violations to ensure the admissibility of evidence.

Now that you have learned *when* and *where* a lawful arrest may be made, the next topic is *how* a lawful arrest may be made. Making a lawful arrest involves a 15-step procedure.

This procedure is not neatly listed in any source of law. Instead it is scattered throughout the *Canadian Charter of Rights and Freedoms* (Charter), the *Criminal Code*, and case law. The 15 steps represent the maximum number of *general* duties potentially associated with making an arrest; they do not cover every possible situation.

The 15 steps are intended to prevent

- ▸ death/bodily harm, and
- ▸ exclusion of evidence at a trial.

Part 1 (steps 1–4) of the 15 steps addresses problems relating to physical violence by the offender, including the following: resisting arrest, assaulting an officer, escaping custody, use of force. Part 2 (steps 5–10) includes the *instructional components*— that is, the legal instructions you have to communicate to an arrested person. There are more of these instructions when the arrested person is a young offender. The instructional components include but are not limited to the following: (1) reason for arrest, (2) right to counsel, and (3) caution. These three instructional components are the subject of many case law decisions. For that reason, it is impossible to include in this chapter every case law–based rule concerning the instructional component of arrest. However, as a solution, the accompanying website, **www.emp.ca/arcaro/ policepowers4E**, includes extensive and ongoing case law related to this area.

The 15-step procedure for making an arrest is as follows:

1. Identify yourself as a police officer.
2. Tell the accused that he or she is under arrest.
3. Take physical custody of the accused person.
4. Search the accused immediately.
5. Procedure for simultaneous arrest of young and adult offender.
6. Inform the accused about the reason for the arrest.
7. Produce the warrant if applicable.
8. Inform the accused of his or her right to counsel.
9. Prove that the accused understood the right to counsel in its entirety.
10. Read the caution to the accused.
11. Allow the accused reasonable time to decide whether to exercise the right to counsel.

12. Provide a reasonable opportunity for the accused to invoke the right to counsel.
13. Question the accused after right to counsel is exercised.
14. Procedure when accused waives the right to counsel.
15. Procedure when accused invokes the right to counsel and then changes his or her mind—the Prosper warning.

RATIONALE FOR THE 15 STEPS

Part 1: Self-Protection—Relevant Provisions

Many unwanted consequences can occur while you are making an arrest. A number of laws address risk prevention and the dangers of violence during arrest, but the four general provisions most closely related to the 15 steps are the ones concerned with

1. resisting arrest,
2. assaulting a peace officer,
3. escaping custody, and
4. ss. 25–27, 34–38, 40–42 C.C. (use of force).

Part 2: Instructional Components—Relevant Provisions

After you make an arrest, you have to instruct the arrested person about a number of matters. There are five provisions relevant to these instructions:

1. Section 10(a) Charter—reason for arrest,
2. Section 10(b) Charter—right to counsel,
3. Section 7 Charter—right to remain silent,
4. Formal caution, and
5. Section 24(2) Charter—admissibility of evidence.

Section 10 Charter states the following:

Everyone has the right on arrest or detention
    (a) to be informed promptly of the reasons therefor;
    (b) to retain and instruct counsel without delay and to be informed of that right: and
    (c) to have the validity of the detention determined by way of habeas corpus and to be released if the detention is not lawful.

Section 7 Charter states the following:

Everyone has the right to life, liberty and security of the person and the right not to be deprived thereof except in accordance with the principles of fundamental justice.

The prescribed formal caution is as follows:

"Do you wish to say anything in answer to the charge? You are not obliged to say anything unless you wish to do so, but whatever you say may be given in evidence."

Sections 514 and 495 C.C. authorize the police to arrest with or without a warrant. When either type of an arrest is made, the police are obliged to *instruct* the arrested person about certain matters. The key point is that the arrested person must be given this information, even if he or she may be expected to know it from past experience. What this means, practically speaking, is that you will have to communicate a certain volume of information to the offender immediately after the arrest is made, even as you are trying to ensure your own safety. The logistical challenge of imparting the compulsory instructions to the arrested person while watching out for potential violence is the reality of the front-line policing environment. Despite the threat of actual or potential violence, and despite the distracted state of the accused, the onus is on you to instruct the arrested person and make sure he or she *understands* your instructions.

Most of the information you must convey concerns the reason for the arrest, the accused's right to counsel, and the caution. Informing the accused about the first two—reason and right to counsel (RTC)—is a statutory requirement. This means that you have no discretion; you must inform an arrested person of both. Failure to do so is a Charter violation. The requirement to give the accused the reason for the arrest emerges from s. 10(a) Charter. The RTC requirement emerges from s. 10(b) Charter. Both these sections have a dual purpose: each provides the right to the arrested person while obligating the police to inform that person of the right. The requirement concerning the **caution** is different. The caution relates to the arrested person's right to remain silent. The caution is not a statutory requirement in Canada. It is strongly recommended, though, and can be a significant investigative benefit insofar as it helps prove that an arrested person's statements were voluntarily made.

The caution warns an arrested person that he or she does not have to answer any questions or speak to the police. In other words, it informs the arrested person of his or her right to silence. Keep in mind the following, however:

- ▸ The "formal" caution does not include the phrase "right to silence."
- ▸ Section 7 Charter gives arrested persons the right to silence, but there are two important facts in this regard:
    1. The actual phrase "right to silence" is not in s. 7 Charter. It is case law that mandates that the right to silence is included in the section.
    2. Section 7 Charter does not mandate that the police inform the arrested person of the right to silence. Section 7 Charter *gives* the right to silence, but does not oblige the police to inform an arrested person of that right. The Canadian right to silence is considerably different than the American version, well publicized in the movies. Canadian law does not have a warning like the US Miranda warning, which uses the phrase, "You have to right to remain silent." Canadian law recommends the caution as a way of helping you prove that statements made by an arrested person were voluntarily made.

Section 24(2) Charter states:

Where, in proceedings under subsection (1), a court concludes that evidence was obtained in a manner that infringed or denied any rights or freedoms guaranteed by this *Charter*, the evidence shall be excluded if it is established that, having regard to all the circumstances, the admission of it in the proceedings would bring the administration of justice into disrepute.

This is the primary rule that governs the admissibility of evidence. A detailed article that comprehensively explains s. 24(2) Charter is included in the website that accompanies this text, **www.emp.ca/arcaro/policepowers4E**.

The following 10 rules summarize s. 24(2) Charter:

1. Section 24(2) is applied only after a Charter violation has occurred and evidence of that violation has been obtained. If no Charter violation has occurred, s. 24(2) does not apply and the evidence is admissible.
2. If a Charter violation is deemed to have occurred, a trial judge has *discretion* to exclude or admit evidence obtained afterward. This means the following: (a) a Charter violation does not make evidence *automatically inadmissible*; (b) evidence obtained after a Charter violation may still be admissible. The key point is discretion. The judge may admit or exclude the evidence.
3. The determining factor is the effect of the admission or exclusion of the evidence on the reputation of the criminal justice system.
4. The landmark cases that offer concrete guidelines regarding s. 24(2) Charter are *R. v. Collins* (1987) and *R. v. Stillman* (1997). Both are S.C.C. decisions.
5. The case of *R. v. Collins* (1987) identified three factors affecting admissibility of evidence under s. 24(2) Charter:
   a. trial fairness,
   b. the severity of the Charter violation, and
   c. how far the exclusion of the evidence will affect the reputation of the administration of justice.[2]
6. The case of *R. v. Stillman* (1997) produced the two-step model used to determine trial fairness with respect to evidence. The first step classifies the evidence obtained as either *conscriptive* or *non-conscriptive*.[3]
7. **Conscriptive evidence** is evidence by which a suspect is compelled to incriminate himself—for example, a confession or a bodily substance, such as a breath sample. Essentially, conscriptive evidence is evidence that emerges from a suspect's body, such as words or substances.
8. **Non-conscriptive evidence** is evidence in whose creation the accused was not compelled to participate—for example, a murder weapon. Non-conscriptive evidence consists of physical items that do not emerge from the suspect.
9. **Derivative evidence** is physical evidence that is discovered as the result of conscriptive evidence—for example, a murder weapon that is discovered because of a suspect's confession.
10. The general admissibility rules that emerged from case law with respect to s. 24(2) Charter are as follows:
    a. Conscriptive evidence obtained through a Charter violation is usually inadmissible.
    b. Non-conscriptive evidence obtained through a Charter violation is usually admissible.

    The key word in both rules is "usually." It does not mean "automatically." This means that Charter violations more negatively effect evidence based on confessions and bodily substances than they do evidence based on physical items such as guns. Here is the final key point: Your goal is to *prevent* Charter violations. With no Charter violation, *s. 24(2) does not apply.*

THE SECTION 24(2) PENDULUM SWING

For years following the *Stillman* case, an extreme pattern developed in the courts with respect to admissibility. Evidence obtained after a Charter violation was almost always excluded. An extensive case law review has shown that the judicial pendulum has swung the other way and that a more balanced approach has been adopted. This trend began in 2004 and was evident in *R. v. Harrison* (2008)—a more flexible approach to s. 24(2) Charter that has resulted in more evidence being admitted.[4] The *Harrison* case is the most important case since *Stillman*, because evidence that was seized after a "flagrant" Charter violation was admitted. This case is the best illustration of how s. 24(2) is supposed to apply, meaning that the severity of the offence is supposed to be weighed against the severity of the Charter violation before the evidence is ruled inadmissible. In the *Harrison* case, the offence of trafficking narcotics was considered to be far more severe than the Charter violation of which the police in the case were guilty. Refer to the accompanying website, **www.emp.ca/arcara/policepowers4E**, for more discussion of *R. v. Harrison* and for the case law review that explains the pendulum swing with respect to admissibility.

ARREST: PREVENTING CHARTER VIOLATIONS

Figure 9.1 outlines the 15-step continuum.

Figure 9.1   15-Step Continuum

Authority to Arrest: With or Without a Warrant:
s. 495 C.C. or s. 514 C.C. requirements

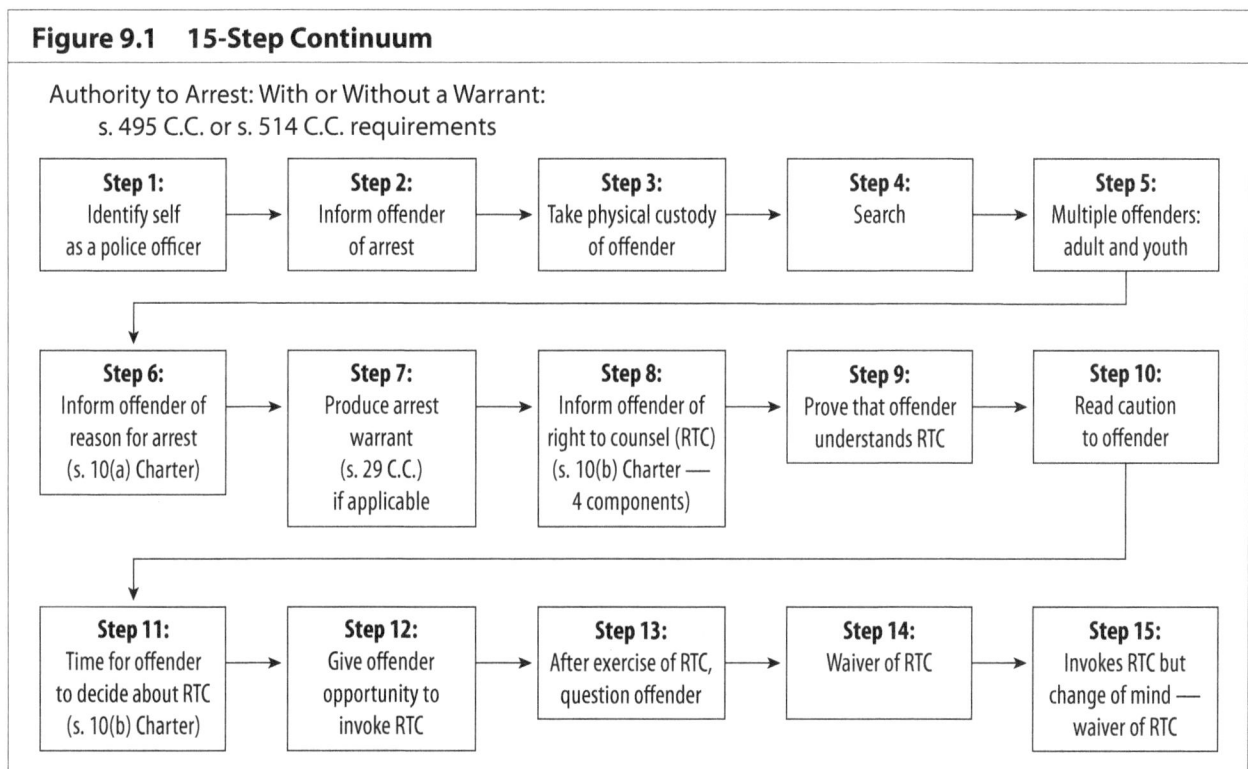

| Step 1:
Identify self
as a police officer | Step 2:
Inform offender
of arrest | Step 3:
Take physical custody
of offender | Step 4:
Search | Step 5:
Multiple offenders:
adult and youth |

| Step 6:
Inform offender of
reason for arrest
(s. 10(a) Charter) | Step 7:
Produce arrest
warrant
(s. 29 C.C.)
if applicable | Step 8:
Inform offender of
right to counsel (RTC)
(s. 10(b) Charter —
4 components) | Step 9:
Prove that offender
understands RTC | Step 10:
Read caution
to offender |

| Step 11:
Time for offender
to decide about RTC
(s. 10(b) Charter) | Step 12:
Give offender
opportunity to
invoke RTC | Step 13:
After exercise of RTC,
question offender | Step 14:
Waiver of RTC | Step 15:
Invokes RTC but
change of mind —
waiver of RTC |

Step 1: Identify Yourself as a Police Officer

An officer should identify him- or herself, as soon as practicable, as being a police officer, especially when not wearing a police uniform. Such self-identification should prove beyond reasonable doubt that the accused knew that a police officer was making the arrest. This proof becomes significant if the accused resists arrest or assaults the police officer, because it is crucial for prosecuting both these offences that the accused knew the officer's occupation.

A police uniform may be sufficient circumstantial evidence to prove the officer's occupation, but even a uniformed officer should identify him- or herself as a police officer, to confirm this fact in the accused person's mind. The identification may be accomplished with a simple oral statement: "I am a police officer with [name of police service]." Where it is practicable to do so, you should also produce a badge for viewing.

Identifying oneself as a police officer is not a statutory or case law requirement for making a lawful arrest. Neither the case law definition of *arrest* nor the *Criminal Code* states specifically that a police officer must inform a person about his or her occupation *before* a lawful arrest can be made. The lawfulness of the arrest does not depend on whether the arresting officer informed the accused of his or her name and occupation. In summary, officers frequently encounter situations where they must arrest a violent offender immediately. It must be emphasized that officers in this situation are not expected to pause and identify themselves before the arrest. Fail to identify will not affect the lawfulness of the arrest. It may be a factor if there is a charge of "Assault police" or "Escape lawful custody."

Step 2: Inform Accused of Arrest

No federal statute states that an accused must be told, "You're under arrest." Therefore, it is not a statutory requirement. However, the Supreme Court of Canada, in *R. v. Whitfield* (1969), stated that a person being arrested must be informed that he or she is being arrested.[5] Consequently, saying "You're under arrest" is a case law requirement.

It must be remembered that an arrest or detention may be made without an officer actually telling an accused that he or she is under arrest. The S.C.C., in *R. v. Therens* (1985), stated that when a police officer makes a demand or direction to a person, or when a psychological compulsion exists within a person that his or her freedom has been removed, a detention has occurred.[6]

Step 3: Take Physical Custody of Accused

Taking physical custody of an arrested person by holding or touching is a recommended procedure. No statute or case law mandates that a police officer take actual physical custody of a person in order to make a proper arrest. In other words, lawful arrest does not require actual physical custody.

Taking hold of an arrested person has two advantages, however:

1. *Accused person's knowledge.* It helps prove that the accused knew he or she was the person who was intended to be arrested. This becomes important when the accused is in a group of people and it is unclear who has been

told, "You are under arrest." Being able to prove the accused knew he or she was under arrest becomes crucial should the accused commit the offences of "Assault with the intent to resist arrest"[7] or "Escape custody."[8]

2. *Self-protection.* Taking hold of the arrested person also provides the officer with a degree of personal safety, and it prevents the accused from escaping by restricting his or her movement.

CONCEPT OF "ORDINARY FORCE"

Taking hold of an offender constitutes use of force. All use of force has to be justified. This minimal force is justified by the S.C.C. decision *R. v. Whitfield* (1969). Merely taking hold of a person is classified as "ordinary force." The *Whitfield* decision stated that the use of ordinary force in arresting a cooperative person is justified by s. 25 C.C.[9] This section justifies a police officer's using as much force as is necessary when doing anything to enforce the law, such as making a lawful arrest. In other words, taking hold of a person's arm and saying "You're under arrest" constitutes **justified use of force**.

CONCEPT OF "HANDCUFFING"

Handcuffing is another use of force. There is no section in the *Criminal Code* devoted to the topic of handcuffing. The word handcuffing is not used in the *Criminal Code*.

Handcuffing is not classified as "ordinary force." Like all use of force, it has to be justified. There is no blanket rule that allows handcuffing in every arrest. A review of the case law literature shows the following:

1. Automatic handcuffing is not lawful. This applies to handcuffing at the time of arrest and handcuffing in the court room, for security purposes.
2. Handcuffing needs justification. Concrete reasons have to be given. They do not have to be extensive or complicated, but you can't simply say, "I automatically handcuffed him." Always record your concrete reasons for handcuffing in your notebook, occurrence reports, and testimony.

The accompanying website, **www.emp.ca/arcaro/policepowers4E**, includes an extensive and ongoing review of criminal and civil cases related to handcuffing. This is a valuable part of the textbook. It's more than just a learning tool. It explains the difference between justified and unjustified use of force, and this could protect you against civil and criminal liability.

The S.C.C. created the following guidelines for taking physical custody of an offender:

1. Any physical custody, such as actual seizure, holding, or touching, with the intent to detain, does constitute an arrest.
2. A person who accompanies an officer who makes only "a mere pronouncing of words of arrest,"[10] without taking physical custody, is under arrest.
3. It is not necessary to touch or hold the person being arrested. After a person has been told he or she is under arrest, the person is "under a legal obligation to submit to the lawful arrest."[11]

The *Whitfield* case concerned a person who resisted an arrest when the officer used words only and did not touch the offender when arresting. An officer stopped the accused, who had been driving a car. The officer knew that the accused was wanted in connection with a valid arrest warrant. The officer approached the car and the accused remained in the driver's seat. The officer told the accused, "I have a warrant for you. Stop the car and shut off the ignition." The officer had no opportunity to touch or hold the accused. The accused accelerated, was pursued, and was apprehended. The accused was charged with escaping lawful custody.

The S.C.C. ruled that the accused was guilty. The "mere pronouncement of words of arrest" constitutes an arrest.

Step 4: Immediate Search of Accused

Police officers are authorized to immediately search a person after the person has been lawfully arrested, and may seize

- ▸ evidence of any offence, including the offence for which the person was arrested, and any unrelated offence;
- ▸ any item that may cause injury to anyone, including the arrested person; and
- ▸ any item that may help the arrested person escape.[12]

This authority originates from common law and has been confirmed by the S.C.C.

The automatic search means that, before searching the arrested person, an officer does not have to have reasonable grounds for believing that he or she possesses any of the above. This authority has been extended to the area surrounding where the arrest was made. The police may search the entirety of whatever may reasonably be considered the *surrounding* area—for example, the interior of a car or an entire room.[13]

Step 5: Simultaneous Arrest of Young/Adult Offender

In some cases, an adult offender (18 years or older) and a young offender (ages 12–17 years) are arrested together. The *Youth Criminal Justice Act* (Y.C.J.A.) states that young offenders must be detained separately from adults. However, an exception to this rule is provided for by s. 30(7) Y.C.J.A., which allows a police officer to detain a young offender with an adult in a police vehicle at the time of arrest. For example, an officer may simultaneously arrest a 17- and an 18-year-old for the same offence. Both may be detained in the same vehicle for the purpose of transporting to the police station. Afterward, at the police station, the young offender must be detained separately from the adult offender.

Step 6: Inform Accused of Reason for Arrest

Informing the accused about the reason for the arrest is a statutory requirement created by s. 10(a) Charter and s. 29(2)(b) C.C. Section 10(a) Charter imposed on police a duty to *inform an arrested person promptly of the reasons for the arrest.* The S.C.C., in *R. v. Evans* (1991),[14] gave two reasons for this requirement:

1. An arrested person is not obliged to submit to an arrest if he or she does not know the reason for it.
2. An arrested person cannot exercise his or her right to counsel in a meaningful way if he or she does not know the full extent of the severity or nature of the reasons for the arrest.

The court created a *general rule* about what constitutes properly informing the accused of the reason for his or her arrest: it is not the particular words used but whether the accused can understand the basic information about the reason for the arrest. Furthermore, the reasons given to the accused must be in keeping with all the circumstances of the case, and sufficiently comprehensive to allow the accused to make a reasonable decision about whether to submit to the arrest and whether to exercise the right to counsel.

This rule permits officers at the scene of the arrest to give an arrested person general explanations for the arrest rather than the precise name of the offence. However, when the decision has been made to charge an accused with specific offences, those specific offences should be explained to the accused person.

PROCEDURE

The process of informing an offender of the reason for the arrest occurs at two sites:

1. the scene of the arrest, and
2. the police station.

At the Scene of the Arrest

Upon arrival at or near a crime scene where the offender has been arrested, an officer has two alternatives about how to inform the accused about the reason for the arrest:

1. Give a general reason that is in keeping with the circumstances. Examples might include the following:
   - "punching that person"
   - "stealing that (item)"
   - "stabbing that person"
   - "shooting at that person"

   Although a general reason does not state a specific offence, it provides a reasonable explanation.
2. If the officer quickly analyzes the circumstance at or near the crime scene and accurately recognizes the offence committed, a specific offence name may be given as the reason for the arrest. Examples might include the following:
   - Assault,
   - Theft under $5,000.00,
   - Impaired driving,
   - Attempted murder, or
   - Mischief under $5,000.00.

   If a specific offence is given as a reason, the officer has the onus of proving that the accused reasonably understood what was said. If doubt exists whether the accused reasonably understands what the specific offence means, the officer may need to give an additional explanation, providing more information. For example, the names of some offences, such as "Mischief," may not be understood by the accused and would require such an additional explanation.

After the accused is informed of the reason for the arrest, ask if he or she understands the reason and, if necessary, have the accused explain to you what it means. Record the accused's responses in a notebook for reference during court testimony at a trial.

At the Police Station

After the accused has been transported to the police station and a decision about specific charges has been made, inform the accused, as soon as is practicable, about each specific offence with which he or she will be charged. Failure to properly inform an arrested person of the proper reason for an arrest constitutes a s. 10(a) Charter violation, which may result in the exclusion of evidence obtained after the violation.[15]

YOUNG OFFENDERS—NOTICE TO PARENTS

If the arrested person is a young offender, the police have an additional obligation to fulfill in connection with giving the reason for arrest. Section 26(1) Y.C.J.A. mandates a procedure called "notice to parent." Where a young offender is arrested and detained in custody pending a court appearance, his or her parent must be notified of the arrest, the place of detention, and the reason for the arrest. The officer-in-charge at the time that the young offender is detained must make the notification, or the officer-in-charge may instruct another officer to perform this procedure. This notice to parent may be given orally or in writing. The notice must be given as soon as possible after the arrest.

Step 7: Production of Warrant

If the arresting officer makes the arrest with a warrant, he or she must have possession of the warrant and produce it when requested to do so.[16] This is a statutory requirement created by s. 29(1) C.C. If an arrest with a warrant is made, the warrant must be executed properly. Proper execution is defined as having possession of the warrant when arresting the offender and producing it when requested to do so.

Section 29(1) C.C. allows an exception to this rule about possessing the warrant. The section states that the officer must have possession *where it is feasible to do so.* This permits the officer to make the arrest when he or she inadvertently finds the accused. Under these circumstances, the warrant may be executed when the accused is at the police station. But if the officer deliberately sets out to search for and arrest the accused, he or she should have possession of the warrant.

Although this section requires that the officer produce the warrant for the accused only at the accused's request, *officers should produce the warrant in every arrest* to prevent arguments in court about whether a request was actually made. A copy of the warrant does not have to be given to the accused and, to prevent its being put to improper and illegal use, it should not be given.

Step 8: Inform Accused of Right to Counsel

A police officer must inform the arrested person of his or her right to counsel, without delay, upon arrest or detention.[17] This is a statutory requirement created by s. 10(b) Charter. This section creates only the basic right to counsel. Since the enactment of the Charter in 1982, case law decisions have added dimensions, or components, to the basic statutory requirement. These components compose the entire right-to-counsel package.

The right to counsel encompasses four distinct components that apply to both adult and young offenders (ages 12–17 years). However, additional rules apply to young offenders. The four components are as follows:

1. base component,
2. Brydges component (legal aid existence and availability),
3. Bartle component (toll-free number), and
4. privacy component.

An accused must be informed of the right to counsel upon his or her arrest or detention. The phrase "upon arrest or detention" has been defined by the S.C.C., in *R. v. Schmautz* (1990),[18] as "at the moment where he or she is arrested or detained."

Adult offenders must be informed of the right to counsel only upon arrest. In other words, an adult offender (18 years or older) does not have to be informed of the right to counsel in a case where mere suspicion exists and the offender voluntarily accompanies the officer for any purpose, such as questioning. For example, if mere suspicion exists that Eddie (19) has committed a robbery, and Eddie consents to be questioned by a police officer, the officer does not have to inform Eddie of the right to counsel because he has not been arrested or detained.

ADDITIONAL RULE FOR YOUNG OFFENDERS

The right-to-counsel rule differs for young offenders. A young offender must be informed of the right to counsel at any time during an investigation, even when no arrest or detention has occurred—for example, during voluntary accompaniment. Essentially, a young offender (12–17 years old) must be informed of the right to counsel any time an officer has any sort of contact with him or her, even during voluntary accompaniment, when only mere suspicion exists.[19]

BASIC FORMULA—ADULT

The arresting officer must clearly communicate the right to counsel to an arrested person.[20] The basic formula for informing an adult offender of the right to counsel is the following: "It is my duty to inform you that you have the right to retain and instruct counsel without delay. Do you understand?"

The officer has the onus of proving that the accused understood what he or she was told about the right to counsel. Usually, the question, "Do you understand?" and an affirmative answer of "Yes" by the accused is sufficient to prove this understanding. The offender's verbatim response should be recorded (in a notebook) rather than a paraphrase such as "the accused understood." If the accused seems not to understand his or her right to counsel, then the officer must provide an additional explanation, such as the following: "This means you have the right to call a lawyer of your choice." Record the explanation and the offender's response verbatim in your notebook. Avoid recording a paraphrase such as, "I explained it further, and then the accused understood."[21]

BASIC FORMULA—YOUNG OFFENDER

The basic formula for informing a young offender of the right to counsel is the same as for adults, but it involves additional information. A young offender must be informed of the right to call not only a lawyer but three other types of people:

1. a parent,
2. any adult relative, or
3. any other appropriate adult chosen by the young offender.[22]

The officer must inform the young offender of his or her right to have any number of these four persons present.[23]

The language in which a young offender is informed about the right to counsel must be compatible with that particular young person's intelligence.[24] Consequently, an officer may have to use very simple language. Afterward, the young person must be asked if he or she understands. If the young person answers "yes," he or she should then be asked to *explain* the right to counsel. The explanation must be correct. If it is not, provide the young person with the correct explanation and again ask him or her to explain it. Write the entire conversation, verbatim, in a notebook, including your own words about the right to counsel and all responses made by the young offender. Court testimony should reflect the recorded verbatim conversation. Do not use a paraphrase such as the following: "I informed the accused of the right to counsel and he or she understood." This phrase will be insufficient during court testimony. Whether the accused understood is a conclusion for the trial judge to make, not you.

This basic formula for conveying the right to counsel does not contain all of the right-to-counsel information that must be conveyed. Case law has added additional requirements, or components. If an officer informs an adult or young offender only of his or her basic right to counsel, a s. 10(b) Charter violation will have occurred.

BRYDGES COMPONENT

The S.C.C., in *R. v. Brydges* (1990),[25] added a second component to the right-to-counsel requirement. An officer must inform both adult and young offenders about the existence and availability of legal aid, regardless of the accused person's financial status.

Legal aid refers to legal advice and service that is provided to an accused person who is eligible for it. The service is available during the course of the prosecution and court proceedings.[26] It is also available immediately after an arrest. Therefore, the police are required to inform an accused person of two elements that together compose the Brydges component of the right-to-counsel information:

1. the availability of temporary, free, and immediate legal service; and
2. that the accused may be eligible for permanent legal aid—that is, legal aid that lasts for the duration of the court proceedings.

The specific content of the Brydges component is printed on "right to counsel" cards, with which police officers are provided. It must be read to every arrested person, regardless of whether he or she can afford a lawyer. Failure to inform an accused person of the Brydges component constitutes a s. 10(b) Charter violation, which may result in the exclusion of evidence obtained after the violation occurs.[27]

BARTLE COMPONENT

The S.C.C., in *R. v. Bartle* (1994), added a third mandatory component to the right-to-counsel requirement. Police officers must inform both adult and young offenders of a toll-free telephone number that will put them in contact with duty counsel.[28] This telephone number provides an accused person with a specific method of obtaining temporary, free, and immediate legal advice. This telephone number must be given to every arrested person, in all cases, whether the accused can afford a lawyer or has his or her own lawyer already. In other words, it is a mandatory obligation to provide this number in all cases. Failure to do so constitutes a s. 10(b) Charter violation and may result in the exclusion of evidence obtained by police after the violation.[29] The trial judge will consider various factors in determining whether to admit or exclude the evidence.

PRIVACY COMPONENT

The Ontario Court of Appeal, in *R. v. Jackson* (1993), added to the basic right-to-counsel requirement a privacy component, one that is mandatory or merely recommended depending on the circumstances.[30]

Mandatory

If any of the following conditions exist, a police officer has a mandatory obligation to inform all adult and young offenders of their right to counsel *in private*:

1. The accused says something to, or in the presence of, the arresting officer (that is, the one who informed the accused of the right to counsel) that indicates to the officer that the accused either

   ▸ does not understand that he or she has the right to counsel in private, or
   ▸ is concerned about whether such a right exists.

2. The accused knows that the right to privacy exists but is concerned about whether privacy will be given.
3. The circumstances in which the accused was informed of the right to counsel may cause him or her to reasonably believe that he or she will have to telephone a lawyer in police presence, without privacy.

The *R. v. Jackson* case shows in what circumstances an accused could reasonably believe that no privacy will be given. The accused was arrested for "Over 80" and informed of his right to counsel. A breathalyzer demand was made, and the accused was transported to a police station.

The accused was seated in an interview room; a police officer sat across from him, pointed to a phone book and a telephone on a desk, and asked him if he wanted to call a lawyer. The officer made no move to leave, and the accused said "no."

During the 30 minutes they remained together in the room, the officer repeated the question about right to counsel, and the accused again refused.

At the trial, the accused testified that he would have called his lawyer but chose not to because he believed he would not have been afforded privacy. The court ruled that a s. 10(b) Charter violation had occurred, for the following reasons:

1. The circumstances were sufficient to cause a reasonable person to believe that the right to phone a lawyer had to occur in the officer's presence and that no privacy would be given.
2. These circumstances were sufficient to cause the officer to have a reasonable apprehension that the accused believed that no privacy would be given.

Recommended

It is not mandatory for an officer to inform an accused person of the right to privacy if no circumstances exist that might cause the accused to reasonably believe that privacy will not be given. However, the court recommended an additional procedure for officers to use in all cases; the court affirmed that it is a "simple matter" for police officers to add the words "in privacy" to the right-to-counsel information content. The court also stated that "it is desirable that this be done."[31]

Step 9: Prove the Accused Understood the Right to Counsel

The S.C.C., in *R. v. Evans* (1991), stated that an accused person cannot be expected to exercise the right to counsel if he or she fails to understand it.[32] Consequently, officers have the onus of clearly communicating the right and then proving that the accused understood it.[33] In most cases, the question "Do you understand?" followed by a response of "Yes" from the accused is enough to demonstrate that the accused understood what was said.[34] It is recommended that this response always be followed with a question such as "What does this mean?" The purpose of this question is to elicit a correct explanation from the accused person regarding the meaning of the right to counsel, and to prove that he or she had sufficient intelligence to understand it. A correct explanation from the accused should include a reference to the right to call a lawyer. Record the response verbatim. During court testimony, state precisely the question asked and the response made. Do not paraphrase by saying, "The accused understood." Such paraphrasing must be avoided during court testimony because it represents a conclusion that only a trial judge is authorized to make.

The S.C.C. also prescribed the following, in the event of a "positive indication" that the accused does not understand his or her right to counsel: "The police cannot rely on their mechanical recitation of the right to the accused; they must take steps to facilitate that understanding."[35]

An example of such a "positive indication" would be the accused's saying something that indicates no understanding, or saying something that raises doubts about his or her ability to understand. An accused's having limited mental capacity is a form of "positive indication." In the *Evans* case, the police were aware of the accused's limited mental capacity, and the accused said he did not understand the right to counsel. If the accused positively indicates that he or she does not understand the right to counsel, police must explain the right in simple terms, such as the following:

- ▸ "It means you can call a lawyer and talk to him or her";
- ▸ "You can talk to a free legal aid lawyer right now";
- ▸ "You can call this free 1-800 telephone number and talk to a lawyer for free"; or
- ▸ "You can apply to legal aid, and you might receive a free lawyer for the trial if you are eligible."

Record verbatim in a notebook your additional explanation and the accused's response. After receiving the response, ask the accused to explain the right to counsel. Record his or her explanation verbatim. The accused's explanation should accurately reflect the officer's simpler explanation. Whenever proof is needed of the accused's knowledge of an issue, the best proof is a verbatim written account of the accused's response, a response that reflects the officer's simpler explanation.

Another instance of a "positive indication" of a failure to understand is an accused's being intoxicated. A slightly or moderately intoxicated person—a person who is coherent and capable of having a conversation—may be capable of understanding what is told to him or her. To remove all doubt, however, the following procedure is appropriate if the accused is even slightly intoxicated:

1. Explain the right to counsel in simpler language, even if the accused says that the right is understood.
2. Ask the accused to explain it.
3. Repeat the procedure once the accused is sober.

Young offenders must have all the right-to-counsel information explained to them in language compatible with their particular intelligence levels. This procedure prevents the potential exclusion of evidence, such as a confession, that is subsequently obtained after a violation occurs.

Step 10: Read Caution to Accused

The caution is a warning to the accused that he or she does not have to say anything to the police, but that if he or she says anything, it may be used in evidence at the trial. The following is an example of a formal caution: "Do you wish to say anything in answer to the charge? You are not obliged to say anything unless you wish to do so, but whatever you say may be given in evidence."

The caution is not a statutory requirement. No statute, such as the Charter or the *Criminal Code*, creates a mandatory requirement to provide an accused person with a formal caution. In other words, failure to caution the accused is not a Charter violation. The caution is a guideline, or a recommended practice, included in the "Judges' Rules" as established in England in 1912. The purpose of the caution is to help officers prove that confessions made by accused persons are voluntary. The voluntariness of a confession must be proven to ensure its admissibility. Reading the caution to an offender after an arrest does not guarantee the admissibility of a confession. All of the circumstances of an interrogation determine whether the confession will be deemed voluntary and therefore admissible. In other words, the caution is merely an advantage that is available to police officers to help them prove the voluntariness of a suspect's confession.

In summary, a police officer's failure to caution an accused is simply a failure to use an opportunity to help make a confession admissible.[36] Failure to caution an accused person does not guarantee the exclusion of a confession or any other evidence obtained as the result of interrogation.

Step 11: Allow Accused Time to Decide to Exercise Right to Counsel

After the accused is informed of the right to counsel, he or she has two options regarding this right:

1. invoke the right to counsel for the purpose of exercising it (ask to call and speak to a lawyer); or
2. waive the right to counsel (decline the right to call a lawyer).

The police have a duty to provide the accused with a *reasonable amount of time in which to decide whether to exercise the right to counsel*. An exact number of minutes is not specified. The amount of time must be *reasonable* with respect to the circumstances of each case.

The British Columbia Court of Appeal, in *R. v. Hollis* (1992), created two rules in this regard:

1. If the accused understands the right to counsel, he or she is expected to decide quickly whether to exercise it. (Again, no specific amount of time is prescribed.)
2. The accused's decision about calling a lawyer must be the product of free choice. This means that the police cannot persuade or influence the accused in any manner to make a specific decision.[37]

The S.C.C., in *R. v. Burlingham* (1995), addressed the issue of police influence on the accused's decision to call a lawyer. The court ruled that s. 10(b) Charter specifically prohibits the police from "belittling" an accused's lawyer with the "express goal or effect of undermining the accused's confidence in and relationship with defence counsel."[38] This prohibition is a component of s. 10(b) Charter. In the *Burlingham* case, the police denigrated the role of the defence lawyer by making disparaging remarks about the lawyer's loyalty, commitment, availability, and legal fees. The police also suggested that they were more trustworthy than the accused's lawyer. These comments constituted a s. 10(b) Charter violation, and a significant quantity of the evidence that was obtained after the violation occurred, including a confession, was excluded under s. 24(2) Charter.

In some cases, the accused makes no decision and gives no response about exercising the right to counsel. When this happens, the following question arises: "Are the police to assume that the accused has invoked the right to counsel?" The British Columbia Court of Appeal answered this question in the *Hollis* case with the following ruling: "If the accused does not state a decision, the police have no obligation to assume or guess that the accused will decide to call a lawyer and may continue the investigation as if the right to counsel has been waived."[39] In summary, the accused may

- ask to call and speak to a lawyer (invoke and exercise the right);
- decline to call a lawyer (waive the right); or
- make no decision, which means *the right is waived.*

Step 12: Provide Opportunity for the Accused to Exercise the Right to Counsel

Invoking the right to counsel means asking for an opportunity to call and speak to a lawyer. An accused person may invoke the right to counsel at any time while he or she is in police custody, from the time of the arrest to the time of his or her release. The accused is not limited or restricted to a particular time period—for example, he or she does not have to invoke the right immediately after being informed of it.

The S.C.C., in *R. v. Manninen* (1987), imposed two mandatory obligations upon police officers when the accused invokes the right to counsel:

1. They must give the accused person a reasonable opportunity to exercise the right to counsel, after the right is invoked.
2. They must cease questioning, delay the investigation, and not attempt to obtain evidence from the accused until he or she has had a reasonable opportunity to call and speak to a lawyer.[40]

The following nine rules and procedures must be followed once the accused has invoked the right to counsel:

RULE 1

Provide the accused with an opportunity to call a lawyer without unnecessary delay.[41] The opportunity is not defined by a specific number of minutes or hours.

RULE 2

Delay the investigation and do not attempt to elicit evidence from the accused until he or she has exercised the right to counsel by actually speaking to a lawyer and receiving legal advice. In other words, this rule prohibits police from questioning an accused person between the time he or she asks for the opportunity to call a lawyer (invoked) and the time he or she actually speaks to a lawyer (exercised).

If the police initiate questioning during this interval and the accused confesses, a s. 10(b) Charter violation will have occurred and the confession will likely be excluded under s. 24(2) Charter.

RULE 3

How much time constitutes a reasonable opportunity? How long must the police delay their investigation? The S.C.C. answered these questions in *R. v. Smith* (1989) by ruling that an accused must be *reasonably diligent* in attempting to call a lawyer after invoking the right to counsel.[42] This imposes a time limit upon the accused to call a lawyer, but not a specific one. What it does is prevent the accused from causing unnecessary delays in an investigation. Without this limit, it would be possible for an accused to intentionally hinder an investigation and cause evidence to be destroyed or lost.

Consequently, the police obligation to cease questioning and delay the investigation is cancelled if the accused is not reasonably diligent in exercising the right to counsel. In this case, the accused person does not lose the right to counsel; the police simply do not have to delay the investigation any further while waiting for the accused to call his or her lawyer.

Certain circumstances may indicate a lack of reasonable diligence. For example, it does not take several hours to call a lawyer. Circumstances showing a lack of reasonable diligence are evident in the *Smith* case.

The accused was arrested at 7:00 p.m. for "Robbery." He was informed of his right to counsel at that time but did not then invoke the right. He did invoke his right two hours later. The officers gave the accused a telephone book and a telephone. The accused decided not to call his lawyer at that time because the phone book indicated only an office number. The officers suggested that he call the number because possibly an answering service would be available. The accused rejected this suggestion and decided to postpone the phone call until the morning.

One hour after the accused invoked his right, the officers interrogated the accused, who initially declined to answer questions about the robbery until he could speak to his lawyer in the morning. Interrogation continued, and the accused eventually made an "off the record" confession.

The S.C.C. ruled that the accused *had not been reasonably diligent* in exercising the right to counsel, and they cited his *casual attempts* to call the lawyer. Consequently, the police did not have to delay the investigation and were allowed to continue questioning. No s. 10(b) Charter violation occurred. The confession was admissible.

The court summarized this decision by establishing the following rule: When the police offer an opportunity to exercise the right to counsel and the accused does not act on it, *the accused has the onus* of proving that it was impossible to speak with his or her lawyer at that time.[43] This presents an advantage to the police when officers must decide if the accused is not being reasonably diligent. After the accused is given a reasonable opportunity to phone a lawyer, the accused is required to make a reasonable attempt to contact the lawyer, including leaving a message with an answering service. If the accused refuses to leave a message and wants to postpone the phone call until office hours, the investigation may justifiably continue. To delay an investigation, the accused has the onus of proving that no possible method exists to contact a lawyer.

RULE 4

In what location should the accused be given the opportunity to call a lawyer? Ensuring personal safety and preventing escape are primary concerns after an arrest is made. It is recommended that the accused's opportunity to call a lawyer be given at the police station, if the accused is transported there justifiably. Permitting the accused to phone in public or from a residence poses a risk. Any arrested person is capable of using violence toward the arresting officer, and is capable of attempting an escape.

After an arrest, the accused's movement in public or in a house should be restricted. The accused should be placed in the police car as soon as possible. If he or she makes a phone call before being transported to the police station, the accused may be calling someone other than a lawyer to seek assistance in escaping while en route to the police station. Many other negative consequences can result from an accused's being permitted, after the arrest, to use the phone in public or in his or her house; such permission entails too much freedom of movement. For example, an accused permitted to phone a lawyer from the house may use the opportunity to gain access to a weapon stored near the phone. In other words, waiting till you reach the police station before giving the accused the opportunity to call a lawyer minimizes unnecessary risks.

The only risk you incur through this delay is that *a confession given by the accused while en route to the police station may be ruled inadmissible*. If the circumstances do not justify the continued detention and transportation of the accused to the police station, he or she may call from the location of the arrest.

RULE 5

Some time will elapse after the accused invokes the right to counsel and before he or she exercises this right. If the accused initiates conversation during this time, record his or her remarks verbatim in your notebook. The police cannot initiate conversation or questioning during this time. However, if the accused initiates conversation and confesses or makes self-incriminating oral statements, that evidence will likely be admissible.[44]

RULE 6

Do not limit the accused person to only one phone call.[45] Telling an accused that only one phone call will be allowed or limiting the accused to only one phone call constitutes a s. 10(b) Charter violation, according to the Ontario Court of Appeal, in *R. v. Pavel* (1989). Giving the accused a "reasonable opportunity" to exercise the right to counsel does not mean limiting him or her to any specific number of phone calls. Instead, the accused must be allowed reasonable opportunities to contact a lawyer. It must be emphasized that, in the case of a young offender, the accused's right to counsel includes the right to contact and speak to parents or other appropriate adults whom the young offender believes may provide assistance or give advice. In other words, a young offender may need several phone calls for the entire right to counsel to be exercised.

An adult's right to counsel is the right to receive advice from a lawyer only. Section 10(b) Charter does not specifically grant an adult offender the right to contact other adults, such as parents or spouses. Consequently, a problem may arise when an offender who is 18 years old, or older, requests to call a parent, spouse, or other adult. The solution to this problem is for police to determine whether such a phone call can reasonably be considered a necessary part of the accused's contacting a lawyer. Most lawyers have answering services after business hours. Phone books and lists of lawyers' phone numbers are provided to an accused at most police stations. For this reason, there is usually no need for the accused to call another adult for help contacting a lawyer. Unnecessary phone calls to other adults have potential consequences, such as the destruction or loss of evidence. Such consequences must be prevented to ensure a successful investigation.

RULE 7

Allow the accused to make phone calls and speak to a lawyer in private.[46] The right to counsel includes the right to privacy, according to case law decisions. Accused persons must be allowed to make phone calls and speak to a lawyer in private, and should not have to ask for privacy; the right to privacy is automatically allowed. Therefore, officers cannot remain in a room when the accused makes phone calls or while an accused speaks to a lawyer in person, nor can the conversation be monitored or overheard by any means. Any confessions or incriminating evidence obtained through a privacy violation will likely be excluded.

RULE 8

After the accused person makes a phone call, determine the result of it. The right to counsel is exercised only by the accused's speaking to and receiving advice from a lawyer. After that, the officer is permitted to question the accused. In many cases, particularly after business hours, an accused person must leave a message with an answering service in order to contact a lawyer. The accused's leaving a message for a lawyer to call the police station *does not constitute* the exercising of the right to counsel.

When the accused makes a phone call, no officer will be in the room or listening to the conversation. The officer must determine the result of the phone call in order to begin questioning the accused. The officer must obviously rely only on the response of the accused. The accused may give the officer one of three responses:

1. he or she spoke to a lawyer;
2. he or she left a message for a lawyer; or
3. *no response*—the accused does not say whether he or she spoke to a lawyer.

If the accused says that he or she spoke to a lawyer, questioning may begin at this stage. If he or she only left a message, the officer cannot yet initiate questioning; one must wait for the lawyer to call. However, if the accused initiates the conversation and makes incriminating statements, record them.

The Nova Scotia Court of Appeal, in *R. v. MacKenzie* (1991), ruled that the confessions an accused makes to police while waiting for a lawyer to call after a message has been left are admissible if the accused initiates the conversation.[47] The accused's conviction was later overturned, but the reasons for the overturning were not related to this circumstance.

The S.C.C., in *R. v. Hebert* (1990), stated, "in the absence of eliciting behaviour on the part of the police, there is no violation of the accused's right to choose whether or not to speak to the police" if the accused initiates conversation and confesses.[48]

If the accused makes *no response*, not telling the officer whether or not a lawyer was spoken to, two questions arise, both answered in case law:

1. Does the officer have to ask the accused about the result of the phone call?
2. Does the accused have the onus of telling the officer that a message was left?

The British Columbia Court of Appeal, in *R. v. Ferron* (1989), ruled that *the police are not obliged* to "ask again and again" if the accused has spoken to a lawyer, after the accused makes phone calls.[49] The Alberta Court of Appeal, in *R. v. Top* (1989), ruled that the *accused should inform the police* about the results of the phone calls, particularly if a message is left.[50]

Consequently, if the accused makes no response after making a phone call, the officer may assume that the accused has exercised the right to counsel and may question the accused. In summary, if an accused person invokes his right to counsel, then exercises it by calling a lawyer and leaving a message, use the following procedure:

1. If the accused does not state that a message was left, begin questioning the accused.
2. If the accused states that a message was left,
   a. do not initiate conversation with the accused; however,
   b. if the accused initiates conversation, allow him or her to continue.

RULE 9

If the accused is a young offender and speaks to parents or other adults, allow him or her an additional reasonable opportunity to call a lawyer. The S.C.C., in *R. v. T.(E.)* (1993), ruled that a parent is not an alternative to a lawyer.[51] Consequently, a young offender who speaks to a parent or adult is still entitled to speak with a lawyer. Do not prevent the right to counsel from being exercised on the grounds that the young offender has received advice from a parent or adult.

Step 13: After the Right to Counsel Is Exercised, Question the Accused

Interrogation is a crucial investigative technique that may yield substantial evidence.

ADULT OFFENDER

After an adult accused has exercised his or her right to counsel by speaking to a lawyer, no rule prohibits the police from questioning the adult in the absence of counsel.[52] A lawyer's advice to an accused will likely be to remain silent. The right to remain silent is a fundamental principle that is included in s. 7 Charter.

The S.C.C., in *R. v. Hebert* (1990), stated that no rule prohibits the police from questioning an accused adult in the absence of a lawyer, after the accused has spoken to the lawyer.[53] The police must allow the accused an opportunity to decide whether to remain silent, but if the accused "volunteers information," then no Charter violation will have occurred.

The police are also permitted to try to persuade the accused to answer questions, provided that this "police persuasion" does not involve denying the suspect the right to choose to remain silent.

In summary, questioning is allowed after an accused adult speaks to a lawyer, if the accused chooses not to remain silent or volunteers information and initiates conversation.

YOUNG OFFENDER

After a young offender exercises the right to counsel, questioning is allowed, but the lawyer or adult whom the young offender consulted with must be present, unless the young offender waives this right in writing.[54] Section 25(7) Y.C.J.A. creates the following rule: A young offender may be questioned after a lawyer or adult is consulted with, but the young offender decides who will be present during the questioning.

The young offender may have a lawyer, parent, or adult present, if he or she chooses. If he or she chooses not to exercise this right, the young offender must sign a written waiver. The police do not decide who will be present during a young offender's questioning.

Step 14: Waiver of Right to Counsel

Choosing not to invoke the right to counsel means declining an opportunity to call a lawyer. If an accused person chooses not to invoke the right to counsel after being informed he or she has the right to do so, the *right to counsel is then waived*, and the investigation and questioning may continue immediately.[55] A waiver of the right to counsel means that the person relinquishes the s. 10(b) Charter right to retain a lawyer and receive legal advice.

After the accused has signed a valid waiver, the police have no other obligations regarding the right to counsel and may question the accused person. The onus is on the prosecution to prove that the accused made a valid waiver of the right to counsel. The S.C.C., in *R. v. Prosper* (1994), stated that the standard of proof required for a valid waiver must be "very high" and that "courts must ensure that the right to counsel is not too easily waived."[56]

The elements that compose a valid waiver and that must be proven by the police are as follows:

1. The waiver must be clear and unequivocal. In other words, its meaning must be unmistakable and not vague. The accused's words must specifically indicate that he or she does not want to call or speak with a lawyer. If any another inference is possible, reasonable doubt will exist about the waiver's validity.
2. The waiver must be voluntarily made. It must be made without inducements—that is, "direct or indirect compulsions," such as threats or promises from police.
3. The accused must understand the whole meaning of the right to counsel—that is, the meaning of all the components.
4. The accused must understand "what is being given up"—that is, legal advice.[57]

An officer's testimony relating to a waiver must be meticulous and must include verbatim the conversation that produced the waiver. A paraphrase such as "The accused waived his right to counsel" will be insufficient to prove a clear, unequivocal waiver. The verbatim conversation needs to be recorded, rather than paraphrased, in a notebook. A young offender's waiver must be in writing.[58] An oral waiver is sufficient only for an adult offender's waiver.

Failure to prove that all of these elements composed the waiver constitutes a s. 10(b) Charter violation.

WAIVER BY INTOXICATED PERSON

Accused persons at the time of an arrest are often intoxicated. This can pose a problem for police if the accused waives the right to counsel. If an accused person who is intoxicated waives the right to counsel, the officer must prove that the accused was aware of the consequences of waiving the right.

The S.C.C., in *R. v. Clarkson* (1986), stated that the prosecution has the onus of proving that an intoxicated accused person who waives the right to counsel was aware of the consequences of the waiver.[59] In other words, the officer must prove that:

- the elements composing a valid waiver were present, and
- the accused had knowledge that
    - legal advice was being given up, and
    - information obtained from the accused afterward, such as a confession, might be used as evidence at the trial.

The following procedure is a way for police to fulfill this obligation:

1. Read the accused all the components of the right to counsel.
2. Ask the accused if each component is understood.
3. Record the response verbatim.
4. Provide additional explanations in ordinary language and record the explanations verbatim.
5. Ask the accused if the explanation is understood, and record the response.
6. Ask the accused to explain the right to counsel to you and record his or her response verbatim.
7. Record the waiver verbatim.
8. Explain to the accused that the consequences of the waiver are that legal advice will be given up and that evidence obtained subsequent to the waiver may be used at the trial. Record the explanation verbatim.
9. Ask if it is understood. Record the response verbatim.
10. Ask the accused to explain the consequences of the waiver. Record his or her explanation verbatim.

There are various degrees of intoxication, from slight to moderate to advanced. Slightly or moderately intoxicated offenders are often coherent and may converse rationally, with a functional mind. If the officer believes that the accused, though intoxicated, has understood all aspects of the waiver, questioning may occur immediately afterward.

If the accused is very intoxicated, so that his or her comprehension of the required elements is impaired, questioning should be delayed until the accused is sober. The right-to-counsel procedure should be repeated at that time.

Step 15: The Prosper Warning

If the accused person invokes the right to counsel, then changes his or her mind and waives it, inform him or her that a reasonable opportunity will be given to contact a lawyer. The S.C.C., in *R. v. Prosper* (1994), made it mandatory for police officers, under these circumstances, to provide this opportunity. Under these circumstances, the police must inform the accused of the following:

- that he or she has the right to a reasonable opportunity to call a lawyer;
- that the police are obliged to "hold off" their questioning of the accused during this period of reasonable opportunity.[60]

Failure to inform the accused about both these things constitutes a s. 10(b) Charter violation.

SUMMARY

The opening commentary in this chapter serves as a reminder that the use of force, even where claimed to be justified, that is, for arrest or for protection, is not automatically authorized. The *Criminal Code* contains several sections that are relevant to the use of force and that should govern a police officer's arrest of an offender. The next chapter looks more closely at these sections and at the importance of police officers' and citizens' understanding the legal meaning of use of force.

Following Chapter 10, a two-chapter discussion on "release provisions" begins. Specifically, you will learn what criteria must be met in order to release a suspect from detention (arrest) and when it is lawful to continue custody.

PROBLEM-SOLVING CASE STUDIES

You are a police officer in each case. Each offender is an adult, unless otherwise indicated.

Problem 1

While investigating a "Fraud over $5,000.00" you obtain an eyewitness statement and a cheque from Helen, both of which implicate Bill. You arrest Bill after this evidence is obtained. You fail to properly inform him of the right to counsel. Afterward, he confesses, and you recover the property obtained by the fraud.

a. Will the right-to-counsel Charter violation result in exclusion of Helen's eyewitness observation or the cheque as evidence?

_____

_____

_____

b. Will the right-to-counsel Charter violation result in automatic exclusion of Bill's confession?

_____

_____

_____

c. Will the confession likely be admitted or excluded?

_____

_____

_____

Problem 2

You arrive at a bar in response to a disturbance. Upon arrival, you are met by the victim, Doug. He and two other witnesses inform you that they saw Bill assault Doug with a weapon (baseball bat). They can identify Bill. You find Bill inside the bar and decide to arrest him.

a. Explain the procedure you would use to arrest Bill inside the bar and what information you will tell Bill at the scene of the arrest.

_____

_____

_____

_____

_____

_____

_____

_____

_____

_____

_____

_____

_____

_____

_____

_____

_____

_____

b. If Bill makes no decision after you inform him of the right to counsel, about invoking or declining the right, what can you assume? Can you question Bill?

_____

_____

c. If Bill is employed and can afford a lawyer, do you have to inform him of the existence and availability of legal aid?

_____

_____

Problem 3

You are investigating a "Theft under $5,000.00." You suspect that Greg, an adult, committed the offence. Greg voluntarily accompanies you to the police station for questioning. Do you have to inform him of the right to counsel before questioning him?

_____

_____

_____

Problem 4

While on patrol, you stop Doug. A CPIC message reveals that a valid arrest warrant exists. You arrest him and transport him to the police station. What do you have to do to execute the arrest warrant?

_____

Problem 5

You arrest Wally for one count of "Break, enter, and theft" and one count of "Robbery." Can you withhold the reasons for the arrest if you believe that telling him will affect your investigations?

_____

_____

Problem 6

You arrest Ellen for "Attempted murder." She invokes her right to counsel.

a. How much time must you provide her to exercise her right?

_____

_____

b. Can you limit Ellen to only one phone call?

_____

c. Does Ellen have a right to phone other adults besides a lawyer?

_____

_____

d. Ellen makes a phone call. She does not inform you of the result of the call. Can you continue the investigation and question her?

_____

_____

_____

_____

e. If Ellen tells you that she does not want to leave a message with her lawyer and wants to wait until business hours begin, can you continue the investigation and question her?

_____

_____

_____

f. If Ellen initially invokes the right to counsel, then changes her mind, and waives it later, do you have to inform her of any information?

_____

_____

_____

_____

Problem 7

You arrest Greg for "Robbery." The arrest is made at his house right now. The offence occurred three days ago.

a. If you fail to "caution" him, will you have committed a Charter violation?

_____

_____

b. If you fail to caution him and he later confesses, will the confession be automatically excluded?

_____

_____

_____

c. What is the significance of the failure to caution Greg?

_____

_____

Problem 8

You arrest Walter, an adult, for sexual assault. You inform him of the right to counsel. He waives the right.

a. What does a waiver mean and represent?

_____

_____

b. Who has the onus to prove that Walter waived his right?

_____

c. How is a waiver proven to be valid?

_____

_____

_____

_____

_____

_____

_____

d. Does the waiver in this case have to be in writing?

_____

e. After the waiver is made, do you have any additional obligations?

_____

_____

Problem 9

You see Claire (16) driving a stolen car on King St. right now. You stop her and arrest her.

a. How do you inform Claire of the right to counsel?

_____

_____

_____

b. If Claire invokes her right to counsel, whom may she contact?

_____

_____

c. If Claire waives her right to counsel, how must the waiver be obtained?

_____

_____

d. Upon arrest at the police station, what procedure must you follow?

_____

_____

_____

_____

Problem 10

You arrest Rick (18) and Laura (17) right now at the scene of a break-in. Can you place both in custody together in the back of your police vehicle?

_____

_____

_____

Problem 11

You are investigating a "Mischief under $5,000.00" complaint. You suspect that Drew (16) committed the offence. Drew voluntarily accompanies you for questioning. Do you have to inform him of the right to counsel?

_____

_____

_____

Problem 12

You arrest and charge Chad for "Attempted murder." You search Chad's car and find a knife that was used in the offence. Afterward, Chad confesses to you that he committed the offence.

a. Can the admissibility of the knife be determined before the trial?

_____

_____

_____

b. If a s. 8 Charter violation is proven to have occurred after the knife was lawfully seized, does s. 24(2) Charter apply to determine its admissibility?

_____

_____

c. It is proven that you committed a s. 8 Charter violation before the knife was seized and before the confession was obtained. Will the knife automatically be excluded under s. 24(2) Charter?

_____

_____

d. Will the knife likely be admitted or excluded?

_____

_____

_____

e. Will the confession be automatically excluded?

_____

_____

_____

f. Will the confession likely be admitted or excluded?

_____

_____

_____

_____

_____

_____

_____

_____

_____

_____

_____

_____

_____

_____

_____

_____

_____

_____

ENDNOTES

1. Gino Arcaro, "Personality Traits of an Interrogator" (diss. Niagara College, 2007).
2. *R. v. Collins* (1987), 33 C.C.C. (3d) 1 (S.C.C.).
3. *R. v. Stillman* (1997), 113 C.C.C. (3d) 321 (S.C.C.).
4. *R. v. Harrison*, 2008 ABQB 81.
5. *R. v. Whitfield* (1969), 1 C.C.C. 129 (S.C.C.).
6. *R. v. Therens* (1985), 18 C.C.C. (3d) 481 (S.C.C.).
7. Section 129 C.C.
8. Section 145(1)(a) C.C.
9. *R. v. Whitfield*, supra note 5.
10. Ibid.

11. Ibid.

12. *Cloutier v. Langlois* (1990), 53 C.C.C. (3d) 257 (S.C.C.).

13. *R. v. Charlton*, 1992 CanLII 367 (B.C.C.A.); *R. v. Speid* (1991), 8 C.R.R. (2d) 383 (Ont. C.A.); *R. v. Smellie* (1994), 95 C.C.C. (3d) 9 (B.C.C.A.).

14. *R. v. Evans* (1991), 63 C.C.C. (3d) 289 (S.C.C.).

15. Section 24(2) Charter.

16. Section 29(1) C.C.

17. Section 10(b) C.C.

18. *R. v. Schmautz* (1990), 53 C.C.C. (3d) 556 (S.C.C.).

19. Section 25(1) Y.C.J.A.

20. *R. v. Anderson* (1984), 10 C.C.C. (3d) 204 (Ont. C.A.).

21. Ibid.

22. Section 146 Y.C.J.A.

23. Ibid.

24. Section 32 Y.C.J.A.

25. *R. v. Brydges* (1990), 53 C.C.C. (3d) 380 (S.C.C.).

26. *R. v. Hermanus* (1993) (B.C. Prov. Ct.), as in *Lawyer's Weekly*, vol. 12, no. 35 (1993).

27. Section 24(2) Charter.

28. *R. v. Bartle* (1994), 92 C.C.C. (3d) 289 (S.C.C.).

29. Section 24(2) Charter.

30. *R. v. Jackson* (1993), 15 O.R. (3d) 709 (C.A.).

31. Ibid.

32. *R. v. Evans*, supra note 14.

33. Ibid.

34. Ibid.

35. Ibid., at 305.

36. *Canadian Criminal Justice System*, Ontario Police College précis (1986).

37. *R. v. Hollis* (1992), 76 C.C.C. (3d) 421 (B.C.C.A.).

38. *R. v. Burlingham* (1995), 97 C.C.C. (3d) 385 (S.C.C.).

39. Ibid.

40. *R. v. Manninen* (1987), 34 C.C.C. (3d) 385 (S.C.C.).

41. Ibid.

42. *R. v. Smith* (1989), 50 C.C.C. (3d) 308 (S.C.C.).

43. Ibid.

44. *R. v. Hebert* (1990), 57 C.C.C. (3d) 1 (S.C.C.).

45. *R. v. Pavel* (1989), 53 C.C.C. (3d) 296 (Ont. C.A.).

46. *R. v. McKane* (1987), 35 C.C.C. (3d) 481 (Ont. C.A.); *R. v. LePage* (1986), 32 C.C.C. (3d) 171 (N.S.C.A.).

47. *R. v. MacKenzie* (1991), 64 C.C.C. (3d) 1 (N.S.C.A.).

48. *R. v. Hebert*, supra note 44.

49. *R. v. Ferron* (1989), 49 C.C.C. (3d) 432 (B.C.C.A.).

50. *R. v. Top* (1989), 48 C.C.C. (3d) 493 (Alta. C.A.).

51. *R. v. T.(E.)* (1993), 86 C.C.C. (3d) 289 (S.C.C.).

52. *R. v. Hebert*, supra note 44.

53. Ibid.

54. Section 25(7) Y.C.J.A.

55. *R. v. Hermanus*, supra note 26.
56. *R. v. Prosper* (1994), 92 C.C.C. (3d) 353 (S.C.C.).
57. Ibid., and *R. v. Clarkson* (1986), 25 C.C.C. (3d) 207 (S.C.C.).
58. *R. v. Brydges*, supra note 25.
59. *R. v. Clarkson*, supra note 57.
60. *R. v. Brydges*, supra note 25.

CHAPTER 10

Use of Force: Sections 25–43 Criminal Code

LEARNING OBJECTIVES

The student will learn

- To understand the potential for violence faced by police officers when making an arrest

- That the improper use of force is a criminal offence

INTRODUCTION

The potential for being murdered is an occupational hazard of policing. Prospective police officers need to understand that offenders may become violent. Some people who are arrested try to assault police officers; others try to kill them. This state of affairs is inescapable. Policing is the only line of work I know of where workers have the occupational hazard of being murdered or assaulted.

That such violent attitudes and behaviour are directed at members of a profession is a sad social commentary. Once I was a guest on a radio talk show, examining a cluster of incidents in which police officers had been shot at and killed. Causes and solutions were discussed. A person called in and stated his belief that the recent murders of police officers were causing an "overreaction," and that a police officer's job is "not really dangerous, not as dangerous as a construction worker's." Although these absurd notions don't represent the common view, they demonstrate that some people accept violence toward police.

If you are serious about being a police officer, you must consider the fact that officers are targets of violence and are sometimes murdered. The police profession involves far more than sporting a uniform.

The dangers of the job outweigh the small pleasure of declaring yourself a police officer. The job has to be taken very seriously. Apart from the threat of being killed or assaulted, police themselves may be charged with a *Criminal Code* offence for using excessive force.

Some college students believe that the laws concerning police use of force can be handily condensed as follows: "Use as much force as is necessary." Wrong! This summary is not only a misrepresentation of the use-of-force laws; it represents a dangerous way of thinking. You cannot ignore key phrases and words in the use-of-force laws.

The federal use-of-force laws are found in ss. 25–43 C.C. They are included in this book starting on page 221 for their academic value and for students' benefit. Every student is encouraged to read each section carefully. These provisions are only *general* guidelines; they do not cover situation-specific, step-by-step procedures. There are also countless case law decisions to supplement the *Criminal Code* provisions. Visit **www.emp.ca/arcaro/policepowers4E** for commentary on a number of important cases.

Experts at police colleges and police training branches teach how to interpret these provisions and how to apply them situationally. The following notes will help you better understand these use-of-force laws:

- Read the definition of *assault* in s. 265 C.C. You will notice that intentional force without consent constitutes an assault—a criminal offence that carries potential jail time. Any type of ordinary force involves the *actus reus* of assault offences.
- Throughout ss. 25–43 C.C. the word "justified" is prevalent. This word is important for two reasons:
  - It creates *accountability*. If you use force as a police officer, you must be able to specify why.
  - It provides police with *protection*. If an officer uses force for correct, legal reasons, the act that would otherwise be an assault is a justified act; in other words, the *mens rea* of assault, defined in s. 265 C.C., is negated, and the person who has used force is *protected* from criminal responsibility, and will not be charged, convicted, or sent to prison.
- Read s. 26 C.C. carefully. Every person, police or citizen, who uses *"excessive force"* is *"criminally responsible."* This means there is no blanket protection given to police officers who use force. In other words, an individual is not licensed to use as much force as he wants in all situations; there is no legal protection for his doing so. The use-of-force provisions offer a set of guidelines that apply to *general* categories of violent situations. A person cannot simply use as much force as he or she feels is needed; there are limitations and restrictions imposed. If you exceed these limits, you may be charged, convicted, and sent to prison for committing a criminal offence; civil responsibility is another consequence.

In summary:

- The possibility of having to use force to save your own life or the life of others, is real.
- When you learn defensive tactics at police college or through your police services, commit yourself to excellence. Take it seriously and train hard.
- Get in the best physical shape possible. Commit yourself to physical fitness *excellence*. Strive for *peak performance* physically.
- Finally, you must remember that policing has a "Catch-22" side—lethal force could be used against you, but if you use too much force against someone else, you could go to jail.

SECTIONS 25–43 OF THE CRIMINAL CODE

Protection of Persons Administering and Enforcing the Law

25(1) PROTECTION OF PERSONS ACTING UNDER AUTHORITY

25(1) Every one who is required or authorized by law to do anything in the administration or enforcement of the law

(a) as a private person,

(b) as a peace officer or public officer,

(c) in aid of a peace officer or public officer, or

(d) by virtue of his office,

is, if he acts on reasonable grounds, justified in doing what he is required or authorized to do and in using as much force as is necessary for that purpose.

25(2) IDEM

(2) Where a person is required or authorized by law to execute a process or to carry out a sentence, that person or any person who assists him is, if that person acts in good faith, justified in executing the process or in carrying out the sentence notwithstanding that the process or sentence is defective or that it was issued or imposed without jurisdiction or in excess of jurisdiction.

25(3) WHEN NOT PROTECTED

(3) Subject to subsections (4) and (5), a person is not justified for the purposes of subsection (1) in using force that is intended or is likely to cause death or grievous bodily harm unless the person believes on reasonable grounds that it is necessary for the self-preservation of the person or the preservation of any one under that person's protection from death or grievous bodily harm.

25(4) WHEN PROTECTED

(3) A peace officer, and every person lawfully assisting the peace officer, is justified in using force that is intended or is likely to cause death or grievous bodily harm to a person to be arrested, if

(a) the peace officer is proceeding lawfully to arrest, with or without warrant, the person to be arrested;

(b) the offence for which the person is to be arrested is one for which that person may be arrested without warrant;

(c) the person to be arrested takes flight to avoid arrest;

(d) the peace officer or other person using the force believes on reasonable grounds that the force is necessary for the purposes of protecting the peace officer, the personal lawfully assisting the peace officer or any other person from imminent or future death or grievous bodily harm; and

(e) the flight cannot be prevented by reasonable means in a less violent manner.

25(5) POWER IN CASE OF ESCAPE FROM PENITENTIARY

(5) A peace officer is justified in using force that is intended or is likely to cause death or grievous bodily harm against an inmate who is escaping from a penitentiary within the meaning of subsection 2(1) of the *Corrections and Conditional Release Act*, if

(a) the peace officer believes on reasonable grounds that any of the inmates of the penitentiary poses a threat of death or grievous bodily harm to the peace officer or any other person; and

(b) the escape cannot be prevented by reasonable means in a less violent manner.

26 EXCESSIVE FORCE

26. Every one who is authorized by law to use force is criminally responsible for any excess thereof according to the nature and quality of the act that constitutes the excess.

27 USE OF FORCE TO PREVENT COMMISSION OF OFFENCE

27. Every one is justified in using as much force as is reasonably necessary

(a) to prevent the commission of an offence

(i) for which, if it were committed, the person who committed it might be arrested without warrant, and

(ii) that would be likely to cause immediate and serious injury to the person or property of anyone; or

(b) to prevent anything being done that, on reasonable grounds, he believes would, if it were done, be an offence mentioned in paragraph (a).

28(1) ARREST OF WRONG PERSON

28(1) Where a person who is authorized to execute a warrant to arrest believes, in good faith and on reasonable grounds, that the person whom he arrests is the person named on the warrant, he is protected from criminal responsibility in respect thereof to the same extent as if that person were the person named in the warrant.

28(2) PERSON ASSISTING

(2) Where a person is authorized to execute a warrant to arrest,

(a) every one who, being called on to assist him, believes that the person in whose arrest he is called on to assist is the person named in the warrant, and

(b) every keeper of a prison who is required to receive and detain a person who he believes has been arrested under the warrant

is protected from criminal responsibility in respect thereof to the same extent as if that person were the person named in the warrant.

29(1) DUTY OF PERSON ARRESTING

29(1) It is the duty of every one who executes a process or warrant to have it with him, where it is feasible to do so, and to produce it when requested to do so.

29(2) NOTICE

(2) It is the duty of every one who arrests a person, whether with or without a warrant, to give notice to that person, where it is feasible to do so, of

(a) the process or warrant under which he makes the arrest; or

(b) the reason for the arrest.

29(3) FAILURE TO COMPLY

(3) Failure to comply with subsection (1) or (2) does not of itself deprive a person who executes a process or warrant, or a person who makes an arrest, or those who assist them, of protection from criminal responsibility.

30 PREVENTING BREACH OF PEACE

30. Every one who witnesses a breach of the peace is justified in interfering to prevent the continuance or renewal thereof and may detain any person who commits or is about to join in or renew the breach of the peace, for the purpose of giving him into the custody of a peace officer, if he uses no more force than is reasonably necessary to prevent the continuance or renewal of the breach of the peace or than is reasonably proportioned to the danger to be apprehended from the continuance or renewal of the breach of the peace.

31(1) ARREST FOR BREACH OF PEACE

31(1) Every peace officer who witnesses a breach of the peace and every one who lawfully assists the peace officer is justified in arresting any person whom he finds committing the breach of the peace or who, on reasonable grounds, he believes is about to join in or renew the breach of the peace.

31(2) GIVING PERSON IN CHARGE

(2) Every peace officer is justified in receiving into custody any person who is given into his charge as having been a party to a breach of the peace by one who has, or who on reasonable grounds the peace officer believes has, witnessed the breach of the peace.

Suppression of Riots

32(1) USE OF FORCE TO SUPPRESS RIOT

32(1) Every peace officer is justified in using or in ordering the use of as much force as the peace officer believes, in good faith and on reasonable grounds,

(a) is necessary to suppress a riot; and

(b) is not excessive, having regard to the danger to be apprehended from the continuance of the riot.

32(2) PERSON BOUND BY MILITARY LAW

(2) Every one who is bound by military law to obey the command of his superior officer is justified in obeying any command given by his superior officer for the suppression of a riot unless the order is manifestly unlawful.

32(3) OBEYING ORDER OF PEACE OFFICER

(3) Every one is justified in obeying an order of a peace officer to use force to suppress a riot if

(a) he acts in good faith; and

(b) the order is not manifestly unlawful.

32(4) APPREHENSION OF SERIOUS MISCHIEF

(3) Every one who, in good faith and on reasonable grounds, believes that serious mischief will result from a riot before it is possible to secure attendance of a peace officer is justified in using as much force as he believes in good faith and on reasonable grounds,

(a) is necessary to suppress the riot; and

(b) is not excessive, having regard to the danger to be apprehended from the continuance of the riot.

32(5) QUESTION OF LAW

(5) For the purposes of this section, the question whether an order is manifestly unlawful or not is a question of law.

33(1) DUTY OF OFFICERS IF RIOTERS DO NOT DISPERSE

33(1) Where the proclamation referred to in section 67 has been made or an offence against paragraph 68(a) or (b) has been committed, it is the duty of a peace officer and of a person who is lawfully required by him to assist, to disperse or to arrest persons who do not comply with the proclamation.

33(2) PROTECTION OF OFFICERS

(2) No civil or criminal proceedings lie against a peace officer or a person who is lawfully required to assist him in respect of any death or injury that by reason of resistance is caused as a result of the performance by the peace officer or that person of a duty that is imposed by subsection (1).

33(3) SECTION NOT RESTRICTIVE

(3) Nothing in this section limits or affects any powers, duties or functions that are conferred or imposed by this Act with respect to the suppression of riots.

Self-Induced Intoxication

33.1(1) WHEN DEFENCE NOT AVAILABLE

33.1(1) It is not a defence to an offence referred to in subsection (3) that the accused, by reason of self-induced intoxication, lacked the general intent or the voluntariness required to commit the offence, where the accused departed markedly from the standard of care as described in subsection (2).

33.1(2) CRIMINAL FAULT BY REASON OF INTOXICATION

(2) For the purposes of this section, a person departs markedly from the standard of reasonable care generally recognized in Canadian society and is thereby criminally at fault where the person, while in a state of self-induced intoxication that renders the person unaware of, or incapable of consciously controlling, their behaviour, voluntarily or involuntarily interferes or threatens to interfere with the bodily integrity of another person.

33.1(3) APPLICATION

(3) This section applies in respect of an offence under this Act or any other Act of Parliament that includes as an element an assault or any other interference or threat of interference by a person with the bodily integrity of another person.

Defence of Person

34(1) SELF-DEFENCE AGAINST UNPROVOKED ASSAULT

34(1) Every one who is unlawfully assaulted without having provoked the assault is justified in repelling force by force if the force he uses is not intended to cause death or grievous bodily harm and is no more than is necessary to enable him to defend himself.

34(2) EXTENT OF JUSTIFICATION

(2) Every one who is unlawfully assaulted and who causes death or grievous bodily harm in repelling the assault is justified if

(a) he causes it under reasonable apprehension of death or grievous bodily harm from the violence with which the assault was originally made or with which the assailant pursues his purposes; and

(b) he believes, on reasonable grounds, that he cannot otherwise preserve himself from death or grievous bodily harm.

35 SELF-DEFENCE IN CASE OF AGGRESSION

35. Every one who has without justification assaulted another but did not commence the assault with the intent to cause death or grievous bodily harm, or has without justification provoked an assault on himself by another, may justify the use of force subsequent to the assault if

(a) he uses the force

(i) under reasonable apprehension of death or grievous bodily harm from the violence of the person whom he has assaulted or provoked, and

(ii) in the belief, on reasonable grounds, that it is necessary in order to preserve himself from death or grievous bodily harm;

(b) he did not, at any time before the necessity of preserving himself from death or grievous bodily harm arose, endeavour to cause death or grievous bodily harm; and

(c) he declined further conflict and quitted or retreated from it as far as it was feasible to do so before the necessity of preserving himself from death or grievous bodily harm arose.

36 PROVOCATION

36. Provocation includes, for the purposes of sections 34 and 35, provocation by blows, words or gestures.

37(1) PREVENTING ASSAULT

37(1) Every one is justified in using force to defend himself or any one under his protection from assault, if he uses no more force than is necessary to prevent the assault or the repetition of it.

37(2) EXTENT OF JUSTIFICATION

(2) Nothing in this section shall be deemed to justify the wilful infliction of any hurt or mischief that is excessive, having regard to the nature of the assault that the force used was intended to prevent.

Defence of Property

38(1) DEFENCE OF PERSONAL PROPERTY

38(1) Every one who is in peaceable possession of personal property, and every one lawfully assisting him, is justified

(a) in preventing a trespasser from taking it, or
(b) in taking it from a trespasser who has taken it, if he does not strike or cause bodily harm to the trespasser.

38(2) ASSAULT BY TRESPASSER

(2) Where a person who is in peaceable possession of personal property lays hands on it, a trespasser who persists in attempting to keep it or take it from him or from any one lawfully assisting him shall be deemed to commit an assault without justification or provocation.

39(1) DEFENCE WITH CLAIM OF RIGHT

39(1) Every one who is in peaceable possession of personal property under a claim of right, and every one acting under his authority, is protected from criminal responsibility for defending that possession, even against a person entitled by law to possession of it, if he uses no more force than is necessary.

39(2) DEFENCE WITHOUT CLAIM OF RIGHT

(2) Every one who is in peaceable possession of personal property, but does not claim it as of right or does not act under the authority of a person who claims it as of right, is not justified or protected from criminal responsibility for defending his possession against a person who is entitled by law to possession of it.

40 DEFENCE OF DWELLING

40. Every one who is in peaceable possession of a dwelling-house, and every one lawfully assisting him or acting under his authority, is justified in using as much force as is necessary to prevent any person from forcibly breaking into or forcibly entering the dwelling-house without lawful authority.

41(1) DEFENCE OF HOUSE OR REAL PROPERTY

41(1) Every one who is in peaceable possession of a dwelling-house or real property, and every one lawfully assisting him or acting under his authority, is justified in using force to prevent any person from trespassing on the dwelling-house or real property, or to remove a trespasser therefrom, if he uses no more force than is necessary.

41(2) ASSAULT BY TRESPASSER

(2) A trespasser who resists an attempt by a person who is in peaceable possession of a dwelling-house or real property, or a person lawfully assisting him or acting under his authority to prevent his entry or to remove him, shall be deemed to commit an assault without justification or provocation.

42(1) ASSERTION OF RIGHT TO HOUSE OR REAL PROPERTY

42(1) Every one is justified in peaceably entering a dwelling-house or real property by day to take possession of it if he, or a person under whose authority he acts, is lawfully entitled to possession of it.

42(2) ASSAULT IN CASE OF LAWFUL ENTRY

(2) Where a person

(a) not having peaceable possession of a dwelling-house or real property under a claim of right, or

(b) not acting under the authority of a person who has peaceable possession of a dwelling-house or real property under a claim of right,

assaults a person who is lawfully entitled to possession of it and who is entering it peaceably by day to take possession of it, for the purpose of preventing him from entering, the assault shall be deemed to be without justification or provocation.

42(3) TRESPASSER PROVOKING ASSAULT

(3) Where a person

(a) having peaceable possession of a dwelling-house or real property under a claim of right, or

(b) acting under the authority of a person who has peaceable possession of a dwelling-house or real property under a claim of right,

assaults any person who is lawfully entitled to possession of it and who is entering it peaceably by day to take possession of it, for the purpose of preventing him from entering, the assault shall be deemed to be provoked by the person who is entering.

Protection of Persons in Authority

43 CORRECTION OF CHILD BY FORCE

43. Every schoolteacher, parent or person standing in the place of a parent is justified in using force by way of correction toward a pupil or child, as the case may be, who is under his care, if the force does not exceed what is reasonable under the circumstances.

CHAPTER 11

Release Provisions: Post-Custody Detention

LEARNING OUTCOMES

The student will learn

- How to apply a decision-making model for releasing offenders
- How to interpret release provisions
- How to apply specific rules and procedures that justify continued detention and mandatory release at the scene of an arrest (Level 1), at the police station (Level 2), and at a bail hearing (Level 3)
- The types and contents of release/compelling documents
- The procedures of a bail hearing

> "... the legislation is not crafted clearly"[1]
>
> —Justice David P. Cole, Ontario Court of Justice,
> referring to the *Criminal Code* release provisions

INTRODUCTION

After a police officer arrests or detains an adult or a young offender, the officer must make four decisions:

1. whether to release the accused or continue detention;
2. how long the detention should be;
3. whether or not to compel the accused to appear in court;
4. what document to serve to compel a court appearance.

Release provisions govern these four decisions. The laws governing "release provisions" may be the most complicated set of laws in the C.C. with respect to front-line policing.

Release refers to the termination of arrest, detention, and custody. When an offender is released from custody, his or her freedom is restored. An arrested person cannot be held in custody arbitrarily. Specific rules and procedures found in Part XVI (ss. 498–529) of the *Criminal Code* govern the length of detention or custody permitted, and determine when an arrested person must be released. They apply to both adult and young offenders. The Y.C.J.A. includes additional release provisions for young offenders.

CONCEPTS OF "COMPELLING" VERSUS "CHARGING"

You must differentiate the concepts of *compelling* and *charging* in order to understand release provisions. To **charge** is to make a formal allegation by laying an Information. To **compel** an accused person is to force him or her to appear in court to answer the charge by issuing a document such as a "promise to appear," a "summons," or an "appearance notice." In other words, to make someone appear in court you need both an Information that lays a formal allegation and a compelling document, in that order. The Information does not force the court appearance and the "appearance notice/promise to appear" does not charge the person. The two documents have separate functions, but they work in tandem.

THE TRI-LEVEL RELEASE MODEL

Making an arrest simultaneously ends one decision-making process and starts another. Applying arrest and detention laws represents the first decision-making process, which culminates in the taking of custody. At this point, an incredibly complex statutory scheme is set in motion to decide whether custody may lawfully continue or whether the person in custody must be released.

The three post-custody detention laws are concerned with bail, release provisions, and judicial interim release. These laws consist of three levels of decisions that form a tri-level release model (TRM), which begins to apply at the time of arrest or custody and continues until a lawful conclusion is reached about releasing or continuing detention. Figure 11.1 is designed to simplify the complexities of TRM.

Although the powers of arrest and investigative detention laws are generally considered to be the ones most relevant to front-line policing, the laws governing post-custody release have a similar significance. Courts consider the unlawful denial of freedom, at any time during an investigation, to be the most serious Charter

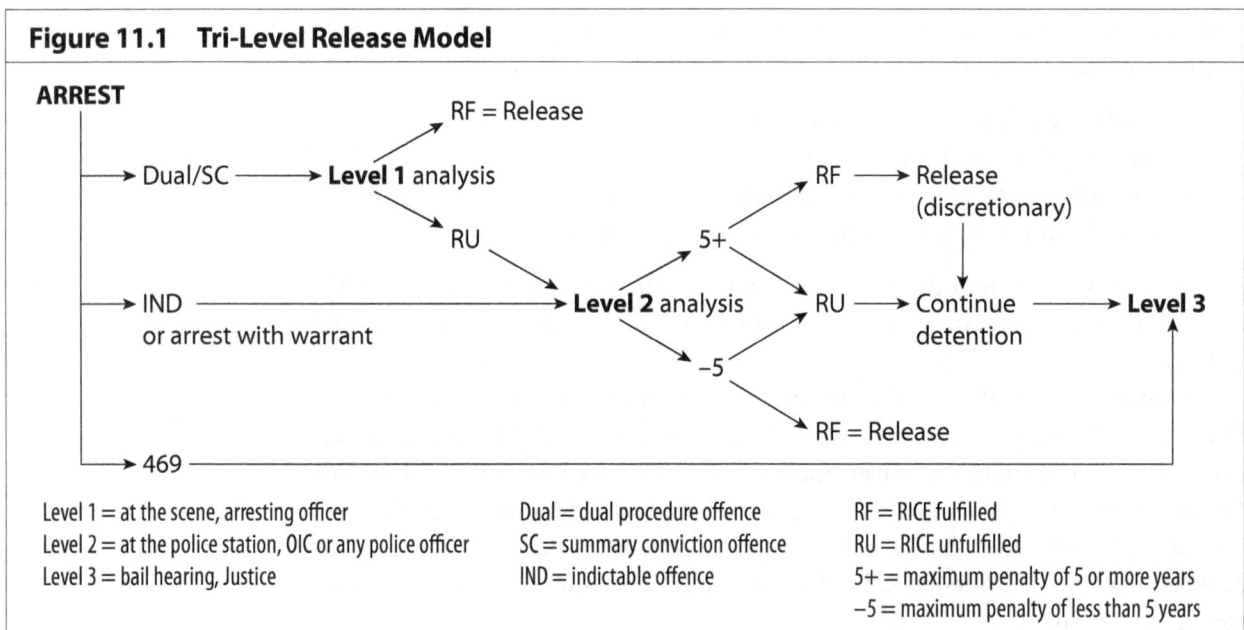

Figure 11.1   Tri-Level Release Model

Level 1 = at the scene, arresting officer	Dual = dual procedure offence
Level 2 = at the police station, OIC or any police officer	SC = summary conviction offence
Level 3 = bail hearing, Justice	IND = indictable offence

RF = RICE fulfilled
RU = RICE unfulfilled
5+ = maximum penalty of 5 or more years
−5 = maximum penalty of less than 5 years

violation.[2] They view with equal severity unlawful detention at the time of arrest or during the post-custody detention stage, and the potential consequences of these violations include civil liability[3] and s. 24 Charter remedies, such as a stay of criminal proceedings.[4] How release provisions are applied during the post-custody detention stage dramatically affects an investigation and prosecution. The problem for police officers is that the statutory scheme that governs release provisions and bail is remarkably complicated. The language is non-functional and "convoluted."[5]

The goal of this chapter is to translate the release and bail provisions into functional language.

CONCEPT OF POST-CUSTODY DETENTION

There are two stages of detention. The initial custody stage represents the actual moment when an arrest is made. It is a brief stage justified by *preceding* circumstances.

The second stage is the *post-custody* detention stage (PCD). It is a substantially longer period of time, characterized by a structured, sequential decision-making process that involves a minimum of one level and a maximum of three levels.

The two stages of detention have equal legal significance. Section 9 Charter mandates that neither can be the result of arbitrary decisions.

Two decisions have to be made during the post-custody detention (PCD) of both adult and young offenders:

1. Is continued detention justified?
2. Is release mandatory?

If release is mandatory, decide what document should be served to compel a subsequent court appearance by the accused.

CONCEPT OF "BAIL"

Bail is defined as *any* form of release authorized by the *Criminal Code*. It may involve the deposit of money or valuable security as a condition of release.[6]

Bail comprises the following four concepts:

1. *Release.* **Release** is an informal phrase referring to the termination of detention or custody and the restoration of freedom. A formal charge may or may not accompany release.
2. *Judicial interim release.* When a formal charge accompanies release, "judicial interim release" is the *Criminal Code* phrase that refers to an accused's pre-trial freedom. The accused is free during the interim between the laying of the charge and the trial.
3. *A court appearance.* Compelling a court appearance refers to the process of legally forcing an offender to appear in court to answer a formal allegation. Compelling the accused to appear means that he or she has no choice. It is accomplished by serving a document, known as a *release document* or a *compelling document.*

   Although charging an accused and compelling a court appearance are parts of one process, they represent two separate concepts, distinguished by two types of documents. An "Information" is a document that formally alleges an offence but it does not compel a court appearance. Conversely, a release or compelling document, such as an Appearance Notice or a Promise to Appear, forces the accused to appear in court but it does not formally charge the offender.

Consequently, commencing criminal court proceedings requires two documents: one to charge and one to compel a court appearance.

4. *Part XVI C.C.* Part XVI C.C. is entitled "Compel Appearance of Accused" and consists of ss. 493–529, a complicated set of laws that explains when and how to release an arrested person. Informally called "release provisions," Part XVI C.C. represents Canada's intricate bail system.

Section 11(e) Charter

This provision governs judicial decision-making. It guarantees that "any person charged with an offence has the right not to be denied reasonable bail without just cause."

Section 11(e) Charter contains two distinct elements:

1. The right to "reasonable bail," and
2. The right not to be denied bail without "just cause."

Part XVI C.C. explains the parameters of both "reasonable bail" and "just cause," but s. 11(e) Charter evaluates whether they are applied properly. Section 11(e) Charter creates a system of accountability by obliging the police to justify both continued detention at all times during PCD and the conditions that are imposed on release.

According to the S.C.C.,

- "reasonable bail" refers to the "terms" of bail, or the "restrictions imposed on the accused's liberty while on bail"; and
- "just cause" refers to the grounds or evidence that supports granting or denying bail.[7]

Presumption of Innocence

Section 6(1) C.C. ensures that a person "shall be deemed not to be guilty of the offence until he is convicted."

The S.C.C. described this presumption of innocence as the "golden thread woven throughout the web of criminal law."[8] Denial of bail is generally accepted as having a "detrimental effect" on the presumption of innocence and the entire criminal justice system because of the "serious practical effects" it has on the accused's ability to raise a defence.[9]

This principle explains why

- it is extremely difficult to detain an arrested person in custody following a bail hearing;
- Part XVI C.C. favours the release of arrested persons as opposed to continued detention;
- PCD requires strict justification and close scrutiny; and
- the consequences of unreasonable, unjustified PCD are severe.

Legislative Evolution

A history of the modern Canadian bail system will help you understand release provisions by revealing Parliament's intention and objectives.

Common law created two separate and distinct grounds for bail denial:

1. ensuring the accused's court appearance, and
2. protecting the public.

Originally, ensuring court appearance was the only common law reason for bail denial. Eventually, English courts recognized the *secondary* reason, public protection, which it defined as a "high probability," based on evidence, that the accused would commit another offence while on bail.[10]

In 1869, Canadian federal legislation stated the following:

1. Bail was discretionary for all offences.
2. Judges, not the police, were the sole decision-makers.
3. Bail denial could be justified on two grounds:
   a. *primary* grounds, referring to ensuring court appearance;
   b. *secondary* grounds, referring to public protection, for which one takes into consideration the nature of the offence, the severity of the maximum penalty, the strength of the evidence, and the accused's character.[11]

For the next 100 years, federal law created the presumption of pre-trial detention. In other words, the accused was given the burden of applying for and justifying his or her release. Statutory law during this period gave judges "virtually no guidance" about how to decide on bail granting or denial.[12]

In the 1960s, empirical research findings that the Canadian bail system was "ineffective, inequitable, and inconsistent" led to Justice Ouimet's 1969 *Report of the Canadian Committee on Corrections*, which recommended changes to the system. Specifically, the report recommended that pre-trial detention be found justified only when "necessary in the public interest" on two grounds:

1. primary grounds, the need to ensure the court appearance of the accused; and
2. secondary grounds, the need to protect the public from repeated criminal activity by the accused.[13]

This recommendation shifted the onus of justification—in this case, the justification for denying bail—to the prosecution.[14]

In 1972, the *Bail Reform Act* radically changed the bail and release provisions, resulting, in 1976, in the passage of Bill C-71, which amended the *Criminal Code* to include the following new concepts:

1. The presumption of pre-trial detention was replaced with the presumption of release, shifting the onus from the accused to the prosecution.[15]
2. The new presumption of release was based on an "undertaking" (that is, a promise or a guarantee from the accused) to attend court for trial. The accused's promise to appear in court became a fundamental release condition.[16]

3. The rigid, inflexible, all-or-nothing approach to bail was eliminated, replaced by the concept of "conditional" release, which gave bail judges discretionary authority to grant release, subject to specific conditions.[17]

4. Responsibility for decision making about release was extended. The officer-in-charge (OIC) of a police station was given the authority to release an accused person "conditionally or unconditionally," and the range of OIC jurisdiction over release was widened to include offences whose maximum penalty exceeded five years' imprisonment.[18]

5. The specific criteria for bail denial were changed. A third grounds for justifying bail denial was created. The Ouimet Report had defined "public interest" according to the common-law primary (court appearance) and secondary (public protection) grounds. However, the *Bail Reform Act* established "necessary in the public interest" as independent grounds for denying bail, separate and in addition to the original two grounds.

There were now three grounds for justifying pre-trial detention: to ensure the court appearance of the accused, to prevent the repetition of a criminal offence, and to protect the public interest. The three grounds may seem redundant, but the amendment was approved and is now s. 515(10) C.C.[19]

These changes created a "ladder approach" to the bail and release system: the greater the maximum penalty attached to the offence, the higher the judicial officer required to decide about bail and release. A Justice was still required to be the sole decision-maker about bail in the case of severe indictable offences.[20]

In 1995, Bill C-42 amended the *Criminal Code* release provisions, extending police authority to release. All police officers were given the same release authority as the OIC. Additionally, the police were authorized to impose conditions upon release, an authority previously reserved for Justices alone.

Objective

Parliament's purpose was to "maintain public confidence in the bail system and the justice system as a whole."[21]

Parliament's intention was to create a "properly functioning bail system" whereby "narrow" and "carefully tailored" rules prevented both "continuing criminal behaviour and an intolerable risk of absconding."[22]

Parliament's objective was to preserve the presumption of innocence and to impose pre-trial detention only in limited cases, where evidence strongly justified it as the only means of ensuring the accused's appearance in court or of protecting the public from continued criminal behaviour by the accused.

APPLYING THE TRI-LEVEL RELEASE MODEL

The General Rule

The most important decision in the model concens the following question: "Is RICE fulfilled?" That is to say, is the arrested person a public safety risk or a fail-to-appear risk? Preventing these two risks is the crucial objective of release decision making.

If the arrested person is either a public safety risk or a fail-to-appear risk (that is, if RICE is not fulfilled), continued detention is justified. If he is neither of these things, RICE is fulfilled and detention ends—release is mandatory.

CONCEPT OF RICE

Part XVI of the *Criminal Code* lists four factors that should be considered in determining whether the continued detention of an adult or young offender is justified. **RICE** is an informal term. It is not used in the *Criminal Code*. Each letter in RICE represents one of four factors that must be considered in determining whether an arrested adult or young offender must be released or whether continued detention and custody are necessary in the public interest. The acronym works as follows:

1. **R**epetition of the offence (for which the accused has been charged) or any other offence (is there a risk of repetition?);
2. **I**dentity of the arrested person (has the accused been identified?);
3. **C**ourt appearance (is there a risk that the accused will not appear in court?);
4. **E**vidence relating to the offence (is there a risk of such evidence being destroyed?).

RICE Fulfilled

The phrase "RICE fulfilled" means that the arrested person is not a public safety or a fail-to-appear risk. Release is mandatory in this case. Continued detention is not justified.

Specifically, *RICE fulfilled* means that all of the following circumstances exist:

▸ No reasonable grounds exist for believing that a repetition of any offence will occur.
▸ The correct identity of the accused has been established.
▸ No reasonable grounds exist for believing that the accused will fail to appear in court.
▸ Evidence connected to the offence has been secured or preserved.

RICE Not Fulfilled

The phrase "RICE not fulfilled" means that the arrested person is a public safety or a fail-to-appear risk. Continued detention is justified.

Specifically, *RICE not fulfilled* means that at least one of the following circumstances exists:

▸ Reasonable grounds exist for believing that a repetition of the offence will occur.
▸ The accused's identity has not been properly established.
▸ Reasonable grounds exist for believing that the accused will fail to appear in court.
▸ Evidence relating to the offence exists and has not been secured or preserved.

The existence of even one of these circumstances means that the release of an arrested person is not beneficial to the public interest. Continued custody is necessary in the public interest.

Determining Whether RICE Is Fulfilled: Procedure

The *Criminal Code* does not explain precisely how to determine whether RICE is fulfilled—for example, what kind of evidence is needed. As a result, police officers must employ investigative techniques to obtain evidence or information relevant to the RICE factors, and consider this information in the context of a *reasonable grounds* belief.

Any evidence that may exist in connection with the following can help you determine whether RICE has been fulfilled.

REPETITION OF THE OFFENCE

Evidence that the offence may be repeated could include the following:

- oral statements the accused has made to the police or any citizen indicating an intent to commit either the same offence again or another offence;
- the accused's physical or mental condition, including intoxication and hostility;
- a past record of criminal convictions, violent acts, psychological disorders, and narcotic dependency;
- no stable financial means of support; and
- the recent arrest of the accused for single or multiple offences.

The absence of the above evidence may prove that RICE is fulfilled.

IDENTITY OF THE ARRESTED PERSON

The identity of an arrested person can be verified by:

- official documents, such as a birth certificate or a driver's licence; or
- verification by family members or persons familiar with the accused, including other officers (who are usually familiar with many offenders).

An accused person's failure or refusal to identify him- or herself means that RICE is not fulfilled. Accused persons cannot be released if their identity is unknown, because an Information and release document requires the accused's name. A refusal to identify oneself does not constitute an offence; the offender cannot be charged with "refusing to identify." What the refusal represents is justification to continue the offender's detention.

Wrongly identifying oneself intentionally constitutes the indictable offence of "obstructing justice"; the accused could evade prosecution by doing this, while an innocent person is implicated.

COURT APPEARANCE

Factors increasing the likelihood that the accused will fail to appear in court could include the following:

- a past record of failure to appear;
- the severity of the offence; and
- an absence of factors binding the accused to his or her community, such as
  - a fixed address,
  - steady employment, or a stable means of income,
  - family, and
  - ownership of property and assets.

When trying to determine whether an accused will appear in court, the following question: "Will the severity of the offence and its consequences be sufficient to cause the accused to leave his or her current status within the community?" The severity of the offence must be considered alongside what the accused would be leaving behind.

EVIDENCE RELATING TO THE OFFENCE

If the release of the accused would increase the likelihood that either of the following will occur, then detention is advised:

- loss of evidence,
- destruction of evidence.

A person cannot be detained while the police are attempting to obtain evidence. Sufficient evidence should have existed prior to the arrest to have constituted reasonable grounds. Essentially, the *Criminal Code* is asking, "Will the accused remove or destroy existing evidence if he or she is released?" To use this factor to justify continued detention, the officer must reasonably believe that evidence does exist that requires securing and preserving from the accused.

In summary, the police have a twofold obligation:

1. If the evidence suggests that RICE is fulfilled, the accused generally must be released; continued detention is not justified.
2. Conversely, if the evidence shows that RICE is not fulfilled, the officer has an obligation to protect the public by not releasing the accused. Continued detention is justified when the public would be threatened or put at risk by the accused's release.

Summary

Whether RICE is fulfilled can be difficult to determine: the status of RICE factors changes and is not always constant. The RICE criteria must be analyzed at each level of release to determine if any changes have occurred.

LEVELS OF RELEASE AND DETENTION

The *Criminal Code* essentially creates three levels, or stages, of release. At each stage, release provisions must be analyzed to determine whether an accused must be released or detained in custody. The levels differ according to general location and to the person responsible for considering the release provisions and making the decision to release or detain.

Although the term "level of release" is not used in the *Criminal Code* (that is, the terms Level 1, Level 2, and Level 3 are not *Criminal Code* terms), we are using them here for teaching purposes, to facilitate interpretation of the relevant *Criminal Code* provisions.

Table 11.1 demonstrates the tri-level concept.

Table 11.1   Levels of Release and Detention

Level	Decision-Making Location	Person Responsible for Decision
1	at the scene of the arrest (before arrival at police station)	police officer (i.e., arresting officer)
2	at the police station	officer-in-charge (refers to a supervisor, such as a staff sergeant), or any police officer (according to a new amendment, any police officer—e.g., a constable—can decide about release)
3	at the bail hearing	Justice (refers to a JP or a provincial court judge)

RELEASE DOCUMENTS: COMPELLING A COURT APPEARANCE

After a person is arrested, the police have two decisions to make:

1. whether to charge and compel the offender to appear in court; and
2. whether to release the offender or continue detention.

Deciding Whether to Charge and Compel

Officers may use their discretion in deciding whether to

1. Charge the offender and compel a court appearance, which requires two separate procedures:
   a. laying an Information; and
   b. compelling the accused to appear in court—in other words, forcing the accused to attend court and answer to the charge.
2. Not charge the offender and use an alternative means to solve the problem. This method is referred to as an **unconditional release**. It represents a "warning or break" given to the offender. "Unconditional" means that the offender will not be required to attend court in answer to a charge. The success of this method largely depends on whether the officer's communication skills are sufficient to solve the problem without a court proceeding. For exmaple, an officer might influence a person, through a warning, to not "do it again." Note that the offence must be minor.

When deciding which problem-solving method to use, the officer's most important consideration is that *the worst consequence be eliminated*—that is, any risk or threat to the public (including death, injury, or property damage) posed by the possible repetition of the offence. This is explained in more detail in Chapter 13.

Decision to Compel a Court Appearance

If a decision is made to charge the offender, two documents are necessary:

1. a sworn Information, to formally charge the offender; and
2. a release or compelling document, to force the offender to appear in court.

A sworn Information represents the formal charge and is a separate document that accompanies the release or compelling document.

A *release* or *compelling document* is a written order directing an accused to appear at a specific court location at a specific date and time. The release or compelling document does not formally charge the accused. Numerous types of release or compelling documents can be found in Part XXVIII, s. 841 C.C., including the following:

- ▸ a summons (Form 6);
- ▸ an appearance notice (Form 9);
- ▸ a promise to appear (Form 10);
- ▸ a recognizance, issued by the officer-in-charge (OIC) (Form 11);
- ▸ a recognizance, issued by a Justice (Form 32);
- ▸ an undertaking, issued by a Justice (Form 12); and
- ▸ an undertaking, issued by a police officer or the OIC (Form 11.1). (This type of undertaking must be used in conjunction with a promise to appear or a recognizance issued by an OIC. It is not a compelling document if used alone.)

Most release or compelling documents are served to the accused upon release. The exception is a summons, which may be served either after release or in lieu of arresting the offender.

Contents of a Release or Compelling Document

All release or compelling documents share the same purpose and the *same contents*. They must instruct a specific accused person to appear at a specific court location on a specific date at a specific time.

The following information must appear on all release or compelling documents: the name of the accused; the name of the offence; and the date, the time, and the address of the court where the appearance is to occur.

It is optional whether to list on all release or compelling documents a date, time, and location for the accused to appear to be fingerprinted and photographed. The police are permitted to take fingerprints and photographs of offenders after they have been arrested or charged for an indictable or dual procedure offence. Depending on the availability of officers, offenders may be fingerprinted or photographed before release. If these procedures cannot be completed prior to release, the accused may be compelled to go to a police station on a specified date and time to be fingerprinted and photographed. This information may be included on the release document. Failure to appear in court is a dual procedure offence. Failure to appear for fingerprints and photographs constitutes a different dual procedure offence.

A **recognizance** and an **undertaking** may entail additional requirements. A recognizance (issued by the officer-in-charge) may call for a deposit from the accused, an amount not exceeding $500.00 if he or she lives inside the province or no more than 200 kilometres from the place of arrest and custody. A Justice may require any sum of money as a deposit if the accused lives out of province or more than 200 kilometres from the place of arrest. An undertaking (issued by a police officer, an OIC, or a Justice) and a recognizance (issued by a Justice) may also include conditions. Regardless of whether the undertaking has conditions, it is named an "undertaking" and refers to only one document. In other words, it is not called "undertaking with conditions."

SEQUENCE OF ISSUANCE—SWORN INFORMATION AND RELEASE OR COMPELLING DOCUMENT

A sworn Information must accompany a release or compelling document to complete the process of compelling an accused to court. The order in which these documents are issued is significant. When a Justice is not required to issue the release, an officer may do so and is permitted to serve some release or compelling documents before laying an Information. Allowing an officer to issue these documents expedites the accused's release; a Justice may not always be available when a release is justified.

Release or compelling documents that a Justice is required to issue must be served after an Information is laid. Table 11.2 explains the order of issuance for sworn Information and for release or compelling documents.

Table 11.2   Order of Issuance for Sworn Information and Release or Compelling Documents

Information Laid First	Release Document Issued First
Release document follows ▸ summons ▸ undertaking (Justice) ▸ recognizance (Justice)	Information laid afterward ▸ appearance notice ▸ promise to appear (PTA) ▸ recognizance (OIC) ▸ undertaking (peace officer or OIC; used in conjunction with PTA or recognizance)
These documents are served after an Information has been laid. They cannot be served before an Information has been laid.	These documents may be served before an Information has been laid. Once the documents above have been served, an Information must be laid as soon as practicable afterward.

UNCONDITIONAL RELEASE

As explained in the previous section of this chapter, an officer may choose to "solve the problem" by granting an unconditional release. No document is given to the accused, by way of explanation, in the case of an unconditional release. The officer simply releases the accused and orally explains the release. An unconditional release is not a binding, formal agreement, and it gives the offender no formal legal assurance that a charge will never be laid. The officer may still charge the offender after issuing an unconditional release. In other words, an unconditional release does not prohibit a police officer from later charging the offender.

NOTICE TO PARENTS OF YOUNG OFFENDERS

Upon releasing a young offender, the police have a mandatory obligation to notify a parent in writing, and this notice must identify the charge(s) and the court date, time, and location.

If the parents' whereabouts are unknown, police may give the notice to an adult relative or, if none is available, to an appropriate adult—one who is known to the young offender and who is likely to assist him or her. If the young offender is married, the notice may be served to the spouse. This notice must be given as soon as possible after the arrest of a young offender. It may be given orally or in writing by either the OIC of the police station or another officer instructed by the OIC. It must inform the parent (or alternate) of the place of detention and the reason(s) for the arrest. This first notice alone will suffice when a young offender is released unconditionally.

LEVEL 1 RELEASE PROVISIONS

The *Criminal Code* describes specific circumstances in which the release of an accused person is mandatory at each of the three levels of release. Among these determining circumstances are whether RICE is fulfillled and what is the classification of the offence. Each level of release has prescribed procedures for release, including relevant documents that may be issued by the releasing person. The justification for continued detention depends on circumstances other than those that determine mandatory release. These release provisions were amended by Bill C-42, which became law on April 1, 1995.

Procedures and Rules

"Level 1" is an informal term that refers to the first stage of release considerations, as established by s. 497 C.C. The term *Level 1* is not actually used in the *Criminal Code*; it is used informally to distinguish this stage from the other levels described by the *Criminal Code*.

Level 1 release refers to the scene of the arrest and applies to the interval between the time of arrest and the time of arrival at the police station. At this level, the decision about release is made by the arresting officer.

Mandatory Release

The arresting officer must release without a warrant at the scene of the arrest (before arrival at the police station), if

- ▸ RICE is fulfilled, and
- ▸ the offence is either
     a. summary conviction, or
     b. dual procedure.

Release is mandatory under these circumstances. In other words, the officer is not justified in transporting the accused to the police station.

Methods of Release

The arresting officer may use any of the following methods when a Level 1 release is mandatory.

APPEARANCE NOTICE

An appearance notice is issued to the offender at the scene, before an Information is laid. The Information must be laid as soon as practicable after the issuance of the appearance notice. The accused must sign the appearance notice, to ensure appearance in court. Refusal to sign means that RICE is not fulfilled.

THE INTENTION OF SERVING A SUMMONS SUBSEQUENT TO RELEASE

A summons cannot be served at the time of release because an Information must be laid first. The offender is released without a document being served. Afterward, the officer must appear before a Justice, lay an Information, and have a summons issued. Therefore, the summons is served some time after the actual release.

UNCONDITIONAL RELEASE

In the case of an unconditional release, there is no intention to charge the arrested person or compel him or her to court. No document is served. The unconditional release is simply recorded on the arrest report and in the officer's notebook. The arresting officer, at the scene, cannot serve any other release or compelling documents, such as a promise to appear, recognizance, or undertaking.

This *mandatory rule* applies when the status of RICE is not entirely known before the arrest is made but is determined at the scene, shortly after the arrest. When RICE is fulfilled at the scene, in the case of summary conviction and dual procedure offences, the officer is not justified in continuing detention by transporting the accused to the police station.

Note: If, during an investigation and before an arrest is made, the officer determines that RICE is fulfilled regarding a summary conviction or dual procedure offence, the arrest cannot be made. Instead, the officer may serve only an appearance notice or a summons to the accused person.

JUSTIFIED CONTINUED CUSTODY

The arresting officer is justified in continuing custody of an accused by bringing him or her to the police station (Level 2), if

▸ the offence is indictable, regardless of RICE fulfillment;
▸ the offence is summary conviction or dual procedure and RICE is not fulfilled; or
▸ the arrest is made with a warrant, regardless if it is endorsed or unendorsed. (As explained in Chapter 7, a Justice may endorse an arrest warrant, which authorizes release from the police station (a **Level 2 release**) only. An endorsed warrant does not authorize release at the scene (a Level 1 release).)

Tables 11.2 and 11.3 summarize the release and detention provisions for Level 1.

Table 11.2   Level 1 Release and Detention Provisions

Release Provisions	Detention Provisions
The accused must be released ▸ at the scene of arrest ▸ by the arresting officer.	Accused must be taken ▸ to the police station.

If arrested without a warrant for
▸ a summary conviction offence, or
▸ a dual procedure offence and RICE is fulfilled
 	
Method
▸ Issue an appearance notice
▸ Issue a summons to appear in court
	1. If arrested without a warrant for
	   ▸ a summary conviction offence, or
	   ▸ a dual procedure offence and RICE is not fulfilled

	2. If arrested without a warrant for ▸ an indictable offence
	3. If arrested with a warrant

LEVEL 2 RELEASE PROVISIONS

Level 2 release considerations begin with the accused person's arrival at the police station. In 1995, with the introduction of Bill C-42, significant changes were made at this level of release. Before April 1, 1995, the OIC was the only officer who could release a person at the police station. The **OIC** is defined as "the officer for the time being in command of the police force responsible for the lock-up or other place to which an accused is taken after arrest," or "a peace officer designated by the OIC, who is in charge of that place at the time an accused is taken to that place to be detained in custody." The OIC is often the staff sergeant or sergeant who is the supervisor of the on-duty shift or platoon of officers. Before Bill C-42, the OIC could not use an undertaking as a release document at this level.

Since April 1, 1995, any police officer or OIC may release an arrested person at the police station, and an undertaking may be used as the release document in conjunction with a promise to appear or a recognizance. For simplicity, only "OIC" will be used to explain Level 2 and Level 3 release.

Procedures and Rules

MANDATORY RELEASE—SECTION 498 C.C.

The OIC must release a person who has been taken to the police station if

- the arrest was made without a warrant,
- RICE is fulfilled, and
- the offence is
    a. summary conviction, or
    b. dual procedure, or
    c. indictable with a maximum penalty not greater than five years, and the offence was committed in the same province as the arrest.

The OIC has *no discretion* about continuing detention if these conditions exist; release is mandatory. The accused must be released and cannot be detained or brought to a Justice for a bail hearing (a Level 3 release).

Methods of Release

When an accused person *must* be released from custody at the police station, the following methods and release or compelling documents may be used:

▶ When there is an intention of serving a summons at a later date, after an Information is sworn, no document is served at the time of release; the accused is orally informed of the police intention to serve a summons later.

▶ A promise to appear (PTA) is issued to the accused person at the police station, at the time of release. A PTA is served before the accused is actually charged.

▶ A recognizance is issued. The OIC may direct the accused to deposit a sum of money up to $500.00 if the accused lives either outside the province where the arrest was made or more than 200 kilometres from the place of custody.

▶ An unconditional release is issued. The accused is released without the stipulation that he or she appear in court. Essentially, the officer has used discretion in deciding not to charge the offender. No document is served to the accused in the event of this form of release; the offender is informed orally. However, unconditional release does not prevent the police from charging the offender at a later time. The police may decide later to charge the offender and swear an Information. In other words, an unconditional release is not a binding agreement or contract promising the offender immunity from later charges.

The following means of release *cannot* be issued at the police station:

▶ an appearance notice,

▶ a summons, when the arrest is made with a warrant (a summons may be issued only instead of a warrant); and

▶ an unconditional release, when the arrest is made with a warrant. If a warrant exists, an Information has already been laid. Only a Crown attorney may withdraw an Information.

DISCRETIONARY RELEASE—SECTION 499 C.C.

The OIC may release a person who has been taken to the police station if

▶ the arrest was made with a warrant; and

▶ the offence is summary conviction, dual procedure, or indictable (but not a s. 469 C.C. offence, such as murder); and

▶ the warrant has been endorsed by a Justice, authorizing the release of the accused.

Methods of Release

The OIC may release an accused person by serving him or her

▶ a promise to appear, or

▶ a recognizance.

The OIC may also require that the accused enter into an undertaking. The undertaking procedure is optional, not mandatory. This involves the accused's being served with a promise to appear or a recognizance and agreeing to whichever of the following conditions the OIC decides to impose:

1. to remain within a specific territorial jurisdiction;
2. to notify a peace officer of any change in

    a. address,
    b. employment, or
    c. occupation;

3. to abstain from

    a. communicating with any witness or any other person named in the undertaking, or
    b. going to a place named in the undertaking, except in accordance with conditions specified in the undertaking;

4. to deposit the accused's passport with the police officer or other person specified in the undertaking;
5. to abstain from possessing a firearm and surrender any firearm in the possession of the person and any authorization, licence, registration certificate, or other document enabling that person to acquire or possess a firearm;
6. to report at specified times to a police officer or other person designated in the undertaking;
7. to abstain from the consumption of

    a. alcohol or other intoxicating substances, and/or
    b. drugs, except in accordance with a medical prescription.

The accused person cannot be forced to agree to any of these conditions, but if the accused fails to agree and fails to sign the undertaking, he or she may be detained and brought before a Justice for a bail hearing.

An undertaking with conditions may be given to an accused only in conjunction with a promise to appear or a recognizance. It cannot be issued alone.

A "breach of undertaking"—a failure to comply with any condition imposed by this type of undertaking—is a dual procedure offence, under s. 145(5) C.C.

DISCRETIONARY RELEASE—SECTIONS 503(2) AND 503(2.1) C.C.

Any police officer or the OIC may release an accused person who has been taken to a police station if

- ▸ the arrest was made

    a. without a warrant, or
    b. with a warrant, regardless of whether the warrant is endorsed; *and*

- ▸ the offence is summary conviction, dual procedure, or indictable (other than a s. 469 C.C. offence, such as murder).

Sections 503(2) and 503(2.1) allow any police officer to release an arrested person by means of a PTA, a recognizance, or an undertaking subject to the same conditions listed above.

Methods of Release

For discretionary release, any of the following methods of release and the following documents may be used:

1. When there is an intention of serving a summons at a later date, after an Information has been served, no document is served (arrest without a warrant only).
2. An unconditional release is issued (arrest without a warrant only).
3. A promise to appear is issued (arrest with or without a warrant).
4. A recognizance is issued (arrest with or without a warrant).

An undertaking, with any or all of the conditions imposed by s. 499 C.C., may be given to an accused in conjunction with a promise to appear or a recognizance.

Although this provision gives police discretion about release, they need to remember s. 498 C.C. (concerning mandatory release): if the offence is summary conviction, dual procedure, or an indictable offence that has a maximum penalty of five years or less, and the arrest is made without a warrant, then release is mandatory if RICE is fulfilled. This new provision serves the following purposes:

- It increases the number of officers who may authorize the release. Not only the OIC but any police officer (including the arresting officer) may now authorize a release from the police station (Level 2 release).
- It expands the number of offences for which the accused, after being arrested, may be released. Previously, it was mandatory that all persons arrested for indictable offences be brought before a Justice for a bail hearing so that the Justice could determine release. Under the new provision, persons arrested for indictable offences that have a maximum penalty of more than five years, except for s. 469 C.C. offences, such as murder, are eligible for release; however, to protect the public, the release should occur only if RICE is fulfilled.

Persons arrested on the authority of any unendorsed warrant, unless it is a warrant for s. 469 C.C. offence, may be released instead of being brought before a Justice for a bail hearing, if RICE is fulfilled. This discretionary provision expedites the release of offenders when RICE is fulfilled, prevents unnecessary and time-consuming bail hearings, and prevents unjustified or unreasonable detention of an accused person. The apparent intent in facilitating the release of an offender who poses no risk to the public (when RICE is fulfilled) is to preserve the presumption of innocence of every arrested person.

JUSTIFIED CONTINUED CUSTODY

The OIC is justified in continuing detention of the accused and requiring a bail hearing before a Justice (Level 3 release) when any of the following conditions exist:

- The offence is an indictable one that has a maximum penalty of more than five years and the arrest is made without a warrant, or with an endorsed warrant, regardless of whether RICE is fulfilled.
- The offence is summary conviction, dual procedure, or indictable with a maximum penalty not greater than five years, and
  a. the arrest was made without a warrant, *and*
  b. RICE is not fulfilled.
- The arrest was made with an unendorsed warrant, for any type of offence.
- The offence is a s. 469 C.C. offence, such as murder.

Table 11.3 summarizes the release and detention provisions for Level 2.

Table 11.3   Level 2 Release and Detention Provisions

Release Provisions	Detention Provisions (Justified Detention)

The accused **must** be released
 	
▸ at the police station
▸ by the OIC if the accused has been arrested
▸ without a warrant for a summary conviction offence
 	
Method
▸ Issue a summons
▸ Issue an unconditional release
▸ Issue a promise to appear*
▸ Issue a recognizance*
 	
The accused **may** be released
 	
▸ at the police station
▸ by the OIC if the accused has been arrested
  1. without a warrant for any offence except a s. 469 C.C. offence
  2. with a warrant (endorsed or unendorsed) for any offence except a s. 469 C.C. offence
and **RICE is fulfilled**
 	
Method
▸ Issue a promise to appear*
▸ Issue a recognizance*
	The accused may be brought to a JP for a bail hearing, if the accused has been arrested
	
	1. without a warrant for:
	  ▸ a summary conviction offence,
	  ▸ a dual procedure offence, or
	  ▸ an indictable offence (with maximum sentence of 5 years or less)
	  and **RICE is not fulfilled**
	2. for an indictable offence (with maximum sentence of more than 5 years)
	3. with an unendorsed warrant
	4. for a s. 469 C.C. offence

* Undertaking may accompany PTA or recognizance

LEVEL 3 RELEASE PROVISIONS

Bail hearings represent the third and final level of release. Only a Justice, defined in s. 2 C.C. as a JP or a provincial court judge, can be responsible for this level of release and can conduct the bail hearing. The rules for bail hearings, found in s. 515 C.C., apply to both adult and young offenders; however, the Y.C.J.A. imposes additional rules.

The term "bail hearing" is not used in s. 515 C.C. *Bail hearing* is an informal term commonly used within the criminal justice system. Section 515 *Criminal Code* refers to *judicial interim release*, which means the release or detention of an accused by a Justice during the time interval between the arrest and the trial. A bail hearing is also called a "show cause hearing." "Show cause" refers to the prosecution's need to show reasons why the accused should be detained or released.

Purpose of a Bail Hearing

A bail hearing has a single purpose: to determine whether the accused person should be released or detained in custody until the trial. The purpose is not to determine the accused's guilt or innocence or to determine whether sufficient evidence exists to have a trial.

It is possible for an accused to plead guilty at a bail hearing appearance, but it is rare. In almost every bail hearing, determination of guilt or innocence is not the issue. The only issue is release or continued detention.

If an accused pleads guilty, a Justice cannot convict or acquit the accused at the conclusion of the bail hearing, nor can the Justice determine whether sufficient evidence exists to have a trial; this determination is made at a preliminary hearing.

Time of Appearance Before a Justice

When the OIC is justified in detaining an accused, s. 503(1) C.C. creates the following rules about when the accused must be taken before a Justice for a bail hearing:

> ‣ without unreasonable delay and within 24 hours of the arrest, if a Justice is available; and
> ‣ if no Justice is available within 24 hours of the arrest, as soon as possible.

When the accused is brought before a Justice, a bail hearing must be conducted, unless

> ‣ the accused pleads guilty and the Justice accepts it, or
> ‣ the accused is charged with a s. 469 C.C. offence, such as murder.

When a person charged with a s. 469 C.C. offence is brought before a Justice, the Justice must detain the accused in custody. After the Justice issues a detention order, the accused must apply for a bail hearing before a judge of the superior court of criminal jurisdiction—in Ontario, for example, a General Division Court Judge.

Adjournment

After an accused is brought before a Justice, the prosecutor or accused may apply for an adjournment to prepare for the bail hearing. The Justice may grant an adjournment at any time before the bail hearing starts or during the bail hearing. The adjournment cannot be longer than three clear days, a *span* which does not include the day the adjournment is granted. The adjournment may exceed three clear days only if the accused consents. The accused is remanded in custody during the adjournment.

The three-day adjournment is not granted automatically to the prosecution. An application must be made after the accused is brought before the Justice. When the prosecution applies for the adjournment, the onus is on them to justify the need for the three-day adjournment. Possible reasons they might cite are the complexities of the investigation or the amount of time needed to prepare the case for the prosecution.

Two points must be emphasized:

1. The accused must first be brought before the Justice within 24 hours, or as soon as possible, in order to apply for the three-day adjournment.
2. The Justice cannot grant an adjournment without an application by either the prosecutor or the accused.

Status of Accused

The accused is presumed innocent during a bail hearing. This fact should be emphasized; it indicates the high standard of proof required to prove why an accused person should be held in custody until the trial.

Pre-trial detention orders are not made when the evidence is weak; the accused has not yet been convicted of the offence. Pre-trial jail custody is informally referred to as "dead time," because this type of custody is not a sentence. It is served during a period when the accused is presumed innocent.

Location

Bail hearings may be conducted at the following locations:

▸ at a police station or in a JP's office, which serves as a temporary courtroom; or
▸ in provincial court, usually before a provincial court judge.

Participants

The following people are the participants in a bail hearing:

1. A Justice.
2. A prosecutor, who may be either

   ▸ a Crown attorney, if held in provincial court; or
   ▸ a police officer, or Crown attorney, if held at a police station.

   A police officer, usually a detective assigned to the investigation, is the prosecutor at the majority of bail hearings that take place at police stations.
3. The accused person. He or she must be in physical attendance at a bail hearing. An exception exists under the following conditions:

   ▸ The accused may appear by any suitable telecommunication device, including a telephone, if

      a. this means of appearance is suitable to the Justice (the Justice has discretion to allow or reject such an appearance), and
      b. both the prosecutor and accused agree to this means.

   A bail hearing cannot be conducted without some form of appearance by the accused. An adult offender is permitted to have a lawyer present. A young offender is permitted to have present a lawyer, a parent, or another adult whom the Justice considers suitable. If the young offender is not represented by counsel, the Justice must inform the young offender of the right to be represented by counsel and must give the young offender a reasonable opportunity to obtain counsel.

FACTORS DETERMINING RELEASE OR CONTINUED DETENTION

The factors that determine the release provisions (RICE) are essentially the same ones that determine release or custody at a bail hearing. But in the case of a bail hearing, these factors are divided into two categories:

1. **primary grounds**, and
2. **secondary grounds**.

"Primary grounds" concern ensuring a court appearance. "Secondary grounds" concern protecting the public if there is a risk that the accused, if released, will commit a criminal offence or interfere with the administration of justice. Saying that primary grounds exist means there are reasonable grounds for believing that the accused may fail to appear in court. Saying secondary grounds exist means there are reasonable grounds for believing that the accused may commit a criminal offence and endanger the public.

A judgment that either primary or secondary grounds exist justifies a detention order and the holding of the accused in custody. The question whether primary grounds exist is examined first, and if they are deemed to exist, a detention order is made. If primary grounds are deemed absent, the question of secondary grounds is explored. If secondary grounds are proven to exist, a detention order is made. If both primary and secondary grounds are absent, the accused must be released.

In summary, the release and detention rules are as follows:

- If only primary grounds exist, a detention order is made.
- If only secondary grounds exist, a detention order is made.
- If neither primary nor secondary grounds exist, the accused must be released.

Onus

The onus at a bail hearing refers to the burden of proof—the responsibility of proving the presence or absence of primary and secondary grounds. Generally, the prosecutor has the onus of proving why the accused should be detained in custody. However, in certain limited circumstances there is a reverse onus, and the accused has the onus of proving that he or she should be released.

Reverse Onus Situation

In a reverse onus situation, the burden of proof shifts to the accused, who now has the burden of proving why he or she should be released. In other words, the accused now has the onus of proving the *absence* of primary or secondary grounds, in order to be released from custody until the trial date. An accused who fails to do so will be detained in custody until the trial date.

A reverse onus situation will occur in the following circumstances:

- The accused is charged with an indictable or dual procedure offence while awaiting trial for another indictable or dual procedure offence. This situation occurs when the accused has been charged with an indictable or dual procedure offence and released, then committed and charged with another indictable or dual procedure offence before the completion of the trial for the first offence. (If either offence is summary conviction, however, the prosecutor still has the onus at the bail hearing.)
- The accused is charged with committing an indictable or dual procedure offence in Canada but does not live here. If the accused lives in another country and commits an indictable or dual procedure offence in Canada,

the accused automatically has the onus at the bail hearing regardless of whether he or she is awaiting trial. (If the offence is a summary conviction, the prosecutor still has the onus.)

▸ The accused is guilty of "Fail to appear" or "Breach of undertaking" while awaiting trial for any criminal offence (summary conviction, dual procedure, or indictable).

▸ The accused is charged with any of the following *Controlled Drugs and Substances Act* offences:

    a. trafficking in substances,

    b. possession of substance(s) for the purpose of trafficking,

    c. importing substance(s), or

    d. exporting substance(s).

A person charged with any of these *Controlled Drugs and Substances Act* offences automatically has the onus at a bail hearing, regardless of whether he or she is awaiting trial for any other offence. However, if a person is charged with "Possession of narcotics" only, the prosecutor has the onus.

▸ The accused is charged with an indictable offence, other than a s. 469 C.C. offence, that is an offence under s. 467.1 C.C. (participation in a criminal organization) or an offence under any federal statute committed for the benefit of, at the direction of, or in association with a criminal organization for which the maximum punishment is imprisonment for five years or more.

Prosecutor Onus: Procedure

The following is a step-by-step summary of the bail hearing procedure when the prosecutor has the onus.

STEP 1

The police must lay an Information before the bail hearing starts. A bail hearing cannot be conducted without an Information being sworn first.

STEP 2

The accused is brought before a Justice within 24 hours of the arrest, without un-reasonable delay.

STEP 3

The accused is arraigned, which means that the Information is read to the accused. The accused is permitted to plead guilty.

STEP 4

If the accused does not plead guilty, the Justice asks the prosecutor (investigating officer), "Do you wish to show cause?" With this question the Justice is asking whether the prosecutor intends to prove the existence of primary or secondary grounds (indicating that RICE is not fulfilled).

STEP 5

If the prosecutor answers "No," he is effectively conceding that primary and secondary grounds do not exist and that RICE is fulfilled. In this situation, the accused must be released by means of an undertaking without conditions. The Justice has no discretion to impose conditions on the undertaking when the prosecutor chooses not to show cause.

STEP 6

If the prosecutor answers "Yes," it means that he or she intends to introduce evidence relating to primary and/or secondary grounds. The bail hearing begins, and the prosecutor's case is presented first.

STEP 7

The prosecutor may introduce evidence by calling witnesses to testify, or by calling only the investigating police officer to testify. The latter is more commonly chosen. The investigating officer's testimony amounts to hearsay.

"Hearsay" evidence is admissible at a bail hearing if the evidence is "considered credible or trustworthy." **Hearsay evidence** is defined as observations that were not perceived by one's own senses; the observations were made by another person. Hearsay evidence comes from a person who is informed about observations by a person who actually perceived them with his or her own senses—for example, a police officer who is informed about observations by a witness.

The admissibility of hearsay evidence represents a significant advantage for the prosecutor because the investigating officer alone may present all the evidence relating to primary or secondary grounds by reading facts and witness statements, and thus removes the need to call other witnesses. This process does not apply at the trial, where hearsay evidence is generally inadmissible.

If the bail hearing is conducted at the police station, and the investigating officer is the prosecutor, this same officer may also testify for the prosecution. In other words, the prosecutor in this case has the option of calling all the witnesses, or of having the officer testify and read the witness statements him- or herself.

All witnesses who are called must be sworn in before testifying. Consequently, a witness who intentionally lies or fabricates evidence while testifying under oath at a bail hearing may be charged with perjury.

STEP 8

The prosecution may introduce only evidence that is generally concerned with proving primary and secondary grounds, including:

- a summary of the circumstances of the offence, to prove that conviction is probable. Although guilt or innocence is not determined at a bail hearing, and the accused is not on trial, the probability of conviction is a relevant consideration in determining whether primary or secondary grounds exist;
- the accused's criminal record;
- any "Fail to appear" or "Breach of undertaking" offences that the accused has committed in the past, whether or not the accused was charged or convicted of these offences;

- any criminal offences that the accused has been charged with and is awaiting trial for, although there has not yet been a conviction; and
- any topic relevant to primary or secondary grounds.

Note: The only information that cannot be introduced by the prosecutor is information that requires an expert opinion. For example, the prosecutor cannot say, "*I* think he's mentally unstable."

STEP 9

The accused person may cross-examine all prosecution witnesses.

STEP 10

After the prosecutor finishes presenting the case, the accused may introduce evidence showing why release should be granted. The accused has the option to testify, but no one can compel the accused to testify; this decision belongs exclusively to the accused.

STEP 11

The prosecutor may cross-examine all defence witnesses, including the accused if the accused has chosen to testify. However, the accused cannot be cross-examined about the offence unless the accused has testified about the offence.

STEP 12

The Justice makes one of the following rulings.

1. If the prosecutor fails to prove that primary or secondary grounds exist, the Justice must release the accused by means of

    a. a recognizance (Form 32)

       - with or without sureties, referring to the posting of bond for the accused, or
       - with a deposit of a sum of money directed by the Justice, if the accused lives in another province or more than 200 kilometres from the place of arrest, or
       - with conditions; or

    b. an undertaking (Form 12)

       - with, or
       - without conditions.

    The Justice may impose one or more of the following conditions on an undertaking or a recognizance, requiring the accused to

       - report to a police officer at a specific time at a specific police station;
       - remain within a specified territorial jurisdiction;
       - notify a specified police officer of any change in address, employment, or occupation;
       - abstain from communicating with any witness or person specifically named;

- ▸ refrain from going to any place specified by the Justice;
- ▸ deposit his or her current passport with the court.

The Justice may impose any other reasonable condition that he or she considers desirable, such as a curfew that compels the accused to be inside a specified place during specified hours (for example, 11:00 p.m. to 7:00 a.m.).

A court date, time, and location are included on the release order. If the accused agrees to all the conditions imposed by the Justice, the accused signs the release document. If the bail hearing is conducted at the police station, the officer should witness the signature, initial it, and record these details in a notebook; all of which will be relevant if the accused violates any of the conditions. Each violation of a condition is a separate dual procedure offence under s. 145(3) C.C. If the accused refuses to sign the undertaking, then the accused will be detained in custody on the basis of primary or secondary grounds.

2. If either primary or secondary grounds are proven and the accused is an adult, the Justice must order that the accused be detained in custody until the trial. The detention order must list the reasons for making the order. Once the detention order is made, the *Criminal Code* allows a bail review to take place. The accused may apply to a judge at any time before the trial for a bail review. An automatic bail review must occur

   a. within 30 days, if the offence is summary conviction; or
   b. within 90 days, if the offence is indictable.

   A bail review is conducted in the same manner as a bail hearing. The purpose remains the same; if primary or secondary grounds still exist, detention continues. If not, the accused is released.

3. If primary or secondary grounds still exist but the accused is a young offender, the Justice may not detain the young offender in custody if all of the following conditions exist:

   a. a responsible person is willing and able to take care of and exercise control over the young offender;
   b. the young offender is willing to be placed in the care of that person;

   Both the person taking care of the young offender and the young offender him- or herself consent to this arrangement in writing.

   If these conditions exist, the Justice has discretion to release the young offender, instead of making a detention order, and may impose conditions on the undertaking. Young offenders who do not consent to the arrangement will be detained in custody.

   If the person who has agreed to take care of the young offender after release becomes unwilling or unable to do so, or if for any other reason, it is no longer appropriate that the young offender be in the care of that person, any person may apply to a youth court judge or a Justice for

   - ▸ an order relieving both the person and the young offender of their obligations, and
   - ▸ an arrest warrant for the young person.

   After young offenders are arrested, they must be brought before a youth court judge or Justice forthwith for a bail hearing.

Reverse Onus—Procedure

The following is a step-by-step summary of the bail hearing procedure when a reverse onus situation exists.

STEP 1

An Information must be laid.

STEP 2

The accused is brought before a Justice and is arraigned.

STEP 3

The Justice asks the accused, "Do you wish to show cause?" thus asking the accused whether he or she intends to introduce evidence showing why release should be granted.

STEP 4

If the accused responds "No," he or she is effectively saying that primary or secondary grounds exist. The Justice must make a detention order and hold the accused in custody.

STEP 5

If the accused responds "Yes," he or she must introduce evidence first, by their own testimony or that of other witnesses.

STEP 6

The prosecutor may cross-examine all defence witnesses.

STEP 7

The prosecutor may then introduce evidence.

STEP 8

The defence may cross-examine.

STEP 9

The Justice makes a ruling, just as in a bail hearing when the onus is on the prosecutor.

SUMMARY

The lawful release of an offender is just as important to front-line policing as a lawful arrest. The next chapter contains problem-solving exercises that will test your understanding of "release," and demonstrate the proper procedures to be used to prevent serious Charter violations.

ENDNOTES

1. *R. v. L. (M.C.)* (2005), 196 C.C.C. (3d) 571 (Ont. C.J.).
2. *R. v. Siemens*, 2000 BCSC 1015.
3. *R. v. Tugnum*, 2002 BCSC 1572.
4. *R. v. Siemens*, supra note 2.
5. *R. v. L. (M.C.)*, supra note 1.
6. *R. v. Pearson* (1992), 77 C.C.C. (3d) 124 (S.C.C.).
7. Ibid.
8. Ibid.
9. Ibid.
10. *R. v. Hall* (2002), 167 C.C.C. (3d) 449 (S.C.C.).
11. Ibid.
12. Ibid.
13. Québec, Ministère de la Sécurité publique, Direction générale des services correctionnels, *Evolution of Penal Policies and the Debate on Imprisonment in Canada and Québec: 1969 to 1999* (2000), http://www.msp.gouv.qc.ca/reinsertion/publicat/politiques_penales/politiques_penales_en.pdf, at 9.
14. *R. v. Hall*, supra note 10.
15. Ibid.
16. *Bail Reform Act*, S.C. 1970-71-72, c. 37, as in *R. v. Hall*, supra note 10.
17. Ibid.
18. *R. v. L. (M.C.)*, supra note 1.
19. Ibid., and *R. v. Hall*, supra note 10.
20. *R. v. L. (M.C.)*, supra note 1.
21. Ibid., and *R. v. Hall*, supra note 10.
22. *R. v. Pearson*, supra note 6.

1 & 2 - appear
3 - bail pack

INTRODUCTION

Understanding release provisions and applying them correctly involves understanding some of the most complex laws in the *Criminal Code*. Your goal as a front-line police officer is to learn how to apply release provisions with such proficiency that it becomes second nature. Using the tri-level release model (TRM) explained in the previous chapter, complete the following case studies and problem-solving exercises to help you achieve this goal.

SELF-EVALUATION: PROBLEM-SOLVING CASE STUDIES AND TEST-YOURSELF QUESTIONS

You are a police officer in each case. Each offender is an adult, unless otherwise indicated.

Problem 1

You arrest Greg for "Fraud under $5,000.00." For how long can you detain him?

_____

_____

Problem 2

You arrest Helen for "Cause a disturbance." When must this arrest or detention end and when must Helen be released?

_____

_____

Problem 3

You attend at a business premises in response to a shoplifting complaint. You arrive to find that a security guard has custody of Wayne, who has committed "Theft under $5,000.00" by stealing a $15.00 compact disc. Wayne is married, has two sons, lives in the same city where the arrest was made, is employed full-time, and has no criminal record. The CD is recovered. The security guard provides you with an eyewitness written statement. Wayne identifies himself legitimately by means of a driver's licence with a photograph. Is RICE fulfilled?

_____

_____

_____

_____

Problem 4

You arrest Eddie for "Impaired driving"; he is intoxicated. He has no criminal record and lives with his parents in the city where you have arrested him. He has a full-time job and is a part-time student. He properly identifies himself. Is RICE fulfilled?

_____

_____

_____

Problem 5

You attend at a bar regarding a disturbance. Chris is found intoxicated and is shouting obscenities at Carlos. Chris is hostile and aggressive toward Carlos. You arrest Chris for "Cause a disturbance." Is RICE fulfilled?

_____

_____

_____

Problem 6

You arrest Steve for "Theft under $5,000.00." He has no means of support and has no fixed address. Is RICE fulfilled?

_____

_____

_____

Problem 7

You arrest a person for "Attempted break and enter" at a house. The offender has no identification documents and refuses to identify himself. Is RICE fulfilled?

_____

_____

_____

_____

Test Yourself

1. You attend at a business regarding a shoplifting complaint. You arrive to find that a security guard has custody of Eric (24), who has stolen a $30.00 CD.

   Explain in detail everything you will ask Eric and what information you will need to determine whether to release or detain him at the scene.

_____

_____

_____

_____

_____

_____

_____

_____

_____

_____

_____

_____

_____

_____

_____

_____

_____

_____

_____

_____

_____

2. You stop a car on Main Street. The driver, Victor (29), is drunk. You arrest him for impaired driving. He identifies himself. He lives in the city where you have arrested him, and is employed as a teacher. He has no criminal record.

   Explain in detail what additional information you will attempt to elicit from Victor, what action you will take relating to custody, and how you will decide whether to detain or release him.

_____

_____

_____

_____

_____

_____

_____
_____
_____
_____
_____
_____
_____
_____
_____
_____
_____
_____
_____
_____

3. Indicate, by circling the correct answer, when the Information has to be laid in relation to the release/compelling document in the list.

Document	Information	
~~Undertaking (Justice)~~	Before	After
~~Promise to appear~~	Before	After
~~Recognizance (OIC)~~	Before	After
Appearance notice	Before	After
Summons	Before	After
Undertaking (police officer/OIC)	Before	After
Recognizance (Justice)	Before	After

a. What is the purpose of a release/compelling document?

_____
_____
_____
_____
_____
_____
_____
_____
_____
_____
_____
_____

b. What content must appear on all release/compelling documents?

_____

_____

_____

_____

_____

_____

_____

_____

Problem 8

You arrest Eric at a department store for "Theft under $5,000.00." You determine that RICE is fulfilled.

a. Do you have to release him?

_____

b. Can you serve an appearance notice to Eric at the scene, before an Information is laid?

_____

c. Can you serve a summons to Eric at the scene, before an Information is laid?

_____

d. Can you release Eric with the intention of serving him with a summons?

_____

_____

_____

e. Can you release Eric unconditionally?

_____

f. Can you serve Eric with the following documents at the scene?

  ‣ promise to appear?

_____

  ‣ recognizance?

_____

  ‣ undertaking?

_____

g. Can you bring Eric to the police station?

_____

Problem 9

You arrest Eric for "Theft under $5,000.00" and release him with the intention of serving him with a summons. After the summons is issued, how can it be served?

_____

_____

_____

_____

_____

_____

_____

_____

Problem 10

You serve a summons to Rick. How can you prove that the summons was served, if Rick fails to appear in court?

_____

_____

_____

_____

_____

_____

Problem 11

You arrest Paul for "Trespass by night." RICE is fulfilled.

   a. Do you have to release him?

_____

   b. Can you bring Paul to the police station?

_____

Problem 12

You arrest Rafael for "Robbery" on King Street. Can you automatically bring him to the police station?

_____

_____

Problem 13

You arrest Mary for "Assault" at a bar. RICE is not fulfilled. Can you bring her to a police station?

_____

Problem 14

You arrest Larry on Niagara Street regarding a warrant for "Fraud under $5,000.00." The warrant is endorsed by the Justice.

    a. Can you release Larry?

_____

    b. Can you automatically bring Larry to the police station?

_____

Problem 15

You arrest June on Parkdale Avenue for "Theft under $5,000.00." You complete an appearance notice because RICE is fulfilled. June refuses to sign the appearance notice and states that she will not attend court. Can you bring her to the police station?

_____
_____
_____

Test Yourself

1. You arrest Michael (33) in the parking lot of a bar on Barton Street for "Cause a disturbance." Explain the following:

    ▸ the release provisions that you have to consider in this case, and

    ▸ how you will decide whether to release or detain.

_____
_____
_____
_____
_____
_____
_____
_____
_____
_____
_____

_____

_____

_____

_____

_____

_____

_____

_____

2. You arrest June (31) for "Fraud under $5,000.00," committed eight days ago when she bought a $2,000.00 television with an NSF cheque. Explain:

   ▸ the release provisions you have to consider; and
   ▸ how you will decide whether to release or detain June.

_____

_____

_____

_____

_____

_____

_____

_____

_____

_____

_____

_____

_____

_____

_____

_____

_____

_____

Problem 16

Noah is arrested for "Cause a disturbance" and is taken to the police station. RICE becomes fulfilled two hours later.

a. Does Noah have to be released?

b. Who may release Noah?

c. What documents may be used to release Noah?

d. Can an appearance notice be used to release Noah from the police station?

e. Can Noah be released unconditionally after he has been taken to the police station?

f. If RICE is fulfilled, can Noah be detained and brought before a Justice for a bail hearing?

Problem 17

Gaetan is arrested for "Theft under $5,000.00" and is taken to a police station. RICE becomes fulfilled one hour later.

a. Does Gaetan have to be released?

b. Can Gaetan be detained and brought before a Justice for a bail hearing?

c. Who may release him?

Problem 18

Luc is arrested for "Robbery" in the city in which he lives, and is taken to the police station.

a. Can Luc be detained and be brought before a Justice for a bail hearing?

_____

_____

b. Is it possible for Luc to be released at the police station by the OIC or any other police officer, before being brought before a Justice?

_____

_____

c. Can Luc be released by means of an appearance notice?

_____

d. Can Luc be released by means of a promise to appear?

_____

e. Can Luc be released by means of a recognizance with a $500.00 deposit?

_____

_____

f. Can the OIC or any police officer release Luc by means of an undertaking with conditions, without bringing him before a Justice for a bail hearing?

_____

_____

_____

_____

g. Can the OIC or any police officer impose conditions on an undertaking, in conjunction with a promise to appear, prohibiting Luc from communicating with Eric (a known offender) and prohibiting Luc from attending Eric's house?

_____

_____

_____

h. Can the OIC or any police officer impose a condition of a curfew, requiring Luc to be inside a specific place between specified hours?

_____

_____

Release Provisions   CHAPTER 12   267

Problem 19

Lucy is arrested with an endorsed warrant for "Fraud over $5,000.00" and is taken to a police station.

    a. Can she be released at the police station, before being brought before a Justice for a bail hearing?

_____

_____

_____

    b. Can Lucy be automatically brought before a Justice for a bail hearing?

_____

_____

_____

Problem 20

Peter is arrested with an unendorsed warrant for "Break, enter, and theft," and is taken to a police station.

    a. Can Peter be released at the police station, before being brought before a Justice for a bail hearing?

_____

_____

_____

    b. Can Peter be automatically brought before a Justice for a bail hearing?

_____

_____

_____

Problem 21

Nikolai is arrested for "First or second degree murder" and is taken to the police station. Can he be automatically brought before a Justice?

_____

Problem 22

Eric is under arrest at the police station. The OIC prepares to release him on a promise to appear. Eric refuses to sign it. What can the OIC do?

_____

_____

_____

_____

Problem 23

Ron is under arrest at the police station for "Theft over $5,000.00." A patrol officer decides to release him by means of a promise to appear and an undertaking with the condition that Ron not communicate with Eric (a known offender). Ron refuses to agree to this condition and refuses to sign the undertaking. What can the officer do?

_____

_____

_____

_____

Problem 24

Shane is under arrest at the police station for "Assault." The OIC decides to release him with conditions. Is an undertaking with conditions the only document given to the accused under these circumstances?

_____

_____

Test Yourself

1. At 2:15 a.m. you respond to an alarm at a business. You find Claudio (18) and Igor (17) inside the building. They forced entry, but had no time to steal anything. Explain the following:
   - the release provisions that you need to consider, and
   - how you will decide about release or detention.

_____

_____

_____

_____

_____

_____

_____

_____

_____

_____

_____

_____

_____

_____

_____

_____

_____

_____

_____

2. You arrest Xavier (28) today for "Assault causing bodily harm," a crime that was committed two days ago. The victim, Victor, is still hospitalized. Xavier lives in the city where the offence occurred, is unemployed, and has two convictions two years ago for assault. Explain the following:

   ‣ the release provisions you must consider, and
   ‣ which you will choose.

_____

_____

_____

_____

_____

_____

_____

_____

_____

_____

_____

_____

_____

_____

_____

_____

_____

_____

Problem 25

Peter is arrested for "Attempted murder" and is brought to the police station.

a. Can he automatically be brought before a Justice for a bail hearing?

_____

b. When does he have to be brought to a Justice?

_____

c. If the police require additional time to prepare for the bail hearing, can they bring Peter to a Justice three days later instead of within 24 hours?

_____

_____

_____

_____

_____

Problem 26

Frank is arrested for "First degree murder" and is taken to the police station.

a. Where is Frank brought next?

_____

b. Under what circumstances can a bail hearing occur?

_____

c. Who will preside over a bail hearing for first degree murder?

_____

d. Who will have the onus at a bail hearing for first degree murder?

_____

Problem 27

June is arrested for "Robbery" and is taken to the police station. She is brought before a Justice for a bail hearing. She is not awaiting trial for any other offence. She was convicted three years ago for "Assault," and one year ago she was investigated for a "Theft under $5,000.00" complaint but was not charged.

a. Who will have the onus at this bail hearing?

_____

b. Can this bail hearing be conducted without an Information being laid first?

_____

c. Where can this bail hearing be conducted?

_____

d. Can the investigating police officer be the prosecutor?

_____

_____

_____

e. Can the bail hearing be conducted in the absence of any appearance by June?

_____

_____

f. Can June plead guilty?

_____

_____

g. The Justice asks the prosecutor, "Do you wish to show cause?" The answer is "No." What will occur in this case?

_____

_____

_____

‣ Does the Justice have discretion about imposing conditions?

_____

h. The prosecutor informs the Justice that he wishes to show cause. Who presents the case first?

_____

i. Do all the Crown witnesses have to be subpoenaed to this bail hearing?

_____

_____

_____

j. The investigating officer begins testifying. Can the officer

‣ read a summary of the offence?

_____

‣ state the conviction for assault?

_____

‣ state June's employment status?

_____

‣ state the circumstances of the "Theft under $5,000.00" complaint?

_____

k. Can June cross-examine the officer?

_____

l. Can June be compelled by either the Justice or the prosecutor to testify?

_____

m. If June testifies, can she be asked about the offence?

_____

n. Can the Justice convict June after the bail hearing?

_____

o. Can the Justice withdraw the Information or release June unconditionally
    (no charge)?

_____

_____

_____

p. If only primary grounds are proven, can June be detained in custody?

_____

q. If only secondary grounds are proven, can June be detained in custody?

_____

r. If neither primary nor secondary grounds are proven, what must occur?

_____

_____

s. How many conditions can the Justice impose?

_____

Problem 28

Eric was arrested two weeks ago for "Break, enter, and theft" and was released on an undertaking without conditions. The trial is scheduled to take place four months from the arrest date. Today, Eric is arrested for "Theft over $5,000.00" and is brought before a Justice for a bail hearing. Who will have the onus?

_____

_____

Problem 29

Chris was arrested one month ago for "Cause a disturbance" and was released by a promise to appear. The trial is scheduled to take place five months from the arrest date. Today, Chris is arrested for "Robbery" and is brought before a Justice for a bail hearing. Who will have the onus?

Problem 30

George was arrested 10 days ago for "Cause a disturbance" and was released on a promise to appear. Today, he is arrested for "Fail to appear" in court and is brought before a Justice for a bail hearing. Who will have the onus?

Problem 31

Sam is arrested today in Toronto for "Fraud over $5,000.00." He lives in Buffalo, New York. He is brought before a Justice for a bail hearing. Who will have the onus?

Problem 32

Sally is arrested for "Impaired driving" in Vancouver. She lives in Toronto. She is brought before a Justice for a bail hearing. Who will have the onus?

Problem 33

Walter lives in Vancouver. He is arrested in Vancouver for "Trafficking narcotics." This is his first offence. Who will have the onus?

Problem 34

Eleanor is brought before a Justice for a bail hearing regarding a charge of "Robbery." A reverse onus situation exists. The Justice asks, "Do you wish to show cause?"

a. To whom is the question directed?

_____

b. If the answer is "No," what must occur?

_____

Test Yourself

You respond to a bank alarm at 2:50 p.m. A robbery occurred five minutes ago. You search the area and lawfully arrest Chris (21). You transport him to the police station. Explain:

▸ what information you will need to obtain in order to conduct a bail hearing, and
▸ the procedures that will be followed at his bail hearing.

_____

_____

_____

_____

_____

_____

_____

_____

_____

_____

_____

_____

_____

_____

_____

CHAPTER 13

Charging an Offender and Use of Discretion

LEARNING OUTCOMES

The student will learn

- The concept of "use of discretion" in the case of *R. v. Beaudry* (2007)
- How to interpret and apply ss. 504–508 and 788–789 C.C.
- The definition of an Information
- The procedure for completing and laying an Information
- The procedure involved in an *ex parte* hearing
- The definition of an indictment and how one is drafted
- The purpose of a preliminary hearing
- The possible outcomes of a preliminary hearing

INTRODUCTION

In law enforcement, there are two alternative ways of addressing a criminal offence:

1. charge the offender by laying an Information, or
2. do not charge him (for example, the offender is warned, or, in slang terms, "given a break").

Both alternatives have the same goals—to maintain public safety, to prevent a repetition of the offence, to protect the victim, to recover the victim's property, to prevent a wrongful charge, etc. The fundamental difference between the two alternatives is *who* will solve the problem. When an offender is charged, you are placing the problem-solving responsibility on the criminal justice system. You are asking the criminal justice system to solve it. When you do not charge the offender, you are expressing your intention to solve the problem without the intervention of the criminal justice system.

The best alternative is the one most likely to eliminate the worst possible consequence. Choosing not to charge is choosing "use of discretion."

USE OF DISCRETION

Officers have a degree of discretion in relation to criminal offences. This discretionary right is authorized in s. 504 C.C., where the word "may" is used with respect to an officer's laying of an Information. The word "shall" is not used.

The *Criminal Code* authorizes police officers' use of discretion but does not provide concrete guidelines concerning how to use it. Learning the use-of-discretion rules requires case law research. Two cases in particular are important:

1. *R. v. Beaudry* (2007) (a landmark decision that outlines a "use-of-discretion decision-making model"); and
2. *Hill v. Hamilton-Wentworth Regional Police Services Board* (2007).

The decision whether to charge or not charge an offender has enormous, wide-ranging implications. The primary concern is to protect the public from a future offence. Protection and prevention are the goals. Protect the public by preventing crimes. Therefore the guiding principle, when it comes to selecting the best alternative is the following: *eliminate the worst possible consequence.* The worst possible consequence is death, injury, or the risk of either. All other potential consequences, such as theft or damage to property, are secondary. Eliminating them is a goal but they obviously do not have the same priority as preventing injury and death.

When choosing how to deal with an offence, ask yourself, "What could be the worst possible consequence of my decision?" In other words, if you choose *not* to charge someone, you must be able to *argue, justifiably, that the offender will commit no future crimes and harm no one if not charged.*[1] You must have concrete reasons for believing this.[2]

Common Sense

There are only three causes of problem-solving failure—DK, DE, or both. *DK* means *deficiency of knowledge*—not defining the specific problem correctly or not knowing the alternative solutions. *DE* means deficiency of execution—knowing which alternative is the right one but not executing properly. Problem-solving failure and improper use of discretion are the same thing. Improper use of discretion can have a number of negative consequences, including being liable for the offence of "Obstruct justice."

Shortly after I was hired as a police officer, I was at the front desk of the police station with the staff sergeant in charge of the uniform platoon. As he read a report, he lamented the decision made by an officer to charge a person with numerous offences that arose from one minor incident. "This guy would charge his own mother," the staff sergeant moaned. "You have to use discretion. You can't charge everybody. It's common sense. Policing is all about common sense. You'll never get anywhere unless you use common sense. Don't forget that!" I didn't.

The same advice was conveyed to me repeatedly. *Discretion* and *common sense* became synonymous. They sound like simple, self-explanatory terms. But, as you learn early in your police career, using discretion effectively and applying common sense are not easy tasks. Discretion, like any other skill, has to be learned and developed through experience, and you also have to strictly follow the guidelines created in case law.

On January 31, 2007, the S.C.C., in *R. v. Beaudry*, released one of its most important decisions ever—one that dramatically affects every Canadian police officer. It explains how to use discretion properly and how to prevent being charged or convicted for obstructing justice. It is likely the most important case law decision you will ever read. A full version of this case can be found at **www.emp.ca/arcaro/ policepowers4E**.

The following is a case law review of three S.C.C. cases. The first, *R. v Beaudry*, creates a *decision-making model* for *applied discretion*. It also explains the fine line separating the lawful use of discretion from the offence of obstructing justice. *Beaudry* follows *R. v. Beare* (1988), a decision in which the S.C.C. established principles to govern police discretion. The last case, *Hill v. Hamilton-Wentworth Regional Police Services Board* (2007), added another step to the model created by *Beaudry*.

CASE LAW REVIEW

R. v. Beaudry (2007) S.C.C.

THE "POLICE DISCRETION—OBSTRUCT JUSTICE" PARADOX

Synopsis: The S.C.C. upheld the conviction of a police officer who deliberately failed to gather evidence needed to lay criminal charges against another officer. The accused was charged after he intentionally failed to take breath samples from another police officer during an impaired driving investigation. The accused contended that his decision involved proper exercise of discretion. The trial judge convicted the accused after the Crown successfully argued that his decision was "founded on preferential treatment."[3] Appeals to the Quebec C.A. and the S.C.C. failed.

The circumstances of this case help show how improper use of discretion can constitute the offence of "Obstruct justice." The details of the *Beaudry* case and other cases on the use of discretion can be read about at **www.emp.ca/arcaro/policepowers4E**.

POLICE DISCRETION

Police discretion is defined as the authority to decide whether to "engage the judicial process"—that is, to decide whether or not to charge and/or arrest an offender. The key point is that the exercise of discretion involves making a decision.

1. The police authority to use discretion emerges from their common-law duty to investigate crimes.

   > There is no question that police officers have a duty to enforce the law and investigate crimes. The principle that the police have a duty to enforce the criminal law is well established at common law.[4]

2. This common-law duty is codified in provincial "Police Act" statutes—the police have provincial statutory authority both to investigate crime and to use discretion.

   > The ability—indeed the duty—to use one's judgment to adapt the process of law enforcement to individual circumstances and to the real-life demands of justice is in fact the basis of police discretion.[5]

   > Discretion is an essential feature of the criminal justice system. A system that attempted to eliminate discretion would be unworkably complex and rigid.[6]

3. The exercise of discretion is essential but it is a limited power. All discretion must be justified.

> [T]his discretion is not absolute. Far from having *carte blanche*, police officers must justify their decisions rationally.[7]

4. The justification for a decision has to have three elements:
   a. It must be informed—that is, based on evidence that constitutes reasonable grounds.
   b. It must include concrete reasons that do not constitute favouritism and bias.
   c. It must be both subjectively and objectively honest/logical. First, the officer must have based his decision on a personal honest belief. Second, a trial judge must determine that the officer's belief reflected actual reality.

Justification for use of discretion has to be appropriate in light of the offence and it has to be in the interests of public safety.[8]

THE OFFENCE OF "OBSTRUCT JUSTICE"

The phrase "Obstruct justice" is a short-form slang term based on s. 139 C.C., a three-part section that creates the offence formally called "attempting to obstruct justice."

- Subsection (1) defines as a dual procedure offence the act of attempting to obstruct justice with specific regard to "sureties."
- Subsection (2) defines as an indictable/10-year-maximum offence the act of "attempting to obstruct justice" in broader terms, with respect to matters other than sureties.
- Subsection (3) lists examples of how the offence of attempting to obstruct justice, as defined in subsection (2), may be committed, but it is not an exhaustive list.
- That the offence can be wide-ranging in its forms is suggested by the phrase "in any manner."
- The *actus reus* of the offence is "attempt in any manner to obstruct, pervert or defeat the course of justice."
- The *mens rea* of the offence is "wilful" (that is, intentional).
- There is no concrete, exhaustive list of all circumstances that could constitute "obstruct justice."[9]

DISCRETION MODEL

The following seven guidelines, which make up an abbreviated use-of-discretion model, emerge from the *R. v. Beaudry* case law decision. The long version of this model can be found at **www.emp.ca/arcaro/policepowers4E**. This model applies to police nationwide. Arguably, nothing is more important to your police career:

1. Discretion is vital for the proper operation of the criminal justice system. Not all offenders must be charged.
2. The police have discretion but it is not absolute—it is limited.
3. Limited discretion means that the exercise of it must be in keeping with the severity of the offence.

4. Using discretion not to charge an offender must be justified with concrete reasons.
5. Improper use of discretion does not automatically constitute "Obstruct justice."
6. A simple error of judgment does not constitute "Obstruct justice."
7. The offence of attempting to obstruct justice is committed when discretion is used disproportionately and unjustifiably and is intended to pervert or defeat the course of justice.[10]

R. v. Beare (1988) S.C.C.

The leading case prior to *R. v. Beaudry* was *R. v. Beare* (1988). In the *Beare* case, the S.C.C. created the following principles with respect to police discretion:

- Discretion is an essential feature of the criminal justice system. A system that attempted to eliminate discretion would be unworkably complex and rigid.
- Police may exercise discretion to start judicial proceedings, but the authority to use discretion is "not absolute." It is limited by the "subjective justification rule."
- A police officer who has reasonable grounds to believe that an offence has been committed, or that a more thorough investigation might produce evidence that could form the basis of a criminal charge, may exercise his or her discretion to decide not to engage the judicial process. But this discretion is not absolute. Far from having *carte blanche*, police officers must justify such a decision rationally.
- The required justification is essentially twofold. First, the exercise of the discretion must be justified subjectively: that is, it must be shown that the discretion was exercised honestly and transparently, and on the basis of valid and reasonable grounds. Thus, a decision based on favouritism, or on cultural, social or racial stereotypes, cannot constitute a proper exercise of police discretion. However, the officer's sincere belief that he properly exercised his discretion is not sufficient to justify his decision.
- Hence, the exercise of police discretion must also be justified on the basis of objective factors; it is important to consider the material circumstances in which the discretion was exercised.[11]

KEY POINTS

1. Rational justification is mandatory when discretion is used.
2. Improper exercise of discretion involves decisions based on favouritism or bias.
3. Proper justification must be relevant and proportionate to the circumstances of the offence.

Hill v. Hamilton-Wentworth Regional Police Services Board (2007) S.C.C.

DISCRETION—NEGLIGENCE PARADOX: THE EASY WAY OUT

This landmark decision allows the police to be sued for investigative negligence. The S.C.C. acknowledged that officers may be tempted not to charge an offender so as to avoid facing potential civil suits.

In this case, the S.C.C. added one more rule to the *Beaudry* discretion model: deciding not to charge an offender in order to avoid the potential for civil liability constitutes an improper use of discretion. Taking the easy way out by not laying an Information simply to avoid getting sued is no more proper a use of discretion than basing a decision on favouritism or on cultural, social, or racial bias. The desire to avoid being sued, favouritism, and bias—all of these constitute unlawful justifications of the use of discretion.[12]

The keys to properly using discretion are the following: (1) forming reasonable grounds; and (2) the duty of police to protect the public from future risk and the suspect from a wrongful charge. The starting point for use-of-discretion decisions is the point where reasonable grounds are formed. This standard of belief is below the standard of the "beyond a reasonable doubt" belief. The S.C.C. called the difference separating the two standards of belief a "significant gap."[13] This means that when the lower standard of reasonable grounds is used, the officer must then make a decision, using the "proportionate discretion" rule established in *Beaudry*, about whether to charge the offender. A decision not to charge cannot be based on the "selfish desire to avoid potential civil liability."

CHARGING AN OFFENDER

The alternative to exercising one's discretion in not charging an offender is charging him or her with a criminal offence by laying an Information. By doing this, you are asking the criminal justice system to solve the problem. The arrest of a person does not constitute a formal charge. Arrest refers only to the physical custody of a person. Similarly, release/compelling documents do not formally charge a person with an offence. For example, when the police serve an appearance notice or promise to appear to a person, he or she has not been formally charged at that particular time.

Formally charging a person requires the laying of an *Information*. An **Information** is the name of a sworn, written document that formally alleges that a specific adult or young offender has committed a specific offence—of any classification.[14] The following five key points are drawn from this definition:

1. An Information is the document used to charge either an adult or a young offender.
2. An Information is the document used to charge an offender in relation to summary conviction, dual procedure, or indictable offences.
3. The procedure used to lay an Information is the same for adult and young offenders, and for any classification of criminal offence.
4. An Information charges the person; it does not compel a person to court.
5. A formal allegation must be in writing and sworn.

The phrase **laying an Information** refers to completing the document, bringing it before a Justice, and swearing its contents under oath.[15] After the Information is laid, a procedure occurs in the course of which police must prove there are reasonable grounds for believing that the person named on the Information committed the offence described on it. Then the Justice decides whether or not to sign the document. The accused person is formally charged when the Justice signs the Information.

The document used as an Information is called a Form 2, and is found in s. 841 C.C. The document is shown in that section of the *Criminal Code.* The procedures and rules explaining how to lay an Information are found in ss. 504–508 and 788–1789 C.C.

PURPOSES OF AN INFORMATION

The four general purposes of an Information are

1. to commence proceedings against the accused,
2. to inform the accused about the specific allegation,
3. to indicate that the allegation has been sworn under oath before a Justice, and,
4. if the offence is summary conviction, to indicate that a formal charge was laid within six months of the offence date.[16]

LAYING AN INFORMATION

The following general rules apply to the process of laying an Information.

General Rules

RULE 1

Anyone may lay an Information if he or she can prove there are reasonable grounds to believe that the person to be charged committed a criminal offence.[17] This means that a police officer or any citizen can lay an Information, for any classification of offence, if the person can prove reasonable grounds. However, the vast majority of Informations are laid by police officers.

The person who lays an Information is called the **informant**.[18] This is the legal name of the person who makes the formal allegation, and it must not be confused with the term "confidential informant"—a person from whom the police receive evidence during an investigation. In other words, the police officer who lays the Information is referred to as *the informant.*

RULE 2

Receiving an Information is the process of accepting it for review, for the purpose of determining whether there are reasonable grounds for formally charging the offender. A Justice receives the Information.

An Information must be laid before a Justice, defined as a Justice of the Peace (JP) or a provincial court judge.[19] The vast majority of Informations are laid before JPs. Again, a Justice is the person who receives, or accepts, the Information. A Justice has no discretion about receiving an Information that concerns an indictable or dual procedure offence. The Justice *must* receive it.[20] This does not mean that the offender will automatically be charged.

Regarding summary conviction offences, s. 788(2) C.C. does not state that a Justice must receive an Information. It states that a Justice *may* receive it, which apparently means that a Justice has discretion about whether to receive it or not.

RULE 3

An Information is not laid in open court. The location may be anywhere other than open court; usually it is laid in a Justice's office.

RULE 4

The time limit for laying an Information depends on

- ▸ the classification of the offence, and
- ▸ whether a release/compelling document was served first (before the Information was laid).

The first determining factor is the classification of the offence. If the offence is summary conviction, the Information must be laid within six months of the offence date. After six months, an Information cannot be laid for this type of offence, and the offender cannot be charged.[21] If the offence is indictable or dual procedure, no time limit exists on laying an Information. An Information may be laid at any time after the offence occurs.

The second factor is the type of compelling document used. An Information must be laid *as soon as practicable* after the offender's arrest and release, and before the court date specified on the document,[22] if an offender is arrested and then released by any of the following means:

- ▸ an appearance notice, or
- ▸ a promise to appear, or
- ▸ a recognizance (by the OIC or police officer), or
- ▸ an undertaking (by the OIC or police officer) in conjunction with a promise to appear or a recognizance.

No specific time limit is imposed, but unreasonable delays should be avoided.

If a summons is used to compel an accused's court appearance, an Information must be laid first, before the compelling document is served. The time limits relevant to the different classifications of offence apply to the laying of an Information in this situation.

If an offender is arrested and is detained for a bail hearing, an Information must be laid before the bail hearing begins. This means that an Information must be laid before a Justice releases the accused or before the Justice detains the offender in custody until the trial—that is, the result of the bail hearing.

CONTENTS OF AN INFORMATION

General Rules

When we talk about the "contents" of an Information (Form 2) we are referring to the facts and details that must be written on it in order for it to be sufficient, or valid. The following general rules apply to the contents of an Information.

RULE 1

The contents must be sufficiently detailed, so that the accused is reasonably informed of the charge against him or her, and is able to prepare a full defence. The contents must be sufficient to allow for a fair trial.[23]

RULE 2

All the facts-in-issue of the offence must be written on the Information, including

- the accused's name (identity),
- the date of the offence,
- the location of the offence, and
- the specific elements that constitute the offence.[24]

RULE 3

An Information must fully allege at least one **count**, defined as one charge.[25] For example, a person charged with one assault is charged with one "count of assault." If the accused is charged with three assaults, he or she is charged with three "counts of assault."

RULE 4

Each count must include a statement that alleges one complete offence.[26] The statement must contain all the elements that constitute the offence and must give reasonable information about the offence to the accused.[27]

RULE 5

A statement that alleges one count of an offence is informally called a **wording**. A wording cannot contain irrelevant words or language that is not essential to the offence.[28] Therefore, unnecessary words must be kept out of a wording.

A wording cannot be composed of the short-form name of an offence, such as "Theft under $5,000.00," or "Break, enter, and theft." It must be composed of a lengthier statement that includes each specific fact-in-issue that is found in the section of the *Criminal Code* that defines the offence.[29] A wording that lacks at least one fact-in-issue is insufficient or invalid. The prosecution has the onus of proving beyond a reasonable doubt that all the facts-in-issue written on the Information apply to the particular case.

Specific Contents

The specific contents of an Information are outlined on Form 2, which is the specific document that is used as an Information. It is illustrated in s. 841 C.C. Eight areas must be completed when an Information is laid:

1. CANADA
    PROVINCE of [insert territorial division or region]
    2. Information of [informant's name], [occupation], hereinafter called the informant.
    The informant says that he or she believes on reasonable grounds that
        3. [accused's name and address]
        4. on or about the [date] day of [month], 20___,
        5. at the [city], in the [territorial division or region]
        6. wording
            7. _____
                (informant's signature)

8. Sworn before me this [date] day
    of [month], 20____
    at [city]

                                        _____
                                             (JP's signature)
                                   A Justice of the Peace in and for [province]

SPECIFIC CONTENTS—EXPLANATION

Item 1: Territorial Jurisdiction or Region

This refers to the judicial district or region where the offence occurred. These districts are determined by province. For example, Central West Region includes Oakville, Burlington, and Milton, Ontario.

Item 2: Informant's Name

This refers to the person who lays the Information, usually a police officer. The informant's occupation must be included. The person named must have a belief based on reasonable grounds that the accused committed the offence. An Information cannot be laid anonymously, without the informant's name.

Item 3: Accused's Name and Address

Before inserting the accused's name and address, determine these facts accurately. Do not base your information on assumptions. Prove the offender's name by means of relevant documents or by the offender's admission. The accused's date of birth may be mentioned also.

Item 4: Offence Date

Form 2 has the phrase "on or about" printed on the document, accompanied by spaces to indicate a specific date. This format may be used when evidence exists that the offence actually was committed on a specific date. (The time of the offence does not have to be specified.) However, in some cases, the specific offence date is not known. The evidence may prove only that the offence was committed between two dates. When this kind of evidence exists, the informant is permitted to place a single line through "on or about" and replace that phrase with "between." Two dates must be written afterward.

For example, an offender is arrested for breaking into a house. The owner reports that she left on Friday, March 1st, at 5:00 p.m. and returned on Sunday, March 3rd, at 9:00 a.m. *The "between" dates should not include possible offence dates.* The "between" dates must be days when the offence could not have occurred. For example, if the "between" dates are February 28th and March 4th, the offence did not occur on either of those days. The informant must prove the offence occurred between those dates, which includes March 1 (5:00 p.m.–11:59 a.m.), March 2, and March 3 (12:00 a.m.–9:00 a.m.). In other words, if the informant wrote "between March 1st and March 3rd," he or she is alleging that the offence occurred on March 2nd.

There is no limit on the span of time that may be bounded by "between" dates. For example, the S.C.C., in *R. v. Colgan* (1987),[30] ruled that a time period of more than six years was suitable.

In *R. v. B.(G.)* (1990),[31] the S.C.C. established the following rules regarding the offence date component of an Information:

- ▸ The exact time of the offence does not have to be specified.
- ▸ The date or dates used must provide reasonable information to the accused about when the offence occurred.
- ▸ What constitutes reasonable information will vary from case to case.
- ▸ Lengthy time periods are acceptable if no evidence indicates a specific date.
- ▸ If the evidence does indicate a specific date, then a specific date must be written on the Information.
- ▸ If evidence introduced at the trial regarding the offence date conflicts with the date or dates written on the Information, the accused may still be convicted if it "is not an essential element of the offence or crucial to the defence."[32] If the discrepancy in dates is an essential element or crucial to the defence, then the accused must be acquitted.

Item 5: Location of Offence

The location of the offence is entered above the wording. Only the city is specified as the location, not the street or address. Where applicable, the street or address is specified in the wording. Do not enter the city name alone; use the phrase "city of" before the actual name (for example, "city of Calgary"). Next to this entry, specify the judicial district or region. The phrase "in the said region" is sufficient because it refers to the district or region named at the top of the Information.

Item 6: Wording

The wording is the most important feature of an Information. Short-form names of offences, such as "break, enter, and theft," cannot be used in lieu of formal wordings on an Information. Actual formal wordings are not found in the *Criminal Code*. The Ministry of the Attorney General for each province prepares wordings that are used by the province's police officers. Publishers of criminal codes have suggested wordings in their publications. A prosecutor should be consulted if doubt exists when drafting the wording.

The following are examples of suggested wordings.

Example 1: "Break, enter, and theft" (s. 348(1)(b) C.C.) is the short-form name for the following:

did break and enter a certain place, TO WIT: [specify place including address] and did commit therein the indictable offence of [specify offence: i.e., THEFT], contrary to s. 348(1)(b) of the *Criminal Code*.[33]

The facts-in-issue of "Break, enter, and theft" are

- ▸ break,
- ▸ enter,
- ▸ place, and
- ▸ commit an indictable offence therein

Note that the formal wording in the above example contains all the facts-in-issue. Two of them require additional explanation:

1. *Place*. Section 348(3) C.C. defines place as
    - ▸ a dwelling house,
    - ▸ a building,

- a structure,
- a railway vehicle,
- a vessel,
- an aircraft,
- a trailer, or
- a pen or enclosure for fur-bearing animals.

Therefore, the place specified must be one of these, and the address must be included. The phrase *TO WIT* means "that being" or "specifically." Examples of how to complete the place specifications are as follows:

- *If the place is a house* at 10 King St., you would write, "TO WIT: a dwelling-house situated at 10 King St." (Do not include the city after the street. The city is written above the wording.)
- *If the place is a business premises* located at 100 Main St., you would write "TO WIT: a building [store or factory is also acceptable] situated at 100 Main St." (Do not use the name of the business only, such as Fred's Video or City College, because these are not included under the definition of place.)

2. *Commit an indictable offence therein.* Include the specific indictable offence committed, such as "Theft" or "Mischief" (it is not necessary to specify whether the amount stolen was under or over $5,000.00).

Example 2: "Theft under $5,000.00" (s. 334(b) C.C.), expressed in its formal wording, is as follows:

did steal [specify item] the property of [insert the property owner's name] of a value not exceeding $5,000.00, contrary to s. 344(b) of the *Criminal Code*.[34]

Where the item stolen is required to be specified, include

- the general type (for example, television set, bicycle), and
- a brief specific description to distinguish the item from any other similar item that the complainant owns.

Elaborate descriptions should be avoided since each word used in the description must be proven. Simple descriptions should be used that are sufficient to inform the accused of the specific offence.

Example 3: "Assault" (s. 266 C.C.), expressed in its formal wording, would be as follows:

did commit an assault on [insert victim's name], contrary to s. 266 of the *Criminal Code*.[35]

Item 7: Informant's Signature

The informant signs the Information, signifying his or her belief that the contents are true. However, this does not signify that the accused is formally charged.

Item 8: Sworn Oath

The informant swears under oath that the contents are believed to be true. The Justice writes the date, month, year, and city where the Information is sworn, *but does not sign it at this stage*. A hearing then begins in which the informant has the onus of proving that reasonable grounds exist for believing the accused committed the offence. If the Justice is satisfied that reasonable grounds do exist, he or she signs the Information. The accused is formally charged at that time. If the Justice concludes that reasonable grounds do not exist, the Justice will not sign the Information and the accused will not be charged.

Joinder of Counts

An offender has often committed multiple offences, which requires that he or she be charged with more than one count. In these situations, the informant has two alternatives about how to charge the offender and how to complete an Information:

1. Lay a separate Information for each offence. Each document will have one count; or
2. Join counts on one Information. This procedure is referred to as **joinder of counts**.[36]

The following are rules regarding joinder of counts.

RULE 1

Summary conviction offences may be joined only with other summary conviction offences, not with indictable or dual procedure offences.[37]

RULE 2

Indictable or dual procedure offences may be joined only with other indictable or dual procedure offences, not with summary conviction offences.[38]

RULE 3

Each count must be distinguished as being separate.[39] This means that each count must have its own individual wording. In other words, one wording must allege only one count.

RULE 4

Unlimited counts may be joined on one document. If additional pages are required, counts may be typed on blank paper and attached to the original document. Multiple counts on one document may be separated by inserting the term "and further" between them, as in the following example:

> on or about the **10th** day of January, 1997, in the city of Hamilton,
> did [insert wording for count 1],
> contrary to section _____ of the *Criminal Code,*
> **and further,**
> on or about the **12th** day of **January,** 1997, in the city of Hamilton,
> did [insert wording for count 2],
> contrary to section _____ of the *Criminal Code.*

Any number of counts may be added in this way. Joining counts saves you from having to repeat the contents on the first page of the Information, such as the accused's name, the informant's name, and the judicial district.

Joinder of Parties

Offences are commonly committed by more than one offender. In situations where multiple offenders commit an offence or offences, the informant has two alternatives about how to charge them and how to lay an Information:

1. *Separately.* The informant may lay separate Informations for each offender. Each separate Information charges only one offender. The offenders charged in this manner are known as accomplices. Accomplices who are charged separately may be subpoenaed by the Crown attorney to testify against each other.[40]
2. *Jointly.* More than one offender may be named on a single Information. This refers to **joinder of parties**, or charging offenders jointly. Jointly charged offenders are called co-accused persons. The prosecution cannot subpoena one co-accused to testify against another co-accused.[41] Consequently, this procedure is restrictive and eliminates the possibility, for the prosecution, of introducing incriminating evidence from one co-accused against the others.

The testimony of one offender against another is valuable evidence. Each accomplice must be considered an eyewitness of the actions of his or her accomplices. Credible eyewitness observations will provide reasonable grounds during the investigation for various procedures, including arrest, search, and laying an Information. Furthermore, credible accomplice testimony will convict the other accomplices without any other supporting evidence.

Consequently, the goal in every investigation involving multiple offenders should be to elicit evidence from one or all of the offenders and to ensure their testimony against each other. Even if accomplices remain silent at the time of their arrests, they may change their mind before the trial and decide to implicate and testify against the other offenders. Charging offenders separately will permit this possibility. Charging offenders jointly will prevent it. Even though charging offenders jointly provides the benefit of reducing paperwork, it eliminates an enormous advantage for the prosecution.

In summary, charging multiple offenders separately is the recommended procedure since it leaves open the advantage of having accomplices testify against each other.

CONCEPT OF AN EX PARTE HEARING

An informant writes the contents of the Information, brings it before a Justice, signs it, and swears under oath that the contents are true. Before the Justice can sign it, an ***ex parte*** hearing must be conducted. *Ex parte* means "without the party," referring to the accused. The *ex parte* hearing is mandatory and cannot be waived by the Justice.[42] The hearing must be held whether the Information is laid before a summons/arrest warrant is issued or after the accused has been arrested and released by means of an appearance notice, promise to appear, or recognizance.[43] In other words, an *ex parte* hearing cannot be waived or avoided simply because the offender was arrested and already released.

Purpose

The purpose of an *ex parte* hearing is to prove that reasonable grounds exist to believe that the person named on the Information committed the offence described in it.

Onus

The informant has the onus of proving the existence of reasonable grounds.

Location

The hearing is held anywhere other than open court. Usually, it occurs in a JP's office at a police station.

Participants

The accused person is never present and cannot be present. The participants are the Justice, the informant, and, if the Justice considers it necessary, witnesses who may give relevant evidence regarding the existence of reasonable grounds.[44]

Evidence

Only the informant's side of the story is heard at an *ex parte* hearing. The accused cannot cross-examine or introduce evidence because he or she is not present.

Hearsay evidence is allowed at an *ex parte* hearing. Therefore, the informant may give all the relevant evidence, including witness statements. The police officer who is the informant usually is the only person who gives evidence at an *ex parte* hearing. However, witnesses may be called if the Justice considers it desirable or necessary.[45] All witnesses who testify, including the informant, must be sworn under oath before giving evidence through testimony.[46]

Ex Parte Hearing—Procedure

The following steps should be followed whether the accused is an adult or a young offender.

STEP 1

The informant, a person who has a belief based on reasonable grounds that a person committed an offence, writes an Information (Form 2). The Information is completed before being brought to a Justice.

STEP 2

The Information is brought before a Justice, usually a JP, at the JP's office in a police station. The location may be anywhere but open court.

STEP 3

The informant signs the Information, preferably before the JP. However, the Information may be signed before being brought to the JP. The signature does not represent a formal charge.

STEP 4

The informant swears under oath that the contents of the Information are true and that he or she believes, on reasonable grounds, that the accused person committed the offence. The accused is not formally charged at this stage.

STEP 5

An *ex parte* hearing begins.

STEP 6

The informant swears under oath and testifies about the evidence that forms the basis of his or her belief. Hearsay evidence is allowed. A summary of the offence and witness statements may be read by the informant.

STEP 7

If the JP deems it necessary, witnesses may be called to testify under oath at the *ex parte* hearing.

STEP 8

At the conclusion of the *ex parte* hearing, the Justice takes the following action:

1. If satisfied that reasonable grounds exist, the Justice signs the Information, which signifies that the offender is formally charged.

   ‣ If the accused has not yet been arrested, the Justice issues a summons to compel the accused to appear in court or—if the informant proves there are reasonable grounds to believe that the warrant is necessary in the public interest—issues an arrest warrant.
   ‣ If the accused has been previously arrested and released by means of an appearance notice, a promise to appear, or a recognizance, the Justice confirms the document, which compels the accused to court.

   The Crown attorney is not present at the *ex parte* hearing. Despite the absence of the Crown attorney, the following rules are significant:

   a. After the Justice signs the Information, the Crown attorney becomes the owner of the Information.
   b. Only the Crown may withdraw the Information.
   c. No one can change or alter the Information after the Justice signs it. For example, if the accused confesses to additional offences after the Information is signed, the new charges cannot be added to the signed Information. A new Information must be laid, requiring another *ex parte* hearing.

2. If the Justice is not satisfied that reasonable grounds exist, the Justice cannot sign the Information and the offender is not charged at this point. Also,

▸ no summons or arrest warrant is issued, or
▸ the appearance notice, promise to appear, or recognizance is cancelled.

The informant is not restricted to only one *ex parte* hearing. If the Justice declines to sign the Information, the informant may lay a new Information when additional evidence is obtained, although the first Information used during the unsuccessful *ex parte* hearing cannot be reused. The *Criminal Code* does not limit the number of attempts or opportunities to lay an Information.

PATH OF AN INFORMATION

After a sworn Information is laid and signed by a Justice, it follows a distinct path through the criminal justice system (see Figure 13.1). In some trials, an Information is the formal allegation; in other trials, it is replaced by another document called an "indictment." In the process, the Information represents the formal allegation, and leads to indictments and preliminary hearings. This text will address the topic of indictments in conjunction with an explanation of preliminary hearings.

To understand the path of an Information, you must understand the concept of the levels of trials and the accused's election of court level.

Figure 13.1 Path of an Information

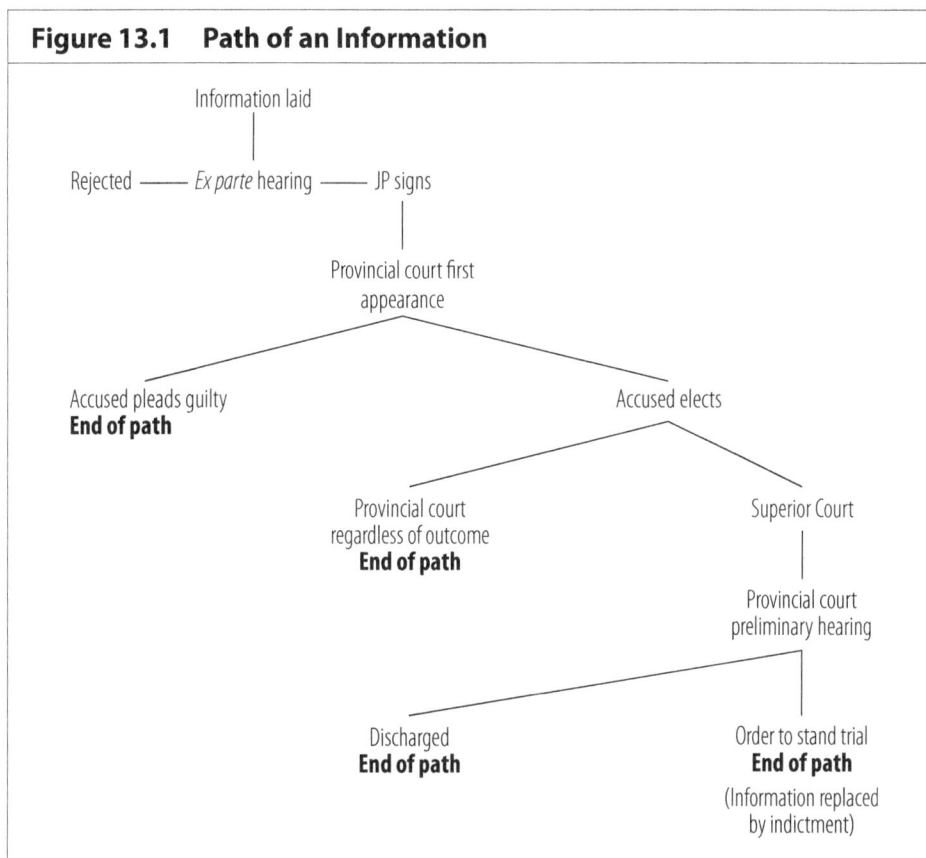

Information laid

Rejected —— *Ex parte* hearing —— JP signs

Provincial court first appearance

Accused pleads guilty
End of path

Accused elects

Provincial court regardless of outcome
End of path

Superior Court

Provincial court preliminary hearing

Discharged
End of path

Order to stand trial
End of path
(Information replaced by indictment)

Level of Trial

Any s. 469 C.C. offence, such as "First degree murder," must be tried in Superior Court, with a jury.

The following offences must be tried in provincial court:

- purely summary conviction offences,
- dual procedure offences that the Crown classifies as summary conviction, and
- section 553 C.C. offences, including "Theft under $5,000.00" and other "under $5,000.00" offences, regardless of the Crown's decision.

The majority of purely indictable offences and dual procedure offences that the Crown selects as indictable are called "election indictable" offences. The accused has a choice, when he or she is charged with an election indictable offence, to be tried in

1. Superior Court of criminal jurisdiction, with a jury (judge and jury);
2. Superior Court of criminal jurisdiction, without a jury (judge alone); or
3. provincial court.

If an accused chooses to be tried in Superior Court with or without a jury, a preliminary hearing must be conducted first, before the trial. All preliminary hearings are conducted in provincial court.

If an accused elects to be tried in provincial court, no preliminary hearing will be conducted before the trial. All trials held in provincial court are tried without a jury.

Accused's Election

1. Superior Court—judge and jury
2. Superior Court—judge alone
————————————————— preliminary hearing line*
3. Provincial court

* If the accused chooses option 1 or 2, which are "above the line," a preliminary hearing must be held. Conversely, choosing option 3, which is "below the line," means no preliminary hearing.

General Rules

A sworn Information, signed by a Justice, is used only in proceedings conducted in provincial court, including

- first appearances,
- trials, for
    a. summary conviction offences,
    b. s. 553 C.C. offences,
    c. indictable offences, where the accused elects to have the trial conducted in provincial court
- preliminary hearings.

The "end of path" of the original Information occurs (1) when the accused pleads guilty at first appearance, or (2) at the conclusion of a preliminary hearing, at which point the Information is replaced with an indictment.

In this case, Information is not used for Superior Court trials because an indictment, which formally charges the accused, replaces it in these trials (for example, general division court, in Ontario).[47]

COMMENTARY

An indictment, like an Information, is a document that represents a formal allegation or charge against an offender. In essence, though their forms differ, the two documents are exactly the same. Informations and indictments serve the same purpose and have the same contents. The replacing of an Information with an indictment is an unnecessary complexity in Canadian criminal law. The concept of starting court proceedings with one document (an Information) and later changing to another document (an indictment) for certain trials is confusing, primarily because there is no need for two documents and there is no logical purpose for this procedure.

The need to replace an Information with an indictment for certain trials is a legal requirement that would benefit from reform and change. The purposes of an Information and an indictment are the same, and the purpose of a trial is the same regardless of what level of court the offender is tried in. It would be logical to use one document throughout the entire court proceeding.

CONCEPT OF INDICTMENT AND PRELIMINARY HEARING

The topic of indictments is directly related to the topic of preliminary hearings; you must learn about the two together to understand the basic police procedures involved in them.

Consequently, the general rules relating to an indictment will be explained before the purpose and procedures of a preliminary hearing are explained. The two topics will be connected in a concluding summary.

Indictment

PURPOSE

An **indictment** is a written document that formally charges an offender.[48] It has the same contents as an Information. However, you do not "lay" an indictment as you do an Information. An indictment is *preferred*. The reason for the difference in terminology is that an indictment is not "laid" before a Justice the way an Information is. An indictment is written by a Crown attorney (that is, a prosecutor), and becomes valid without being brought before a Justice.

When a Crown attorney writes and signs an indictment, the procedure is called *preferring an indictment.* In other words, the indictment is issued by a Crown attorney, not a Justice.[49] A police officer cannot prefer an indictment; only a Crown attorney may do so. Most important, an indictment cannot be used to initiate proceedings against an accused person.

An indictment replaces an Information when a trial is conducted in a Superior Court of criminal jurisdiction—most commonly, after a preliminary hearing concludes and the accused is ordered to stand trial. An indictment cannot be used for proceedings in provincial court, such as trials and preliminary hearings. An Information is the document used in all provincial court proceedings.

Preliminary Hearing

PURPOSE

The purpose of a **preliminary hearing** is to determine whether sufficient evidence exists to conduct a trial. The purpose is not to determine guilt or innocence.[50]

The preliminary hearing also provides "live" disclosure of the prosecution's case to the accused person. The prosecutor's case must previously be disclosed in writing to the accused; the preliminary hearing provides a further opportunity for the accused to analyze the prosecution's evidence.

When is a preliminary hearing required?

A preliminary hearing is required only before a trial that is scheduled to take place in a Superior Court of criminal jurisdiction, with or without a jury.[51] A preliminary hearing is not conducted if the trial is scheduled for provincial court.

An accused person may waive the preliminary hearing, with the consent of the prosecutor.[52] By waiving a preliminary hearing, the accused is conceding that sufficient evidence exists to go to trial, but is not acknowledging guilt.

Where is a preliminary hearing conducted?

A preliminary hearing is conducted in provincial court. A jury cannot be used in provincial court.[53]

What document is used as the formal allegation during a preliminary hearing?

The Information that was initially laid to commence proceedings is the document that is used as the formal allegation against the accused at all preliminary hearings. An indictment is not used during the preliminary hearing.

What are the possible results of a preliminary hearing?

The judge may make one of the following rulings at the conclusion of a preliminary hearing:

1. *Discharge.* This refers to a judge's conclusion that insufficient evidence exists to go to trial. The accused is not ordered to stand trial. However, the accused is not *acquitted*; he or she is no longer charged. The original Information terminates and cannot be used again in the future.[54] After an accused is discharged, new evidence may be obtained and the Crown may prosecute the accused at that time. It is possible to charge the offender in the future by laying a new Information. In this case, a new process begins, starting with the personal written consent of the attorney general to lay a new Information.[55]

2. *Order the accused to stand trial.* This refers to a judge's conclusion that sufficient evidence exists for a trial to be conducted. The prosecutor has proven a *prima facie* case; however, the accused has not been convicted.[56]

RULES AND PROCEDURES

The provisions that govern preliminary hearings are found in Part XVIII of the *Criminal Code* (ss. 535–51 C.C.). They create the following rules and procedures.

Rule 1

The prosecutor has the onus of proving that a *prima facie* case exists. This means that all the facts-in-issue of the offence are proven and sufficient evidence exists to go to trial. The prosecutor does not have to prove guilt beyond reasonable doubt at this point; he or she needs to prove that the evidence is sufficient to obtain a conviction at a trial.[57] The standard for proving that sufficient evidence exists is lower than the standard for proving beyond reasonable doubt.

Rule 2

The prosecutor has *no obligation to introduce all the evidence* that exists in the Crown's case. The prosecutor may produce as much or as little evidence as he or she chooses, provided that the evidence is sufficient to convict at a future trial. Take, for example, a prosecutor's case that consists of five witnesses and the accused's confession. The prosecutor in this instance has the option of either introducing all the evidence or introducing partial evidence, such as the confession and one eyewitness only—provided that partial evidence will prove a *prima facie* case exists.[58] The judge cannot order the Crown to call witnesses or introduce evidence.[59]

Rule 3

The Crown presents his or her case first. The accused may cross-examine any Crown witness who testifies.[60]

Rule 4

All witnesses must be sworn under oath.[61]

Rule 5

At the conclusion of the Crown's case, the defence has the option of introducing evidence.[62] The choice belongs to the accused. The Crown may cross-examine any defence witness who is called by the defence to testify.

Rule 6

The judge cannot exclude evidence, under s. 24(2) Charter. This exclusionary rule does not apply to preliminary hearings.[63]

Rule 7

After hearing the evidence introduced, the judge discharges the accused or orders the accused to stand trial. If the accused waives the preliminary hearing, he or she will be ordered to stand trial without the hearing being conducted.[64]

Rule 8

After the accused is ordered to stand trial, various documents (the Information, the evidence introduced at the hearing, and the release document) are transferred from provincial court to the Superior Court of criminal jurisdiction where the trial will be held.[65]

The Information will not be used at the trial in the Superior Court of criminal jurisdiction. Instead, the prosecutor prefers (writes and signs) an indictment to replace the Information. The indictment is very similar to the Information; the main difference between the two is that the Information is sworn before a Justice.[66]

DIRECT INDICTMENT

Section 577 C.C. affords the prosecution two significant advantages in expediting a trial. The Crown is permitted to cause an accused to stand trial in Superior Court by

1. preferring an indictment before a preliminary hearing is conducted, essentially bypassing a preliminary hearing; or
2. preferring an indictment after the accused has been discharged at the conclusion of a preliminary hearing, essentially reversing a judge's discharge of the accused.

The prosecutor must obtain the personal written consent of the attorney general or the deputy attorney general in order to prefer an indictment in these situations. This type of indictment, which is not commonly used, is called a "direct indictment."[67]

SUMMARY

The next chapter deals with Step 5—"Search Authority"—of the Rapid Decision-Making Model outlined in Chapter 1. A police officer's authority to search an offender and a "place" with or without warrant will be explained and interpreted, with particular emphasis on preventing Charter violations.

PROBLEM-SOLVING CASE STUDIES

You are a police officer in each case. Each offender is an adult, unless otherwise indicated.

Problem 1

Walter and Eddie have known each other for several years. Eddie assaulted Walter three days ago. Can Walter lay an Information today to charge Eddie?

_____

_____

_____

_____

_____

Problem 2

Warren is a security guard in a department store. He sees Eddie commit "Theft under $5,000.00." Can Warren lay an Information anonymously so that Eddie will not know who charged him?

Problem 3

You form reasonable grounds today that Will committed "Fraud over $5,000.00" eight months ago, and you arrest Will without a warrant today. Will is subsequently released at the police station by means of a promise to appear.

a. When must you lay an Information?

b. Before whom must the Information be laid?

c. Where must the Information be laid?

d. You complete the Information and bring it to a JP. You sign the Information. What must occur afterward?

e. After you sign the Information and swear under oath, is Will formally charged?

f. Does an *ex parte* hearing have to be conducted even though you had arrested Will without a warrant?

g. What is the purpose of the *ex parte* hearing?

h. Can you introduce all the evidence, including witness statements, without calling the witnesses?

i. Do you, and any other witnesses, have to be sworn under oath before testifying at the *ex parte* hearing?

_____

j. Does Will need to be present at the *ex parte* hearing?

_____

k. What will occur if you fail to prove that reasonable grounds exist?

_____

_____

l. What will occur if you successfully prove that reasonable grounds exist?

_____

_____

m. When is Will formally charged?

_____

n. Who owns the Information after the Information is signed by the JP?

_____

o. Could you have preferred an indictment instead of laying an Information?

_____

_____

Problem 4

Can an Information be laid to charge an offender with either summary conviction, dual procedure, or indictable offences?

_____

_____

Problem 5

You investigate two robberies that occurred during the past seven days and form reasonable grounds that Walter committed both offences. Can one wording allege both counts?

_____

_____

Problem 6

Warren and June live at 1000 E. 200th Street, Hamilton, Ontario. They leave their house on Saturday, March 23, at 9:00 a.m. and return on Sunday, March 24, at 9:00 p.m. They discover that a break and enter has occurred during their absence.

Their 26-inch colour TV, valued at $700.00, has been stolen. On March 27 you form reasonable grounds for believing that Eddie committed the offence.

a. Should the offence date on the Information allege "between March 23rd and March 24th"?

_____

_____

b. What should the alleged offence date be?

_____

_____

_____

c. Does the address have to be included in the location portion that precedes the wording?

_____

d. Is the following a valid wording on an Information: "did commit a break, enter, and theft"?

_____

e. What wording should be used?

_____

_____

_____

f. After this Information is signed by a JP, you question Eddie about other offences. Eddie confesses that he committed another break and enter at another house on the same street. Can another count be added to the signed Information?

_____

_____

Problem 7

Jack and Eddie commit three robberies, on April 5th, 6th, and 7th, respectively.

a. Can all three counts of robbery be joined on one Information?

_____

_____

b. Can Jack and Eddie be joined on the same Information?

_____

c. If Jack and Eddie are joined on the same Information, can the prosecutor subpoena them to testify against each other?

_____

d. How should they be charged if the prosecution wishes to subpoena Jack and Eddie to testify against each other?

_____

_____

_____

Problem 8

You arrest Will for "Attempted murder." June is the victim.

a. How are proceedings commenced?

_____

b. Can the *ex parte* hearing be waived by the Justice?

_____

c. The JP signs the Information. Will later appears in court. If Will elects to have the trial in provincial court, will a preliminary hearing be conducted?

_____

_____

d. If Will elects to have a trial in Superior Court of criminal jurisdiction (for example, General Division, Ontario), with judge and jury or with judge alone, will a preliminary hearing be conducted?

_____

e. Where will the preliminary hearing be conducted?

_____

f. Will the Information be used at the preliminary hearing?

_____

g. What is the purpose of the preliminary hearing?

_____

h. Who has the onus?

_____

i. Does the prosecutor have to introduce all the evidence at the preliminary hearing?

_____

_____

j. Can Will be found guilty or not guilty at the conclusion of the preliminary hearing?

_____

k. If Will is discharged, can an Information be laid in the future when additional evidence is obtained?

_____

l. If Will is discharged, can the prosecutor prefer an indictment?

_____

m. If Will is ordered to stand trial, what happens to the Information?

_____

_____

n. How is an indictment preferred?

_____

o. Could the preliminary hearing have been bypassed?

_____

_____

_____

Test Yourself Questions

1. You have reasonable grounds to charge Walter Cleaver (31), 5295 Barton Street, Hamilton, with assault for punching Eddie (28) in the face on March 15, 2002 at 1525 King Street, Hamilton.

   a. Go to s. 841 C.C. Find the document that depicts an Information and complete it; and

   b. explain how the *ex parte* hearing will be conducted.

_____
_____
_____
_____
_____
_____
_____
_____
_____
_____
_____
_____
_____
_____
_____

_____

_____

_____

_____

ENDNOTES

1. *R. v. Beaudry* (2007), 216 C.C.C. (3d) 353 (S.C.C.).
2. Ibid.
3. Ibid.
4. Ibid.
5. Ibid.
6. *R. v. Beare* (1988), 45 C.C.C. (3d) 57 (S.C.C.).
7. *Beaudry*, supra note 1, at para. 37.
8. Ibid., at para. 40.
9. Section 139 C.C.
10. *Beaudry*, supra note 1, at para. 52.
11. Ibid.
12. *Hill v. Hamilton-Wentworth Regional Police Services Board*, 2007 SCC 41.
13. Ibid., at para. 132.
14. Section 504 C.C.
15. Section 504 C.C.
16. *R. v. Corcoran*, 1995 Can LII 7085 (Ont. S.C.).
17. Sections 504, 785, 788(1), and 839 (Form 2) C.C.
18. Sections 504, 785, 788(1), and 839 (Form 2) C.C.
19. Sections 2, 504, 788(1), and 782 C.C.
20. Section 507(2) C.C.
21. Section 786(2) C.C.
22. Section 505 C.C.
23. *R. v. B.(G.)* (1990), 56 C.C.C. (3d) 200 (S.C.C.).
24. Ibid.
25. Section 2 C.C.
26. Section 581(1) C.C.
27. Section 581(3) C.C.
28. Section 581(2)(b) C.C.
29. Section 581(2)(a) C.C.
30. *R. v. Colgan* (1987), 38 C.C.C. (3d) 576 (S.C.C.).
31. *R. v. B.(G.)*, supra note 23.
32. Ibid., at 218.
33. *Martin's Annual Criminal Code* (Aurora, ON: Canada Law Book, 1997), appendix A/39.
34. Ibid., at appendix A/37.
35. Ibid., at appendix A/32.
36. Sections 591(1) and 789(1)(b) C.C.
37. Section 789(1)(b) C.C.
38. Section 591(1) C.C.

39. *R. v. Cote* (1977), 33 C.C.C. 353 (S.C.C.).

40. *R. v. Primeau* (1995), 97 C.C.C. (3d) 1 (S.C.C.), and *R. v. Jobin* (1995), 97 C.C.C. (3d) 97 (S.C.C.).

41. Section 4(1) C.E.A.

42. Sections 507(1) and 508(1) C.C.

43. Sections 507(1) and 508(1) C.C.

44. Sections 507(1)(a) and 508(1)(a) C.C.

45. Sections 507(1)(a) and 508(1)(a) C.C.

46. Sections 507(3)(a) and 508(2)(a) C.C.

47. Section 566(1) C.C.

48. Section 2 C.C.

49. Section 574(1) C.C.

50. Section 548(1) C.C.

51. Section 536(4) C.C.

52. Section 549(1) C.C.

53. Section 537 C.C.

54. Section 548(1)(b) C.C.

55. Sections 577(b) and 577(c) C.C.

56. Section 548(1)(a) C.C.

57. Section 548(1)(a) C.C.

58. *Caccamo v. The Queen*, 1975 Can LII 24 (S.C.C.).

59. Ibid.

60. Section 540(1)(a) C.C.

61. Section 540(1)(a) C.C.

62. Section 541 C.C.

63. *Mills v. The Queen* (1986), 26 C.C.C. (3d) 481 (S.C.C.)

64. Section 549(1) C.C.

65. Section 551 C.C.

66. Sections 566(1) and 574(1) C.C.

67. Section 577 C.C.

CHAPTER 14

Search and Seizure, Part 1: The Decision-Making Model

LEARNING OUTCOMES

The student will learn

- How to apply a search and seizure decision-making (SDM) model
- How to prevent a s. 8 Charter violation

INTRODUCTION

The search and seizure process does not occur in isolation. It is connected to arrest and detention (custody). That is why this chapter overlaps with Chapters 1–5. As with custody, the police cannot search randomly or arbitrarily. An *authority* is needed.

There are three general classifications of search authorities:

1. consent,
2. with a warrant, and
3. warrantless (without a warrant and without consent).

There are two time periods in which these authorities can be exercised:

1. post-custody
2. pre-custody

DEFINITIONS

A **search** is defined as follows: Looking for things, including spoken words, to be used as evidence of an offence.[1] This definition is found in case law.

A **seizure** is defined as follows: The taking of a thing from a person, by a public authority, without that person's consent.[2] This definition is found in case law.

The **focus of search** is as follows: A search can be directed only at a person or a place.

The search of a person is directed at the following:

- clothes worn by the person,
- items on the person's body,
- items inside the clothes,
- items held by the person, and
- bodily substances, including blood and hair.

The *Criminal Code* does not define **place** in the context of a search. The Code's definition of place, found in s. 348(3), relates to break and enter offences only. Case law defines *place*, in relation to searches, as follows:

1. A dwelling-house, defined as an entire, or any part of a, building or structure that is kept or occupied as a permanent residence, including

   - any building that is connected to the house by a doorway or covered and enclosed passageway (for example, an attached garage is a dwelling-house),
   - a unit designed to be mobile and to be used as a permanent or temporary residence, and that is being used as a residence.[3]

2. The perimeter of a dwelling-house.[4]
3. A building, referring to a structure that is not used as a permanent residence, including

   - a business premises,
   - an office, or
   - a school.

4. Receptacles—that is, a structure that is used to contain property, such as sheds and lockers.
5. Vehicles, meaning cars, trucks, and other motor vehicles that are not designed to be used as a temporary or permanent residence and are not being used as a residence, whether being operated or parked and unoccupied.[5]

An **unreasonable search/seizure** is an unlawful one; conducted without any lawful authority. This type of search or seizure has three possible consequences:

1. Criminal liability: If intentional, it may constitute a criminal offence such as "Assault," "Theft," or "Mischief."
2. Civil liability: Whether intentional or unintentional, a civil suit may result.
3. Charter violation: Whether intentional or unintentional, a Charter violation will have occurred, and the evidence seized may be excluded from the trial.

SECTION 8 CHARTER

Section 8 Charter consists of one sentence: "Everyone has the right to be secure against unreasonable search or seizure." These words have had a most profound effect on police officers' authority to search for and seize evidence. Although seemingly simple, they can be interpreted very broadly. To establish guidelines for search and seizure, significant case law analysis is required.

Section 8 Charter does not specifically define what constitutes a reasonable search or seizure. It does not establish or list any specific search or seizure authorities that police may use. Instead, it limits the police powers of search and seizure to those circumstances and conditions set out in various sources of law.[6]

The S.C.C. has identified the specific purpose of section 8 Charter: to secure and protect a citizen's right to a reasonable expectation of privacy against unjustified governmental intrusions by state agents, including the police.[7] The court emphasized that this guarantees only a reasonable expectation of privacy. The circumstances constituting *reasonable expectation of privacy* vary depending on certain factors. The methods that the police use to conduct a search or seizure in a specific situation are among these factors.

To prevent unjustified police violations of a person's reasonable expectation of privacy, the S.C.C., in *Hunter et al. v. Southam Inc.* (1984),[8] established the following general principles relating to search and seizure:

1. Prior judicial authorization is required for the police to search or seize, unless exigent circumstances exist. Prior judicial authorization means a valid search warrant.
2. The person who may grant the authorization must be a judicial officer, meaning a JP or a provincial court judge.
3. The judicial officer must assess and evaluate a written application stating the evidence that composes the reasons for wanting to search. The assessment must be done in an entirely neutral, impartial, and unbiased manner.
4. The evidence described in the reasons for applying for the authorization, or warrant, must satisfy the judicial officer that reasonable grounds exist for believing the following:
   a. an offence has been committed,
   b. the items intended to be searched for will be evidence that proves the offence has been committed, and
   c. the items are in the place to be searched. The judicial officer must be satisfied that the police have a strong reason to believe the items are in the place, and the police must confirm this belief under oath. A belief that evidence *may* be found is insufficient to justify a search, because it suggests only a possibility of finding evidence. A possibility constitutes a mere suspicion, and searches cannot be based on mere suspicion.
5. If exigent circumstances exist, the police may search without prior judicial authorization. No warrant is needed. **Exigent circumstances** means that an urgent situation exists and there is no time to obtain a warrant. The specific conditions that constitute exigent circumstances are identified in various sources of law and were explained in Chapter 8 of this textbook.
6. If a search is conducted without prior judicial authorization, the same standards of belief apply as with a warrant. It must be proven there are reasonable grounds for believing that
   a. an offence was committed,
   b. the item to be searched for will be evidence of the offence,
   c. the item is in the place or on the person,
   d. no time existed to obtain a warrant, and
   e. the law authorized the search in that situation.

In summary, an unreasonable search constitutes a section 8 Charter violation. Examples of an unreasonable search or seizure—and a s. 8 Charter violation—are when police

- violate a person's reasonable expectation of privacy; or
- conduct their search without prior judicial authorization, with no excuse of exigent circumstances, and without the support of a specific law authorizing the warrantless search; or
- conduct their search with prior judicial authorization, but have obtained this authorization through improper means (for example, invalid consent, explained in the next chapter).

Consequence of a Section 8 Charter Violation

Evidence obtained through a s. 8 Charter violation *may* be excluded from the trial; however, it is *not automatically inadmissible* or excluded.

Section 24(2) Charter provides an explanation that applies. The following summarizes it: Non-conscriptive evidence is more likely to be admitted after a Charter violation than conscriptive evidence.

The key point is: prevent Charter violations. If you prevent a Charter violation, s. 24(2) doesn't apply and the evidence will be admissible.

Refer to the accompanying website, **www.emp.ca/arcaro/policepowers4E**, for case law review and self-evaluation.

SEARCH AND SEIZURE DECISION-MAKING MODEL

Preventing s. 8 Charter violations calls for structured decision making.

Interpreting and applying search and seizure laws requires a complex form of rapid decision-making. The police must make split-second decisions based on a large volume of information.

The SDM is divided into the "post-custody" and "pre-custody" applications.

This means a search can happen either before or after an arrest or detention. In other words, there are two pathways. Both have five requirements that have to be met if you are going to conduct a search.

1. *Occurrence recognition*. Identifying the offence or emergency—establishing what has *occurred*—is the starting point of all searches. It creates the context and the basis for the search.
2. *Item.* Establish the objective of the search—"what item you are searching for." *Item* connects to *occurrence*. The specific item(s) is the evidence that helps prove the occurrence.
3. *Place/person*. The *location* of the items has to be identified. Items are located only
   a. on persons, or
   b. in places.
4. *Belief.* This requirement has to do with *how* you know the item is in the place or on the person. You need to classify the strength of your belief—is it based on reasonable grounds or on mere suspicion?

5. *Urgency.* This means determining whether *exigent circumstances* exist, defined as "imminent risk to life/health or risk of evidence destruction/ loss." You have to determine whether there is time to get a warrant or not.

SEARCH AUTHORITY RECOGNITION

SAR is an acronym for "search authority recognition." This refers to the three categories of search authorities: consent, with a warrant, and without a warrant. These authorities are relevant both before custody and after custody.

- *Post-custody*: The decision to search persons or places may occur after police have taken custody of the offender. In this case, search is the fifth decision in the rapid decision-making (RDM) model (see Chapter 1).
- *Pre-custody*: In other cases, search precedes arrest or detention. In these cases, custody emerges from search/seizure.

In some cases, then, a search is the product of an arrest or detention. In other cases, arrest or detention results from a search. The starting point for both sequences is offence/occurrence recognition, or Step 1 in the RDM model (what you are trying to find has to be evidence concerning what happened).

The search and seizure decision-making (SDM) model shown in Figure 14.1 illustrates this explanation.

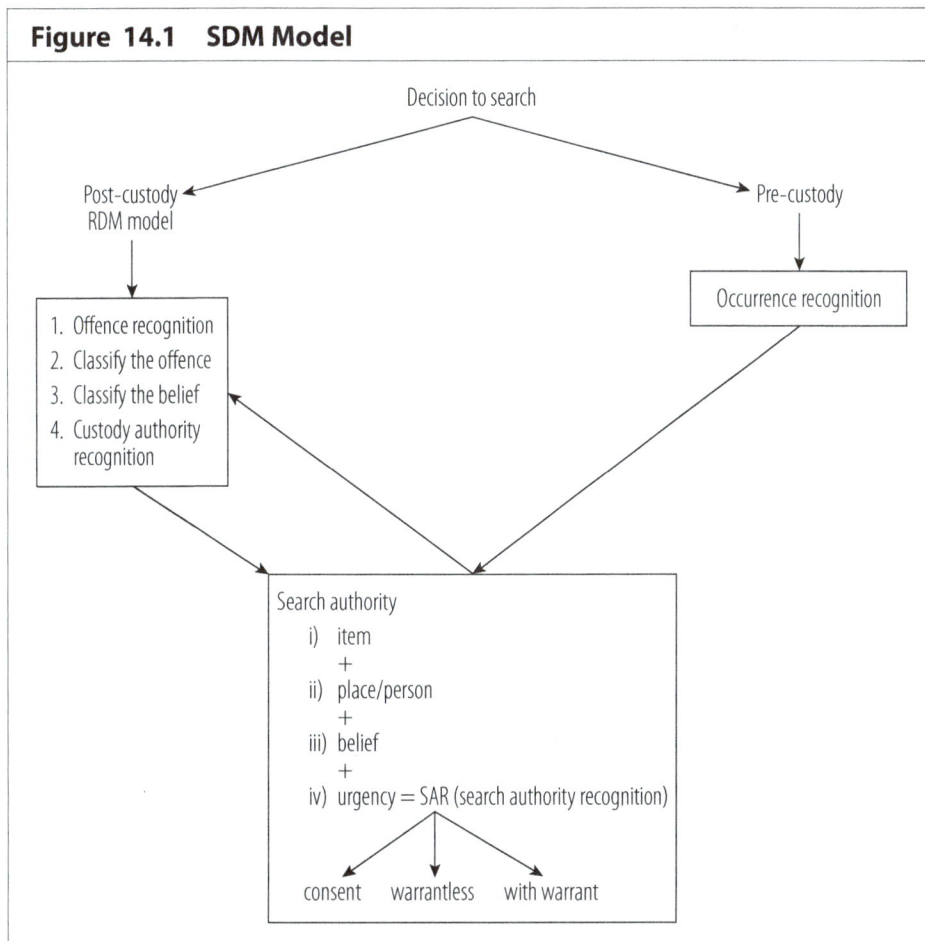

Figure 14.1 SDM Model

Decision to search

Post-custody RDM model

Pre-custody

Occurrence recognition

1. Offence recognition
2. Classify the offence
3. Classify the belief
4. Custody authority recognition

Search authority
i) item
+
ii) place/person
+
iii) belief
+
iv) urgency = SAR (search authority recognition)

consent   warrantless   with warrant

SUMMARY

Search is the fifth step in the RDM model. Your authority to search with or without a warrant is clearly outlined in law and in case law decisions. Consent search is a lawful authority and one that is a benefit to police officers because of the obvious non-requirement of a warrant. Search by consent is the subject of the next chapter.

ENDNOTES

1. *R. v. Sandhu* (1993), 82 C.C.C. (3d) 236 (B.C.C.A.).
2. *R. v. Dyment* (1988), 45 C.C.C. (3d) 207 (S.C.C.).
3. Section 2 C.C.
4. *R. v. Grant* (1993), 84 C.C.C. (3d) 173 (S.C.C.); *R. v. Kokesch* (1990), 61 C.C.C. (3d) 207 (S.C.C.).
5. *R. v. Grant*, supra note 4.
6. *Hunter et al. v. Southam Inc.* (1984), 14 C.C.C. (3d) 97 (S.C.C.).
7. Ibid. and *R. v. Colarusso* (1994), 87 C.C.C. (3d) 193 (S.C.C.).
8. *Hunter et al. v. Southam Inc.*, supra note 6.

CHAPTER 15

Search and Seizure, Part 2: Consent

LEARNING OUTCOMES

The student will learn

- How to differentiate between implied and expressed consent
- To understand the investigative benefit of obtaining consent
- How to apply "third-party" consent

INTRODUCTION

This chapter explains only the basic concept of consent in relation to search and seizure. However, the relevant case law is very extensive and crucially relevant to front-line policing. To facilitate your research, the accompanying website, **www.emp.ca/ arcaro/policepowers4E**, includes ongoing coverage of this case law.

THE BASIC CONCEPT

Consent is a valuable investigative technique that facilitates many police procedures, including interrogation, search, and the seizure of evidence. For two reasons, valid consent significantly expands the circumstances in which a police officer may conduct a search:

1. Being an alternative authority, valid consent removes the need for a search warrant; and
2. Valid consent makes a search reasonable because it represents a s. 8 Charter waiver.

Obtaining valid *consent* to search during an investigation provides the police officer with significant advantages, including the following:

1. It applies both to persons and to any "place," including a house.
2. Consent may be obtained even if mere suspicion exists. Police do not require reasonable grounds to obtain valid consent.

3. Consent may be obtained to search for any type of item (for example, stolen property, weapons, narcotics).
4. Speed. Valid consent can be obtained quickly, minimizing the two most important risks in an investigation (the risk to life and the risk of destruction of evidence).

There are two types of valid consent—*expressed* and *implied*. **Expressed consent** means that no doubt exists about whether it was given; the full case law informational component was communicated. In the case of **implied consent**, police logically infer that consent was given, but some doubt may exist as to whether it was. In other words, *expressed consent* is the best kind to have; *implied consent* is the next best.

CONSENT AUTHORITY

Remarkably, there is no Canadian legislation or statute that specifically authorizes a warrantless search by consent; there is no legislation or statute that creates guidelines and procedures for police to follow when trying to obtain valid consent.

Consent searches are authorized in common law.[1] The following is the common law doctrine governing case law consent decisions: "One who has invited or assented to an act being done towards him cannot, when he suffers it, complain of it as wrong."[2]

The *theoretical premise* of consent search is that the search does not constitute an "actionable intrusion." According to this theory, a person who consents to a police search waives the right to invoke legal protection against any intrusion that may result from the search. The giving of consent is considered to be a "private transaction between individuals." Consequently, consent searches are lawful regardless of whether the police have reasonable grounds to search by means of any alternative authority.[3]

Although common law authorizes and recognizes consent searches, *it does not create specific procedures and rules for the police to follow.*

Not just common law but case law decisions authorize consent searches. Two prominent case law decisions have provided rules and procedures relevant to consent searches. Both decisions will be discussed in this section.

Definition

No Canadian statute defines consent. **Valid consent** is defined in case law as a person's "voluntary and informed decision to permit the intrusion of the investigative process upon his constitutionally protected rights."[4] The key elements of this definition are as follows.

1. Consent is an *informed decision.* The person making the decision must be sufficiently informed of the investigative facts and must have adequate knowledge of exactly what has been decided.
2. The decision must be *voluntarily* made. No person is obliged to give consent to the police to permit a warrantless search. Every person has the choice to give or refuse consent.

Section 8 Charter Waiver

Giving police valid consent to search or seize constitutes a waiver of that person's s. 8 Charter right. Waiving a Charter right means to surrender it or give it up. If the consent is valid, the search or seizure will be considered reasonable and no s. 8 Charter violation will be deemed to have occurred. The seized item will be admissible.

Conversely, if valid consent is not obtained and the police search for or seize evidence, a s. 8 Charter violation will be deemed to have occurred. Evidence obtained by means of invalid consent may be excluded, but *not automatically*. If a physical item is seized through a search and seizure based on invalid consent, the item will usually be admissible, according to the S.C.C. guideline established by *R. v. Collins* (1987).[5]

OBTAIN CONSENT: PROCEDURE

Neither the *Criminal Code* nor the Charter offers guidelines or procedures for obtaining valid consent. The following two case law decisions do:

1. *R. v. Wills* (1992), Ontario Court of Appeal[6]
2. *R. v. Borden* (1994), Supreme Court of Canada[7]

Ontario Court of Appeal Guidelines

R. v. Wills is a prominent case insofar as it establishes seven conditions that must exist for consent to be valid. The existence of each condition must be proven by the prosecution. The following is a list of these conditions. The court did not recommend specific procedures for proving the conditions exist. The following list, however, does suggest some procedures:

1. *Consent must be expressed or implied.* Although implied consent is acceptable, expressed consent is the best type to obtain. In the case of expressed consent, the accused's consent is clearly expressed and unequivocal; the accused's words clearly and unmistakably state that he or she is giving consent. If what the accused says is vague or ambiguous, the consent will be deemed invalid.

    Consent from an adult offender may be given orally or in writing. Consent in writing is done on a written consent form, or statement, signed by the consenting person. Written consent offers police the advantage of clearly proving the consent was valid. **Oral consent** refers to conversation that is not written or signed in a statement form. Instead, it is recorded verbatim by the officer in a notebook.

    Consent from a young offender should be obtained in writing. **Written consent** is a statement recorded, either on a statement document or in an officer's notebook. The content should demonstrate that the seven conditions needed for valid consent exist, and the statement should be written from the perspective of the consenting person (for example, "I, Robert Johnson, consent …"). The consenting person then signs the statement.

Procedure: Record *verbatim* all conversation with the accused. Verbatim means direct, word-for-word quotation including all questions, comments, and responses. When testifying in court, convey the conversation verbatim. Do not paraphrase the accused's words either when recording them initially or during testimony. To **paraphrase** is to condense or summarize the accused's verbatim response into a general statement such as "the accused consented." This is a conclusion for the judge alone to make. A paraphrase is vague and does not prove unmistakable consent.

Obtain written consent from a young offender by drafting a consent statement in your notebook or on a statement form. Obtain the young offender's signature. This procedure may be used for adults, too, but verbal consent oral consent from adults is also sufficient.

For more information, see the author's companion text *Principles of Law Enforcement Report Writing*, 3rd ed.

2. *Consent must be voluntary.* Voluntary means obtained without coercion, oppression, inducements, or any other external pressure on the accused. **Inducements** are defined as threats or promises. The accused must be aware of what he or she is doing and cannot be subjected to threats or promises. *Voluntariness is defined by the absence of inducements* from the police when they are trying to obtain consent. Again, recording and testifying about verbatim conversation is crucial to proving the absence of inducements.

Procedure: Inform the accused that he or she has no obligation to consent and that the decision to consent is exclusively his or hers. Avoid using any words that constitute or imply

- threats of violence, or of being arrested or charged if consent is denied; or
- promises about favourable treatment of the accused in connection with his or her arrest, charge, and release.

Emphasize that the choice about consent is entirely the accused's. Ask the accused if this is understood and record the response to prove his or her knowledge that the decision belongs exclusively to him or her.

Record the entire conversation verbatim. Again, avoid paraphrases during testimony, such as "the accused voluntarily consented" or "I did not threaten or make promises to the accused."

3. *The accused must be aware of the specific act the police intend to perform if given consent.* The precise nature of the search and seizure the police will carry out cannot be withheld from the accused.

Procedure: Inform the accused of the following:

- that a search and/or seizure is being requested;
- what the target of the search is (for example, person or specific place);
- what is the specific evidence being sought, if known; and
- what type of offence is being investigated.

Providing the accused with as much information as possible not only ensures that the consent will be valid but also may convince the accused to cooperate and surrender the property voluntarily, so that no search is required.

4. *The accused must be aware of the potential consequences of giving consent.* The accused must know what may result from a search and seizure—must

know, in other words, that the possible consequences of a search or seizure are prosecution and the admissibility of the evidence seized.

Procedure: Inform the accused of the following:

- that charges may be laid,
- what the specific offence is, if known, and
- that the evidence may be used at a trial.

5. *The accused must know that consent may be refused.* No law exists in Canada compelling or obliging a person to consent to a search or seizure. Refusing consent is not an offence; a person cannot be charged or arrested for this. The accused must know that he or she may refuse to consent to the search.

   Procedure: Inform the accused as follows: "You don't have to consent. You may refuse to give consent. The choice is yours. If you refuse, you cannot be charged for refusing."

6. *The accused must know that consent may be revoked at any time after it is initially given.* Consenting to a search is not irrevocable. The person may stop the search at any time by removing consent. The accused must be informed about this fact, and the prosecution will be required to prove that the accused was informed.

   Procedure: Inform the accused as follows: "If you consent to this search, you can revoke consent at any time you choose and stop the search."

7. *If the accused gives consent, he or she must not have revoked consent at any time during the search.* The prosecution has the onus of proving that the accused said or did nothing during the search that directly indicated or indirectly implied an intent to terminate the search. The absence, from the prosecution's testimony, of any statement or conduct signalling the accused's desire to terminate the search, between the time that consent was given and the time that any seizure was made, will prove the existence of this condition.

   Procedure: You cannot prove these conditions existed by simply saying, "The accused did not revoke consent at any time during the search." This is a conclusion that is the judge's to make. Instead, record verbatim all your conversation with the accused, between the time consent is given and the time the seizure is made. Note even the time periods when the accused is silent. Record the location and conduct of the accused during the search.

   When testifying, convey the entire conversation, the periods of silence, and all relevant observations. Again, the absence from your testimony of any statement from the accused indicating a desire to remove consent will suffice to prove that this condition existed.

Supreme Court of Canada Guidelines

The case of *R. v. Borden* (1994)[8] provides an example of invalid consent and shows how s. 24(2) Charter is applied to determine the admissibility of evidence that originates from the accused (for example, blood samples).

SITUATION

The police arrested an adult accused of one count of sexual assault; he was suspected of having committed a second count. The police sought blood samples from the accused in connection with the second count of sexual assault, for the purpose of DNA comparison. The accused signed a written consent form that simply indicated his consent to their taking of a blood sample "for the purpose relating to their investigations." The accused was not informed that the blood sample was taken in connection with the second count of sexual assault. After the blood sample was obtained, a positive comparison was made, and the accused was charged with a second count of sexual assault. Was the consent valid?

No. Although the use by the police of the plural "investigations" was deliberate, the consent form did not specify that the blood sample was to be used in connection with the second count of sexual assault. The second investigation had exceeded the exploratory stage. The police were obliged to inform the accused that the blood sample was intended to be used in a different investigation from the one for which the accused was detained. He was not so informed. The taking of blood was a seizure, and the consent was invalid, constituting a s. 8 Charter violation. The S.C.C. ruled that the admission of the blood sample would bring the administration of justice into disrepute. Consequently, the blood sample was excluded under s. 24(2) Charter.[9]

In the *Borden* case, the S.C.C. considered the *Wills* ruling made by the Ontario Court of Appeal, and produced a similar list of the elements that compose valid consent:[10]

1. The accused must have the volition to decide whether or not to consent. The consent must be voluntarily given.
2. The accused must be sufficiently informed by police of relevant information.
3. The accused must know that he or she is not required to consent.
4. The accused must know what is the specific investigation in which the police intend to use the product of the seizure.
5. If the police arrest or detain an accused for one offence and ask for consent to seize evidence to use in their investigation of an unrelated offence, the accused must be informed of this fact.
6. The police do not have to ensure that the accused has a detailed understanding of every possible outcome of giving consent. The accused must understand generally the consequences of giving consent; he or she must know that the item seized by means of it will be used for another specific investigation.
7. If the police arrest or detain an accused for one offence and are only in the exploratory stage of another, unrelated offence, the police have no obligation to inform the accused that the evidence he gives by consent, in connection with the offence for which he is arrested, may be used in the investigation of another offence. But if the investigation into the second offence is beyond the exploratory stage and the police suspect the accused of having committed it, the police must inform him or her that the evidence seized will also be used in the second investigation.[11]

R. v. Clement (1996)[12] is an S.C.C. case that provides an excellent example of what circumstances constitute valid consent, and provides a general rule regarding the admissibility of a physical item seized by means of invalid consent, under s. 24(2) Charter.

CASE LAW

R. v. Clement (1996)

■ **Issue**: Consent

■ **Offence**: "Robbery"

■ **Circumstances**: Four robberies occurred at stores in one community. The offender wore a Halloween mask and carried a revolver during each offence. Witnesses gave only general descriptions of the offender, the gun, and the mask.

While on patrol some time after the last robbery, two officers received a radio transmission informing them about a Crime Stoppers tip. Two persons, a male and a female, had tried to sell cocaine in a nearby city. A description of the suspect's car and the car's licence plate number were broadcast. Shortly afterward, the officers saw the car and followed it for three miles, to a gas station. The officers stopped the car and conducted an investigation that consisted of two separate searches of the suspect's car. The driver was male and the passenger female.

The officers did not think that the information they had received via radio constituted reasonable grounds for believing that narcotics were in the car, so they could not conduct a lawful search of the car without a warrant. Both occupants of the car were escorted to the cruiser and were seated inside. One officer asked to search the car. The driver complied with the request.

A search began, resulting in the seizure of a loaded and cocked handgun, found under the driver's seat. After the search, the officers arrested both occupants for the possession of a restricted weapon. They were informed of their right to counsel. They invoked the right and exercised it after they arrived at the police station.

After consulting with a lawyer, the driver signed a written consent permitting a second search of the car. As a result, a Halloween mask was seized from behind the dashboard. The driver was subsequently charged with four counts of robbery.

■ **Trial**: The evidence relating to consent was composed of

1. the following statement from the officer: "If you let me have a quick look in your car, I can solve this here, or right now";
2. the accused's lack of protest at the officer's request; and
3. the accused's awareness that giving consent was not compulsory, a circumstance that was proven during his testimony, when he testified that he "knew they had no right to search my car."

The officer who requested the first search testified that he could not remember informing the accused about what they were investigating or informing him that he could have refused to give consent. However, the accused's testimony proved that he had knowledge about the drug investigation, having heard the officers discussing it.

The defence brought a motion to exclude the gun and the mask because of s. 8 (unreasonable search), s. 9 (arbitrary detention), and s. 10(b) (right to counsel) Charter violations.

The trial judge ruled that

▸ A s. 9 Charter violation had occurred because the occupants were detained; they did not enter the cruiser by consent.

(continued)

▸ A s. 10(b) Charter violation had occurred. The occupants were entitled to be informed of their right to counsel upon being detained. Instead, they were informed a few minutes later, at the conclusion of the first search.
▸ Both Charter violations lasted only two or three minutes.
▸ The officers did not have reasonable grounds to search the car for narcotics without a warrant.
▸ The search and seizure did not constitute a s. 8 Charter violation because valid consent was obtained before both searches.

The gun and the mask were not excluded under s. 24(2) Charter. The accused was convicted, and he appealed to the Ontario Court of Appeal.

■ **Appeal**: The appeal was dismissed by a 2–1 decision. The following rulings were made:

▸ The consent regarding the first search was valid because it was voluntary and informed. The accused knew the officers were searching for drugs, and he could have refused to give consent.
▸ The accused's identity was proven by the fact that the gun, the mask, along with the accused's height, weight, and hair, matched up with the general descriptions given by witnesses.
▸ The content of the Crime Stoppers tip, in this case, did not constitute reasonable grounds to search without a warrant.
▸ If valid consent had not been obtained in this case, which would have resulted in a s. 8 Charter violation, the gun would not have been excluded under s. 24(2) Charter because

  a. the crime was serious;
  b. the officers acted in good faith, without displaying oppressive conduct;
  c. the loaded, cocked gun represented danger to the police and the public; and
  d. the gun was physical evidence that existed before any potential Charter violation.

The court ruled that the admission of the gun, despite the consent being invalid, would be "realistic" and would not diminish the public's respect for the justice system. Section 9 and 10(b) Charter violations occurred prior to the second search and the seizure of the mask. However, the mask was not excluded under s. 24(2) Charter because its admission would not bring the administration of justice into disrepute. The obtaining of formal, written consent was a significant factor that contributed to this decision. The accused appealed his conviction to the S.C.C.

■ **S.C.C.**: The accused's appeal was dismissed. The court ruled that valid consent had been obtained and that no s. 8 Charter violation had occurred because "the appellant testified that he knew the police had no right to search the car. It is apparent that he gave his consent freely and voluntarily."

SUMMARY

The *R. v. Clement* case shows the profound advantage that consent searches give police, during the investigation of a serious offence, with respect to the admissibility of physical items including weapons. The principles created by *Clement* include the following:

(continued)

1. The prominent factor in proving that consent is valid is showing the accused knew that

    ▸ the police have no legal authority to compel consent, and
    ▸ consent may be denied by the accused.

2. Valid consent may be obtained through less than optimum procedures. The officer's conversation with the accused, concerning consent, was relatively brief. The information conveyed to the accused was minimal in comparison to the extensive guidelines created in the *Wills* and *Borden* cases.

3. The accused's statements during the investigation and during court testimony are crucial evidence of knowledgeable consent. The accused cannot be compelled to testify by the prosecution. If the decision is to testify, he or she may be cross-examined by the Crown attorney. The accused's testimony may be used to prove that he or she knew that no legal obligation exists to consent and that consent may be denied.

4. Weapons and physical evidence seized in relation to serious offences will likely be admissible even if obtained through invalid consent.

COMMENTARY

Principle 4 (above) represents one of the most significant investigative advantages for police officers because it does not impose unreasonable obligations upon them in dangerous situations.

The court has effectively demonstrated what the priorities are in cases involving serious offences and weapons. The court weighed the issues of consent and admissibility of the weapons seized, in the context of "bringing the administration of justice into disrepute." In other words, it questioned whether the admission of the weapons would cause more harm to the administration of justice than the exclusion of this evidence. What the court was acknowledging is that investigations often involve dangerous situations in which time is of the essence for the investigating officer. If time constraints cause the consent to be invalid, the court will not penalize the prosecution by excluding evidence. This principle is logical and rational—a way of ensuring that justice is administered properly.

Police officers must be cognizant, then, that invalid consent is not always detrimental to an investigation, if the error was committed in good faith. Their lack of a reasonable grounds belief, when a suspected, armed offender is stopped, should not deter or delay police from attempting to search by consent. If mere suspicion exists, police officers should either obtain additional evidence quickly, by means of visual observations or by questioning the suspect, or should try to search by consent. It is important to use effective communication skills to obtain consent quickly and not delay the search with unnecessary or meaningless conversation.

Effective communication skills are learned through experience and practice. If the information conveyed to the suspect, due to the urgency of the situation and the time restrictions created by the presence of weapons, is not sufficient to produce valid consent, the prosecution of the offender will not usually be adversely affected.

Finally, if weapons seized by invalid consent are excluded at a trial under s. 24(2) Charter, the investigation should not be considered a failure. The seizure of the weapon ensured that the officer would not be harmed or killed at the time of the investigation. That is always a higher priority than exclusion of evidence at a trial.

THIRD-PARTY CONSENT (MULTIPLE OCCUPIERS)

Who may give lawful consent to the police to search a place? If the police have consent to search a place, they must be able to prove that the person who consented had lawful authority to do so. This becomes significant when more than one person occupies, lives in, or uses a place that the police intend to search by consent. Third-party consent refers to consent given by a person to search a place that he or she does not own. It also refers to situations where a person consents to the search of a place and another person's property is seized.

The following general principles and rules, concerning third-party consent searches of places occupied by multiple persons, were established by the S.C.C., in *R. v. Edwards* (1996):[13]

1. The legality of a search consented to by a third party depends on whether the accused had a reasonable expectation of privacy.
2. The court determines whether a reasonable expectation of privacy existed by considering the total circumstances of each individual case. Among the circumstances that are considered are the following:

    - the presence of the accused at the time of the search;
    - who has possession or control of the property or place searched;
    - who has ownership of the property or place searched;
    - what the property or place has been used for in the past;
    - whether the person giving consent has the ability to regulate others' access to the place, including the right to admit or exclude others;
    - whether a subjective expectation of privacy reasonably exists (subjective refers to a belief that exists in the accused's mind alone, not elsewhere); and
    - whether the accused's expectation of privacy, objectively considered, is reasonable (objective refers to the context of actual external circumstances).

If the accused establishes that a reasonable expectation of privacy existed, then the judge must decide whether the search was conducted in a reasonable manner. Additionally, the court ruled that an occupant of a place who is a guest or visitor has *no expectation of privacy*. A visitor, in the *R. v. Edwards* case, was defined as a person who

- does not contribute to the rent or household expenses,
- keeps a few personal belongings in the owner's apartment,
- has a key to the apartment, and
- lacks the authority to regulate access of people into the owner's apartment.[14]

Essentially, these principles may be interpreted and summarized as follows.

1. Persons who have a reasonable expectation of privacy in a place are owners, and lawful occupiers. These persons have the authority to give consent to the police to search the place. These persons may also refuse to give consent and may revoke it at any time after it is given. An owner's authority supersedes a lawful occupier's authority.

2. A lawful occupier refers to a person who

    a. has possession or control of the place or property, and

    b. has the ability to regulate access of persons into that place—that is, the ability to allow other people to enter, or to prohibit entry, or to remove others from the place. If an owner or lawful occupier gives the police consent to search a place, the police may search for and seize evidence that is possessed by a guest or visitor.

3. Guests and visitors have no reasonable expectation of privacy in a place because they do not have control of the place and have no right to allow people to enter, or to prohibit or remove people from that place.

4. A person who is not authorized by the owner to regulate access of people into the place, such as a guest or visitor, does not have lawful authority to give consent to the police to search a place.

THIRD-PARTY CONSENT: PROCEDURE

The following is a list of procedures and rules for obtaining consent to search places that multiple people are occupying, living in, or using.

1. Determine who the owner of the place is and if he or she is present. If present, try to obtain consent from that owner, who has the most lawful authority to give consent.

2. If the owner is absent, and other occupiers are present, ask them

    ▸ who has possession or control of the place, and

    ▸ who has the right to regulate access of people into the place.

    Obtain consent from a person who, based on his or her answers to these two questions, qualifies as a lawful occupier.

3. Do not obtain consent from a guest or visitor, or any other person who does not control the place or is not empowered to control people's access to the place.

4. If consent is obtained from the owner or lawful occupier, search all areas and seize any evidence, including any that a guest or visitor might possess.

5. If the owner or lawful occupier who gives consent is an adult, he or she does not have to be informed of the right to counsel prior to the search because he or she is not detained.

6. If the person who gives consent is a young person, 12–17 years old, inform him or her of the right to counsel prior to the search.

The following case law decision is an example of third-party search circumstances.

CASE LAW

R. v. Edwards (1996)

- **Issue**: Third-party consent

- **Offence**: "Possession of narcotics for the purpose of trafficking"

- **Circumstances**: The police conducted surveillance of the accused (an adult) after receiving information that he was trafficking narcotics out of his car, and that the narcotics were either on his person, at his residence, or at his girlfriend's apartment. His girlfriend was an 18-year-old Grade 11 student who lived alone.

    On the day of the arrest, the police saw the accused drive his girlfriend from a residence to her apartment. The accused entered the apartment and remained there briefly. Then he left alone, drove away, and was stopped by the police, who knew he was a suspended driver. Driving under suspension is an arrestable offence under the *Highway Traffic Act* of Ontario. The police stopped the car and approached it, and at this point they saw the accused talking on a cellular phone and swallowing an object about one-half the size of a golf ball, wrapped in cellophane. The accused kept the car doors locked until he had swallowed the object. The police then arrested him for driving while under suspension, towed his car, and transported him to the police station.

    The police suspected that crack cocaine was in the girlfriend's apartment, but they considered their belief to be insufficient to obtain a search warrant. Two officers attended at the apartment and interviewed the girlfriend.

    The significant part of the interview was what the officers said to the girlfriend for the purpose of obtaining consent to search the apartment. Some of the things the officers said were "lies and others were half-truths." Specifically, the officers informed her of four things:

    1. Her boyfriend had informed the police that narcotics were in the apartment.
    2. If she refused or failed to cooperate, a police officer would remain in her apartment until a search warrant was obtained.
    3. Obtaining a search warrant would be an inconvenience for the officers because of the paperwork that was involved.
    4. One of the officers was going on vacation the following day. The girlfriend and the accused would not be charged, regardless of what the police found in the apartment.

    The girlfriend was never informed of her right to refuse to consent to police entry and search. There was conflicting evidence about whether the officers' statements were made before or after they were admitted into the apartment.

    After the police entered, the girlfriend directed the officers to a living room couch. Six bags of crack cocaine, valued between $11,000.00 and $23,000.00, were found beneath a pillow. The narcotics were seized, and the officers left. They returned 20 minutes later and arrested the woman on the instructions of a superior officer, after consultation with a Crown attorney. The police still did not inform her of the right to counsel.

    During questioning, the accused's girlfriend gave a statement implicating the accused in placing the narcotics under the cushion on the couch. The

(continued)

accused and the girlfriend were charged jointly with possession of narcotics for the purpose of trafficking. The charge against the girlfriend was later withdrawn, on the trial date.

On the evening of the arrest, the police attended at the vehicle compound where the accused's car was stored. Without a warrant, they seized the accused's cellular phone and pager, and intercepted calls for several hours from people ordering small amounts of crack cocaine.

- **Trial**: At the trial, the accused denied being the owner of the narcotics. The accused was convicted. His appeal to the Ontario Court of Appeal was dismissed. He then appealed to the S.C.C.

- **S.C.C. Appeal**: The only issue at appeal was, "Did the accused have the right to challenge the admission of evidence obtained as a result of a search of a third party's place?" The manner in which the police obtained consent was not an issue.

The S.C.C. dismissed the accused's appeal. The following reasons and rulings were made:

- ▸ The accused had no expectation of privacy because he contributed nothing to the rent or household expenses, and had no authority to regulate access of people into the apartment. As the court put it, "He was no more than a privileged guest."
- ▸ The accused could not contest the admissibility of the evidence under s. 24(2) Charter, because no personal right of the accused's was affected by police conduct.
- ▸ The court found it unnecessary to consider whether the accused's girlfriend actually gave valid consent to search the apartment.

COMMENTARY

Investigations can be successful even when less than optimum procedures are used to obtain consent. The procedures used by the police in this case were not in accordance with guidelines created by other case law decisions. However, this issue was not a factor in the appeal or the ruling. This case demonstrates the need to carefully read case law decisions. The decision would be confusing if only a summary of the circumstances were read.

This case also demonstrates the value and advantages of using consent during investigations when the object of the search is a physical item. Consent is especially valuable when only mere suspicion exists. It is equally effective when reasonable grounds exist and a search warrant could be obtained. The procedures that comply with the *Borden* and *Wills* guidelines should obviously be used whenever possible to obtain consent, but less than optimum procedures will not always result in the exclusion of evidence. Finally, if consent is refused, two other alternatives exist:

1. a search warrant, and
2. search without warrant provisions.

The conditions of these methods of search will be examined in Chapters 16 and 17.

Owner (Management): Temporary Occupiers

Some places that the police may need to search are owned or managed by one person and temporarily occupied by another person who has rented, leased, or been given the place to use. Examples of such places include the following:

▸ apartments owned by landlords and rented by tenants,
▸ hotel rooms rented to guests,
▸ offices owned by employers and given to employees, and
▸ lockers owned by schools and leased or given to students.

A question that often comes up in investigations, when it comes to the legality of search and consent, is the following: "Does the owner or management of a place have authority to give the police consent to enter and search the place that is temporarily occupied by another person who has rented, leased, or been given use of the place?"

Generally, the owner or management cannot give the police consent to enter and search the place if the temporary occupier has been given the authority to regulate people's access to that place. If the temporary occupier has that authority, then he or she has a reasonable expectation of privacy and will likely be considered to be the *lawful occupier* of that place.

Two situations that the police commonly confront have to do with

1. landlord and tenant, and
2. hotel management and guests.

A landlord owns the building where tenants live, but a landlord cannot regulate access of persons into a tenant's apartment. Only the tenant may grant or refuse people consent to enter his or her apartment. Consequently, a landlord has no authority to give valid consent to the police to enter and search a tenant's apartment.[15]

Guests who rent hotel rooms have a reasonable expectation of privacy while they are temporarily occupying the room. Accordingly, hotel management has no authority to give consent to the police to enter and search a guest's room. This rule was created by the Ontario Court of Appeal, in *R. v. Mercer* (1992),[16] which provides an excellent illustration of how consent searches apply to hotel rooms. This case provides another example of how s. 24(2) Charter is applied to searches and seizures resulting from invalid consent.

CASE LAW

R. v. Mercer (1992)

■ **Issues:**

1. Can hotel management search a guest's room without a warrant and without the guest's consent?
2. Does a hotel guest have a reasonable expectation of privacy in a hotel room?
3. Does hotel management have the authority to consent to a police search of a guest's room?
4. Will evidence seized from a guest's hotel room be admissible under s. 24(2) Charter, after a warrantless search?

(continued)

■ **Offence**: "Possession of narcotics for the purpose of trafficking"

■ **Circumstances**: Two co-accused persons rented a suite in a hotel. The rooms were registered in their names although payment was guaranteed by a brother of one of the co-accused. The suite consisted of a living and dining area, a bedroom, a hallway, and a closet in which were stored tables and chairs that could be used to convert the living area into a boardroom. The closet was accessible only to the guests that had a key to the room.

During the accused persons' stay at the hotel, a maid went to the room and found a "Do Not Disturb" sign on the door. The maid consulted with the manager, who instructed her to knock and then enter the room. The maid subsequently entered the room in the absence of the accused persons and without their consent. The maid noticed that a pillow was missing. She searched for it and found it in the storage closet. She then searched inside the pillowcase and found a quantity of money. She immediately notified the hotel manager, who attended at the room and also searched the pillowcase. The manager noticed the money and a brown, waxy brick, or block. The manager decided to call the police. She suspected illegal activity had occurred in the room, and reported what she found in the closet. But she did not mention the word "drug" when she reported this suspicion.

Two officers arrived at the hotel and entered the room by invitation of the manager. They searched the pillowcase, found a block of cannabis resin, and $6,900.00 in cash. The evidence was returned to the closet. The officers left to obtain a search warrant. Other officers secured the room during the period of time required to obtain the search warrant. The accused persons arrived at the room before the search warrant could be obtained. Both were arrested immediately.

■ **Trial**: The accused persons were convicted. The following reasons were given:

- ▶ Neither of the police officers had reasonable grounds to believe that narcotics were in the room prior to their entry.
- ▶ The hotel manager did not have reasonable grounds to believe that narcotics were in the room.
- ▶ The belief of the police and the manager was based on mere suspicion.
- ▶ The officers believed that they had authority to enter the room and search it by the manager's consent, because of the manager's invitation.

■ **Appeal**: The co-accused persons appealed their convictions to the Ontario Court of Appeal. The appeal was dismissed, and the convictions were upheld. The court gave the following reasons:

- ▶ Hotel guests have a reasonable expectation of privacy in hotel rooms that they have rented. A guest's knowledge that cleaning staff will enter the room daily does not remove their reasonable expectation of privacy. A hotel room can be considered an "office away from the office" where private papers and confidential business documents are protected from "uninvited viewers."
- ▶ Hotel management cannot give consent to the police to search a guest's hotel room without a warrant.
- ▶ A warrantless search of a hotel room with a "Do Not Disturb" sign on the door, in the guest's absence, based on mere suspicion of criminal activities,

(continued)

constitutes an impermissible intrusion on a reasonable expectation of privacy, and a s. 8 Charter violation.
▸ However, the narcotics were not excluded from the trial. They were admissible under s. 24(2) Charter because the administration of justice would not be brought into disrepute by the admission of the narcotics. The reasons for this conclusion were as follows:

▸ Although the police were mistaken in believing that they could legally enter the room at the manager's invitation, they "did not have the benefit of Canadian case law clearly stating otherwise."
▸ The police were acting in circumstances where an investigation has "little statutory or judicial guidance."
▸ The police made a reasonable mistake, in good faith.
▸ The search was not initiated by the police; it was a response to the hotel manager's request.

SUMMARY

This case raises several key points. The court acknowledged the absence of statutory laws concerning warrantless searches of hotel rooms, without the consent of the guests. This case also established two rules:

1. Hotel guests may reasonably expect privacy and are protected from warrantless searches of their personal property and documents.
2. Hotel management is not authorized to consent to warrantless police searches of guests' rooms.

However, the court showed tolerance for reasonable mistakes made by the police in good faith, and showed reluctance to exclude seized evidence that results from reasonable mistakes. Such tolerance and reluctance represents an advantage for law enforcement personnel. The dismissal of the accused's appeal shows that offenders may be convicted in cases where police make mistakes and where statutory law does not offer clear procedures or guidelines.

SUMMARY

Search by consent is an investigative benefit to front-line police officers. One of the obvious benefits is the speed with which a search can be conducted relative to the time it takes to apply for and obtain a search warrant. The next chapter explains the different types of search warrants that are available to investigators, and the rules applicable to each one.

PROBLEM-SOLVING CASE STUDIES

You are a police officer in each case. Each offender is an adult, unless otherwise indicated.

Problem 1

While on patrol, you receive a radio transmission that a blue car has left the scene of a break and enter at a business premises. The description of a stolen TV and a calculator are also broadcast. You see a car of a similar description, and you stop it. Shane is the driver and Tony is a passenger. Both are 18 years old. The car is owned by Shane's father. You have mere suspicion that they were involved in the offence.

a. Is the car a "place" for the purpose of a search?

_____

_____

_____

_____

_____

b. Can you obtain consent to search the car if mere suspicion exists?

_____

_____

_____

c. Do you have to obtain consent from both persons in order to search the car?

_____

_____

_____

d. Do you have to tell Shane that you wish to search the car specifically for the stolen TV and calculator?

_____

_____

_____

e. Do you have to tell Shane that he may refuse to consent?

_____

_____

_____

f. Do you have to tell Shane that he may revoke consent after he initially gives consent?

_____

_____

_____

g. If Shane refuses to consent, can you tell him that a refusal is incriminating evidence that makes him look guilty, and can be used against him?

_____

_____

_____

h. If Shane refuses to consent, can he be arrested or charged for refusing?

_____

_____

_____

i. If Shane consents to a search of the car, can you automatically search both persons?

_____

_____

_____

j. After you obtain consent, you search the interior. You ask Shane to open the trunk. He refuses. Can you forcibly open the trunk?

_____

_____

_____

_____

_____

k. If you do not obtain valid consent, or obtain it improperly, and then search the car and seize the stolen property, will the seized evidence automatically be inadmissible in court?

_____

_____

_____

_____

l. Do you have to obtain consent in writing, on a specific consent form, in this case?

_____

_____

_____

_____

Problem 2

You are investigating a "Theft under $5,000.00" complaint. After an initial investigation, you develop mere suspicion that George committed the offence and that he may have the stolen property in his apartment. You attend at the apartment complex. George is not home. Walter, the landlord of the apartment, is present. Does consent from the landlord authorize you to search George's apartment?[17]

_____

_____

_____

Problem 3

You attend at a residence in response to a call about a loud party. Upon arriving, you find numerous people inside the house. Several are loud and appear impaired. You suspect that drugs may be in the house. You learn that Bill and Moria are the owners. Both are absent. Their son Tom (19) is present with a number of his friends. Eddie (19) lives next door and is present inside Tom's house. You speak to Eddie, who appears cooperative. Can you obtain consent from him to search the house for drugs?

_____

_____

_____

_____

_____

_____

_____

_____

_____

_____

Test Yourself

1. You are dispatched to a loud party at 5110 Forman St., Toronto. Upon arrival at 11:15 p.m., you see numerous teenagers inside the house. You approach the door and hear a loud party. You make no other observations. No adults can be seen. You are suspicious that drugs or other illegal property may be on the premises. Explain exactly how you will obtain consent to search the house.

_____

_____

_____

_____

_____

_____

_____

_____

_____

_____

2. You stop a suspicious car that is driving slowly on Forman St., Toronto, at 3:20 a.m. You stop the car. Art (22) is the driver. Hector (21) is the passenger. CPIC checks for both are negative. You are suspicious about what may be in the car. Explain exactly how you will obtain consent to search the car.

_____

_____

_____

_____

_____

_____

_____

_____

_____

_____

ENDNOTES

1. The Law Reform Commission of Canada, Working Paper 30, "Police Powers—Search and Seizure in Criminal Law Enforcement (1983)," at 52, as in _R. v. Mercer_ (1992), 70 C.C.C. (3d) 180, at 187 (Ont. C.A.).
2. Ibid.
3. Ibid.
4. _R. v. Wills_ (1992), 70 C.C.C. (3d) 529 (Ont. C.A.).
5. _R. v. Collins_ (1987), 33 C.C.C. (3d) 1 (S.C.C.).
6. _R. v. Willis_, supra note 4.
7. _R. v. Borden_ (1994), 92 C.C.C. (3d) 404 (S.C.C.).
8. Ibid.
9. Ibid.
10. _R. v. Edwards_ (1996), 104 C.C.C. (3d) 136 (S.C.C.).
11. _R. v. Borden_, supra note 7.
12. _R. v. Clement_ (1996), 107 C.C.C. (3d) 52 (S.C.C.).
13. _R. v. Edwards_, supra note 10.
14. Ibid.
15. _R. v. Pugliese_ (1992), 71 C.C.C. (3d) 295 (Ont. C.A.).
16. _R. v. Mercer_, supra note 1.
17. _R. v. Edwards_, supra note 10, and _R. v. Pugliese_, supra note 15.

CHAPTER 16

Search and Seizure, Part 3: Search Warrants

LEARNING OUTCOMES

The student will learn

- How to obtain an ordinary (s. 487 C.C.) search warrant.
- How to obtain a general warrant
- How to obtain a telewarrant
- How to obtain a tracking warrant
- How to obtain a telephone number records warrant
- How to obtain a DNA analysis warrant
- How to obtain an impression warrant
- How to obtain a drugs and substances warrant

INTRODUCTION: THE GENERAL RULE

The following is the most important search and seizure rule: *When no exigent circumstances (urgency) exist, apply for a search warrant. Do not jeopardize the admissibility of evidence by circumventing judicial authorization.*

The key phrase is "judicial authorization." Parliament prefers that a Justice of the Peace (JP) decide whether you search or not. The only time that you can search without judicial authorization is when exigent circumstances exist—in other words, when there is an urgent situation and no time to get a search warrant.

CONCEPT OF JUDICIAL AUTHORIZATION

A **search warrant** is a written document that provides police with *judicial authorization* to enter and search a specific place for specific items, and to seize any items found that are evidence of the offence.

Judicial authorization refers to authority given by a Justice—a provincial court judge or JP—who must be unbiased and neutral. The police *apply* for the warrant and a Justice decides whether or not to grant it. The objective of a search warrant is to search for specific evidence that will prove an offence has been committed. In other words, search warrants concern physical items. Feeney warrants (see Chapter 8) concern humans (suspects).

Search warrants need to be applied for: they are not automatically issued at the request of the police. An application entitled "an Information to Obtain" must be written and presented to a JP. The contents of the application must convince the Justice that reasonable grounds exist to believe that specific items are in a specific place. The key to an effective application is an extensive narrative explaining the reasonable grounds, in writing.

These requirements prevent "fishing expeditions" by police—searches based on uncertainty, when police have no prior knowledge that specific items are in a specific place. An example of a fishing expedition would be when police search a place for *any evidence* without knowing specifically what they are looking for, or when they search *several places* trying to find one item. In summary, it is impossible to get a search warrant based on mere suspicion—uncertainty about items or place.

Types of Search Warrants

Search warrants are found in the *Criminal Code* (C.C.) and in the *Controlled Drugs and Substances Act* (C.D.S.A.). Recent *Criminal Code* amendments have added new types of search warrants to the longstanding list. The search warrants discussed in this chapter are the following:

- ▸ s. 487 C.C. (ordinary search warrant),
- ▸ s. 487.01 C.C. (general warrant—use of device, including video surveillance),
- ▸ s. 487.1 C.C. (telewarrant),
- ▸ s. 492.1 C.C. (tracking warrant—tracking device),
- ▸ s. 492.2 C.C. (telephone number recorder),
- ▸ s. 487.04 C.C. (bodily substances for forensic DNA analysis),
- ▸ s. 487.092 (impression warrant), and
- ▸ s. 11 C.D.S.A. (drugs and substances warrant).

Section 487 C.C. Search Warrant

This is the most common type of search warrant. It is referred to as a **s. 487 C.C. search warrant** or simply as a *Criminal Code* search warrant. This type of warrant is used to search any type of place for physical items that are evidence of an offence. It is the most basic kind of search warrant used during investigations. The following general rules apply to it:

RULE 1

A s. 487 C.C. search warrant authorizes the search of a

- ▸ building
- ▸ receptacle, or
- ▸ place (as defined in Chapter 8 of this textbook).

So when the police intend to search a place for evidence, they must obtain a s. 487 C.C. search warrant (prior judicial authorization) unless a lawful authority exists to search without a warrant.

RULE 2

A s. 487 C.C. search warrant authorizes the seizure of anything

- on or in respect of which any criminal offence under any federal statute has been, or is suspected of having been, committed;
- that there are reasonable grounds to believe will afford evidence of the commission of any classification of criminal offence;
- that will reveal the whereabouts of a person who is believed to have committed any classification of criminal offence;
- that there are reasonable grounds to believe it is intended to be used for the purpose of committing any criminal offence against a person, an offence for which the perpetrator may be arrested without a warrant;
- that is "offence-related property." This term is defined in s. 2 C.C. as any property, within or outside Canada,
    a. by means or in respect of which a criminal organization offence is committed;
    b. that is used in any manner in connection with the commission of a criminal organization offence; or
    c. that is intended for use in committing a criminal organization offence, but does not include real property, other than real property built or significantly modified for the purpose of facilitating the commission of a criminal organization offence.

Essentially, the warrant authorizes the search for and seizure of tangible, physical items that are evidence concerning any classification of offences under any federal statute.

RULE 3

A s. 487 C.C. search warrant cannot be obtained or used to search

- a person, or
- a place to find a person.

The warrant authorizes only the search for a physical item that will prove the whereabouts of the person who is believed to have committed the offence.

Keep in mind that police officers are authorized by law to enter and search a place (including a dwelling-house) without a warrant—under certain circumstances, to arrest a person if reasonable grounds exist that the person is inside the place.

RULE 4

The warrant may be issued to a police officer or to a person named therein. Consequently, police officers or citizens who are specifically named on the warrant are authorized to execute it. A citizen may assist the police in the execution of a search warrant provided that a police officer controls and is accountable for the search.[1]

RULE 5

Section 487 (2.1) C.C. permits the search of computer systems for data and authorizes the following procedures:

- Any computer system at the building or place may be used or caused to be used to search any data contained in or available to the computer system.
- Any data may be reproduced or caused to be reproduced in the form of a printout or other intelligible output.
- The printout or other output may be seized for examination or copying.
- Any copying equipment at the place may be used or caused to be used to make copies of the data.

Section 487 (2.2) C.C. imposed a mandatory obligation on the person who is in possession or control of the place being searched. After the warrant is presented to that person, he or she must allow

- any computer system to be used to search for data,
- a hard copy of the data to be obtained and seized by the police,
- copying equipment at the place to be used by the police to make copies of the data.

RULE 6

An application under oath must always be made to a Justice before a s. 487 C.C. search warrant may be issued. The application is called an "Information to Obtain a Search Warrant." The **Information to Obtain** must satisfy a Justice that specifically listed items are in a specific place and must explain the reasonable grounds police have for believing this.

RULE 7

After the search warrant is executed and the named items are seized, the police must make a **return**. They do this by bringing the seized items, or a written report, to a Justice as soon as practicable after the seizure is made.

INFORMATION TO OBTAIN

The issuance of a *Criminal Code* search warrant is not automatic. It must be preceded by the Information to Obtain a Search Warrant, also called Form 1. It is illustrated in Part XXVIII s. 841 C.C. Refer to that section of the *Criminal Code* to see an example of the actual search warrant.

The contents of an Information to Obtain a Search Warrant must include

- the *place* intended to be searched,
- the *offence* that the evidence to be searched for will prove,
- a description of the *items* to be searched for,
- a statement that there are *reasonable grounds* for believing that the items are in the place, and
- the *applicant's name and signature.*

All of these must be sufficiently proven to a Justice. If one area is deficient, the application will be rejected. All elements of the Information to Obtain must be explained and described to the Justice with a great degree of specificity.

Place to Be Searched

Only *one* place may be named on one Information to Obtain. The address must be precise, leaving no doubt about the whereabouts of the place. For example, if the place is an apartment, the unit number must be specified. The owner's name is desirable to help prove the credibility of the application, but the owner's name is not a mandatory requirement. It is possible to have the search warrant authorized without the owner's name because the warrant is directed toward the place, not the person. But if the place is vaguely described, so that there is doubt about what premises are to be searched, the Justice will reject the Information to Obtain, denying police authorization to search.[2]

Offence Committed

You must name a specific offence on the Information to Obtain, so that it is clear what the searched-for evidence will prove. Short-form names of offences, such as "Break, enter, and theft," will usually not suffice and should be avoided. A formal wording of the offence, similar to that used on an Information, is usually required, as are the date and location of the place.

However, case law decisions have shown that an imprecise wording of the offence will not necessarily affect the validity of the warrant. The wording on an Information to Obtain does not require the same precision as the wording on an Information or an indictment. It is recognized that the police are only in the preliminary stage of an investigation when an Information to Obtain is drafted, which justifies some lack of specificity in the wording.[3]

Items to Be Searched For

The Information to Obtain must list specific items that the police intend to search for. A statement such as "any evidence that will prove the offence" is insufficient, and will result in the warrant not being issued. The rules described below serve as guidelines for describing items sufficiently.

RULE 1

A connection must exist between the item and the offence. The item must in some way be evidence of the offence named on the Information to Obtain.[4]

RULE 2

Do not describe items in broad terms. The phrase "broad terms" means a general, non-specific description, one that will not help the searching officers recognize and identify an item, if it is found.[5]

RULE 3

The description should be sufficiently specific to enable the searching officers to positively recognize and identify the items.[6]

RULE 4

Model names and serial numbers, if applicable, should be included if they are known.[7] If this information is unknown, or does not apply, unique features of the item should be included—for example, details concerning damage or markings due to wear and tear. Describing an item's unique features will help police identify and recognize it. General descriptions, such as size and colour, are not usually sufficient to positively identify an item.

RULE 5

A reasonable latitude in descriptions is permitted where the nature of the item prevents precision or specificity. In this case, the searching officers must use proper discretion to determine whether the item found is the one described on the Information to Obtain. If there is doubt in this regard, the item must not be seized.[8]

Procedure

The space provided on the Information to Obtain is usually insufficient to permit listing and describing all the items properly, so you may need to use a separate blank page and attach it to the Information to Obtain. Entitle the page "Appendix A." In the insufficient space provided on the Information to Obtain, write "refer to Appendix A."

List each item separately. Each item's description should include

- general description—for example, type of item, make, model, colour; and
- specific description—for example, serial number or any unique feature such as damage or marks that will allow positive recognition and identification.

Examples of items that may be searched for include

- *stolen property*, such as, television sets, stereos, videocassette recorders;
- *weapons* used to commit an offence;
- *documents*, such as, written plans to commit a robbery;
- *clothing*, such as, ski masks used as disguises worn during offences; and
- *fingerprints*, such as, a victim's fingerprints to prove presence at a crime scene.

Reasonable Grounds for Belief

This represents the most important part of the Information to Obtain. This belief must be justified in a lengthy written summary, which will require separate pages be attached to the Information to Obtain document. The space provided on the Information to Obtain itself will undoubtedly be insufficient. Write "refer to Appendix B" on the space provided and entitle the written supplementary document "Appendix B."

The objective of the written justification of the reasonable grounds belief is to convince the Justice that the *items listed are in the specific place named, right now*. The amount of evidence used to explain the belief must constitute reasonable grounds.

The following are examples of evidence that may constitute reasonable grounds:

1. One credible eyewitness who

    ▸ saw the item in the place, or

    ▸ was told by the offender that the item is in the place.

2. Circumstantial evidence that exceeds mere suspicion.

    The following are circumstances that would constitute mere suspicion—an insufficient belief—and would result in the application being rejected:

    ▸ the item *may* be in the place,

    ▸ the item *may* be in one of several places,

    ▸ the item *may* be evidence to prove the offence.[9]

CONFIDENTIAL INFORMANT

Reasonable grounds for belief about an item's whereabouts are often based on the report and observations of a **confidential informant**—a witness whom the police choose not to identify. Police are permitted to protect an informant's identity by referring to him or her on the Information to Obtain, as an anonymous informant.[10] The S.C.C. has ruled that there is a common-law authority that allows a police officer to protect the identity of an informant. As well, a person cannot be compelled to state whether he or she is or has been a police informant. The need to protect an informant's identity is based on public interest, and the "essential effectiveness of the criminal law."[11]

Whether a confidential informant's report constitutes reasonable grounds is determined according to the following rules.

Rule 1

The informant's report must be based on more than mere rumour or gossip.[12] A simple conclusory statement made by an informant to a police officer does not constitute reasonable grounds.[13] A **conclusory statement** may be defined as a general conclusion or opinion offered with no explanation of it basis. An example of a conclusory statement would be the following: "An anonymous informant reports that the suspect has two stolen television sets in his house."

Rule 2

The informant must explain the basis of his or her information, such as a conversation with the accused, or an eyewitness observation.[14] The basis must explain specifically how the informant learned that the item(s) are in the place.

Rule 3

The informant should be able to identify the offender(s).[15]

Rule 4

The informant must be credible and reliable. You may prove this by citing past dealings with the informant where he or she has been accurate, or by testimony from witnesses who have seen the informant and the accused together.[16]

Rule 5

The informant's report should be supported by some police investigation.[17] It is not necessary for the police to confirm each detail so long as the sequence of events reported by the informant sufficiently indicates an "anticipated pattern" (the events and their sequence make sense) that makes coincidence unlikely. However, if the informant's credibility cannot be evaluated or if he or she reports fewer details, the standard of verification must be higher.[18]

STRUCTURE OF WRITTEN GROUNDS

The structure of the written explanation of the reasonable grounds for belief should be as follows.

Step 1

Summarize the facts of the offence, to demonstrate that it actually occurred.

Step 2

Describe the place to be searched by stating the specific address, if it is a building. Include the owner's name, if it is known. If the place is a motor vehicle, include a precise description, the owner's name, and the location of the vehicle.

Step 3

Introduce the informant, state the date and time the information was received, and the person who received the information (the recipient).

If you decide to have the informant remain confidential, do not identify or name him or her. Refer to him or her as an *anonymous informant*. Do not describe characteristics or circumstances that would permit a person to accurately guess or determine the informant's identity. The Information to Obtain may become a public document before the trial and may be discussed during a trial. An appropriate introduction in this case would simply be the following: "As the result of an interview on [date/time], information was received by [recipient] from a person who will remain anonymous." If no need exists to protect the informant's identity, name him or her.

DECISION TO MAINTAIN CONFIDENTIALITY

If the informant's identity is protected, proving credibility will require providing additional facts in the written grounds. Some doubt about the information may naturally exist simply because the information and the existence of an anonymous person may easily be fabricated. Naming the informant often removes this doubt.

Although naming the informant may lend the information greater credibility, the decision is usually made to maintain the informant's confidentiality. Informants represent valuable long-term investigative benefits in law enforcement; they are, arguably, the single most important factor in an investigator's career. Case law decisions have acknowledged the need to maintain informants' anonymity. The following general principles may guide the decision whether to protect or divulge an informant's identity:

    a. *Divulge* an informant's identity if

        ▸ no threat exists regarding the person's safety, or

- ▸ he or she has never provided information in the past, or
- ▸ there is no intention of using the person in the future as an informant, or
- ▸ the person will be subpoenaed by the police to testify in court.

b. *Protect* an informant's identity if

- ▸ the person's safety will be jeopardized if his or her identity is divulged, or
- ▸ he or she has provided reliable information in the past, or
- ▸ there is an intention to receive information from the person in the future, or
- ▸ no intention exists to subpoena the person to testify in court.

If the informant's identity is not divulged, emphasize the accuracy of the information received from that person in your past dealings with him or her. Be careful not to include detail that will enable people to identify the informant. A balance must be struck between convincing the Justice about the informant's credibility and reliability, and protecting the informant's identity. Often, a simple account of the *number of times* that the informant has been used in the past, together with a reference to the past information's accuracy, should suffice. *A reference to the absence of any past deceit or fabrication by the informant should be included.* If the informant has never lied to police, say so at the end of your account of the informant's past performance.

Step 4

Precisely explain the informant's observations. Avoid *simple conclusory statements.* Do not paraphrase an informant's observations. To increase the precision of your explanation and provide a basis for the informant's observations, include the following:

a. *The time and the place where the observations were made.* Whether the informant saw an item in a place or was informed of its presence by the accused, the informant should be capable of remembering either of these events. If the informant cannot remember, his or her information should be doubted and fabrication suspected.

b. *A description of the items seen.* The informant should provide general and unique features when describing an item.

c. *The location of the items.* Explain exactly where the item was seen in the place to be searched. Avoid general terms such as "inside the house."

d. *A description of the surroundings.* Describe the interior of the place and of other items surrounding the evidence. This will help prove that the informant was in the place.

e. *Verbatim conversation with the accused.* If the accused has told the informant about the location of evidence, or has made any other significant incriminating statements, his or her words should be quoted directly. Avoid paraphrasing. Again, include the time and place where the conversation occurred.

f. *Names of other persons present during the observation or conversation.* Caution must be used in this regard. Naming people may enable someone to determine the identity of the informant. Name other persons present only if these people are commonly in the accused's company. Avoid doing so if the people were not frequent visitors.

g. An account of the degree of familiarity between the informant and the accused. This should include references to

- the length of time the informant has known the accused,
- the frequency of the informant's visits with the accused, and
- other activities of the accused, known to the informant, that are relevant to the offence.

Step 5

Present any information, obtained by other investigative methods, that corroborates the informant—for example, information obtained by surveillance or information based on another person's observations or knowledge.

Step 6

Provide information about the accused's

- criminal record,
- past participation in offences where no charge was laid, or
- any other relevant information about his or her past, learned from prior investigations.

Step 7

Summarize the connection between the item(s) intended to be searched for and the offence committed. Although the connection may seem obvious, write a summary that explains how the item will be evidence in relation to the offence, and what exactly it will prove.

Step 8

If applicable, include a reasonable grounds explanation of the need to execute the warrant at night. Section 488 C.C. states that a s. 487 C.C. search warrant must be executed by day unless reasonable grounds exist to believe there is a need for it to be executed at night. "Day" is defined in s. 2 C.C. as between 6:00 a.m. and 9:00 p.m. Conversely, "night" is between 9:00 p.m. and 6:00 a.m.

Step 9

If appropriate, apply for an order prohibiting public access to the Information to Obtain (refer to the section on "public access" in this chapter).

Step 10

If applicable, include a statement proving the need for a telewarrant (refer to the section on "telewarrants" in this chapter).

SPECIAL CIRCUMSTANCES: INFORMANT

What circumstances will compel a police officer to disclose a confidential informant during court testimony? The need to protect an informant's identity has been recognized in several S.C.C. decisions. The only exception to the non-disclosure rule is when the accused's innocence is at stake. Under these circumstances, the informant's identity must be disclosed. Proving the need for such disclosure requires evidence that the informant lied to the police, or was mistaken. In other words, there must be proof that the accused was framed by the informant. There must also be evidence that the officer who applied for the search warrant knew or ought to have known that the informant was mistaken or lied.[19]

In the absence of evidence that the accused's innocence is at stake, the police do not have to disclose the informant's identity on the Information to Obtain, or during court testimony. And, cross-examination questions (from the defence) whose answers might disclose the informant's identity do not have to be answered during testimony.[20] The Crown attorney can prevent the answering of these questions.

In cases where items are found and seized as the result of an informant's observations, the innocence-at-stake exception does not apply, and the informant's identity may be protected.[21]

Name of Applicant

A space is provided at the top of the Information to Obtain for the name of the applicant, which must be provided. The applicant, formally known as the **informant**, cannot remain anonymous. Usually the informant is the police officer investigating the offence. (The term *informant*, here, must not be confused with the *confidential informant* who is the source of the information given to the police.)

The Information to Obtain must be signed by the informant. The signature must be made before the document is presented to the Justice. *It is improper to present an unsigned Information to Obtain to a Justice.*[22]

The officer may sign it at any time before meeting with the Justice but as a matter of protocol the officer should sign it in the presence of the Justice, prior to presenting it.

The officer's signature is very significant. In combination with a subsequent oath, it signifies that the officer believes that the contents of the Information to Obtain are true and not intentionally fabricated.

APPLYING FOR THE WARRANT: PROCEDURE

Steps

The following is a step-by-step procedure for applying for a search warrant.

STEP 1

The applying officer, known formally as the informant, completes the Information to Obtain before bringing it to the Justice. The Justice cannot assist in preparing the Information to Obtain. The officer must complete it without any suggestions or recommendations from the Justice. Assistance from the Justice in this regard constitutes a serious s. 8 Charter violation and could result in the exclusion of the evidence seized.[23]

STEP 2

The officer must sign the Information to Obtain before presenting it to the Justice. An unsigned Information to Obtain cannot be presented to a JP. As a matter of protocol, sign the document in the presence of the JP, prior to presenting it.

STEP 3

The Information to Obtain is brought and presented to a Justice, usually a JP, anywhere other than in open court. Commonly, the location is a JP's office in a police station. A JP is not usually a full-time Justice, and it may be necessary to bring the Information to Obtain to another place, such as the JP's residence. Presenting the Information to Obtain means that the document is signed and ready for the JP to examine. Do not ask the JP to review the contents of an unsigned Information to Obtain for deficiencies, so that you can correct any errors in the document before the formal presentation is made. The JP must be neutral, an unbiased evaluator, and cannot participate in the officer's investigation by correcting errors on an unsigned Information to Obtain.[24]

STEP 4

The JP will ask the officer to swear the signed Information to Obtain, under oath. The officer is swearing under oath that he or she believes that the contents are true. The officer is essentially swearing that nothing in the contents is fabricated. Intentionally fabricating an Information to Obtain and then swearing it under oath constitutes perjury. If the information from an informant contributed to the formation of reasonable grounds, and the evidence is not found, the officer will suffer no consequences.

STEP 5

The JP analyzes the contents of the sworn Information to Obtain for the purpose of evaluating and determining whether there are reasonable grounds to believe that the items are in the place, right now. No evidence should be given orally by the officer. The only evidence that the JP can evaluate must be written on the sworn Information to Obtain, in accordance with s. 487 C.C. In summary, no oral communication should occur between the officer and the JP during the JP's analysis and evaluation. Commonly, the JP asks the officer to leave and conducts the analysis in private. The officer should leave, whether asked to or not, to prevent any possibility of his communicating unsworn oral evidence and thereby contributing to the JP's evaluation. No other persons, such as witnesses, are required to be present.

STEP 6

The JP makes one of the following two decisions:

1. If, in the JP's opinion, reasonable grounds *do not exist* to believe the item is in the place, the application will be rejected, authorization to search will be denied, and the search warrant will not be issued. The Information to Obtain is kept by the JP. A rejection does not rule out future applications.

The police may reapply for a search warrant if additional information is obtained. The JP may inform the officer about the specific area of deficiency in the Information to Obtain. The officer may subsequently correct the deficiency, and the JP may then evaluate the corrected version on another application.[25] However, the original Information to Obtain cannot be used to reapply; a new one must be drafted for each new application.

If a JP rejects an Information to Obtain, the officer cannot redo the Information to Obtain and bring the document to another JP to seek a second opinion. It is improper to approach other JPs with essentially the same Information to Obtain after one JP has denied the application.[26]

2. If the JP is satisfied that reasonable grounds do exist for believing the item is in the place, a search warrant will be issued. The JP keeps the Information to Obtain, and it becomes court property. The JP completes the s. 487 C.C. search warrant on Form 5.[27] The officer does not complete the search warrant and does not keep the original Information to Obtain.

Form 5: Contents

A s. 487 C.C. search warrant is set out on Form 5, found in Part XXVIII C.C. The following is a list of what must appear on the search warrant:

1. The names of the province and territorial division.
2. The phrase "to the police officers in the said (territorial division)" is preprinted on Form 5. This means that the warrant is directed to all police officers in that territorial division. Any number of officers are authorized to participate in the search. Each officer's name does not have to be written on the warrant.
3. The name of the applying officer who acted as the informant must be written on the warrant. This officer may or may not participate in the search but should be present during the search.
4. Any citizen whom the JP authorizes to assist the officers during the search must be named individually.
5. A list of items to be searched for must be named on the warrant or on a separate, attached page entitled "Appendix A."
6. A description of the offence must be included; the formal wording and section number should be used.
7. The type of place to be searched—for example, dwelling-house—must be stated on the search warrant.
8. The address of the place must be given.
9. The date or dates of the intended search must be specified. Generally, only one date will be authorized but multiple days may sometime be authorized.
10. The hours during which the search may be conducted must be stated. A s. 487 C.C. search warrant must be executed by day,[28] between 6:00 a.m. and 9:00 p.m.[29] A search during night hours is possible if the JP authorizes it. The authorized time of search is expressed in terms of "between [time] to [time]."
11. The date of issuance and the city where the warrant is issued, are stated.
12. The signature of the Justice is given.

TELEWARRANT: SECTION 487.1 C.C.

A telewarrant is a warrant obtained by telephone or other means of telecommunications. Telecommunications is defined in s. 35(1) *Interpretation Act* as any

- transmission,
- emission or reception of signs,
- signal,
- writing, or
- images or sounds or intelligence of any nature conveyed by wire, radio, visual, or other electromagnetic system.

Section 326 C.C. has the same definition of telecommunication, but it applies only to ss. 326 and 327 C.C.

A police officer may apply for a telewarrant if he or she can prove that

- an indictable or dual procedure offence has been committed, and
- it would be impracticable for the officer him- or herself to appear personally before a Justice to apply for the warrant.

Proving impracticability is difficult in most urban areas. A telewarrant cannot be obtained merely for convenience or because of urgency. The key to obtaining a telewarrant is being able to prove that the officer cannot practicably appear personally before a Justice owing to, for example, geographical distance.

Until 1997, a telewarrant could be obtained only for a s. 487 C.C. search warrant and a s. 256 warrant to obtain blood. Recent amendments now permit telewarrants for the following:

- s. 487 C.C. search warrant,
- s. 256 C.C. warrant to obtain blood,
- general warrant,[30]
- forensic DNA analysis warrant,[31]
- impression warrant,[32]
- warrant to enter a dwelling-house,[33] and
- *Controlled Drugs and Substances Act* search warrant.

Only two warrants cannot be obtained by telewarrant:

- tracking warrant, and
- number recorder warrant.

OBTAIN A TELEWARRANT: PROCEDURE

Steps

The following procedure applies to telewarrants.

STEP 1

Submit an Information to Obtain under oath by telephone or other means of telecommunications to a Justice designated by the chief judge of that jurisdiction for issuing telewarrants.

STEP 2

The Justice records the Information to Obtain verbatim. The required contents of an Information to Obtain submitted this way are the same as for a conventional s. 487 C.C. search warrant, but one significant addition must be included. The police officer must submit a statement on the circumstances that make it impracticable for him or her to appear personally before a Justice.

STEP 3

The Justice may issue a search warrant on Form 5.1 if he or she is satisfied the reasonable grounds exist for believing the item is in the place.

The important question is, "What document will the police officer have in his or her possession when executing the warrant?" The answer depends on the device the officer and the Justice use to communicate with each other. Two devices are possible:

1. If the communication is made by telephone or by a means of telecommunication that *does not produce a writing*, obviously the Justice cannot send the warrant to the officer. Under these circumstances, the following procedure is used to enable the officer to possess a search warrant document:

    a. The Justice must complete and sign a search warrant by using Form 5.1. The time, date, and place of issuance must be included. It must be emphatically stated that the Justice cannot transmit this warrant to the officer.

    b. Then the officer also completes a warrant using Form 5.1 on the direction of the Justice. This means that during the communication the Justice will instruct the officer about what to write on the officer's copy of the search warrant. Essentially, the Justice dictates the contents and the officer records it verbatim.

2. If the warrant is issued by a means of telecommunication that produces a writing, the Justice completes Form 5.1 and transmits a facsimile to the officer. The officer must obtain a second facsimile of the warrant afterward for the records.

Special Circumstances

- ▸ If the warrant is executed at an occupied premises, the officer must give a facsimile of it to any occupant present and in control of the place, before entering or as soon as practicable after entry.
- ▸ If the warrant is executed at an unoccupied place, the officer must affix a facsimile of the warrant to a prominent location inside the place, where it will likely be seen.
- ▸ After the warrant is executed, the officer must file a written report, the Information to Obtain, and the warrant with the clerk of the court within seven days. The report must include the time and date of execution, and a list of all items seized.[34]

EXECUTION OF THE SEARCH WARRANT

Execution refers to carrying out the search warrant by entering and searching of the place. The following rules apply to the execution of a s. 487 C.C. search warrant.

Who May Search?

A s. 487 C.C. search warrant is directed to all police officers in the territorial division that is named on the warrant. Consequently, any number of officers may participate in the search. The participating officers do not have to be individually named on the search warrant.

The officer who is named on the warrant as the informant does not have to be present during the search but should be a participant because he or she will likely have more knowledge about the investigation and the items to be searched for. It is also important that one officer, usually the named officer, control and supervise the search.

When Must the Search Be Executed?

The warrant must be executed on the date or dates stated on the warrant, and between the hours specified on the warrant by the JP. The hours will be between 6:00 a.m. and 9:00 p.m. (day) only, unless the JP specifically authorizes night hours (9:00 p.m.–6:00 a.m.) on the warrant.

Commonly, only one day is named on the search warrant, making it valid only for that specific day. The Justice has discretion, however, to extend the warrant to include more than one day. In this case, the reasonable grounds part of the Information to Obtain must specify why more than one day is required.

Can Force Be Used for Entry?

No specific *Criminal Code* provision directly explains use of force (procedure or guidelines) in connection with a s. 487 C.C. search warrant. Section 25 C.C. gives police general authority to use as much force as is necessary to do whatever they are authorized to do. However, a specific procedure is not outlined.

Section 8 Charter is the highest governing provision regarding use of force, and it requires that the search be reasonable. However, the Charter does not explain precisely what force is reasonable with respect to entering a place.

Specific guidelines and procedures are found in common law and case law. A common law rule prohibits police from using automatic, unlimited force to enter a place in execution of a s. 487 C.C. search warrant. The reason for this rule is that unexpected entry into a place, such as a house, may provoke violence. To prevent violent reactions, a proper announcement before entry is generally required.

The S.C.C. defined a proper announcement as being composed of three notices:

- ▸ notice of presence, signalled by knocking or ringing the doorbell; and
- ▸ notice of authority, conveyed by identifying oneself as a law enforcement officer; and
- ▸ notice of purpose, conveyed by stating a lawful reason for entry (for example, a search warrant).[35]

Before entering the place to execute the search warrant, officers must give the three notices and *request entry*. If the request is granted, there will obviously be no justification for use of force. If the entry is denied, officers may then enter, and force may be used if necessary.

Admission may be denied in two ways. A verbal denial is clear and unmistakable. Entry may then be made, and force may be used if necessary. But the denial may also take the form of no response. This poses the problem of how long officers should have to wait before entering and using force if necessary. The S.C.C. stated that officers "minimally" should request admission and have it denied. No other guideline was given. The court did not impose any obligation on police to wait for any specified time. Consequently, s. 8 Charter will be the governing factor. Officers must act reasonably when no response is made to their request for admission. If people are in the place, hesitation to enter may bring a risk to the officer's personal safety. Officers should enter as soon as possible, without delay, because no response to their announcement may reasonably suggest that violence is pending or that evidence inside the place may be destroyed. In other words, officers can become targets for violence in this situation.

Commonly, there will be some evidence that persons are inside the place, such as parked cars outside, sounds from inside, observations through a window, or information received from a witness or informant. If there is no evidence that persons are in the place, officers have few means of positively determining whether occupants are in the place. Merely assuming that no one is inside may be dangerous. Executing a search warrant does not require that occupants be in the place. The S.C.C. stated only that admission should be requested and denied before police enter. The court did not impose on police an obligation to determine positively that persons are inside. Thus police should make their entry with minimal hesitation after requesting admission.

There is an exception to this proper announcement rule. Police may enter with the use of force and without a proper announcement if exigent circumstances exist, as when an officer believes that

- there is a real threat of violent behaviour toward the police or toward anyone else; or
- there is a risk that evidence may be lost or destroyed.[36]

When police use force to enter a place, with or without an announcement, they have the onus of proving at the trial that they had reasonable grounds for believing that exigent circumstances were present *and* that they had this belief at the time that force was used. At the trial, the Crown and police must introduce reasons, in the form of sworn oral testimony, to justify their use of force. Their testimony must include the facts that supported their belief that exigent circumstances existed. For example, their testimony might show they had a reasonable belief that weapons were inside the place when they arrived to execute the warrant. The belief does not have to be proven beyond a reasonable doubt.

Failure by police to give evidence that sufficiently explains their reasons for using force constitutes a serious s. 8 Charter violation, according to the S.C.C. The court recommended that judges be reluctant to admit evidence that was obtained as the result of unjustified, excessive force. Such evidence will usually be excluded.[37]

Do Occupants Have to Be Present at the Time of the Search?

Can the warrant be executed at an unoccupied place? The occupants of a place may not always be there when the police arrive to execute the search warrant. The *Criminal Code* does not directly address this situation. The search warrant does not state that it may be executed only when the occupants are present. Specific procedures and guidelines are found in case law.

If officers positively determine that no occupants are inside the place, their authority to enter depends on whether exigent circumstances exist. If they do exist, police entry and search of the place will be considered reasonable. The following constitute exigent circumstances:

▸ no knowledge of when the occupants will return,
▸ certainty that the items are in the place, and
▸ a reasonable belief that the items will be lost or destroyed before another search warrant can be executed.[38]

If no exigent circumstances exist and the place is unoccupied, the search warrant cannot be executed. A search conducted in the absence of exigent circumstances will be considered unreasonable. Factors that may indicate the *absence* of exigent circumstances are

▸ more than one date named (as authorized dates of search) on the warrant,
▸ temporary absence of the occupants,
▸ sufficient time to conduct surveillance on the place until the occupants return.[39]

Must the Warrant Be Produced?

The officer who executes the warrant has two obligations. He or she must

▸ have possession of the search warrant, if feasible; and
▸ produce it when requested to do so by an occupant.

It is recommended that the officer hold the warrant while the occupant reads it, to prevent it being destroyed. Any occupant may request to see the warrant. The officer should produce it for the owner or person who has control of the place, regardless of whether this person requests it. Allowing the occupant to read the warrant may encourage him or her to relinquish all the items named on the warrant.

Officers are not required to give the occupant a copy of the warrant, and should not do this. Not giving it will prevent the occupant from using the warrant for unlawful purposes, such as personating a police officer and stealing property.[40]

What Governs the Arrest or Detention of Occupants?

The search warrant itself does not authorize the arrest or detention of any occupant. Officers must comply with the arrest-without-warrant provisions found in s. 495 C.C. They may make an arrest if they find any criminal offence being committed, or if they have reasonable grounds for believing that an occupant has committed or is about to commit a dual procedure or indictable offence. For example, officers may encounter the following during a search:

- Intentional obstruction or interference from occupants ("obstruct police"). Movement by occupants that is not intended to interfere with or obstruct the search does not constitute "obstruct police," and is therefore allowed.
- Possession of weapons, stolen property, or narcotics, which may occur while occupants are attempting to destroy or conceal them.
- Reasonable grounds for believing that an arrest warrant exists for any of the occupants.

The S.C.C. has permitted officers to control occupants during a search, primarily during narcotic searches, by confining them to a specific area, in circumstances where evidence is at risk and needs to be preserved.[41] Officers may also detain persons to prevent their committing dual procedure or indictable offences if officers have reasonable grounds to believe that an occupant(s) is about to commit one of these types of offences.[42]

Obstructing police is an example of a dual procedure offence that officers may prevent by means of arrest. For example, if an occupant informs officers that they will not be permitted to search and that he or she will interfere with the officers if they try to search, the officers may arrest the occupant.

It must be emphasized that officers cannot make arrests automatically, without justification. If an occupant wants to leave the premises and police have no lawful justification for detaining or arresting the person, he or she must be allowed to leave. Police may arrest a person leaving only if they have lawful arrest authority under s. 495 C.C.—for example, if the person possesses an item obtained by crime, a narcotic, or a weapon, or is attempting to conceal or destroy evidence named on the warrant, to obstruct the search.

What Governs the Search of Occupants?

The search warrant itself does not authorize the search of persons found inside the place. In order to search a person, justification must exist. The authorities that justify such a search will be explained later in this chapter, including

- search after a lawful arrest or
- reasonable grounds to believe that the occupant(s) has possession of a weapon or firearm[43] or narcotics.[44]

Otherwise, in the absence of any authorization, the search of a person may be conducted only by consent of the person.

What Areas May Be Searched?

A search warrant does not restrict a search to partial areas of a place. The warrant authorizes a search of an entire place. However, s. 8 Charter requires that the areas searched must be *reasonable*. Consequently, the size of the listed items, specifically the smallest item, will determine the areas of search. For example, if jewellery is the smallest item, the areas of reasonable search broaden. If a television set is the smallest item, certain areas, such as desk drawers, cannot reasonably be searched. A house garage may be searched if the garage is attached to a dwelling-house and the warrant is directed to the house. Detached garages, sheds, and motor vehicles on the property are separate places, and cannot be searched unless named on the warrant by the JP. If they are not so named, a separate warrant is necessary for each.

Can Items Not Listed Be Seized?

During the execution of a search warrant, police may find other evidence, not listed on the warrant, that is related or unrelated to the offence named on the search warrant. Any item not listed on the warrant may be seized if reasonable grounds exist to believe that it was obtained by or was used in the commission of any offence, including offences unrelated to the offence named on the warrant.[45]

Is There a Time Limit/Expiry Date for the Warrant?

Five time limits govern the expiry of search warrants. The search warrant expires and the search must end in the following circumstances:

- at 9:00 p.m., if the authorization is for day only;
- if authorized for night and if the time, such as midnight, is stated on the warrant;
- when all the items have been found, regardless of the actual time of seizure and how much time remains before the expiry time stated on the warrant;
- the search of the place has concluded and nothing has been found (if the search was thorough, continued search may be unreasonable); and
- the police stop the search and leave the property, regardless of whether the search was thorough or complete.

If officers remain on the premises after the warrant has expired, without consent or any other authority, they will be considered trespassers.[46]

"Return" of Seized Items

If items are seized during the execution of any search warrant, the officer must comply with the combined requirements of ss. 487(1)(e) and 489.1 C.C. These requirements form a procedure that is formally called a "report by police officer." It is informally called a "return" to a Justice. A return may be defined as a notification, or report, to a Justice that explains what item was seized and determines the disposition of the item by ordering its detention or its release to the lawful owner.

Section 487(1)(e) C.C. states that the search warrant authorizes the seizure of the item and the return of it to a Justice, in accordance with s. 489.1 C.C. In other words, this provision gives police the authority to keep custody of the seized item and return it to a Justice.

Section 489.1 C.C. creates the procedural guidelines relating to the manner in which the return must be made. Two alternative procedures exist under s. 489.1 C.C. Which of the two methods is appropriate depends on whether the seized item is needed for an investigation or for trial.

If it is needed, the item must be lawfully detained. If the item is not needed, it must be returned to its owner.

DETAINING A SEIZED ITEM

A seized item's return to a Justice, when it is detained for an investigation or a trial, has two components. First, a Justice authorizes the search for and seizure of the item. This is why the Justice must be notified of the results and the item must be "returned" to him or her. Second, only a Justice has the authority to allow the police to keep the item until the trial, rather than return it to the owner.

When Must the Return Be Made?

No specific time limit is imposed. The return must be made as soon as practicable after the item is seized, meaning that no unjustified delay is permitted.

How Is a Return Made?

A return may be made through either of the following two methods:

1. Bring the actual seized items before a Justice.
2. Complete a document named a "Report to a Justice" and bring the document, instead of the actual items, before a Justice.[47] The "Report to a Justice" is Form 5.2 in Part XXVIII C.C. The contents of this document include

   - the seizing officer's name,
   - the type of search warrant executed (e.g., s. 487 C.C.),
   - the address of the place searched,
   - a list of and description of items seized,
   - the date and time of seizure, and
   - the officer's signature.

The seizing officer has discretion to use either method. No particular circumstances dictate the use of one return method or the other. The "Report to a Justice" document is sometimes more convenient.

A return may be made to either the Justice who issued the search warrant or to any other Justice in the same territorial division.[48] After the return is made, the Justice must decide whether to detain the item or release it to the lawful owner. If *charges are laid* shortly after the search, the JP must immediately order detention of the items, without a hearing, until the trial.[49]

If *charges are not laid* after the search because a lengthier investigation is required, the property may be detained for three months unless the Justice authorizes extended detention, in consideration of the nature of the investigation.[50] If the *three months*, or *extended detention time expires*, and no charges have been laid because the investigation is continuing, extended detention may be authorized, after a hearing.[51] If no charges will be laid, the seized items must be returned to the lawful owner.[52]

When the seizing officer is satisfied that there is no dispute as to who is the lawful owner of the item, and the item is not needed for any investigation or trial, the officer must return the seized item to the lawful owner. A receipt must be obtained from the owner. Afterward, the officer must report to a Justice that the item has been returned.[53]

Photographs

Where charges are laid, rules of evidence generally require the production of the original item at the trial unless it is impracticable to do so. Photographs of the items, instead of items themselves, are not permitted in every case; however, photographs may be taken and introduced in court instead of the actual item if the offence is

- theft under or over $5,000.00;
- robbery;
- breaking and entering with intent, or committing an indictable offence;
- false pretences under or over $5,000.00; or
- fraud under or over $5,000.00.

Using a photograph of the item means the item itself can be released to the lawful owner instead of being kept in police custody for several months until the trial.[54] Such photographs will be admissible under two conditions:

1. The photographer is a police officer or took directions from a police officer, and completes a certificate stating that he or she took the photograph and that the photograph is a true photograph.[55]
2. The accused is given reasonable notice, before the trial, that the pictures will be used.[56]

No Items Found

If the search warrant is executed and no items are seized, the officer signs the back of the search warrant and writes the date of execution. The search warrant is then returned to the JP.

SEARCH WARRANT NOT EXECUTED

In some cases, circumstances will arise after the issuance of a search warrant that may prevent its being executed before the expiry time. When this happens, the search warrant must be returned to the JP; it cannot be executed after the expiry time. If the reasonable grounds still exist to believe the item is in the place, a new application must be made to obtain another search warrant.

PUBLIC ACCESS

The contents of an Information to Obtain must often be kept confidential to protect the identity of an anonymous informant, of ongoing investigations, and of intelligence-gathering techniques that will be used in future investigations. Consequently, the issue of public access to the Information to Obtain is critical to the protection of investigations.

In 1997, s. 487.3 C.C. was enacted to serve as a procedure to prevent public access to an Information to Obtain. The S.C.C. decision in *MacIntyre v. Nova Scotia*

(A.G.) (1982) is the predecessor to s. 487.3 C.C. It provides a useful context in which to interpret the new provisions.

The *MacIntyre* decision created two rules concerning public access to an Information to Obtain that can serve as guidelines:

1. Public access was denied after a search warrant was executed and no seizure was made.
2. Public access was allowed after the warrant was executed and items were seized. Access was allowed to any member of the public, the lone exception being a situation where the course of justice would have been obstructed by having the public read it.[57]

Section 487.3 C.C. allows a judge or Justice to make an order prohibiting public access to and disclosure of any information relating to the warrant or authorization. Making this order requires that an application be made (usually by the informant) at the time the warrant is issued, or at any time after that. The application must prove there are grounds for requiring the prohibition order. The relevant grounds are as follows:

- disclosure would subvert the ends of justice for one of the reasons in s. 487.3(2) C.C.; or
- the information disclosed might be put to an improper purpose; and
- the benefits of the prohibition outweighs considerations about public access to the information.

The disclosure will subvert the ends of justice if it will

- compromise the identity of a confidential informant,
- compromise the nature and extent of an ongoing investigation,
- endanger a person engaged in particular intelligence-gathering techniques and thereby prejudice future investigations in which similar techniques would be used, or
- prejudice the interests of an innocent person.

Section 487.3(2) C.C. states that "any other sufficient reason" justifies a prohibition order. After a prohibition order is made, all documents relating to the application shall be placed in a packet and sealed by the Justice immediately on determination of the application. The sealed packet must be kept in the custody of the court in a place to which the public has no access.

Section 487.3(4) C.C. provides that any person may apply to terminate the prohibition order in order to gain public access. The subsection does not impose restrictions on any person who wishes to apply for termination of the order. Consequently, any member of the public, including the accused, may be the applicant.

The following is a summary of the procedural rules relating to a prohibition order regarding public access to an Information to Obtain:

- A prohibition order cannot automatically be made; an application must precede the order.
- Making the application begins the process of determining whether the order will be made or not.

▸ After an application is made, the Justice has discretion about granting or denying it.

▸ A Justice cannot make an order without an application first being made.

When Does the Application Have to Be Made?

The application may be made

▸ at the time the warrant is issued, or
▸ at any time after the warrant is issued.

Who May Make the Application?

Section 487.3 does not directly specify who may apply for a prohibition order, but it does not restrict any person either. This lack of limitation implies that any person may apply. Usually, the applicant will be the officer who completes the Information to Obtain.

How Does the Application Have to Be Made?

The section does not specify the manner in which the application must be made. It does not state whether the application must be in writing, or what document must be used, or whether the application must be under oath. Section 487(1) C.C. refers specifically to the manner of applying for a search warrant; it uses the phrase "by information on oath." No such phrase is used in s. 487.3 C.C. The absence of specific procedures suggests that unsworn oral evidence may suffice as an application for a prohibition order. It would also appear that the grounds for the application may be included on the Information to Obtain.

What Has to Be Proven in the Application?

The application for a prohibition order must prove that disclosure of the Information to Obtain will result in any one of the following four consequences:

1. the identity of a confidential informant will be divulged; or
2. the investigation is ongoing and the nature and extent of it will be jeopardized; or
3. a person who is using intelligence-gathering techniques during the investigation will be endangered and future investigations will be prejudiced; or
4. an innocent person's interest will be prejudiced.

Additionally, "any sufficient reason" may be specified on the application. However, this phrase obviously conveys no precise guidelines about what is "sufficient."

What Occurs If a Prohibition Order Is Made?

The Justice seals all relevant documents in a packet and stores the packet in a place that is inaccessible to the public.

DRUG SEARCH WARRANTS

Two search warrants are available to police during a drug investigation:

1. s. 11 *Controlled Drugs and Substances Act* (C.D.S.A.) warrant, and
2. s. 487 C.C. warrant.

Both warrants authorize police officers to search places for drugs; therefore, the procedures for each need to be compared. Comparison of them will help show which warrant to use in each situation.

The C.D.S.A. is a federal statute that was enacted in 1997; it replaces two statutes, the *Narcotic Control Act* (N.C.A.) and the *Food and Drugs Act* (F.D.A). It is legislation that regulates substances formerly called narcotics and drugs, now called "controlled substances." The basic design of the C.D.S.A. is similar to the N.C.A. and the F.D.A.

Section 11 C.D.S.A. creates a search warrant relating to controlled substances. The following are general rules that apply to this warrant. The case law decisions referred to are from before the C.D.S.A. was enacted, but they are still considered useful sources of procedural guidelines.

Relevant Definitions and Terms

Controlled substance. A substance included in Schedule I, II, III, IV, or V.
Precursor. A substance included in Schedule VI.

- *Schedule I substances* include cocaine and heroin.
- *Schedule II substances* include cannabis (marijuana) and its derivatives.
- *Schedule III substances* include LSD and amphetamines.
- *Schedule IV substances* include barbiturates and anabolic steroids.
- *Schedule V substances* include pyrovalerone.
- *Schedule VI substances* include ephedrine and lysergic acid.

Rules

RULE 1

A C.D.S.A. warrant authorizes the search of any place, including a dwelling-house and any building that is not a dwelling-house.[58] This contrasts to the N.C.A. search warrant, which can only be used for dwelling-houses.

RULE 2

A C.D.S.A. search warrant must be applied for. The document is called an Information to Obtain a C.D.S.A. search warrant.

RULE 3

The required contents of an Information to Obtain a C.D.S.A. search warrant are the same as for an Information to Obtain a s. 487 C.C. search warrant: place, offence, items, reasonable grounds. The same standard of sufficiency applies as well.

RULE 4

The C.D.S.A. search warrant authorizes the search for and seizure of the following:

- ▸ a controlled substance or precursor relating to a C.D.S.A. offence,
- ▸ anything in which a controlled substance or precursor is contained or concealed,
- ▸ offence-related property, or
- ▸ anything that will afford evidence relating to a C.D.S.A. offence.

For a C.D.S.A. search warrant, the Information to Obtain must specify the items that are believed to be in the place. The use of the words "controlled substance" or "precursor" is insufficient; the name or type of substance must be specified. Other items that may be specified in the application, items that will afford evidence relating to C.D.S.A. offences, include weight scales and packages. There must be reasonable grounds for believing these items are in the place.

Not just the type but the specific quantity of the substance should be specified on the Information to Obtain, so that it complies with the reasonableness requirement of s. 8 Charter.

Specifying a quantity will define the extent of the search and add credibility to the reasonable grounds belief. It also imposes a reasonable limit on the search. If the search ultimately yields a greater quantity than has been specified, it "may be seized."[59]

RULE 5

Anonymous informants may be used to prove the reasonable grounds for belief. The S.C.C., in *R. v. Scott* (1990),[60] recognized the need to protect the identity of informants in drug-related investigations to ensure their assistance and facilitate the relationship of trust between them and the police. The sufficiency of an informant's observations is measured by the same standard as is applied to an Information to Obtain a s. 487 C.C. search warrant. For example, a simple conclusory statement— one that does not explain the basis for the informant's report—is insufficient. The basis of the informant's report must be explained. The informant's credibility and reliability must be proven by past dealings or by supporting investigation.

RULE 6

The Justice cannot assist the officer in the preparation of the Information to Obtain and must act as a neutral evaluator.

RULE 7

The Information to Obtain is presented to the Justice just as an Information to Obtain a s. 487 C.C. search warrant is presented. The officer signs, preferably in the presence of the Justice, and swears under oath that the belief is true. The Justice analyzes and evaluates the Information to Obtain, and decides whether the grounds for belief it outlines are sufficient. If the application is rejected, no warrant is issued, and the document is kept by the Justice. The officer may re-apply when additional evidence is uncovered. If the grounds are deemed sufficient, the Justice issues the search warrant and keeps the Information to Obtain, which becomes the property of the court.

RULE 8

The C.D.S.A. search warrant must be *directed to* at least one officer. In other words, the C.D.S.A. search warrant[61] must name at least one officer, who will be responsible for the control and conduct of the search. The S.C.C. created the following rules regarding this provision:

1. More than one officer may be named but not an entire drug unit. Listing an entire drug unit will defeat the purpose of the naming requirement.
2. Naming two officers is acceptable.
3. The named officer(s) must
   a. participate in the search, and
   b. closely control and supervise the search.
4. Any number of unnamed officers may participate in the search and seize narcotics, but the seizures must be taken into the possession of an officer named on the warrant, who controls and supervises the search.
5. Failure to name any officer at all constitutes a s. 8 Charter violation.[62]

RULE 9

A C.D.S.A. search warrant may be executed at any time, by day or by night. Night searches do not require special authorization by a Justice, as is required for a s. 487 C.C. search warrant. However, as a matter of practice, Justices commonly type the hours of search on the warrant. For example, the hours typed on the warrant may include from the time the warrant was issued (for example, 2:00 p.m.) until 11:59 p.m., so that the allotted time includes the night hours (after 9:00 p.m.) of the authorized day of the search. It is possible for the Justice to authorize the warrant for more than one day. The reasonable grounds must include justification for requiring the authorization of more than one day.

RULE 10

Section 12 C.D.S.A. authorizes the officer who executes the C.D.S.A. warrant to "enlist such assistance as the officer deems necessary." This would authorize, for example, bringing a number of officers to assist in the execution of the warrant if the officer can justify doing this. It also authorizes the use of as much force as is necessary in the circumstances.

This provision does not require police to make any announcement to the occupant prior to entry. Despite this, s. 8 Charter requires that all searches be reasonable. In keeping with this, force cannot be automatically used in all cases.

The S.C.C. established rules relating to the s. 12 C.D.S.A. authorization of use of force in two cases: *R. v. Genest* (1989)[63] and *R. v. Gimson* (1991).[64] Entry without prior announcement is justified when police have reasonable grounds for believing that evidence may be destroyed or that actual danger is present. For example, a reliable informant's report that narcotics are being sold in a dwelling-house and that the front door might be barricaded encourages the inference that the occupant wishes to have time to destroy evidence. The use of force under s. 12 C.D.S.A. is justified under such circumstances, as was the situation in the *Gimson* case. However, the court did not address the question whether a blanket authority exists to enter without a prior announcement when executing a drug search warrant.

The fact that narcotics may be easily disposed of often necessitates an unannounced entry. A common practice used by officers executing narcotics searches is to enter unannounced and make an announcement shortly after entry.

The s. 12(b) C.D.S.A. use-of-force authority is not limited to entry. It extends to "exercising any of the power" that is authorized in s. 11 C.D.S.A. This authorized power includes using force to break open items inside the place while conducting the search. This general use-of-force authority replaces a provision, included in the N.C.A., that authorized police use of force to break open doors, floors, containers, walls, ceilings, plumbing fixtures, and "any other thing." Section 12 C.D.S.A. authorizes the same use of force if it is proved to be reasonably necessary.

RULE 11

Although the C.D.S.A. does not require that occupants of a dwelling-house be present when the search warrant is executed, the s. 8 Charter requirement of reasonableness does not permit automatic entry by force into a house when the occupants are absent.

Two cases provide rules and guidelines regarding the execution of a C.D.S.A. search warrant when the occupants are not home. In *R. v. Grenier* (1991),[65] the Quebec Court of Appeal ruled that the execution of a search warrant and use of force to enter were justified when the occupants were not home, for the following reasons: (1) the police knew that 17 marijuana plants were in the house; (2) they had no knowledge about when the occupants would return; and (3) they had no way of knowing if the narcotics would still be there if the search was delayed until the occupants returned. Had there been no urgency, the police would have had to delay the search.

In *R. v. McGregor* (1985),[66] the Manitoba Court of Queen's Bench stated that forced entry and search of an unoccupied house is not justified if the house can be kept under surveillance while attempts are made to locate an occupant of the house.

The determining factor, when police are trying to decide whether to execute a C.D.S.A. search warrant when the occupants are not at home, is whether exigent circumstances exist—urgency. Entry and search of an unoccupied house are justified when police have reasonable grounds to believe that the evidence will be destroyed or lost if the search is delayed until the occupants return.

RULE 12

The officer who executes the search warrant must have possession of the warrant and must produce it at the occupant's request.[67]

RULE 13

The C.D.S.A. search warrant does not authorize the arrest of the occupants. Arrests must be authorized by s. 495 C.C.

RULE 14

The C.D.S.A. warrant authorizes the search of occupants found in the place, but not automatically. The authority to search occupants is contingent upon an officer's having reasonable grounds to believe that the occupant has any of the substances or items named on the warrant "on their person."[68] In the absence of this belief, police may search occupants only if occupants consent to it.

RULE 15

In addition to the substances and items named on the warrant, the officer may seize the following during the search:

- any controlled substance, precursor, container with those substances in it, and any item that is evidence of any C.D.S.A. offence,[69] and
- any unrelated item that is evidence of any offence, under any statute.[70]

RULE 16

An C.D.S.A. search warrant expires

- at 11:59 p.m., or any other time specified, on the authorized day stated on the warrant; or
- when all the named items have been found; or
- when the house is thoroughly searched and nothing is found; or
- when the officers leave the dwelling-house.

RULE 17

A "return" to a Justice must be made after items are seized. Section 13(1) C.D.S.A. states that the return provisions under ss. 489.1 and 490 C.C. apply to anything seized by means of a C.D.S.A. warrant. The return procedure is the same as the one outlined in the part of this textbook devoted to the s. 487 C.C. search warrant. There is one difference, though: when a police officer seizes a controlled substance by means of a warrant, the officer must cause a copy of Form 5.2, "Report to a Justice," to be sent to the Ministry of Health. The report must identify the place searched, the controlled substance seized, and the place where it is detained.[71]

Table 16.1 summarizes the differences between the two types of search warrants used to search for and seize drugs.

Table 16.1   Types of Search Warrants

C.D.S.A. Search Warrant		Section 487 C.C. Search Warrant
Any place.	PLACE	Any place.
Directed to one officer who will closely supervise the search. Two are acceptable, but not an entire drug unit.	DIRECTED TO	Directed to all police officers in the territorial jurisdiction.
Same as above	NAMES OF OFFICERS	Name of the applying officer who acted as the informant must be written.
Mandatory that the officer to whom the warrant is directed participate. The number of additional officers is optional.	PARTICIPATING OFFICERS	Not mandatory that the applying officer attend, but he or she should.
Day or night.	TIME OF EXECUTION	Day only. Justice may authorize night search if the grounds justify it.
Section 12 C.D.S.A. specifically authorizes the use of as much force as is necessary, but force must be reasonable. Case law proper announcement rule applies.	USE OF FORCE	No specific provision regarding type of force used; force must be reasonable according to case law requirements— proper announcement must be made, and s. 25–28 C.C. followed.
Mandatory requirement plus copy to the Ministry of Health.	RETURN	Mandatory requirement.

ELECTRONIC SURVEILLANCE

Electronic surveillance may significantly contribute to the success of an investigation by helping the investigator obtain information that will prove the commission of an offence.

Several types of electronic surveillance exist, including

- video recording,
- tracking devices, and
- number recorders.

Electronic surveillance constitutes a search and seizure. Unreasonable electronic surveillance committed by a state agent constitutes a s. 8 Charter violation.

A series of S.C.C. decisions have had significant impact on the laws concerning electronic surveillance. In response to these decisions, new search warrants have been added to the *Criminal Code* that authorize various forms of electronic surveillance.

GENERAL WARRANT: SECTION 487.01 C.C.

This is a relatively new warrant that was added to the *Criminal Code* in 1993. It is referred to as a "general" warrant, but this term is misleading: it implies that this warrant authorizes the seizure of a variety of items. It does not. Section 487 C.C. authorizes the general search of places for items.

The s. 487.01 C.C. general warrant was enacted in response to the S.C.C. decision made in *R. v. Wong* (1993).[72] The court made the following rulings:

1. Video surveillance of activity constitutes a search.
2. Video surveillance of places where persons have a reasonable expectation of privacy cannot be conducted without a warrant (for example, in a motel room).
3. Video surveillance in those places, conducted without a warrant, is unreasonable and constitutes a s. 8 Charter violation.

A s. 487.01 **general warrant** is not used to search for and seize items; it is intended to be used by *police officers only* to obtain *information* concerning the commission of any offence under any federal statute. This information may be obtained by

- any device,
- any investigative technique or procedure, or
- doing anything that would otherwise be an unreasonable search or seizure.

Specific devices and investigative techniques that may be authorized by means of this search warrant are surveillance by means of a television camera or some similar electronic device.[73] Video surveillance of an activity in a *public place* does not require a warrant because the person being observed does not have a reasonable expectation of privacy.

Consequently, a general warrant is associated primarily with *video surveillance*, but also with the obtaining of *information by means of observations* made with or without electronic devices.

Examples of observations made without an electronic device are

1. Entering the perimeter of a dwelling-house and looking inside the house for evidence of an offence, such as narcotics possessed for the purpose of trafficking. The perimeter of a house is a place. The visual observations of the interior of the place constitute a search.
2. Making photocopies of the outsides of envelopes and of packages of mailable material while the material is in a post office.[74]

A s. 487.01 C.C. general warrant may be used to authorize these investigative techniques when they are means of obtaining, *by observation*, information that is relevant to the offence being investigated. A general warrant may also be considered an investigative means of obtaining information that will help *form the reasonable grounds belief needed to obtain a s. 487 C.C. warrant to search the place for items.*

If the police apply specifically to use an electronic device to make observations, the procedure used to obtain a general warrant must be the same as the one used in applying to intercept private communications, a procedure described in Part VI C.C., ss. 183–196. For example, if the application includes a request to conduct video surveillance, the offence must be one of those defined in s. 183 C.C., such as "conspiracy," "counselling," or attempting to commit one of the other offences listed.[75]

OBTAIN AND EXECUTE A GENERAL WARRANT: PROCEDURE

Steps

The following procedure applies to a general warrant.

STEP 1

The first step in applying for a general warrant is completing an Information to Obtain. Section 487 C.C. does not specify what document to use for this. Therefore, Form 1 (as illustrated in sec. 841 C.C.) may be adapted to suit the case.

STEP 2

The applicant, referred to as the informant, *must be a police officer.* A citizen cannot apply for or obtain this warrant.

STEP 3

The Information to Obtain must do the following:

▸ It must demonstrate in writing that there are reasonable grounds to believe that a criminal offence under any federal statute has been or will be committed. The offence may be in contravention of the *Criminal Code* or the *Controlled Drugs and Substances Act.*
▸ It must demonstrate in writing that there are reasonable grounds to believe that *information* concerning the offence will be obtained. The type of information is not specified, but it must be information that can be acquired by observation. It cannot be an item.

STEP 4

The Information to Obtain must specify the technique, procedure, device, or action that will obtain the information. If a television camera or similar electronic device is being requested, the specific type of device must be named.

STEP 5

The Information to Obtain must explain that no other provision in any statute authorizes the type of procedure being requested. For example, other provisions in the *Criminal Code* authorize warrants to search for items, track the location of persons or items, and seize bodily substances for DNA analysis. However, no statute authorizes the making of observations with or without electronic means.

STEP 6

The informant must sign the Information to Obtain and bring it to a provincial court judge or a judge of a superior court of criminal jurisdiction. *It cannot be brought to a JP.*

STEP 7

The judge may deny the warrant or issue it. If the warrant is issued, Form 5 may be adapted to suit the case. Section 487.01 C.C. does not specify the type of document that must be used as the warrant.

The judge must specify on the warrant precise *terms* and *conditions* to ensure a reasonable search or seizure.[76] There is no mandatory limit on how long the police may use video surveillance or the procedure specified. The terms and conditions will likely specify the method that should be used to install the device, so that the entry into the place is authorized.

TRACKING WARRANT: SECTION 492.1 C.C.

A tracking warrant is a relatively new warrant that any citizen or police officer may obtain. A **tracking device** is defined as any device that may help ascertain the location of any thing or person, by electronic or other means, when the device is installed in or on any thing.[77]

The installation of a tracking device for surveillance purposes constitutes a search. The S.C.C., in *R. v. Wise* (1992),[78] ruled that the installation of a tracking device without a warrant constitutes a s. 8 Charter violation: the warrantless installation of a tracking device constitutes an unreasonable search because it violates a person's reasonable expectation of privacy.

Section 492.1 C.C. creates the authority for a citizen or police officer to apply for and obtain a warrant for

- the installation, maintenance, and removal of a tracking device, in or on any thing, including a thing carried, used, or worn by any person; and
- the monitoring of the installed tracking device.

This new warrant was enacted in 1993, in response to the *R. v. Wise* decision. Its purpose is to obtain information that is relevant to an offence, including information about the whereabouts of a person. Section 492.1 C.C. does not restrict the type of place where entry may be made to install the tracking device. The warrant authorizes entry into any place, including a dwelling-house.

An Information to Obtain must be completed to apply for a tracking warrant. If the application is accepted, a tracking warrant is issued and is valid for a maximum of 60 days.[79]

OBTAIN AND EXECUTE A TRACKING WARRANT: PROCEDURE

Steps

The following procedure is used to apply for a tracking warrant.

STEP 1

An Information to Obtain must be completed. The applicant may be a citizen or a police officer.

STEP 2

Section 492.1 C.C. does not specify what form must be used to apply for the tracking warrant itself. Form 1 (Information to Obtain, illustrated in s. 841 C.C.) may be adapted for use in applying for a tracking warrant.

STEP 3

The Information to Obtain must include a written account of why there are reasonable grounds to suspect that

- any offence under a Canadian federal statute has been or will be committed, and
- a tracking device will help obtain *relevant information* regarding the commission of that offence, including the whereabouts of any person involved in it.

The key points of this rule are as follows:

- The applicant's belief does not have to be as strong as the one required to obtain a s. 487 C.C. search warrant, the applicant needs to prove only that a reasonable suspicion exists.
- A tracking warrant may be used during investigations of offences under the *Criminal Code*, the *Controlled Drugs and Substances Act*, or any other federal statute.
- There are no restrictions about the type of information that can be acquired through the use of a tracking device. It may be directed at any relevant information, including the location of any person.

STEP 4

The Information to Obtain must specify the item, and the location of the item, in or on which the tracking device is intended to be installed.

The key points of this rule are as follows.

- ▸ Section 492.1 C.C. uses the singular form of "a tracking device," signifying that the installation of only one tracking device may be applied for on one Information to Obtain. If more than one tracking device is required, a separate Information to Obtain must be completed for each individual tracking device.
- ▸ Only one item may be named as the site of the tracking device's installation, because the section uses the singular form of "thing." No restriction is placed on the type of "thing" in or on which the device may be installed. The only requirement is that the "thing" be capable of having a tracking device installed in it or on it. The item may include clothes or any "thing" carried, used, or worn by a person.
- ▸ The location of the item must be specified. This is required so that the Justice can authorize *entry into the place* where the item is situated so the tracking device can be installed in it.

STEP 5

The Information to Obtain must be signed by the applicant and brought to a Justice (JP or provincial court judge). The applicant must swear the Information under oath.

STEP 6

The JP evaluates the Information to Obtain and determines whether a reasonable suspicion exists that relevant information can be obtained, through the use of a tracking device, about an offence that has been or will be committed.

The application may be rejected, with the JP denying the warrant. If this happens, other applications may be made subsequently, when additional evidence is obtained to justify the need for the warrant.

If the Justice is satisfied that a reasonable suspicion exists, he or she may issue the tracking warrant. Section 492.1 C.C. does not specify a form on which a tracking warrant must be issued. Consequently, Form 5 (a s. 487 C.C. search warrant, illustrated in s. 841 C.C.) may be adapted to suit the case.

The Justice must specify a time period on the warrant, not exceeding 60 days. The warrant is valid during this specified time period, allowing the tracking device to be *maintained* and *monitored*.

STEP 7

After the authorized time period expires, the original warrant authorizes the removal of the tracking device and entry into a place to accomplish this. A Justice may issue further tracking warrants after the original one expires.[80] The original warrant cannot simply be extended. Instead, if additional time is required, an Information to Obtain must be submitted to the Justice for each subsequent application.

NUMBER RECORDER WARRANT: SECTION 492.2 C.C.

A number recorder warrant is another relatively new warrant that any citizen or police officer may obtain. A **number recorder** is defined as any device that can be used to *record or identify*

1. a telephone number, or
2. the location of the telephone from which a telephone call originates or at which it is received or is intended to be received.[81]

The recorder is also called a DNR, referring to a dial or digital number recorder. The device is attached to a telephone number. The DNR is commonly used on the suspect's telephone to monitor his or her outgoing calls. It is activated when the telephone is taken "off the hook." The monitored telephone emits electronic impulses that are recorded on a computer printout tape. The tape also discloses the telephone number dialled when an outgoing call is made. The DNR does not record

- whether the receiving telephone was answered, or
- the conversation.[82]

DNR signals are not private communications.

Consequently, the authorization to intercept private communications, as permitted by s. 184 C.C., does not apply to DNR signals and does not have to be obtained to use DNR. If an incoming call is made to the monitored phone, the DNR records only that the phone is "off the hook" and the length of time that it is "off the hook."[83]

Phone companies possess tracing devices that are installed on complainant's telephones, with the consent of the complainant. A **trace device** is used as an investigative means of determining a suspect in order to use a DNR. For example, if a person is receiving obscene phone calls and the caller's identity is unknown, a trace device is installed on the complainant's telephone with the complainant's consent. The trace device can determine the source of the call by identifying the address and the name of the person to whom the phone circuit is registered. Afterward, a DNR may be used to monitor the outgoing phone calls made by the suspect.[84]

The recording or identifying of a telephone number by means of a DNR constitutes a search.[85] Bell Canada may conduct this type of search without a warrant if it is conducted without direction from the police. Bell Canada is not a state agent if it conducts a DNR search without the police initiating the process.[86]

However, any DNR search initiated or requested by the police requires a number recorder warrant. The s. 492.2 C.C. warrant also authorizes the seizure of any telephone records of calls that originated from a particular telephone, or that were received or intended to be received at a particular telephone.

OBTAIN AND EXECUTE A NUMBER RECORDER WARRANT: PROCEDURE

Steps

The following procedure applies to a number recorder warrant.

STEP 1

An application must be made using an Information to Obtain. Section 492.2 C.C. does not specify a document that must be used to apply. Therefore, Form 1 (as illustrated in s. 841 C.C.) may be adapted for use as the application for this type of warrant.

STEP 2

A citizen or police officer may be the applicant (the "informant").

STEP 3

The Information to Obtain must include a written account of the evidence constituting reasonable grounds to *suspect*

- that any criminal offence under any federal statute has been or will be committed, and
- that information useful to the investigation of that offence could be obtained through the use of a DNR.[87]

STEP 4

The Information to Obtain must also include

- the suspect's name, address, and telephone number, or
- the address of a place (for example, Bell Canada) where any person or body lawfully possesses records of telephone calls originating from, or received by, or intended to be received by the suspect.

STEP 5

The Information to Obtain must be brought to a Justice and signed by the informant. The informant must swear the Information to Obtain under oath.

STEP 6

The Justice evaluates the Information to Obtain and denies or issues a warrant.

If the warrant is issued, the Justice may use Form 5 and adapt it to suit the case. Section 492.2 C.C. does not specify a form that must be used as the warrant.

The Justice must specify a time period on the warrant, not exceeding 60 days, for which the warrant will be valid.[88]

STEP 7

The warrant authorizes the installation, maintenance, and removal of the DNR, and the monitoring of the DNR during the time period specified on the warrant. After the time period expires, the Justice may issue further warrants, if further applications are made to justify the new warrants. The original warrant cannot simply be extended without new applications.[89]

FORENSIC DNA ANALYSIS: SECTION 487.04 WARRANT

This search warrant came into force in July 1995. It authorizes the seizure of certain bodily substances, in restricted circumstances, for the purpose of forensic DNA analysis.

This warrant represents a significantly advantageous investigative procedure for the police. Prior to its introduction there was no specific authority enabling police to seize bodily substances for forensic DNA analysis. Police had relied on indirect authorities, such as consent and search of a person after an arrest. Sometimes these seizures were ruled to be s. 8 Charter violations and were excluded under s. 24(2) Charter.

The letters DNA stand for deoxyribonucleic acid.[90] **Forensic DNA analysis** is defined as the analysis of the bodily substance obtained in execution of a warrant, and the comparison of the result of that analysis with the results of the analysis of the DNA of the bodily substance found at the crime scene, on or within the victim's body, or on or within the body of any person or thing associated with the commission of the offence.[91]

Forensic DNA analysis warrants may be obtained only in relation to certain designated offences, including:

- murder,
- manslaughter,
- robbery,
- break, enter with intent,
- break, enter and commit,
- arson (all types),
- mischief causing danger to life,
- sexual offences,
- assault causing bodily harm,
- assault with a weapon,
- aggravated assault,
- unlawfully causing bodily harm,
- piratical acts,
- kidnapping,
- hostage taking,
- hijacking,
- criminal negligence causing bodily harm, and
- criminal negligence causing death.

OBTAIN AND EXECUTE A SECTION 487.04 WARRANT: PROCEDURE

Steps

The following procedure applies to a s. 487.04 warrant.

STEP 1

An application is made by completing an Information to Obtain. A police officer must be the informant. The contents of the Information to Obtain must include a demonstration that there are reasonable grounds to believe that

- a designated offence has been committed,
- a bodily substance has been found
  - at the place where the offence was committed,
  - on or within the victim's body,
  - on anything worn or carried by the victim at the time when the offence was committed,
  - on or within the body of any person or thing, or
  - at any place associated with the commission of the offence,
- a person was a party to the offence, and
- forensic DNA analysis of a bodily substance from the person will provide evidence about whether the bodily substance was from that person.[92]

STEP 2

The Information to Obtain must be sworn before a provincial court judge only. A JP cannot issue this warrant. The judge may issue the warrant if he or she is satisfied that the reasonable grounds belief exists and that it is in the best interests of the administration of justice to issue the warrant.[93] The determining factors are

- the nature and circumstances of the designated offence;
- whether there is a police officer who is able, by virtue of training or experience, to obtain a bodily substance by means of a specified investigative procedure; or
- whether there is another person who has the training or experience to obtain the bodily substance by means of a specific investigative procedure, under the direction of a police officer.[94]

If issued, the warrant authorizes a police officer to obtain, or to cause another person to obtain under his or her direction, a bodily substance from the person mentioned in the warrant. The only bodily substances that may be seized are hair, saliva, and blood. The procedures used to obtain the particular bodily substances are restricted to the following:

- *hair*—the plucking of individual hairs from the person, including the root sheath;
- *saliva*—the taking of buccal swabs by swabbing the lips, tongue, and the insides of the cheeks, to collect epithelial cells; and
- *blood*—the taking of blood by pricking the skin surface with a sterile lancet.[95]

Only one of these substances may be seized per warrant. The warrant must include any terms and conditions that the judge considers advisable to ensure that the seizure is reasonable.[96]

STEP 3

Before executing a forensic DNA analysis warrant, a police officer has a mandatory obligation to inform the person of the following:

- the contents of the warrant,
- the nature of the investigative procedure that will be used,
- the purpose of obtaining the bodily substance,
- the possibility that the results of forensic DNA analysis may be used as evidence at a trial, and
- that the police officer and anyone under his or her direction has authority to use as much force as is necessary to execute the warrant.

Young Offender

A young offender has the right to a reasonable opportunity to consult with and have present at the time the warrant is executed any of the following persons:

- a lawyer,
- a parent,
- an adult relative, or
- any appropriate adult chosen by the young offender.[97]

STEP 4

The executing officer has the authority to

- detain the person for a reasonable period, and
- require the person to accompany him or her, as part of the process of executing the warrant.[98]

Right to Counsel

Although this section does not make it mandatory for police, before executing a warrant, to inform an adult offender of his or her right to counsel, adult offenders should be informed of this right because they will have been detained during the execution of the warrant. Section 10(b) Charter imposes an obligation on police to inform any person who has been detained of his or her right to counsel.

Both adult and young offenders may waive the right to counsel. A young offender's waiver must be

- recorded on audiotape, or
- recorded on videotape, or
- recorded in writing and containing a statement signed by the young offender that he or she has been informed of the right.[99]

These requirements do not apply to adult offenders. However, recording an adult's waiver in this manner will help prove the credibility of the waiver. Otherwise, the waiver should be recorded verbatim in a notebook.

STEP 5

The bodily substance that is seized may be analyzed for DNA only in relation to the offence stated in the warrant. It cannot be used in the investigation of any other offence. Using the bodily substance or the DNA results of the analysis in connection with an investigation other than the one for the designated offence named on the warrant constitutes a summary conviction offence.

STEP 6

The bodily substance must be destroyed

> ▸ forthwith after the results show the person was not the offender; or
> ▸ one year after the person is acquitted at trial or discharged after a preliminary hearing.[100]

However, a provincial court judge may order that the bodily substance and the DNA analysis result not be destroyed if there are reasonable grounds to believe that they may be required in the investigation or prosecution of that person for another designated offence.[101]

IMPRESSION WARRANT: SECTION 487.092 C.C.

An "impression" includes a

> ▸ handprint,
> ▸ fingerprint,
> ▸ footprint,
> ▸ foot impression,
> ▸ teeth impression, or
> ▸ other print or impression of the body.

Prior to 1997 and the enactment of s. 487 C.C., no warrant existed that allowed the police to obtain these types of impressions from a person. The *Identification of Criminals Act* has long allowed the police to take fingerprints from a person after the person has been arrested or charged with an indictable offence. However, before 1997, impressions could be obtained only by consent.

Section 487.092 C.C. created a warrant enabling police to obtain impressions from a person. This provision apparently came about in response to *R. v. Stillman* (1997), a case in which it was ruled that taking dental impressions from an offender, without a warrant, as part of a search incident to arrest, constituted a s. 7 and s. 8 Charter violation.

In applying for an impression warrant, an Information to Obtain must first be presented, under oath, to a Justice. It must be proven there are reasonable grounds to believe that

> ▸ a criminal offence has been committed,
> ▸ information concerning the offence will be obtained by the print or impressions, and
> ▸ the issuance of the warrant is in the best interests of the administration of justice.

If satisfied that reasonable grounds do exist, the Justice may issue a warrant authorizing a police officer to do anything, or cause anything to be done under his or her direction, to obtain an impression from the person named in the warrant.

The warrant must include terms and conditions that the Justice considers advisable, as a way of ensuring that the search and seizure is reasonable in the circumstances.

SUMMARY

Regardless of the type of warrant for which an officer applies, reasonable grounds that specific evidence is located in a specific place is necessary to obtain the warrant. As explained in the introduction of this chapter, the only time an officer would not obtain a warrant is when consent to search is granted, or when there are exigent circumstances. The next chapter deals with "warrantless" search and the situations that apply to this authority.

PROBLEM-SOLVING CASE STUDIES

You are a police officer in each case. Each offender is an adult, unless otherwise indicated.

Problem 1

You are investigating a "Theft under $5,000.00" offence that occurred at a business premises in a shopping mall 10 minutes ago. You receive information that gives you reasonable grounds to believe that the stolen property is in a car owned by Carl. The car is parked on King St., in front of Carl's house.

  a. Can a s. 487 C.C. search warrant be obtained to search Carl's car for stolen property?

  _____

  _____

  b. What other authority may be used to search Carl's car for the stolen property?

  _____

  _____

Problem 2

You are investigating a summary conviction offence, and you form reasonable grounds to believe that an item that represents evidence about the offence is currently in Tom's office. Can a s. 487 C.C. search warrant be obtained in relation to this classification of offence?

_____

_____

Problem 3

You form reasonable grounds that Victor committed a robbery yesterday.

a. Today, you form a reasonable grounds belief that a letter written by Victor is in Carl's house. The letter states Victor's new address. Can a s. 487 C.C. search warrant be obtained to search the house for the letter?

_____

_____

_____

b. Today, you form reasonable grounds to believe that Victor is currently in a house situated at 10 King St. Can a s. 487 C.C. search warrant be obtained to enter the house and search for Victor?

_____

_____

_____

Problem 4

You are investigating a robbery, and you form reasonable grounds to believe that a mask and clothing worn by Ralph, the suspect, are currently in Ralph's house.

a. Can you enter and search the house without first obtaining a s. 487 C.C. search warrant and without consent if you suspect that the evidence will be destroyed before you arrive with the warrant?

_____

_____

b. Can you obtain a s. 487 C.C. search warrant without first completing an Information to Obtain?

_____

_____

Problem 5

You are investigating a "Theft over $5,000.00" offence. You receive information that the stolen items may be in either Mary's office, Betty's house, or Gloria's car.

a. Can you complete one Information to Obtain to search all three places?

_____

_____

b. Will you be able to obtain three search warrants to search each of the three places, under these circumstances?

_____

_____

_____

Problem 6

You are investigating a murder. You determine that John is a suspect and that he is temporarily living at Gord's house. Can you apply for a search warrant and write "any evidence relating to the murder" as the "items" on the Information to Obtain?

_____

_____

_____

_____

Problem 7

Marg reports the following to you at 10:00 p.m. today. She was in Jeanette's house 30 minutes ago. Jeanette's brother Reg and his friend Dave were present. Reg showed Dave a 20-inch colour TV set that was operating in the living room and told him that he stole it last night when he committed a break and enter at The Store. Reg asked Dave and Marg if either wanted to buy it. Both declined. Reg left a few minutes later. Marg has known Reg for 15 years, and she has given you accurate confidential information in the past. She is associated with many known criminals. You begin writing an Information to Obtain.

a. Can you list the item to be searched for as a "20-inch colour TV"?

_____

_____

_____

_____

b. Do you have to name an offence for which the TV will be evidence?

_____

_____

_____

_____

c. What should be the first part of your written account of the reasonable grounds?

_____

_____

d. If you do not know that Jeanette is the owner of the house, will the warrant be automatically rejected?

_____

_____

_____

_____

e. Can you protect Marg's identity on your written account of the reasonable grounds?

_____

_____

_____

_____

_____

_____

_____

f. Will the following statement in Appendix B (reasonable grounds narrative) constitute reasonable grounds: "Information has been received from an anonymous informant that a stolen TV is inside Jeanette's house"?

_____

_____

_____

_____

_____

_____

_____

_____

_____

g. Will Marg's information likely constitute reasonable grounds?

_____

_____

_____

_____

h. To what should the last part of the written grounds refer?

_____

i. Can you get advice from the JP about what to include in the contents of your written account of the grounds for belief?

_____

_____

j. Where do you have to meet the JP to present the Information to Obtain?

_____

k. Can you give the JP an unsigned Information to Obtain and solicit his or her opinion about accuracy and sufficiency?

_____

_____

l. You sign the Information to Obtain and swear the contents under oath. What will occur next?

_____

_____

_____

m. The JP decides that reasonable grounds exist and that he or she will issue the search warrant. Who keeps the original Information to Obtain?

_____

n. Which officers must be named on the search warrant?

_____

_____

_____

o. Can this warrant be executed at night?

_____

_____

p. You attend at Jeanette's house to execute the warrant. How many officers can participate in the search?

_____

q. Can you enter the house forcibly without any announcement?

_____

r. You receive no answer and believe no one is home. Can you execute the warrant?

_____

_____

_____

_____

s. If Reg is home and answers the door, what do you have to inform him of or give to him?

_____

t. Four other people are inside the house. Does the search warrant authorize the arrest and search of the occupants?

_____

u. If Reg immediately gives you the TV, the only item listed, can you continue searching the house?

_____

_____

v. You complete the search, and the TV is not found. You and all the officers leave the premises. You phone Marg, who tells you that Reg called her and said that he saw the police arrive and he hid the TV in the attic before they entered. Can you return and search the house on the authority of the original warrant?

_____

_____

w. Could you have gone to Reg's house and arrested him for "break, enter, and theft" without first applying for the search warrant?

_____

_____

Problem 8

You receive confidential information from Theodore that Carl has one pound of cocaine in a gas station that Carl owns. What type of search warrant should you obtain?

_____

_____

_____

Problem 9

You receive information from Carl that one pound of marijuana is in June's house.

a. What type of search warrant should you obtain?

_____

b. You apply for a C.D.S.A. search warrant. Do the rules regarding the Information to Obtain differ from those for applying for a s. 487 C.C. search warrant?

_____

c. The JP authorizes a search warrant. What officers must be named on it?

_____

_____

_____

d. Does the named officer have to participate in the search?

_____

e. How many officers may participate in the search?

_____

_____

f. Can a C.D.S.A. search warrant be automatically executed at night?

_____

ENDNOTES

1. *R. v. J.E.B.*, 1989 CanLII 1495 (N.S.C.A.).
2. *R. v. Purdy* (1972), 8 C.C.C. (2d) 52 (N.B.S.C.).
3. *Church of Scientology and the Queen (No. 6)* (1987), 31 C.C.C. (3d) 449 (Ont. C.A.).
4. Ibid.
5. Ibid.
6. *R. v. Purdy*, supra note 2.
7. *Church of Scientology*, supra note 3.
8. Ibid.
9. *R. v. Purdy*, supra note 2.
10. *R. v. Scott* (1990), 61 C.C.C. (3d) 300 (S.C.C.).
11. *Bisaillon v. Keable* (1983), 7 C.C.C. (3d) 385, at 411-12 (S.C.C.).
12. *R. v. Zammit* (1993), 81 C.C.C. (3d) 112 (Ont. C.A.).
13. *R. v. Debot* (1989), 52 C.C.C. (3d) 193 (S.C.C.).
14. Ibid.
15. Ibid.
16. Ibid.
17. Ibid.
18. Ibid., at 195.
19. *R. v. Kelly* (1995), 90 C.C.C. (3d) 367 (B.C.C.A.).
20. Ibid.
21. Ibid.
22. *R. v. Gray* (1993), 81 C.C.C. (3d) 174 (Man. C.A.).
23. Ibid.
24. Ibid. and *Hunter et al. v. Southam Inc.* (1984), 14 C.C.C. (3d) 97 (S.C.C.).
25. *R. v. Gray*, supra note 22.
26. *R. v. Eng* 1995 CanLII 1794 (B.C.C.A.).
27. Part XXVIII C.C.
28. Section 488 C.C.
29. Section 2 C.C.
30. Section 487.01(7) C.C.
31. Section 487.05(3) C.C.
32. Section 487.09(4) C.C.
33. Section 529.5 C.C.
34. Section 487.1 C.C.
35. *Eccles v. Bourque* (1974), 19 C.C.C. (2) 129, at 133-34 (S.C.C.); *R. v. Genest* (1989), 45 C.C.C. (3d) 385 (S.C.C.).
36. *R. v. Genest*, ibid.
37. Ibid.
38. *R. v. Grenier* (1991), 65 C.C.C. (3d) 76 (Que. C.A.).
39. *R. v. McGregor* (1985), 23 C.C.C. (3d) 266 (Man. Q.B.).
40. Section 29(1) C.C.
41. *R. v. Silveira* (1995), 97 C.C.C. (3d) 450 (S.C.C.).
42. Section 495(1)(a) C.C.
43. Section 101(1) C.C.
44. Section 11 N.C.A.

45. Section 489 C.C.
46. *R. v. Moran* (1987), 36 C.C.C. (3d) 225 (Ont. C.A.).
47. Section 489.1(2) C.C.
48. Ibid.
49. Sections 490(1)(b) C.C. and 490(2)(b) C.C.
50. Section 490(2)(a) C.C.
51. Section 490(9.1) C.C.
52. Section 490(1)(a) C.C.
53. Section 489.1(1)(a) C.C.
54. Section 491.2 C.C.
55. Sections 491.2(2) and 491.2(3) C.C.
56. Section 491.2 (5) C.C.
57. *MacIntyre v. Nova Scotia (A.G.)* (1982), 65 C.C.C. (2d) 129 (S.C.C.).
58. Section 11(1) C.D.S.A.
59. Section 11(6) C.D.S.A.
60. *R. v. Scott* (1990), 61 C.C.C. (3d) 300, at 313-14 (S.C.C.).
61. Section 12 N.C.A.
62. *R. v. Strachan* (1988), 46 C.C.C. (3d) 479 (S.C.C.).
63. *R. v. Genest*, supra note 36.
64. *R. v. Gimson* (1991), 69 C.C.C. (3d) 552 (S.C.C.).
65. *R. v. Genest*, supra note 36.
66. *R. v. McGregor*, supra note 39.
67. Section 29(1) C.C.
68. Section 11(5) C.D.S.A.
69. Section 11(6) C.D.S.A.
70. Section 11(8) C.D.S.A.
71. Sections 13(4) and 13(5) C.D.S.A.
72. *R. v. Wong* (1993), 60 C.C.C. (3d) 460 (S.C.C.).
73. Section 487.01(4) C.C. and *R. v. Noseworthy* (1995), 101 C.C.C. (3d) 460 (Ont. Gen. Div.).
74. *Canada Post Corp. v. Canada (Attorney General)* (1995), 95 C.C.C. (3d) 568 (Ont. Gen. Div.).
75. Section 487.01(4) C.C.
76. Section 487.01(3) C.C.
77. Section 492.1(4) C.C.
78. *R. v. Wise* (1992), 70 C.C.C. (3d) 193 (S.C.C.).
79. Section 492.1(2) C.C.
80. Section 492.1(3) C.C.
81. Section 492.2(4) C.C.
82. *R. v. Fegan* (1993), 80 C.C.C. (3d) 356, at 363-64 (Ont. C.A.).
83. Ibid.
84. Ibid.
85. Ibid.
86. Ibid.
87. Section 492.2(1) C.C.
88. Section 492.2(3) C.C.
89. Section 492.2(3) C.C.
90. Section 487.04 C.C.

91. Section 487.04 C.C.
92. Section 487.05(1) C.C.
93. Section 487.05(1) C.C.
94. Section 487.05(2) C.C.
95. Section 487.06(1) C.C.
96. Section 487.06(2) C.C.
97. Sections 487.07(1) and 487.07(4) C.C.
98. Section 487.07(2) C.C.
99. Section 487.07(5) C.C.
100. Section 487.09(1) C.C.
101. Section 487.09(2) C.C.

CHAPTER 17

Search and Seizure, Part 4: Warrantless Search

LEARNING OUTCOMES

The student will learn

- How to interpret and apply the common-law "search incident to arrest"
- How to interpret and apply the plain-view doctrine
- How to interpret and apply firearm and weapon searches without a warrant and without consent
- How to define terms relevant to firearms and weapons
- How to obtain a firearms and weapons search warrant
- How to make a "return"
- How to interpret and apply warrantless search authorities under the C.D.S.A.
- How to interpret and apply s. 487.11 C.C. (warrantless search for ordinary evidence)
- How to prevent Charter violations in connection with warrantless searches

INTRODUCTION: CONCEPT OF WARRANTLESS SEARCH

Also known as "search without warrant," a **warrantless search** is defined as a search without judicial authorization and without consent. Warrantless searches are based on one basic authority—exigent circumstances, or urgency, that allows no time to get a warrant.

The warrantless search authorities are not neatly listed in one statute. They are found in various sources of law including common law, case law, the *Criminal Code*, and the C.D.S.A.

There are eight warrantless search authorities:

1. search of person after arrest (search incident to arrest)
2. search of person incident to investigative detention
3. plain-view doctrine
4. section 489 C.C.
5. firearms and weapons (ss. 117.02 and 117.04(2) C.C.)
6. drugs (s. 11(7) C.D.S.A.)
7. warrantless entry to preserve evidence while awaiting search warrant
8. section 487.11 C.C. (evidence to any offence)

SEARCH INCIDENT TO ARREST

Police officers are authorized to immediately search a lawfully arrested person and may seize the following:

1. Evidence relating to any offence—not just the offence for which the accused was arrested but any other, unrelated offence. The evidence may be any item in the accused's possession or any clothing that is evidence of an offence. Police stations have suitable apparel for accused persons to wear while in police custody if their clothing is seized as evidence.
2. Items capable of causing injury to any person, including the accused. To prevent injury or suicide, police may seize from the accused, before he or she enters a police jail cell, clothing, jewellery, or other items in pockets. Belts, shoelaces, jewellery, and lighters should always be seized and kept in a property locker while the accused is in a police jail cell. The accused is usually allowed to wear his or her own clothing. Clothing should be seized only when there is some evidence that the accused is suicidal. All efforts must be made to prevent a suicide while an accused is in police custody.
3. Any item that can facilitate escape.[1]

The only item that cannot be seized without consent is money that is not evidence and is lawfully owned by the accused.[2] Usually, an officer asks for the accused's consent to put the money in a police property locker for safekeeping while the accused is in the police cells. Consent is commonly given.

Items seized that are evidence of any offence may be kept until court proceedings conclude. Items that are seized not because they constitute evidence or are illegal but to the end of preventing injury or escape must be returned to the accused at the time of his or her release from custody.

A person may be *automatically* and immediately searched upon being arrested. This means that the arresting officer *does not have to prove* that there were reasonable grounds for believing that the accused possessed any of the items that may be seized.[3] The only requirement in this case is that lawful authority existed to arrest.

The S.C.C. stated that the *exercise of this authority*, with respect to the actual extent of the search, is not unlimited. The court explained this rule as follows:

1. This search authority does not impose a duty upon the police. Officers do have discretion not to search an arrested person when the officer is satisfied that such a search is unnecessary.

2. The focus of the search must be weapons and evidence. The search cannot be used to "intimidate, ridicule, or pressure" the arrested person to obtain a confession.

3. The search cannot be conducted in an "abusive fashion," with unjustified physical or psychological constraint. [4]

The authority to search after an arrest is not found in any Canadian statute. It is a common-law authority, originating in English cases in 1853. Canadian courts recognized this common-law authority in 1895. The S.C.C., in *Cloutier v. Langlois* (1990), supported the lawfulness of the search of an arrested person. The common-law authority "is formally called a "search incident of arrest."

Commentary

It is difficult to imagine how a police officer can be positively satisfied beyond all doubt that an arrested person is unarmed without searching his or her person. Any arrest poses a potential risk to the arresting officer.

Any officer who has routinely arrested persons has learned through experience that no arrested person may be assumed to be unarmed or incapable of using violence.

Delay Between Arrest and Search

The common-law **search-incident-to-arrest authority** does not specify how much time may elapse between the arrest and the search. During some investigations, a delay may occur. The S.C.C., in *R. v. Caslake* (1998),[5] made significant rulings about this issue. The *Caslake* decision is also relevant to questions concerning

1. whether the common-law search authority extends to vehicles, and
2. the validity of an "inventory search" of a car conducted hours after the arrest.

See Chapter 5 for the complete case law decision.

Immediate Surroundings

This authority permits an officer to search not only the arrested person but the **immediate surroundings** of the place where the person was arrested. No warrant or consent is required. What constitutes "immediate surroundings" has not been specifically defined by the S.C.C. The size of the area searched is governed by the s. 8 Charter requirement of *reasonableness*. Appeal courts in Ontario and British Columbia have ruled that immediate surroundings include the following areas, when the accused is arrested in a vehicle:

- the interior of the vehicle (O.C.A. and B.C.C.A.),[6]
- the trunk of a vehicle (B.C.C.A.),[7] and
- the inside of a vehicle door, after the police remove a door panel (B.C.C.A.).[8]

Other case law decisions have established the following guidelines regarding the immediate surroundings of places other than vehicles.

R. v. LIM (1990)

In *R. v. Lim* (1990), the Ontario High Court of Justice stated, "The scene of an arrest may yield valuable evidence which will assist the police in their investigation and in determining what should be done with the arrested person. This common sense proposition lies at the root of the common-law rationale for searches as an incident of arrest."[9]

The court added that warrantless searches after an arrest are justified because they permit prompt and effective seizure of evidence relevant to the accused's guilt or innocence. Finally, a guideline significantly advantageous to police was created when the court set out to determine whether a s. 8 Charter violation occurs when immediate surroundings are searched after an arrest. The court established that the purpose of s. 8 Charter is to protect individual privacy expectations from unwarranted searches. However, a lawful arrest reduces the arrested person's expectation of privacy. Although this guideline does not define a specific area, it implies that officers have considerable latitude when it comes to their authority to search the immediate surroundings after an arrest.

R. v. SMELLIE (1994)

In *R. v. Smellie* (1994),[10] the British Columbia Court of Appeal ruled that the immediate surroundings includes the entirety of what may reasonably be considered the surroundings. This suggests that if the accused is arrested inside a place, the entire room where the accused is arrested may be searched without a warrant. It does not imply that the entire house or premises may be searched.

Arrest Outside a House

In some cases, a person is arrested outside a house but in close proximity to it. The question arises whether the house may be searched without a warrant as a search incident to arrest.

In *R. v. Golub* (1997),[11] an accused person was arrested outside his house, about 4.5 metres (14 feet) from the door. The police had reasonable grounds to believe that a firearm was in the house and suspected that someone else may have been in the house. Officers entered without a warrant, searched the entire house for other persons, and seized a loaded rifle. In that case, the Ontario Court of Appeal ruled that the search was a justified search incident to arrest.

The court created the following procedural guidelines about warrantless entry and the search of a house when an arrest is made outside the house but in close proximity to it:

1. A search is justified when "**exceptional circumstances**" exist.
2. "Exceptional circumstances" are defined as situations "where the law enforcement interest is so compelling that it overrides the individual's right to privacy within the home."
3. The risk of physical harm to persons at an arrest scene constitutes exceptional circumstances that justify a warrantless entry and search of the house.

Note: Refer to Chapter 5 for the complete circumstances of *R. v. Golub*. This case features a justified warrantless search of a dwelling-house when the accused is arrested outside, in close proximity.

In summary, the common-law search-after-arrest authority is an advantage for police; it permits them to search persons and partial places automatically, without a warrant. The primary purpose of this authority is to protect police. An immediate search should be conducted after any arrest, regardless of how minor the offence may be, to prevent any harm being done to the arresting officer.

The Alberta Court of Appeal, in *R. v. Lerke* (1986), agreed with this opinion, stating that

> the reluctance of Canadian courts to invalidate searches after arrest is understandable. Judges cannot be blind to the deaths and injuries suffered by police officers on duty as guns and knives become more common. Situations which appear quite innocent, with no hostile demonstration by the person being arrested, can explode into violence leaving the arresting officer dead or injured. It is difficult to second-guess any police officer who ensures that a person is not armed when he perceives danger as he makes an arrest or escorts a prisoner.[12]

SEARCH INCIDENT TO INVESTIGATIVE DETENTION

Chapter 4 of this text explained the investigative detention authority and corresponding **search incident to investigative detention**. *R. v. Mann* (2004) was included in that chapter. That leading case is a primary point of reference with respect to investigative detention and the authority supporting it. *R. v. Clayton* (2007) is also a landmark S.C.C. decision. It expands the police authority to perform investigative detention and the accompanying search to emergencies where reasonable suspicion is directed at a *group* of possible suspects. Specifically, it authorizes roadblocks and investigative detention in "911 gun call" investigations.[13]

911 is one example of a **distress call.** There are two categories of distress calls— *expressed* and *implied.* A distress call can come from a dwelling-house or from a non-residential place. There are innumerable circumstances surrounding every distress call. No type of investigation is more challenging or more dangerous to the front-line officer. This chapter will include only the *R. v. Clayton* decision because it is the case that best explains the expanded authority for search incident to investigative detention. But there are many other case law decisions relevant to distress calls. You can find a review of these decisions in the following two sources:

1. the fifth edition of the accompanying textbook, *Criminal Investigation: Forming Reasonable Grounds*, which contains an entire chapter devoted to "First Officer" response to expressed and implied distress calls; and
2. the website that accompanies this textbook: **www.emp.ca/arcaro/ policepowers4E.**

CASE LAW

R. v. Clayton (2007)

- **Issues:** A 911 call has two simple elements: (a) emergency and (b) uncertainty. It represents for police imminent risk of death or serious injury, along with two significant investigative limitations: (a) time, and (b) information. These are the real limitations posed by a 911 call—minimal time and minimal information for making life-or-death decisions in a rapidly changing situation.

  Put yourself in the shoes of a front-line police officer who receives a radio broadcast that simply reports the following: "911—group of men armed with guns at a bar." Policing is a continual process of establishing a belief and deciding on a response. You receive a wide range of information, form an appropriate belief, and make the corresponding response. The investigative response is proportionate to and governed by the belief. The 911 call stimulates a single and unvarying belief: danger exists. That belief is non-negotiable and undeniable. The 911 call legitimately puts police into optimum self-protection mode.

  A 911 call binds the police. The public has two expectations of the police—protection and privacy. Members of the public want to be protected without their privacy unreasonably invaded. The police can neither neglect a problem nor exceed their authority to intervene. Striking this balance is enormously challenging. But the reality of front-line policing is this—public safety and officer safety always come first. It's instinctive and obvious. Safety always has and always will supersede all other objectives. Every officer's first goal is to prevent death and injury. If you polled any number of Canadian citizens, they would by an overwhelming margin support this idea.

- **Offences:** "Carrying concealed weapon" and "possession of prohibited firearm."

- **Circumstances:** Within minutes of receiving a 911 call reporting that a number of persons were openly displaying handguns in a strip club's parking lot, the police stopped the first car leaving the lot's rear exit. The car's two occupants, accused person #1 (driver) and accused person #2 (passenger), were searched. Each had a loaded semi-automatic handgun—weapons prohibited by the *Criminal Code*. The following is a summary of the events.

  - 1:22 a.m.: A 911 call was received reporting that four of about 10 men (identified by race) were in a parking lot in front of a strip club, openly displaying handguns. The caller identified four vehicles in his report. The dispatcher broadcast a "gun call," and a number of police officers immediately responded.
  - 1:26 a.m.: Constables #1 and #2 positioned their police vehicle at the rear exit of the club's parking lot. Almost immediately, a car left the offence scene and drove toward the exit. However, this car was not one of the four reported by the 911 caller.
  - 1:27 a.m.: Constables #1 and #2 stopped the car. They saw that the occupants (the accused persons) were both male and both of the race reported by the caller. Constable #2 approached one of the accused persons (the driver) and told him that there had been a gun complaint. He asked the driver to exit the car and became concerned for his own safety, because the driver "protested twice" before exiting the car. Constable #2 asked the driver to put his hands on the top of the car.

(continued)

- ▸ Constable #1 approached the passenger (accused #2) and began questioning him. The passenger gave "strange and evasive answers and stared straight ahead, avoiding eye contact." He wore gloves, even though it was not "glove weather." Constable #1 asked the passenger to exit the car and to place his hands on the rear of the car. The passenger exited the car, but stood blocking Constable #1's sightline to the inside of the car.
- ▸ When Constable #1 put his hand on the passenger's shoulder to direct him to the back of the car, the passenger shoved Constable #1 and ran away. Both officers pursued him while another constable (#3) watched the driver.
- ▸ Officers in front of the club subdued the passenger (accused #2). Constable #1 searched him and found a loaded, prohibited handgun in his pocket. Constable #3 arrested the driver for possession of a loaded, prohibited weapon after one was found under his jacket.

- ■ **Trial:** Both accused persons were convicted. The trial judge ruled that the officers' stopping of both accused was lawful, but that their further detention and search violated ss. 8 and 9 Charter. Despite the Charter violations, he admitted the guns into evidence under s. 24(2) Charter. The two accused were convicted of carrying concealed weapons and the possession of loaded, prohibited firearms. The trial judge concluded that the police investigation was a "legitimate response to safety concerns in a fast-paced situation."

- ■ **Ontario Court of Appeal:** Incredibly, the accused persons' appeals were allowed, and both were acquitted. The court ruled that the seizure constituted Charter violations. The evidence of the handguns was excluded under s. 24(2) Charter.

  The Ontario Court of Appeal made an absurd ruling—the roadblock was unlawful because there was "no imminent danger" and "no tailored response." Astonishingly, their verdict was that a call that reported multiple people at a strip club "openly displaying" guns constituted "no imminent danger." The Court actually expected the police to design under such circumstances a customized strategy, "tailored" to the specific circumstances of this 911 call. The Court also attributed the Charter violations to "institutional failures" of the police to adequately train their personnel.

- ■ **Supreme Court of Canada:** A unanimous decision by the S.C.C. reversed the absurd Ontario Court of Appeal decision. The Crown's appeal was allowed, and the convictions were restored. The following reasons were given:

  1. *Totality of circumstances.* The totality of the circumstances justified a reasonable suspicion that justified, in turn, the initial detention. Thus the roadblock, the stopping of the car, and the initial questioning were justified.
  2. *Reasonable necessity.* The circumstances in *R. v. Mann* directed reasonable suspicion to only one person. But it is possible that the totality of circumstances could cause reasonable suspicion to be directed to more than one person. In the *Mann* case, a detention was lawful because the appearance of the accused matched five features of a reported description of a suspect (given by the dispatcher, regarding a crime in progress: age, race, height, weight, and clothing), and the accused was in close proximity to the crime in progress (2–3 blocks away). Although the

(continued)

circumstances in the *Clayton* case were different, the detention of the suspect's car, as in *R. v. Mann*, was deemed to be "reasonably necessary."

3. *Reasonable measures.* The police concretely explained the rationale behind the strategy. The roadblocks were considered "reasonable measures" because the police had reasonable suspicion to believe that stopping cars leaving the parking lot was an "effective" investigative strategy.

4. *Quick response.* The police had detained the suspect's car within five minutes of the 911 call and within one minute of their arrival.

5. *Public safety risk.* The limited information given by the dispatcher "constituted reasonable grounds that public safety was at risk and that the handguns could be in the possession of those leaving the parking area."

Additionally, the S.C.C. ruled there was "no evidence" of institutional failure regarding police training. Not minimal evidence—*none*. The S.C.C. concluded that "tailored responses" to 911 calls would be "unreasonable burdens" imposed on the police.

COMMENTARY

The Globe and Mail (p. A8, Saturday, July 7, 2007) reported the following about the S.C.C. decision:

1. "civil rights groups fear ruling will clear way for broader police powers to invade privacy"; and

2. the vice-president of the Criminal Lawyers Association was "disappointed," saying that the "Supreme Court should not be expanding incursions into privacy and liberty—that's Parliament's job."

The S.C.C. must be applauded for overturning an absurd decision that would have placed police officers in needless binds during all future investigations of 911 gun calls.

Refer to the accompanying website, **www.emp.ca/arcaro/policepowers4E**, for the full case, verbatim. The actual case serves as excellent discussion and research material about how case law decisions are made. Pay special attention to the rulings of the trial judge, of the Ontario Court of Appeal, and of the S.C.C. Note the wide range of the judges' opinions. If the S.C.C. and the Ontario Court of Appeal can differ this strongly, imagine how hard it is to make decisions on the front line in life-threatening circumstances.

PLAIN-VIEW DOCTRINE AND SECTION 489(2) C.C.: SEIZURE WITHOUT WARRANT

Section 489(2) C.C. is a new "seizure without warrant" authority that was apparently enacted in response to a case law seizure authority called the "plain-view doctrine." The two seizure-without-warrant authorities are similar in conception, but s. 489(2) has a certain vagueness in comparison to the plain-view doctrine, which will be interpreted and explained here. Together, these two authorities effectively represent a significant advantage for police officers during investigations, because they permit the warrantless seizure of evidence, relating to any offence, that officers inadvertently find.

Section 489(2) C.C. says that police officers who are "lawfully present in a place pursuant to a warrant or otherwise in the execution of duties may, without a warrant, seize anything that the officer believes on reasonable grounds

▸ has been obtained, or
▸ has been used, or
▸ will afford evidence in respect of,

an offence against the *Criminal Code* or any act of Parliament."

To interpret this new authority, we must first explain the case law "plain-view doctrine" that preceded it, because it defines terms relevant to s. 489(2) C.C.

Plain-View Doctrine

The **plain-view doctrine** is a search-without-warrant authority found in case law. The plain-view rule authorizes police as follows: "A peace officer who is lawfully on any premises, whether pursuant to a warrant or otherwise, is permitted to seize any evidence, which is in plain view and which is inadvertently found."[14]

"Lawfully on any premises" includes being in a place by any of the following authorities:

1. a search warrant (any type);
2. consent, including by invitation to enter to take any type of report;
3. entry and search without warrant when authorized by a statute or case law; and
4. entry without a warrant pursuant to provincial statutes concerned with tenant protection. These statues permit the landlord to enter an apartment when an emergency exists and to bring a police officer to act as a witness.[15]

"Any premises" includes a dwelling-house or any other building. "Plain view" means clearly visible. "Inadvertently found" means *unexpectedly found*, with no prior knowledge the item was in the place and without physical effort to search for the item.

Under the plain-view doctrine, police may seize any item that proves the commission of any offence, including offences unrelated to the one police are investigating while lawfully on the premises.

The plain-view doctrine, based in American law, has been recognized and applied in Canada, in the following cases:

▸ *R. v. Shea* (1983) (Ontario H.C.J.),
▸ *R. v. Longtin* (1983) (Ontario C.A.),
▸ *R. v. Belliveau* (1986) (N.B. C.A.),
▸ *R. v. Nielsen* (1988) (Sask. C.A.), and
▸ *R. v. Grenier* (1991) (Quebec C.A.).[16]

Section 489(2) C.C. Interpretation

The following is a comparison of s. 489(2) C.C. and the plain-view doctrine:

1. **any peace officer**—Defined in section 2 C.C., this category does not include citizens.

2. **lawfully present in a place pursuant to a warrant or otherwise**

   a. "a place"—The exercise of this authority is not restricted to any type of place. Consequently, it can be used to seize evidence from any place, including

      ▸ a dwelling-house,
      ▸ a business premises,
      ▸ an office,
      ▸ a school, and
      ▸ a vehicle

   b. "lawfully present"—*Pursuant to a warrant or otherwise* means that the police can use this authority to seize evidence if their presence on the premises is authorized by any of the following:

      ▸ search warrant—any type, including s. 487 C.C. general warrant, s. 529 C.C. warrant to enter house, and C.D.S.A. search warrant;
      ▸ consent—including an invitation to enter a place to interview a complainant regarding any offence; and
      ▸ warrantless entry and search authorized by any federal or provincial statute.

3. **seize anything that is evidence**—While in the place, an officer may seize any item without a warrant if he or she can prove there are reasonable grounds to believe that the item will afford evidence of any criminal offence. This includes items that have been obtained by or used in the commission of any criminal offence recognized by the *Criminal Code* or the C.D.S.A. The item does not have to be evidence concerning the offence being investigated; it may be evidence of an unrelated offence. The type of item may be wide-ranging, including stolen property, weapons, drugs, and clothing. The officer must believe beyond mere suspicion that the item was obtained or used in an offence.

   The belief can be based on the officer's positive identification, on a witness's recognition, on the suspect's admission, or simply on the nature of the item, as in the case of drugs or an unlawful firearm.

4. **discovery of the item**—Section 489(2) C.C. does not authorize the search of a place or a person for evidence. The question that arises is the following: "How does the item have to be discovered in order for the warrantless seizure to be lawful?" The answer is not clearly stated in s. 489(2) C.C. No reference is made to the terms "plain view" or "inadvertent," which would have helped. However, the absence of a discernible authority to search suggests that the plain-view doctrine will be the authority determining the manner in which items may be discovered. Accordingly, a seizure under s. 489(2) C.C. may be made only if the item is in "plain view" and "inadvertent." **Inadvertent discovery** means finding unexpectedly, without prior knowledge that the item was in the place. The following are examples of an inadvertent discovery:

   ▸ A police officer responds to a complaint at a place such as a house. After being invited to enter, the officer sees an item that is evidence of a criminal offence, in plain view. Having been invited to enter, the officer is lawfully on the premises, by the occupant's consent. The discovery of the item was inadvertent because the officer had no prior knowledge the item was in the place and conducted no physical search to find it. The officer may seize the item under s. 489(2) C.C. without having to obtain a warrant.

▸ A police officer is lawfully searching a place with a warrant. During the authorized search the officer finds other items, not named on the warrant or unrelated to the investigation, that are evidence of an offence. These items may be seized. The officer must make a return to a Justice after seizing an item under this authority, according to the procedures described in s. 489(2) C.C.

Procedure

The admissibility as evidence in court of items seized without a warrant under s. 489(2) C.C. depends on the prosecution being able to prove the following:

▸ that the person who made the seizure was a peace officer;
▸ that the officer was lawfully in the place (specify the authority);
▸ that the item found was evidence relating to a criminal offence;
▸ that the person who made the seizure had reasonable grounds to believe the item was evidence of a criminal offence;
▸ that the discovery was inadvertent—the item was in plain view and seized with no prior knowledge that it was in the place; and
▸ that a return was made to a Justice either in writing or by the actual item's being brought to him or her.

FIREARMS AND WEAPON SEARCHES

In December 1998, firearm legislation changed. The amendments concerned the acquisition, possession, and use of firearms. The search authorities remain the same except for definition changes.

Relevant Definitions and Terms

Weapon (Section 2 C.C.). Anything (including a firearm) that is used, designed to be used, or intended for use

▸ in causing death or injury to any person, or
▸ for the purpose of threatening or intimidating any person.

Firearm (Section 2 C.C.). A barrelled weapon from which any shot, bullet, or other projectile can be discharged and which is capable of causing serious bodily harm or death to a person, and which includes any frame or receiver of such a barrelled weapon and anything that can be adapted for use as a firearm.

Imitation Firearm (Section 84 C.C.). Anything that imitates a firearm, including a replica firearm.

Prohibited Weapon (Section 84 C.C.). A knife that has a blade that opens automatically by gravity or centrifugal force or by hand pressure applied to a button, spring, or other device in or attached to the handle of the knife; or any weapon, other than a firearm, that is classified as a prohibited weapon. A regulation lists items that are classified as prohibited weapons; it also includes weapons listed in the former prohibition orders. Examples of these are

- tear gas, mace,
- *nunchakus,*
- *shuriken,*
- finger ring with one or more blades capable of being projected from the surface,
- constant companion,
- knife-comb,
- spiked wristband, and
- brass knuckles.

Prohibited Firearm (Section 84 C.C.). This term refers to

1. a handgun that
   a. has a barrel equal to or less than 105 mm (6 inches) in length, or
   b. is designed or adopted to discharge a 25 or 32 calibre cartridge
2. a sawed-off shotgun that is less than 660 mm (26 inches) in length or that has a barrel length less than 457 mm (18 inches),
3. an automatic firearm, and
4. a firearm proscribed by regulation, such as a Taser Public Defender.

Prohibited Device (Section 84 C.C.). This term refers to

1. a handgun barrel that is equal to or less than 105 mm (6 inches),
2. a silencer,
3. a replica firearm,
4. any component, or part of, or accessory for use with, a weapon that is defined by a regulation as a prohibited device, including an electrical or mechanical device that is designed or adapted to operate the trigger mechanism of a semi-automatic firearm for the purpose of causing the firearm to discharge cartridges in rapid succession.

Ammunition (Section 84 C.C.). This term refers to a cartridge containing a projectile that is designed to be discharged from a firearm and that includes a caseless cartridge and shot shell.

Prohibited Ammunition (Section 84 C.C.). This term refers to ammunition, or a projectile of any kind, that is prohibited.

Restricted Firearm (Section 84 C.C.). This term refers to

- a handgun that is not a prohibited firearm,
- a semi-automatic handgun with a barrel less than 470 mm long,
- a firearm that can be reduced to a length of less than 660 mm by folding, or
- a firearm prescribed by regulation to be a restricted weapon including an M16 rifle.

Restricted Weapon (Section 84 C.C.). This term refers to any weapon, other than a firearm, that is proscribed by a regulation.

Authorization. This term refers to a document that allows an individual or business to carry out a particular activity related to firearms or other regulated items. Four types of authorizations for such activity exist, including authorization to

- carry,
- transport,
- import, and
- export.[17]

Licence. This term refers to a document that allows an individual or business to

- keep,
- acquire, or
- carry out an activity
- relating to firearms or other regulated items.

Various types of licences exist, including the following:

1. *Business licence*: allows a business to carry out specific activities relating to certain classes of firearms or regulated items.
2. *Possession and acquisition licence*: allows adults to acquire and possess firearms within a specific class.
3. *Non-resident 60-day possession licence*: allows non-resident adults to borrow non-restricted firearms while in Canada during a specified 60-day period.
4. *Cross-bow acquisition licence*: allows acquisition of cross-bows by individuals.
5. *Registration certificate*: a machine-readable plastic card required to register all classes of firearms. Previously needed for restricted weapons only.[18]

Firearm and Weapon Search Authorities

The *Criminal Code* has three search authorities that are specifically related to fire-arms and weapons. They are found in s. 117, which includes warrant and warrant-less search authorities:

1. Search Warrant for Public Safety Reasons—section 117.04(1) C.C.
2. Warrantless Search for Evidence of an Offence—section 117.02(1) C.C.
3. Warrantless Search for Public Safety Reasons—section 117.04(2) C.C.

SEARCH WARRANT FOR PUBLIC SAFETY REASONS

A s. 487 C.C. search warrant may be obtained to search for and seize any evidence relating to a criminal offence. When weapons or firearms are evidence that proves the commission of a criminal offence, a s. 487 C.C. search warrant authorizes police to search a place for them. Some investigations may concern an offence unrelated to weapons and firearms, but a person's possession of those items may nonetheless represent a risk to public safety.

The following examples illustrate the contrasting circumstances:

- **Example 1** An accused person robbed a bank using a handgun. He conceals the handgun in his house. The handgun is evidence relating to the robbery. A conventional s. 487 C.C. search warrant authorizes the search of the house and seizure of the gun.

> ▸ **Example 2** An investigation reveals that a person has threatened to harm others or to kill himself. He possesses weapons or firearms in his house.

In the second example, the weapons are not evidence directly related to the threatening behaviour. Attempted or threatened suicide is not a *Criminal Code* offence. In this example, either no offence has been committed or an unrelated act has occurred of which the weapons and firearms are not evidence. A conventional s. 487 C.C. search warrant will not authorize the search for or seizure of weapons in these circumstances. Another search authority is needed in those circumstances.

Section 117.04(1) C.C. provides alternative authority to obtain a search warrant relating to weapons, including firearms, based specifically on public safety reasons. A police officer may apply for this search warrant by completing an Information to Obtain. He or she must prove there are reasonable grounds to believe that it is not desirable, in the interests of the safety of the person or of any other person, for the person to possess any

- ▸ weapons (including firearms),
- ▸ prohibited devices,
- ▸ ammunition,
- ▸ prohibited ammunition, or
- ▸ explosive substances.

The reasonable grounds described on the Information must include the specific circumstances of the person's conduct, a description of the relevant items, and the location of the items.

Section 117.04(1) C.C. does not restrict the application or the warrant to any specific type of place. The place may be a dwelling-house, any other kind of building, or a vehicle. A specific place must be named on the application, to ensure the reasonableness of the search. The application will be denied if it requests a search of multiple places on the basis that weapons may be in them.

The significant feature of the reasonable grounds, for this kind of application, is that the applying officer does not have to prove that an offence was committed.

The weapons that are the subject of the proposed search do not have to constitute evidence relating to any offence. What must be reasonably proven is that possession of these weapons poses a risk to public safety. Essentially, the reasonable grounds must be based on the following facts:

- ▸ weapons are in a place,
- ▸ the person has possession of the weapons, and
- ▸ the possession of the weapons is unsafe for any person.

Essentially, the belief should establish the need for a preventative measure.

After the Information to Obtain is completed, it is brought to a Justice. The same procedures apply here as were outlined previously. If reasonable grounds are proven, the Justice may issue a warrant. As stated, s. 117.04(1) C.C. does not restrict the type of place to be searched. The warrant authorizes the seizure of any weapons or devices that may, if they remain in the person's possession, pose a risk to public safety. The search warrant also authorizes the seizure of the following documents relating to the item:

- ▸ authorization,
- ▸ licence, or
- ▸ registration certificate.

This means that the police may seize the weapon and the document authorizing possession of the item.

If the Justice is satisfied that reasonable grounds exist, the next issue is what document will serve as the warrant. The section does not specify a type of search warrant that must be used. Consequently, one must refer to s. 487 C.C., which states that it may be used for the purposes of the *Criminal Code* or of any federal statute. Section 487(3) C.C. also states that the Form 5 search warrant may be "varied to suit the case." These provisions allow the Form 5 search warrant to be used, with the document's content altered so that any reference to the commission of the offence is deleted. In summary, a s. 487 C.C. search warrant, varied to suit the case, may be used as a search warrant for weapons for public safety reasons.

WARRANTLESS SEARCH FOR EVIDENCE OF AN OFFENCE

In certain circumstances, the police are allowed to search a person, vehicle, and place other than a dwelling-house for firearms and regulated items, without a warrant or consent. This authority may be used during investigations where firearms represent evidence of an offence. The warrantless search authority is not automatic.

The following conditions must exist before a warrantless search can be conducted:

1. A police officer (not a citizen) must form a belief based on reasonable grounds.
2. Reasonable grounds must exist to believe that

    ▸ a weapon,
    ▸ an imitation firearm,
    ▸ a prohibited device,
    ▸ any ammunition or prohibited ammunition, or
    ▸ explosive substance,

    was used in the commission of an offence; or an offence is being or has been committed involving a

    ▸ firearm,
    ▸ imitation firearm,
    ▸ crossbow,
    ▸ prohibited weapon,
    ▸ restricted weapon,
    ▸ prohibited device,
    ▸ ammunition or prohibited ammunition, or
    ▸ explosive substance.

3. These weapons, firearms, or regulated items are likely to be found

    ▸ on a person,
    ▸ in a vehicle, or
    ▸ in any place other than a dwelling-house.

4. The conditions for obtaining a search warrant exist.
5. Exigent circumstances exist.

"Exigent circumstances" means that no time exists to obtain a warrant because of imminent danger to any persons, or that loss or destruction of evidence is imminent. Obtaining a search warrant often takes about one hour. Conducting a warrantless search for firearms and weapons as evidence requires proof of a reasonable belief that someone may be killed or injured, or that the evidence would be lost or destroyed during the time required to obtain a search warrant. The circumstances that constitute such reasonable grounds have been previously explained.

Although this search authority does not extend to dwelling-houses, s. 487.11 C.C. provides a broad warrantless search authority that includes dwelling-houses. Section 487.11 C.C. may be used as the authority to search a house for firearms or weapons without a warrant because it allows a warrantless search for any evidence of an offence when exigent circumstances exist. This authority will be interpreted and explained later in this chapter.

If exigent circumstances are not present, a house or any other place may be searched either by consent or by a s. 487 C.C. search warrant. Finally, the s. 117.02(1) C.C. warrantless search authority does not apply to circumstances where an offence is about to occur. Although this situation is not included, it will rarely be a hindrance to the application of this authority. Most firearm or weapons situations fall under the category of "currently being committed" because of the variety of possession-related offences involved. For example, the dual procedure offence of "possession of a weapon dangerous to the public peace" may justify the use of a warrantless search authority. Using a warrantless search authority in the context of this offence does not require proof that the weapon has been used unlawfully.

For example, an officer forms reasonable grounds based on the statement of a witness who saw a suspect put a baseball bat in his car and heard him express the intention of committing an assault. If the officer stops the suspect before the assault is committed, the officer does so on reasonable grounds that the suspect is "currently committing" the offence of possessing a weapon dangerous to the public peace. Exigent circumstances exist. Reasonable grounds exist to believe that the weapon is in the vehicle. Although the assault was only about to occur, the vehicle may be searched without a warrant. The officer may also arrest the suspect because reasonable grounds exist to believe that he committed a dual procedure offence. Then the vehicle may be searched under the common-law search-incident-to-arrest authority.

After the warrantless seizure of a firearm or weapon, the seizing officer must make a return to a Justice using the same procedures as for a return made after a seizure by warrant.

WARRANTLESS SEARCH FOR PUBLIC SAFETY REASONS

This provision allows the police to use the same procedures as for the s. 117.04(1) C.C. search warrant authority for public safety reasons, but without a warrant and without consent. The condition that allows a warrantless search for public safety reasons is "by reason of a possible danger to the safety of that person or any other person," which makes the obtaining of a warrant impracticable.

This warrantless search authority consists of the following elements:

1. The places that may be searched include a

   - dwelling-house,
   - building, or
   - vehicle.

2. The item searched for does not need to represent evidence of an offence. In this case, the reason for searching is a reasonable belief that "it is not desirable, in the interests of the safety of the person or of any other person," for the person to possess weapons, firearms, or regulated items.

3. An immediate danger to any person must be present. It must be proven that no time existed to obtain a warrant.

The justification for a warrantless search is a reasonable belief that any person would have been injured or killed if the police took the time to obtain a warrant to prevent a person from possessing weapons, firearms, or regulated items. An example is a domestic dispute where weapons or firearms are in the house and hostilities between intoxicated participants are escalating. Although no offence may have yet been committed, the circumstances justify the belief that the possession of weapons or firearms under these circumstances represents a danger to public safety and that the danger is immediate. The combination of the public risk and the urgency justifies a warrantless search for the purpose of preventing harm, despite the fact that no criminal offence has occurred.

The conditions that must be proven and the procedure are as follows:

1. A police officer only, not a citizen, may form the belief.

2. There must be reasonable grounds to believe that any weapon (including a firearm) or regulated item is in a specific place, including a dwelling-house.

3. There must be reasonable grounds to believe that a person's possession of those items represents a public safety risk. The officer does not have to prove that a criminal offence has been or is being committed.

4. A possible danger to any person must be proven to exist. The word "possible" implies that the belief does not have to be about a positive threat to life, only a reasonable possibility that a person may be hurt or killed as a result of the possession of weapons.

5. Any weapon, firearm, or regulated item may be seized. Any documents related to the weapon may be seized, including any

   ▸ authorization,
   ▸ licence, or
   ▸ registration certificate.

If the documents cannot be seized at the time of the weapons seizure, the documents are revoked.[19]

ADDITIONAL CASE LAW: Warrantless Weapons Searches

A number of leading cases provide outstanding points of reference for warrantless weapons searches. These include the trilogy of:

1. *R. v. McCormack* (2007)
2. *R. v. Hudson* (2007)
3. *R. v. Peacock-McDonald* (2007)

Refer to the accompanying website, **www.emp.ca/arcaro/policepowers4E**.

Return to a Justice

After a seizure of weapons, firearms, or regulated items is made by any of the three authorities, either with or without a warrant, a return to a Justice is mandatory.

If a warrantless seizure is made of weapons or firearms that are evidence of an offence, a return must be made according to the previously explained procedures, under s. 490 C.C. The return may be made either in writing or by bringing the item to a Justice. If the weapons are evidence, they must be lawfully detained for court.

If weapons or regulated items are seized for public safety reasons, either with or without a warrant, a return is mandatory despite the fact that the items will not be evidence for an offence and no detention for court is required because no charge will be laid. Section 117.04(3) C.C. explains the return procedures:

1. In the case of a seizure by warrant, the actual seized items or documents must be brought forthwith to the Justice who issued the warrant. A return in writing cannot be made. The return cannot be made to a Justice who did not issue the warrant. "Forthwith" is defined in case law as meaning *immediately*, without any unjustifiable delay. The date of execution must also be shown to the Justice.
2. In the case of a warrantless search, the actual items or documents must be brought to a Justice who "might have" issued a warrant, meaning a Justice who has jurisdiction. The seizing officer must prove the reasonable grounds that formed the basis of the warrantless search. The reasonable grounds must be written on the "Report to a Justice."

Disposition—Weapons Seized for Public Safety Reasons

When the police seize a weapon, firearm, or regulated item for public safety reasons, under ss. 117.04(1) and (2) C.C., with or without a warrant, the seized items cannot be detained for court because no offence will have been committed. Consequently, no charge will be laid and no trial will occur. The items must be dealt with in a different manner. Section 117.05(1) C.C. explains these procedures:

1. The items must be returned to the lawful owner unless a police officer makes an application for a disposition hearing. The police cannot dispose of the seized items without a hearing.
2. The process for a disposition hearing begins with an application by a police officer. The police have a 30-day time limit, starting on the day of the seizure, to make the application. The police have discretion to make the application.
3. If the application is not made, no disposition hearing will occur, and the seized items must be returned to the lawful owner.
4. If an application is made by a police officer within the 30-day time limit, a Justice must conduct a disposition hearing. The Justice has no discretion about conducting it upon receiving the application; the hearing becomes mandatory.
5. Upon receiving the application, the Justice schedules a date for the disposition hearing. The hearing is not a trial; the purpose of the hearing is to determine whether the weapons or firearms will be disposed of or returned to the owner.

6. The Justice directs that "notice of the hearing be given to such person or in such a manner" as the Justice may specify. This means that the Justice creates the list of persons who will be subpoenaed to the hearing, including the person from whom the items were seized. Again, this person is not charged with an offence. The hearing will determine only whether he or she will regain possession of the items.

7. At the hearing, the Justice may proceed *ex parte*, meaning that the hearing will be conducted in the absence of the person from whom the items were seized, just as a summary conviction court may proceed with a trial in the absence of a defendant. Section 803(2) C.C. explains that a summary conviction trial may be conducted in the absence of the defendant if he or she has been notified of the time and place of the trial, and the consent of the attorney general is obtained.

8. At the hearing, the Justice shall hear all relevant evidence, including evidence relating to the value of the seized items. Relevant evidence means evidence relating to whether it is in the interest of public safety for the person to possess the seized items.

9. At the conclusion of the hearing, the Justice makes one of two conclusions:

   a. It is not desirable (in the public interest) for the person to possess weapons or regulated items. In other words, the Justice has concluded that the person's possession of the seized items poses a public risk. If this finding is made, the Justice shall order the following disposition:

      ‣ anything seized be forfeited to Her Majesty or be otherwise disposed of. The Justice orders fair and reasonable disposal of any seized item, including destruction or sale of the item; and

      ‣ prohibition of the person's possessing any weapon or regulating items during any period not exceeding five years, if "the Justice is satisfied that the circumstances warrant such an action." The prohibition is contingent upon the evidence convincing the Justice that the prohibition is necessary. If the prohibition is not ordered, the Justice must include in the record reasons for not ordering it.

   b. Public safety is not at risk. This finding means that the person's possession of the seized items is not undesirable with respect to the public interest. The items will be returned to the person if this finding is made. The Justice must include reasons in the record for making this finding. The attorney general may appeal this finding to the Superior Court.

An example of circumstances that constitute a public safety risk and exigent circumstances, justifying a warrantless search, is found in *R. v. Golub* (1997).[20] This case is explained in Chapter 5.

Seizure for Failure to Produce Authorization

Section 117.03(1) C.C. allows the police to demand that a person in possession of a firearm produce an authorization or licence for it, as well as a registration certificate. The same demand may be made of a person found possessing a prohibited weapon, a restricted weapon, a prohibited device, or any prohibited ammunition.

The police may make this demand in any place where the person is found possessing the firearm, whether a dwelling-house, a building, or a vehicle. The condition for making the demand is simply that the officer find the person in possession of the item.

For example, if a police officer is lawfully on any premises—for example, present by invitation in a dwelling-house—and sees firearms stored in the house, he or she may demand that the possessor produce the proper documents for inspection. The definition of possession under s. 4(3) C.C. applies here, meaning

- **actual possession**, by having the item on his or her person; or
- **constructive possession**, by having the item not on his person but in any place, whether or not he owns or occupies the place and has control or access to the item for his use or benefit; and
- **joint possession**, whereby two or more persons may possess one item.

If the possessor of the firearm fails to produce the documents at the police officer's demand, the officer has authority to seize the firearm or regulated item. The officer cannot search for it because s. 117.03(1) C.C. does not authorize a search of any nature. The officer may seize only the firearm or regulated item that he or she finds in the person's possession. The only instance in which the police cannot make the seizure is if the possessor who fails to produce the documents "is under the direct and immediate supervision of another person who may lawfully possess the firearm."

How much time must a person be given to produce the documents after the officer's demand? The answer is found in the phrase "fails, on demand, to produce." The documents must be produced upon demand—that is, immediately. The section does not stipulate that the officer give the person any specific amount of time to produce. Say, for example, that an officer finds a person in possession of a firearm or regulated item in a car or public place and demands production of documents. If the person fails to produce the documents, stating that he or she has them at home, the officer may seize the firearms immediately. There is no requirement that the officer, before seizing the firearms, give the person time to retrieve the documents from his or her home.

After police seize the item, the person from whom it was seized may produce the relevant documents "within 14 days" in order to reclaim the seized item.

If the claimant produces these documents within 14 days, the seized item must be returned to him or her "forthwith," meaning immediately and without unjustified delay.[21]

If the claimant does not produce the documents within 14 days, the police have an additional mandatory obligation. A police officer must take the seized item to a provincial court judge forthwith. This means that the return

- cannot be made to a JP, and
- must be made as soon as 13 days expire, counting from the time of the seizure.[22]

After the return is made, the provincial court judge may, "after affording the person from whom it was seized or its owner, if known, an opportunity to establish that the person is lawfully entitled to possess it, declare it to be forfeited to Her Majesty, to be disposed of or otherwise dealt with as the attorney general directs." In other words, the judge can order forfeiture of the seized item. But a hearing must be held to allow the person an opportunity to prove that he or she has lawful authority to possess it.

PROCEDURE

The procedure for a s. 117.03(1) seizure is as follows:

1. Enter the premises lawfully, where applicable. In some cases, the occasion for using this authority will occur inside a place. The officer must be lawfully on the premises by means of a search warrant, without a warrant, or by invitation or consent. Lawful presence is not an issue when the officer is not on a premises—when, for example, an officer is on a street while stopping a car or on a sidewalk with a pedestrian.

2. Find a person in possession of a firearm or a regulated item. Possession includes actual possession, constructive possession, or joint possession. The remainder of the procedure cannot be followed if the person is not seen to be in possession of the item.

3. Make a demand of the possessor of the firearm that he or she produce relevant documents, including

   ‣ authorization,
   ‣ licence, or
   ‣ registration certificate.

4. If the possessor fails to produce the documents, seize the item.

5. Retain custody of the seized item for 14 days. If the person produces the documents within 14 days of the seizure, return the seized item forthwith to that person.

6. If no documents are produced within 14 days, take the seized item forthwith to a provincial court judge.

DRUGS AND SUBSTANCES

Police officers have authority to search for drugs without a warrant and without consent, under s. 11(7) *Controlled Drugs and Substances Act* (C.D.S.A.). This provision has simplified the more complex authority that previously existed under the repealed *Narcotic Control Act*.

The C.D.S.A. has not only simplified the interpretation of the warrantless search authority but has extended it to include a dwelling-house. The *Narcotic Control Act* permitted a warrantless search only of places other than a dwelling-house. Section 11(7) C.D.S.A. states that "a peace officer may exercise any of the powers described in subsection (1), (5), or (6) without a warrant if the conditions for obtaining a warrant exist but by reason of exigent circumstances it would be impracticable to obtain one."

Essentially, the police may search any place, including a dwelling-house, if reasonable grounds exist to believe that a controlled substance or anything that is evidence relating to a C.D.S.A. offence is in that place and exigent circumstances exist—that is, there is no time to obtain a search warrant.

Exigent circumstances require evidence supporting the officer's belief, based on reasonable grounds, that there is an imminent danger of the loss, removal, destruction, or disappearance of the drugs, if the search is delayed so that a search warrant can be obtained.

The determining factor relating to exigent circumstances, in the case of a C.D.S.A. offence, is the potential movement of the drugs, during the time required to obtain a search warrant, from the place they are in. Approximately one hour is required to obtain a search warrant. Factors to consider when deciding whether to invoke exigent circumstances include the following:

- The type of place to be searched. Is it a vehicle, for example? In this case, there is a strong reason to believe that the drugs will move in the time it would take to obtain a warrant.
- The quantity of the drugs.
- The activity in which the suspect is involved. For example, are the drugs for selling or for personal use?
- Observations made by witnesses, including informants. The significant element here is what the suspect conveyed to the witness about his or her intentions for the drugs.
- Observations made by the police officer during the investigation. For example, was there "excessive customer traffic"—that is, potential drug users—at the place?

The S.C.C., in *R. v. Grant* (1993), created useful guidelines for interpreting this authority. Places may be categorized as

1. fixed or stationary, or
2. moving or mobile.

Fixed or stationary places include

- dwelling-houses,
- stores,
- business premises,
- lockers,
- offices,
- bars,
- schools,
- garages (attached or detached),
- perimeters of houses,[23] and
- gardens.[24]

Moving or mobile places include

- motor vehicles,
- water vessels, and
- aircraft.[25]

The following principles are relevant when it comes to determining whether drugs may move and exigent circumstances exist:

1. Reasonable grounds for believing that narcotics are in a motor vehicle, water vessel, aircraft, or other "fast-moving" place will often constitute exigent circumstances, but not in every case.

2. No blanket authority exists for searching conveyances without a warrant, simply on the grounds that the place is capable of moving.[26] It is possible for drugs to be in a conveyance under circumstances in which it is unlikely they will move or be lost during the time it would take the officer to obtain a search warrant. An example of this would be a case where the drugs are in a parked vehicle, and there is evidence suggesting that the drugs will continue to be stored there for as long as it would take an officer to obtain a warrant.

3. Conversely, a search warrant is not automatically required to search fixed or stationary places such as dwelling-houses, businesses, offices, or schools. Such a place may be fixed or stationary, but there may also be evidence that the drugs will move or be lost if the search is delayed until a search warrant is obtained. A warrantless search of any fixed or stationary place, including a dwelling-house, is justified if it is impracticable to obtain a search warrant due to exigent circumstances.

In summary, the type of place is only one consideration in determining whether exigent circumstances exist. Though important, it is not the only element to consider. The officer's determination about exigent circumstances must be focused on the drugs, not the place.

The S.C.C., in the *R. v. Grant* case, also ruled about the status of the "perimeter of a house" as a place. The relevance of this "perimeter" issue is illustrated by the following example. Imagine that a police officer develops a mere suspicion that drugs are in a house. He enters the perimeter of the house and walks to a window. He looks inside to make observations intended to form reasonable grounds that the drugs are in that house. Entering the perimeter and looking in the window constitute a search. But is the perimeter a "place," and what authorities are needed to enter it?

The S.C.C. ruled that the perimeter of a house is a place, and that all search and seizure regulations apply to it. In other words, reasonable grounds are required before an officer enters the perimeter. A search warrant is required unless exigent circumstances exist. Police officers have no authority to enter the perimeter to conduct a search without a warrant, based on mere suspicion only.

Search of Person During a Warrantless Search for Drugs

During a warrantless search for drugs, persons will likely be found in the "place." The question is whether the persons found in the place during a warrantless search may be searched without consent. Together, ss. 11(7) and (5) C.D.S.A. authorize the search of a person found in the place, if reasonable grounds exist to believe that he or she has any controlled substance on his or her person. The following are guidelines established by the S.C.C. in *R. v. Debot* (1989):[27]

1. An automatic search of all persons found in the place is prohibited.
2. Before searching a person, the officer must have a reasonable belief that the person has actual possession of the substance.
3. Reasonable belief requires only proof of a "reasonable probability" that the person has actual possession of a substance.

This reasonable belief may be founded on

▸ an informant or witness's observations,
▸ an officer's observations, or
▸ circumstances, such as the person's close proximity to the particular area where the drugs are believed to be concealed.

This authority applies when the reasonable belief is directed to a place. In some cases, the reasonable grounds are directed to a specific person. For example, a witness may inform police that he saw a specific person place cocaine in his pocket. Possession of that substance is a dual procedure offence. The proper procedure is to arrest the person first and search him or her afterward, using the search-incident-to-arrest authority. The immediate surroundings may also be searched.

One exception exists. Possession of under 30 grams (1 ounce) of marijuana is now a summary conviction offence. A lawful arrest may be made only if a police officer finds committing. If an officer is informed by a witness that a person possesses under 30 grams (1 ounce) of marijuana, police may conduct a search by consent, or may make an arrest if the person admits having possession. If the officer has reasonable grounds that the person possesses over 30 grams— a dual procedure offence—a lawful arrest and search can be made.

USE OF FORCE

Section 12 C.D.S.A. authorizes the use of as much force as is necessary in the circumstances. Excessive force may result in criminal and civil liability.

OTHER ITEMS

Section 11(8) C.D.S.A. authorizes the seizure of anything that the police believe on reasonable grounds to be evidence obtained by or used in the commission of any offence. Consequently, evidence unrelated to the primary offence may be seized if it is found during a lawful warrantless search.

RETURN OF SEIZED ITEMS

Section 13 C.D.S.A. makes it mandatory for police to make a return to a Justice using the procedure described in ss. 489.1 and 490 C.C. A report must also be sent to the Minister of Health using the same procedure described in the C.D.S.A. search warrant section.

PROCEDURE: WARRANTLESS SEARCH

1. Form reasonable grounds that a controlled substance or anything that will be evidence of any C.D.S.A. offence is in a specific place, including a dwelling-house. A belief based on mere suspicion is insufficient to justify a search.
2. Form reasonable grounds that exigent circumstances exist, in which case it is impracticable to obtain a search warrant.
3. If reasonable grounds exist for believing that a person found in the place has possession of a controlled substance, that person may be searched without consent. All persons cannot automatically be searched.

4. Any controlled substance or any evidence of a C.D.S.A. offence that is found may be seized.[28]

5. Any other item that the officer believes on reasonable grounds to be evidence of any offence may be seized if it is found during the search.

6. If any seizure is made, a return must be made in accordance with the procedures described in ss. 489.1 and 490 C.C.

7. If the officer's reasonable grounds concern a specific person,

   ▸ arrest the person,
   ▸ search the person incident to arrest, and
   ▸ search the immediate surroundings of the place.

ODOUR OF DRUGS

A controversial topic and a common problem for police is whether the odour of drugs in a car constitutes reasonable grounds to believe that drugs are in there. No statute or S.C.C. case law directly addresses this issue. Useful guidelines are found in *R. v. Polashek* (1999),[29] an Ontario Court of Appeal decision that also includes rulings related to a number of other police procedures. You will find a complete explanation of this decision on the website that accompanies this textbook: **www .emp.ca/arcaro/policepowers4E**. The following is a summary of the Court's decision regarding the odour of drugs:

▸ The court agreed in part with the accused's argument that the odour of drugs alone did not constitute reasonable grounds to believe that the accused was committing an offence.

▸ However, the court stated that they would "not go so far as was urged by the appellant that the presence of the smell of marijuana can never provide the requisite reasonable and probable grounds for an arrest."

▸ The court did not establish a definite procedure. Essentially, an odour of marijuana alone will usually not constitute reasonable grounds to believe a person is committing an offence, but in some circumstances it will. The following principles should help officers distinguish which circumstances do and which do not constitute reasonable grounds:

   ▸ "The sense of smell is highly subjective. It gives the police unreviewable discretion."[30]
   ▸ Smells are transitory, leave no trace, and are incapable of objective verification.
   ▸ Some officers can convince the trial judge that they have acquired sufficient expertise through experience or training, and that their opinion—that the odour of marijuana shows present possession—is reliable.

▸ In the case of *R. v. Polashek*, the officer cited the odour of marijuana as one of various circumstances on which the reasonable grounds were based. The other circumstances the officer cited, in support of the reasonable grounds, were the following:

   ▸ When the officer stated that he smelled marijuana, the accused looked to his right and over both shoulders and said, "No, you don't."

> ▸ The geographical area. The place was a fairly small area where drug use was prevalent.
> ▸ The officer's experience. He had made 40 to 50 marijuana seizures in previous cases in the same area.
> ▸ The time, which was 1:00 a.m.

▸ The court ruled that the smell of marijuana, combined with the other factors, did support the officer's reasonable grounds belief, but recognized that it was a "close case" because the officer did not see actual smoke or see any object in plain view that supported his idea that the accused was in present possession of marijuana.

In summary, the circumstances under which the smell of marijuana is detected will determine whether it may contribute to an officer's belief, based on reasonable grounds, that a person is in possession of drugs. The smell alone may be sufficient for reasonable grounds if the officer can justify the opinion with expertise based on experience or training. Otherwise, the officer will need to cite other factors, in addition to the smell of marijuana, if he or she hopes to prove reasonable grounds about the presence of drugs.

ADDITIONAL CASE LAW: Drug Searches

The volume of case law relating to drug searches has increased exponentially. The leading cases include the following:

1. *R. v. Nguyen* (2007)
2. *R. v. Harrison* (2008)
3. *R. v. Dreyer* (2008)
4. *R. v. Ford* (2008)
5. *R. v. Jackson* (2007)
6. *R. v. Harris* (2007)

Refer to the accompanying website, **www.emp.ca/arcaro/policepowers4E**.

WARRANTLESS ENTRY TO PRESERVE EVIDENCE

Police are often concerned that during the time it takes them to obtain a warrant to search lawfully for narcotics, the narcotics may be lost or destroyed. An effective procedure in this case would be to enter the house without the warrant, on the grounds of needing to preserve the evidence from destruction by the occupants. But the C.D.S.A. and the *Criminal Code* contain no authority for police to enter a place without a warrant, while awaiting the arrival of the search warrant, in order to preserve and protect the evidence.

However, the S.C.C., in *R. v. Silveira* (1995),[31] addressed this issue and created a guideline that permits the procedure recommended above, but only in urgent circumstances. The court stated that warrantless entry by police into a house to preserve evidence, while they await the arrival of a drug search warrant, is justified if exigent circumstances exist. "Exigent circumstances" have been defined, previously in this text, as a situation of emergency or importance that may make it impracticable for police to obtain a search warrant before entering. Factors in determining whether exigent circumstances exist include

1. the nature of the offence;
2. whether an accused has been arrested in close proximity to the house to be searched; and
3. whether police have reasonable grounds to believe that a warrantless entry is necessary to prevent the destruction or removal of evidence while they await the issuance and arrival of the search warrant.

No blanket authority exists automatically allowing the police to use this procedure. Exigent circumstances will be judged on a case-by-case basis. The court emphasized that this procedure will be justified only in rare cases.

CASE LAW

R. v. Silveira (1995)

■ **Issue:** Preservation of evidence while awaiting a search warrant.

■ **Offence:** "Trafficking narcotics"

■ **Circumstances:** During a one-week investigation, an undercover police officer made three separate purchases of cocaine from the accused person's accomplice. Each purchase was made in a similar fashion; the officer met the accused's accomplice at a community centre where the officer gave advance payment. The accomplice left, met the accused, and they travelled to the accused's house. They entered the house and returned to the officer, giving a quantity of cocaine to the officer.

After the third purchase, police arrested the accused near his house. Before being transported to the police station, the accused was questioned, and he confessed that narcotics and money were inside his house. This confession, added to other evidence, would have constituted reasonable grounds to obtain a search warrant.

The accused was transported to the police station. The arresting officer intended to complete an Information to Obtain a search warrant but feared that the narcotics would be destroyed during the time required to obtain the warrant. Six officers were sent to the accused's house to preserve the narcotics until the search warrant arrived.

The officers attended at the house and announced their presence by knocking. When the door was opened, they entered without a warrant and with guns drawn. The accused's family members were present. The officers informed them that they had no search warrant but one was being obtained. Police confined the occupants to the interior of the house. The officers searched for weapons only, for their safety, but did not search for narcotics. The officers remained there and detained the occupants for one hour and 15 minutes. During this time, as police waited for the search warrant, the accused's brother arrived. He had knowledge that the accused had been arrested.

The officer who obtained the warrant failed to disclose in the Information to Obtain that the officers were already present at the house to preserve evidence.

(continued)

The search warrant was issued and executed. A quantity of cocaine and money was seized. The accused was charged with trafficking narcotics.

The S.C.C. upheld the accused's conviction and made the following rulings:

▸ The warrantless entry was a search unauthorized by law and it constituted a s. 8 Charter violation.

▸ However, the narcotics were not excluded under s. 24(2) Charter and were admitted as evidence.

▸ Drug sales are serious crimes. The severity of the offence, combined with considerations about the easy destruction or removal of the drugs, should arguably always permit police to enter without a warrant if their aim is to preserve evidence; but no statutory law currently authorizes such action.

▸ No search for narcotics occurred during the interval when police were preserving evidence. Their warrantless entry was made in good faith. The police intention to preserve evidence rather than to search for it diminished the severity of their Charter violation.

▸ The nature of the offence, combined with the fact that the arrest occurred in close proximity to the house, constituted exigent circumstances.

▸ The failure to disclose, on the Information to Obtain, that the police were present at the accused's house did not mislead the Justice who issued the search warrant.

▸ The warrantless search for weapons was justified to protect the officers.

▸ The momentary display of firearms was justified.

WARRANTLESS SEARCH FOR ORDINARY EVIDENCE: SECTION 487.11 C.C.

Before 1998, no blanket authority existed allowing police to search a place without a warrant for ordinary evidence relating to a criminal offence. For example, if the police had reasonable grounds to believe that stolen property, such as televisions and stereos, was in a place, they had to apply for a s. 487 C.C. search warrant or to obtain consent —the only two alternatives available to them. The *Criminal Code* did not include an authority to search a place for any ordinary evidence, without a warrant and without consent. In other words, there was no alternative to a s. 487 C.C. search warrant if police wanted to search a place for ordinary evidence of an offence.

Section 487.11 C.C. is a warrantless search authority that allows police, in exigent circumstances, the same authority as a s. 487 C.C. search warrant—that is the authority to search any place, including a dwelling-house. This new amendment may be the most significant investigative procedure that has been added to the *Criminal Code*. It is a wide-ranging search authority that will likely become the most advantageous authority available to the police. This amendment was made partly in response to *R. v. Silveira* (1995).

Section 487.11 C.C. authorizes a police officer to conduct the same searches as are authorized by a s. 487 C.C. warrant and a s. 492.1 C.C. tracking warrant, under conditions where, though the officer has sufficient grounds to obtain either warrant, he cannot practically do so owing to exigent circumstances. If items are seized in this kind of search, a return to a Justice is mandatory as it is under other search authorities.

Procedure: Ordinary Evidence

To conduct a warrantless search for ordinary evidence of a criminal offence, the following procedures apply:

1. Form reasonable grounds to believe that an item is in a building, receptacle, or place. This includes a dwelling-house, business premise, school, locker, or vehicle.
2. Form reasonable grounds to believe that the item

   ▸ is relevant to any criminal offence that has been or is suspected to have been committed under any federal statute; or
   ▸ will afford evidence with respect to the commission of an offence; or
   ▸ will reveal the whereabouts of a person who is believed to have committed any criminal offence under any federal statute; or
   ▸ is intended to be used for the purpose of committing any offence against a person, for which the offender may be arrested without a warrant; or
   ▸ is offence-related property.

3. Form reasonable grounds to believe that exigent circumstances exist that would make it impracticable to obtain a s. 487 C.C. search warrant.

   No blanket authority or circumstance automatically constitutes exigent circumstances; each case will be judged on an individual basis. The S.C.C. has emphasized that a warrantless search, especially of a dwelling-house, will be justified in rare cases.

4. If items are seized, a return to a Justice must be made in accordance with s. 489.1 C.C.

In summary, the s. 487.11 C.C. warrantless search authority cannot be used liberally or for convenience's sake, especially in relation to a dwelling-house. If there is sufficient time to obtain a search warrant, a s. 487 C.C. search warrant must be obtained.

Procedure: Tracking Device

Section 487.11 allows a police officer to "exercise any of the powers described in 492.1(1)." This authorizes warrantless tracking device installation. The following describes the step-by-step procedure for doing this:

1. Form reasonable grounds to suspect that a criminal offence has been or will be committed.
2. Form reasonable grounds that relevant information regarding the offence or the whereabouts of any person can be obtained through the use of a tracking device.
3. Form reasonable grounds that exigent circumstances make it impracticable to obtain a tracking warrant.
4. Install and maintain the tracking device, without a warrant, in or on anything, including a thing carried, used, or worn by any person.

SECTION 487.11 NON-APPLICABILITY

Section 487.11 authorizes police entry into any place, including a dwelling-house, without a warrant. But the starting point is crucial—that is, specific offence recognition. You need to know what specific offence you are investigating before applying s. 487.11.

Section 487.11 does not apply in cases where police are uncertain about whether a criminal offence has occurred. The following are two examples of such cases, and two solutions.

Warrantless Forcible Entry into House to Protect Life

A "disconnected 911 call" is a common distress call. Such calls are explained fully in the *Criminal Investigation: Forming Reasonable Grounds* textbook, as part of "First Officer" response to emergencies. Disconnected 911 calls do not permit specific offence recognition. Consequently, s. 487.11 does not apply to these situations.

The police have a common-law duty to protect life and property, prevent crime, and preserve the peace. This duty is enshrined in provincial statutes that regulate and govern policing, such as the *Police Services Act* of Ontario.

The S.C.C., in *R. v. Godoy* (1999), created an authority that allows the police to enter a house forcibly and without a warrant, in response to a disconnected 911 call, for the purpose of searching the house for an injured person.[32] Additionally, the S.C.C. stated that police may disregard any person who answers the door and informs the police that there is no problem inside. Police entry into the house to search for injured persons is justified despite the refusal of the person who answers the door.

The complete circumstances and ruling of *R. v. Godoy* (1999) are found in "911 Radio Broadcasts/Protecting Life" in Chapter 8 of this text. The following is a summary.

> Patrol officers received a radio broadcast stating "911 unknown problem" at a house. Upon the officers' arrival at the house, a man answered the door and told officers there was "no problem" inside. He tried to shut the door on them. The officers entered and heard a woman crying. They searched the house and found the man's wife, who reported that her husband had assaulted her. The S.C.C. ruled that the disconnected 911 call constituted sufficient reasonable grounds to enter the house forcibly, without a warrant, to search for injured persons. The entry was justified by the officers' common-law authority to protect life.[33]

PROCEDURE

When police arrive at a house after receiving a radio broadcast stating "911 unknown problem," the following procedures apply:

1. If the officers make an announcement by knocking on the door but receive no answer, forcible warrantless entry is justified.
2. If they announce themselves and a person answers the door and reports there is no problem inside, their warrantless entry into the house is justified.

3. If the person who answers the door refuses the officers entry and closes the door, their forcible warrantless entry is justified.
4. The S.C.C. stated that a disconnected 911 call constitutes reasonable grounds to believe that "the caller is in some distress and requires immediate assistance."[34] This situation constitutes exigent circumstances, which would justify the officers' forcible, warrantless, and unannounced entry into the house.
5. After they enter, they are justified in searching the interior to find injured persons.
6. After police find an injured person, an oral statement from that person, claiming that he or she has been assaulted, constitutes reasonable grounds for the police to make an arrest.

EXPECTATION OF PRIVACY—VEHICLE

Commonly, as a police officer, you will stop a car for a traffic violation. Your observations will then cause you to suspect a criminal offence. Section 487.11 will not apply because you cannot recognize a specific offence. The following is an example of this situation, and a solution.

You are a uniformed police officer on patrol. You stop a car for speeding. Three occupants are in the car. The driver has no documentation and tells you that the car is owned by a friend. Three open garbage bags, full of new clothes with price tags attached, are on the back seat. One occupant informs you that they own the clothes. Another tells you that they were in the car when they borrowed it. CPIC reveals that the car has not been reported stolen and a valid arrest warrant exists for the driver for unpaid fines. You *suspect* that the clothes have been stolen. Can you search the trunk without a warrant? Can you seize the clothes?

The new search authority under s. 487.11 C.C. would *not* apply here because there are no reasonable grounds to believe that stolen property is in the car. Only mere suspicion exists, and a search may cause a Charter violation. Section 8 of the Charter guarantees a person's reasonable expectation of privacy. The S.C.C. has stated that the purpose of s. 8 Charter is to protect a citizen's right to a reasonable expectation of privacy against unreasonable searches by the police. However, this guarantee protects only a *reasonable* expectation of privacy. The circumstances that constitute "reasonable" will vary in every case. In *R. v. Edwards* (1996), the S.C.C. created the following relevant guidelines:

1. Section 8 Charter is a personal right that protects people, not places.
2. The success of the accused's challenge to the legality of a search depends on his or her establishing that his or her personal right to privacy has been violated.
3. Section 8 Charter issues require two separate inquiries:
    a. Did the accused have a reasonable expectation of privacy in the place that was searched?
    b. If the expectation existed, was the search conducted reasonably?[35]

Whether the accused had a reasonable expectation of privacy is determined by evaluating the totality of the circumstances. The factors to be considered may include, but are not restricted to, the following:

▸ the accused's whereabouts at the time of the search;
▸ the possession, ownership, and historical use of the place;
▸ the accused's ability to regulate access to the place, including the right to admit or exclude persons;
▸ whether the accused had a subjective expectation of privacy; and
▸ the objective reasonableness of the expectation.

If an accused person does establish that he or she had a reasonable expectation of privacy, a second inquiry will determine whether the search was conducted in a reasonable manner.

The S.C.C. applied these principles in *R. v. Belnavis* (1997).[36]

CASE LAW

R. v. Belnavis (1997)

■ **Issues:**

1. What expectation of privacy can a driver and passenger have in a car, with respect to a police search for stolen property?
2. What are the consequences when the police search of a car for stolen property violates whatever right to privacy the occupants' may have?

■ **Offence:** "Possession of stolen property"

■ **Circumstances:** A police officer stopped a car, with New York plates, for speeding. The car had three female occupants. The driver failed to produce any documents but identified herself orally. She accompanied the officer to the cruiser as requested. One passenger followed.

The officer intended to write a speeding ticket and suspected that the car may have been stolen. The driver stated that the car was owned by a friend.

The officer returned to the car to search the glove box for ownership documentation. He asked the passenger in the back seat to identify herself. At that time, he saw three open garbage bags full of new clothes with price tags attached. The passenger stated that each occupant owned one bag. The officer searched the trunk and found five additional bags full of clothing. After returning to the cruiser, he questioned the driver. She contradicted the other occupant's explanation by stating that the bags were in the car when she borrowed it.

A CPIC check revealed that the car had not been reported stolen. A valid arrest warrant existed for the driver for unpaid traffic fines. The driver was arrested. Afterward, the officer learned that the driver's boyfriend owned the car and had lent it to her.

The clothes were seized. After an investigation, all three women were charged with possession of stolen property.

■ **Trial:** The accused persons were acquitted. The trial judge ruled that the officer had no reasonable grounds to conduct the search or to believe that the clothes had been stolen.

■ **Ontario Court of Appeal:** The Crown appealed. The court allowed the appeal, quashed the acquittal, and ordered new trials.

(continued)

■ **Supreme Court of Canada:** An appeal by the accused persons was dismissed. The issues on which this appeal was centred were the following:

  ▸ What expectation of privacy can a passenger and a driver have in a car?
  ▸ What are the consequences when the warrantless search of a car by police violates whatever right to privacy the occupant may have?

■ The court ruled that the passenger had no expectation of privacy in relation to the car or the property seized. She was not the owner. No evidence existed that she had any control over the car, or had used it before, or had any relationship with the owner that gave her special access or privilege regarding the car.

The driver did have a privacy right relating to the car. The search constituted a s. 8 Charter violation. However, the seized property obtained through the violation was not excluded under s. 24(2) Charter because the admission of the evidence would not bring the administration of justice into disrepute. The following rulings were made:

  ▸ The officer had reasonable grounds to search the car.
  ▸ The officer had "every right" to search for ownership documentation, and to open the back door of the car and look inside for safety reasons.
  ▸ The garbage bags were in plain view.

COMMENTARY

The property was not conscriptive evidence. Therefore, trial fairness was not an issue. The driver did not own the car. No evidence indicated her historical use of the car. Consequently, her right to privacy was greatly reduced.

The Charter violation was minimal. Society's interest in the prosecution outweighed the Charter violation. The quantity of stolen property indicated that more than petty theft had been committed.

RIGHT TO COUNSEL: PERSON BEING SEARCHED

Two Charter questions arise regarding the search of a person. Do the police have a mandatory obligation to

1. inform the person that he or she has a right to counsel before being searched?
2. delay the search and give the person a reasonable opportunity to call a lawyer?

The majority of the S.C.C. answered both these questions in *R. v. Debot* (1989).

Regarding question 1: If the accused is arrested and then searched incident to arrest, the officer must inform the accused of his or her right to counsel upon arrest, without delay—that is, before the search.

If the accused is not arrested but is searched under a lawful authority, the search constitutes a detention, and the person must be informed of his or her right to counsel upon being detained, without delay.

To summarize, the person must be informed of his or her right to counsel without delay, as soon as he or she is arrested or detained and before the search is conducted. Exceptions to this rule are

  ▸ situations where force must be used to subdue the person; or
  ▸ for legitimate self-protection, as when police are searching for weapons.

In answer to question 2, the police do not have to delay the search and do not have to provide the person with an opportunity to call a lawyer before the search.[37]

It must be noted that, in the *Debot* case, Supreme Court Justice Sopinka disagreed that police should have to inform a person of his or her right to counsel before searching the person; he stated that no purpose is served by informing a person of the right to counsel if the person will not then be provided with an opportunity to call a lawyer before the search is conducted.

THE REALITY OF POLICING

The real world of policing is complicated and dangerous—a world in which split-second life and death decisions have to be made. The volume and complexities of Canadian laws significantly add to these challenges. As a student, you cannot yet imagine the reality of policing. Understanding that reality, as a new officer, requires commitment and learning.

Memorizing laws is not enough; you have to learn to apply them in stressful, rapidly changing circumstances. Textbook and classroom learning is vital—it's the starting point. Learning to make rapid decisions and to apply everything you've learned in this book takes practical experience. It doesn't happen overnight and it doesn't *just happen*. But it will happen if you are dedicated to learning and to working hard. There is no magic formula, so work hard, and never stop learning.

TEST YOURSELF QUESTIONS

1. Jen (31) phones the police dispatch and reports the following: Cam (35), her boyfriend, phoned her 15 minutes ago from an unknown number and unknown place. He told her that he was driving to her house with a gun to kill her. She describes his car and plate number. This information is broadcast to you. You see the car on Yonge St., one km (.75 mile) from Jen's house, and stop it. Cam is the driver. Explain what you can do and the authorities that will determine your investigative procedures.

_____

_____

_____

_____

_____

_____

_____

_____

_____

_____

_____

2. You are dispatched to a domestic at a house at 4000 Main St. Upon arrival, you are met by Terry (34) outside the house. She reports the following: She lives at this house with her husband Dermott (30) and two sons, ages 9 and 6. Dermott arrived home 30 minutes ago. He was drunk. He yelled at her and became increasingly agitated. No assault or threats occurred. Both sons were downstairs in the rec room. Terry feared for her safety and ran outside to phone the police from a neighbour's house. She believes the two children are still inside with Dermott. Dermott has three hunting shotguns downstairs in a storage room. There is ammunition in that room. She does not know whether the guns are loaded. Explain what procedures are available to you. Choose your course of action, and explain the legal justification for your actions.

ENDNOTES

1. *Cloutier v. Langlois* (1990), 53 C.C.C. (3d) 257 (S.C.C.).
2. Ibid.
3. Ibid.
4. Ibid., at 278.
5. *R. v. Caslake* (1998), 121 C.C.C. (3d) 97 (S.C.C.).
6. *R. v. Speid* (1991), 8 C.R.R. (2d) 383, 13 W.C.B. (2d) 659 (Ont. C.A.); *R. v. Charlton*, 1992 CanLII 367 (B.C.C.A).
7. *R. v. Charlton*, ibid.
8. *R. v. Smellie* (1994), 95 C.C.C. (3d) 9 (B.C.C.A.).
9. *R. v. Lim (No. 2)* (1990), 1 C.R.R. (2d) 136, at 145 (Ont. H.C.J.).
10. Supra note 8.
11. *R. v. Golub* (1997), 117 C.C.C. (3d) 194 (Ont. C.A.).
12. *R. v. Lerke* (1986), 24 C.C.C. (3d) 129 (Alta. C.A.).
13. *R. v. Clayton* (2007), 220 C.C.C. (3d) 449 (S.C.C.).
14. *R. v. Shea* (1982), 1 C.C.C. (3d) 316 (Ont. H.C.J.).
15. Ibid.
16. *R. v. Grenier* (1991), 65 C.C.C. (3d) 76 (Que. C.A.).
17. Canadian Firearms Centre; Department of Justice, *Firearms Officer Desk Manual*, vol. 2 (1998).
18. Ibid.
19. Section 117.04(4) C.C.
20. *R. v. Golub*, supra note 11.
21. Section 117.03(3) C.C.
22. Ibid.
23. *R. v. Grant* (1993), 84 C.C.C. (3d) 173 (S.C.C.).
24. Ibid.
25. Ibid.
26. Ibid.
27. *R. v. Debot* (1989), 52 C.C.C. (3d) 193 (S.C.C.).
28. Sections 11(6) and (7) C.D.S.A.
29. *R. v. Polashek* (1999), 134 C.C.C. (3d) 187 (Ont. C.A.).
30. Ibid.
31. *R. v. Silveira* (1995), 97 C.C.C. (3d) 450 (S.C.C.).
32. *R. v. Godoy* (1999), 131 C.C.C. (3d) 129 (S.C.C.).
33. Ibid.
34. Ibid.
35. *R. v. Edwards* (1996), 104 C.C.C. (3d) 136 (S.C.C.).
36. *R. v. Belnavis* (1996), 107 C.C.C. (3d) 195 (Ont. C.A.).
37. Supra note 27.

APPENDIX A
Solve It!

This section includes case studies with situations that uniform patrol officers commonly investigate. You are a uniform patrol officer in each case. The circumstances reflect all the information known in the case. The amount of information varies in each case.

- Analyze the circumstances of each case carefully.
- Each case represents a problem.
- Solve the problem by identifying the procedures that are available and those that are not available.
- Search the entire book for answers to questions, including
  - Can you arrest?
  - Can you charge anyone?
  - Do you have to release or detain?
  - If an arrest can lawfully be made, what steps would you follow to prevent Charter violations?
  - Write a thorough explanation for each case study, discussing laws that authorize actions or prevent certain procedures.

Case 1

12:17 a.m.

- You are on patrol on Main St. in a business district.
- A man is walking on the sidewalk, travelling in the same direction as you.
- You are aware that three break and enters have occurred in this area during the past seven days.
- This man looks at you as you drive past him. You do not recognize him.
- He abruptly stops and runs on the sidewalk in the opposite direction.
- You pursue him; after 30 seconds, he stops as you approach him.

_____

_____

_____

_____

_____

_____

_____

_____

_____

_____

_____

_____

_____

_____

_____

_____

_____

_____

_____

_____

_____

_____

Case 2

11:23 p.m.

You receive a radio broadcast regarding a "male person, about 25 years, long brown hair, walking on King St. toward Main St. He left Joe's Bar a few minutes ago. A handgun was seen in his jacket pocket. The complaint is anonymous." No other information was received. You search the area.

11:29 p.m.

You see a male person, similar in appearance to the broadcast description, walking on King St., one block south of Main St. He is alone. He appears sober. He is acting and walking normally.

_____

_____

_____

_____

_____

_____

_____

_____

_____
_____
_____
_____
_____
_____
_____
_____
_____
_____
_____
_____
_____

Case 3

2:07 a.m.

- While on patrol on Barton St. you see a blue car driving away from the parking lot of a body shop.
- The body shop is closed.
- The car accelerates as it leaves the parking lot.
- There are two people in the front seat.
- You activate your roof lights, and the car stops two blocks from that premises.
- You approach the driver's door. You recognize the driver, Eddie (27), as a person you arrested for theft over $5,000.00 two years ago.
- The male passenger is unknown to you.
- Both are sober.
- You ask both for identification and they comply.
- You have a clear view into the back seat.
- You see a number of tools scattered on the back seat.

_____
_____
_____
_____
_____
_____
_____
_____
_____
_____
_____
_____

_____

_____

_____

_____

_____

_____

_____

_____

_____

_____

Case 4

10:14 p.m.

- ‣ You see a red car fail to stop for a red light on Yonge St.
- ‣ You activate the roof lights and the car stops.
- ‣ Four males are in the car, ages between 21 and 35.
- ‣ The driver is sober.
- ‣ You detect a strong odour of marijuana coming from inside the car.

_____

_____

_____

_____

_____

_____

_____

_____

_____

_____

_____

_____

_____

_____

_____

_____

Case 5

9:47 p.m.
You receive a radio transmission of a disconnected 911 call from a house at 5000 Wellington St.

9:52 p.m.

- Upon your arrival, you knock on the front door.
- A man answers it. He calmly informs you that there is no problem and that you are probably mistaken.
- You see and hear nothing else.

_____

_____

_____

_____

_____

_____

_____

_____

_____

_____

_____

_____

_____

_____

_____

_____

_____

_____

_____

_____

_____

_____

_____

_____

_____

_____

_____

_____

_____

_____

_____

_____

Case 6

8:45 p.m.
You receive a radio broadcast of a break and enter in progress at a house situated at 6000 Walker Rd.

8:49 p.m.

- June (22) meets you outside the house and reports the following:
  - Her sister (19) and her three-year old son are visiting her. They are both inside the house.
  - June rents the house.
  - June's ex-boyfriend forced open the front door about five minutes ago.
  - June ran out of the house and thought that her sister and the child followed but they didn't.
  - June is uncertain whether her boyfriend Tony (25) is armed.
- You hear a woman and child both screaming.

_____

_____

_____

_____

_____

_____

_____

_____

_____

_____

_____

_____

_____

_____

_____

_____

_____

_____

_____

Problem-Solving Case Studies Solutions

CHAPTER 4

Problem 1

Yes. You saw a summary conviction offence occur. You may arrest because you found the offence being committed.

Problem 2

Yes. You saw a dual procedure offence occur.

Problem 3

Yes. You saw an indictable offence ("Theft over $5,000.00") occur, and pursued the offender until apprehension, without losing sight of the offender.

Problem 4

Yes. "Assault" is a dual procedure offence that is treated as indictable for the purposes of arrest. June is an eyewitness, constituting reasonable grounds. No time limit exists to arrest for an indictable offence.

Problem 5

Yes. "Robbery" is an indictable offence. A confession constitutes reasonable grounds. A six-month time limit is not imposed for indictable offences.

Problem 6

Yes. Stealing the car constitutes "Theft over $5,000.00," which is an indictable offence. Although you saw the offence but lost sight of the offender, you are an eyewitness, which constitutes reasonable grounds. A police officer's authorities for arrest without warrant apply to young offenders.

Problem 7

Yes. "Break, enter and theft" into a house is an indictable offence. A confession to a citizen constitutes reasonable grounds. Wally's report to you is hearsay evidence. Hearsay evidence may be used by you to form reasonable grounds. No time limit exists.

Problem 8

No. "Indecent act" is a summary conviction offence. Although June's eyewitness report constitutes reasonable grounds, you did not see the offence occur. Police officers must find committing to arrest without warrant for summary convictions offences. No lawful authority allows a police officer to arrest without warrant on reasonable grounds for a summary conviction offence. However, it must be emphasized that you may charge Eddie by laying an Information anytime up to six months after the offence date. A summons will then be issued and served to Eddie.

Problem 9

No. "Obscene phone calls" are summary conviction offences. A confession constitutes reasonable grounds. No lawful authority exists for a police officer to arrest on reasonable grounds for summary conviction offences. However, you may charge Eddie at any time until six months after the offence date.

Problem 10

No. No lawful authority exists to arrest if mere suspicion exists, or for the purpose of questioning in order to form reasonable grounds by means of a confession. In the absence of reasonable grounds, you may question Eddie if valid consent is obtained from him. "Attempted murder" is an indictable offence. You must find committing or have reasonable grounds to arrest without a warrant.

Problem 11

Yes. "Impaired driving" is a dual procedure offence. Reasonable grounds exist that this person is about to commit this offence. You may arrest without a warrant to prevent the offence.

Problem 12

Yes. "Assault" is a dual procedure offence. Reasonable grounds exist that the assault is about to occur. The officer may arrest without a warrant to prevent the assault.

Problem 13

Officers commonly receive information like this about offences that may be committed in the future. The verbal statement made by Eddie to Wally in this case constitutes reasonable grounds. However, the absence of a specific definition for "about to commit" causes a problem: the exact moment that constitutes "about to commit" is not specified in the *Criminal Code*. Yet, if you wait for Eddie to commit the offence, knowing that it may occur, victims could suffer harm and you may then be criticized for not preventing the offence.

Problem 14

Yes. "Wanted" constitutes reasonable grounds that the warrant actually exists. The warrant was signed and issued in Toronto. Therefore, the warrant is valid in St. Catharines and anywhere in Ontario.

Problem 15

Yes. "Wanted" constitutes reasonable grounds that the warrant actually exists. The warrant was signed and issued in Calgary and is valid in Edmonton and anywhere in Alberta.

Problem 16

Yes. Although "Trespass by night" is a summary conviction offence, the warrant is valid anywhere in Alberta and the officer has reasonable grounds that it does exist.

Problem 17

Yes. Although the warrant is not valid in Halifax, the existence of the warrant constitutes reasonable grounds that June has committed a dual procedure offence, which is classified temporarily as indictable. A procedure then must be followed to make the "out-of-province" warrant valid in Halifax. This procedure is explained under "arrest with warrant" in Chapter 7 of this text.

Problem 18

No. "Indecent act" is a summary conviction offence. The warrant is not valid in Regina. No authority exists to arrest on reasonable grounds for a summary conviction offence.

Problem 19

Although reasonable grounds exist to believe that Eddie has committed a dual procedure offence, an arrest is not necessary in the public interest, as outlined in problem 18. Therefore, you may charge him by laying an Information and compelling him to court by means of a summons or an appearance notice, despite being unable to arrest him.

Problem 20

In this case, the lawful authority exists to arrest without a warrant because there are reasonable grounds to believe that a dual procedure offence has been committed. You must determine whether the arrest is necessary in the public interest.

Problem 21

You may arrest Ward without a warrant for "Breach of the peace." You cannot charge Ward for "Cause a disturbance" because the incident occurred in a dwelling-house. Note: Ward cannot be charged for being drunk in a dwelling-house. The charge of "Public intoxication" is a provincial offence found in liquor laws and can occur only in public places.

Problem 22

Yes. "Theft under $5,000.00" is a dual procedure offence. Ward saw the offence occur and pursued Eddie continuously until apprehension, constituting "find committing."

Problem 23

Yes. "Assault" is a dual procedure offence and Wally found Eddie committing.

Problem 24

No. Ward found Eddie committing a summary conviction offence, "cause a disturbance," on public property. Ward is a nonowner; the offence did not happen in relationship to his property.

Problem 25

Yes. "Cause a disturbance" is a summary conviction offence. Ward is a person authorized by the owner. Ward found Eddie committing the summary conviction offence on or in relation to the owner's property. "Cause a disturbance" may occur anywhere except in a dwelling-house.

Problem 26

Yes. "Impaired driving" is a dual procedure offence. Wally has found Eddie committing.

Problem 27

Yes. "Mischief under $5,000.00" is a dual procedure offence. Ward has found Eddie committing. Additionally, Ward is the owner of the property. The criminal offence occurred in relation to his property.

Problem 28

Yes. "Trespass by night" is a summary conviction offence. June is the owner of the property. She found a criminal offence being committed, by Eddie, on her property.

Problem 29

No. "Theft over $5,000.00" is an indictable offence. A confession constitutes reasonable grounds. June did not find Eddie committing the offence. No citizen may arrest on reasonable grounds.

Problem 30

    a. No. Breaking the window is classified as "Mischief under $5,000.00," a dual procedure offence. Clarence's report constitutes reasonable grounds. June did not find the offence being committed. No citizen may arrest on reasonable grounds.

    b. No. Clarence lost sight of Eddie after the offence ended. Clarence's facial recognition of Eddie after the offence, and loss of sight, constitute reasonable grounds. No citizen may arrest on reasonable grounds.

    c. Yes. A police officer may arrest without a warrant on reasonable grounds for a dual procedure offence.

Problem 31

No. "Robbery" is an indictable offence. Ward did not find the offence being committed. The news broadcast represented reasonable grounds.

Problem 32

No. June has no authority to arrest on reasonable grounds that a person is about to commit an indictable offence. The police should be notified and the reasonable grounds transferred to an officer.

CHAPTER 7

Problem 1

    a. Yes. "Aggravated assault" is an indictable offence. Reasonable grounds exist to arrest without a warrant. In other words, you may arrest without obtaining judicial authorization.

    b. Yes. An arrest warrant in the first instance may be obtained for any criminal offence.

    c. No. The offender must first be charged before the warrant may be issued.

    d. You must prove the evidence that constitutes reasonable grounds that Eddie committed aggravated assault.

    e. No. If nothing else is proven, the Justice will issue a summons to compel Eddie to court.

    f. It must be proven that the offender's arrest is necessary in the public interest. The circumstances of this offence may be sufficient. You may also introduce any violence or threats made by the offender in the past.

    g. No. You must present only the Information to the Justice. No other document is required. The Justice decides whether to issue a summons or an arrest warrant.

Problem 2

    a. No. "Indecent act" is a summary conviction offence. You cannot arrest on reasonable grounds for a summary conviction offence.

    b. Yes. You may swear an Information before the six-month time limit and prove that an arrest warrant is necessary in the public interest.

Problem 3

No. "Indecent act" is a summary conviction offence. "Wanted" constitutes reasonable grounds; however, the warrant is not valid in Winnipeg.

Problem 4

    a. Yes. "Trespass by night" is a summary conviction offence. The warrant is valid in Calgary.

    b. No. The warrant usually is valid in the entire province where it is issued. The Edmonton officer may execute the warrant, without an endorsement, take custody of Wally, return him to Edmonton and bring him before a Justice within 24 hours or as soon as practicable.

CHAPTER 9

Problem 1

a. No. A s. 10(b) Charter violation does not affect evidence obtained before the violation occurred. Section 24(2) Charter may result in exclusion of evidence obtained after a Charter violation occurred.

b. No. They may be excluded under s. 24(2) Charter if the admission of the evidence would bring the administration of justice into disrepute. They may be excluded or admitted.

c. The confession will usually be excluded. According to *R. v. Collins*, physical items obtained after a Charter violation should usually be admitted.

Problem 2

a. Identify yourself to ensure Bill knows you are a police officer.

  ▸ Tell Bill he is under arrest for "Assault with a weapon" or that he is under arrest and use any general description that includes hitting Doug with a bat. Either reason is sufficient.

  ▸ Take physical custody of Bill to prevent unrestricted movement.

  ▸ Search Bill immediately to protect yourself and others. Seize

    – any evidence for any offence, or
    – any items that may injure anyone including Bill, or
    – any items that may help Bill escape.

  ▸ Inform Bill of the right to counsel as soon as practicable. This could be done while seated in the police vehicle. Read the following to Bill:

    – the basic right-to-counsel component, and
    – the existence and availability of legal aid, and
    – the toll-free telephone number for duty counsel, and
    – the right to talk to a lawyer in private.

  ▸ Ask Bill if he understands each component. Record his response. If he does not understand any component, explain it in simpler language. Then ask Bill if he understands and ask him to explain what it means. Record the response verbatim.

  ▸ Caution Bill by reading, "Do you wish to say anything in answer to the charge? You are not obliged to say anything unless you wish to do so, but whatever you say may be used in evidence. Do you understand?" Record Bill's response verbatim. Record any other comments and conversation that occur.

  ▸ Record Bill's decision regarding exercising the right. You may facilitate the decision by simply asking, "Do you want to call a lawyer?" If Bill informs you that he wants to call a lawyer, record the decision. Provide a reasonable opportunity for Bill to call a lawyer at the police station, not in the bar. Do not question him while en route to the police station. If Bill initiates conversation, record the entire conversation verbatim.

  ▸ If Bill declines to call a lawyer, record the waiver verbatim. This waiver does not have to be formally obtained in writing or signed by Bill. After the waiver, you may question Bill about the offence.

b. You do not have to assume that Bill will decide to call a lawyer. You may assume he has waived the right. You may continue the investigation.

c. Yes. The *Brydges* component is a mandatory component regardless of the accused's financial status.

Problem 3

No. Greg, an adult, must be informed of the right to counsel only upon arrest or detention. Greg is not under arrest in this case. If he confesses, then arrest him and inform him of the right to counsel.

Problem 4

Obtain possession of the warrant and produce it to Doug by letting him read it.

Problem 5

No. Informing Wally about the reasons for the arrest is a mandatory requirement created by s. 10(a) Charter. He must be told about the specific charges as soon as possible so that he may exercise the right to counsel in a meaningful way.

Problem 6

a. No specific time exists.

b. No. A reasonable opportunity does not limit Ellen to only one phone call.

c. No. Ellen, an adult, must be provided only with a reasonably opportunity to call a lawyer.

d. Yes. Ellen has the onus to inform you about the result of the call, particularly if a message was left for a lawyer. You have no obligation to ask if she has spoken to a lawyer. You may continue the investigation and question Ellen.

e. Yes. Ellen has not been reasonably diligent in attempting to call a lawyer and is causing unnecessary delays in the investigation. You may question her.

f. Yes. You have a mandatory obligation to inform Ellen that she has the right to a reasonable opportunity to call a lawyer, and you have an obligation to "hold off" questioning and the investigation during the reasonable opportunity.

Problem 7

a. No. The caution is not a mandatory requirement nor is it a procedure created by the Charter. It is a recommended guideline established by the Judge's Rules.

b. No. Failure to caution will not automatically exclude a confession or any other evidence obtained afterward. The confession will be admissible if it is proven to have been voluntarily made.

c. A failure to caution Greg represents a failure to utilize an advantage that you have to help prove the voluntariness of his confession.

Problem 8

a. It means that Walter has declined to call a lawyer and it represents a forfeiture or surrender of his s. 10(b) Charter right to counsel.

b. The Crown (prosecution).

c. You testify about the verbatim response made by Walter. Avoid simply stating that "the accused waived his right to counsel." Additionally, the Crown must prove that

- the waiver was clear and unmistakable, and
- the waiver was voluntarily made, and
- the accused understood the meaning of each component, and what was being given up.

d. No. Walter, an adult, may waive his right orally or in writing.

e. No.

Problem 9

a. You must inform Claire, a young offender, of the same four components as you would with an adult, but you must also inform her of the right to call parents, adult relatives, or any appropriate adult, and to have any of these persons present. Informing Claire of the right must be in language compatible with her intelligence.

b. Claire may contact any or all of the people from whom she has the right to seek advice, including a lawyer, parents, or any adult. She cannot be restricted to only contacting a lawyer.

c. A waiver made by Claire, a young offender, must be in writing and signed by her.

d. You must make the first notice to parent. The notice may be made orally or in writing. It must be made as soon as possible after the arrest. The parent must be informed of the reason for the arrest and place of detention. Additionally, Claire must be detained in jail cells that are separate from adult jail cells.

Problem 10

Yes. The Y.O.A. permits you to place Laura, a young offender, in custody in the police vehicle with Rick at the time of the arrest. They must be detained separately at the police station.

Problem 11

Yes. Drew must be informed of the right to counsel at any time that you speak to him during the investigation, including before questioning, when Drew is not under arrest.

Problem 12

a. No. Admissibility of evidence is determined only during a trial, by a judge. The jury, if there is one, does not determine admissibility of evidence.

b. No. Section 24(2) Charter is used to determine admissibility of evidence that was obtained *after the commission* of a Charter violation.

c. No. The trial judge must determine whether the admission of the knife would bring the administration of justice into disrepute.

d. According to the *Collins* case, it will likely be admitted because it is a physical item that did not emerge or originate from the accused person and existed before the Charter violation occurred. However, a possibility exists that the knife may be excluded.

e. No. No type of evidence obtained after a Charter violation has been committed is automatically inadmissible. The trial judge must determine if the admission of the confession would bring the administration of justice into disrepute.

f. It will likely be excluded because a confession is evidence that emerged or originated from the accused, constituting self-incriminating evidence that did not exist before the violation occurred. However, a possibility does exist that the confession may be admitted.

CHAPTER 12

Problem 1

Greg may be detained in custody as long as at least one of the four release factors (RICE) is not fulfilled. This will justify the necessity of continued custody.

Problem 2

Custody is no longer justified when all four release factors (RICE) become fulfilled. Helen must be released when RICE is fulfilled.

Problem 3

Yes. There is no evidence that indicates that Wayne will fail to appear in court; he has interests that bind him to the community and the offences is relatively minor. No evidence exists that Wayne will repeat this or any offence. All the evidence has been secured and proper identification has been obtained.

Problem 4

No. Eddie is intoxicated. His condition creates a reasonable belief that he may repeat the offence if he is released at the scene. However, RICE is a fluctuating concept, and it will be fulfilled after Eddie becomes sober.

Problem 5

No. Chris's condition and conduct create a reasonable belief that he may repeat the disturbance or assault Carlos if he is released. However, RICE may become fulfilled after Chris becomes sober and calm.

Problem 6

No. The lack of a fixed address creates a reasonable belief that Steve may fail to appear in court; he has nothing to bind him to the community and could easily move. Additionally, the absence of financial support combined with the circumstances of this offence creates a reasonable belief that he may repeat this offence.

Problem 7

No. RICE will remain unfulfilled until the offender properly identifies himself. Continued detention is justified during the period of time that the offender's identity remains unknown. "Refusing to identify" is not a criminal offence. The offender cannot be charged for refusing to identify.

Problem 8

    a. Yes. "Theft under $5,000.00" is a dual procedure offence and RICE is fulfilled. Release is mandatory.

    b. Yes.

    c. No. An Information must be laid first.

    d. Yes. You may release Eric without a document at the time of release. Afterward, you may appear before a Justice, swear an Information, have a summons issued, and serve a summons at a later date.

    e. Yes. You have discretion to release Eric with no intention of charging him or compelling him to court.

    f. No; No; No.

    g. No. RICE is fulfilled.

Problem 9

A summons may be served only a police officer in one of two ways:

1. Personally—serving it to the person to whom the summons is directed. Personal service may be made anywhere.

2. Substitutionally—if the accused person cannot be conveniently found, a summons may be served only at the accused's house to a person who lives there who is 16 years or older.

Problem 10

Two methods exist to prove that a summons was served.

1. Sworn affidavit of service—the serving officer may complete the back of the summons, which is called an "affidavit of service." The officer then appears before a Justice and swears under oath that the summons was served.

2. Verbal testimony in court—if the accused fails to appear in court, the serving officer may testify under oath about the service of the summons.

Problem 11

    a. Yes. The offence is summary conviction. RICE is fulfilled. Release is mandatory.

    b. No. RICE is fulfilled.

Problem 12

Yes. The offence is indictable. Release is not mandatory regardless of whether RICE is fulfilled.

Problem 13

Yes. The offence is dual procedure, and RICE is not fulfilled.

Problem 14

    a. No. The endorsement authorizes release at the police station (Level 2) only.

    b. Yes. The endorsement does not authorize release at the scene of the arrest (Level 1).

Problem 15

Yes. A signature represents a promise or assurance that the accused will attend court. Refusal to sign creates doubt about the court appearance. You may bring her to the police station because RICE is no longer fulfilled.

Problem 16

a. Yes. The offence of summary conviction, and RICE is fulfilled. Release is mandatory.

b. Either the OIC or any police officer because of the combined effect of s. 498 and s. 503 C.C.

c. The following documents may be used:

   ▸ a summons, after an Information has been laid,

   ▸ a promise to appear,

   ▸ a recognizance, or

   ▸ an undertaking, in conjunction with a promise to appear or recognizance.

d. No.

e. Yes. A decision may be made not to charge him while he is at the police station.

f. No. If RICE is fulfilled, continued detention is not justified. The accused must be released.

Problem 17

a. Yes. The offence is dual procedure and RICE is fulfilled. Release is mandatory.

b. No.

c. The OIC or any police officer.

Problem 18

a. Yes. "Robbery" is an indictable offence with a maximum penalty of life imprisonment. No mandatory release exists for this type of offence.

b. Yes. The OIC or any police officer has discretion to release and may release if RICE is fulfilled.

c. No. This document cannot be used to release at the police station.

d. Yes.

e. Only if Luc lives in another province or beyond 200 km from the place of arrest. Otherwise, no cash deposit can be taken.

f. Yes, if the undertaking is served in conjunction with a promise to appear or a recognizance. The undertaking cannot be served alone. Any one or all four specific conditions may be imposed at the officer's discretion.

g. Yes. These conditions are included in the four specified by the *Criminal Code*. Luc may be prohibited from communicating with a specific person and from attending a specific place.

h. No. This type of condition cannot be imposed by the OIC or any police officer. Only a Justice may impose a curfew.

Problem 19

a. Yes. Either the OIC or any police officer has discretionary authority to release and may release if RICE is fulfilled, regarding any warrant except in the case of a s. 469 C.C. offence.

b. Yes. No mandatory obligation exists to release a person arrested with an endorsed warrant. Therefore, the accused may be brought directly to a Justice for a bail hearing.

Problem 20

a. Yes. Either the OIC or any police officer has discretionary authority to release and may release if RICE is fulfilled, regarding any warrant except in the case of a s. 469 C.C. offence (new provision—s. 503(2) and (3) C.C.).

b. Yes. No mandatory obligation exists to release a person arrested with an unendorsed warrant. Therefore, the accused may be brought directly to a Justice for a bail hearing.

Problem 21

Yes. Nikolai cannot be released by the OIC or any other police officer.

Problem 22

Eric's signature represents his promise to appear in court. Refusal to sign it represents reasonable grounds that he may fail to appear in court. RICE is not fulfilled. The accused may be detained and brought before a Justice for a bail hearing.

Problem 23

The officer may impose any of the four conditions on an undertaking, in order to release Ron by means of a promise to appear or a recognizance. Ron cannot be forced to agree to this condition or any other, but failure to agree to and sign the undertaking authorizes the patrol officer to continue detention of Ron and bring him to a Justice for a bail hearing.

Problem 24

No. The undertaking with conditions may be given to Shane only in addition to a promise to appear or a recognizance.

Problem 25

a. Yes.

b. Without unreasonable delay and within 24 hours of the arrest, if a Justice is available. If no Justice is available within 24 hours of the arrest, as soon as possible.

c. No. If an adjournment is required to prepare for the bail hearing, Peter must still be brought to a Justice without unreasonable delay and within 24 hours. The prosecutor must make an application for a three-day adjournment. The Justice has discretion to grant the adjournment or reject it.

Problem 26

- ▸ Before a Justice. The Justice must detain Frank and cannot release him.
- ▸ Frank must apply for a bail hearing.
- ▸ A judge of the superior court of criminal jurisdiction (for example, in Ontario, a General Division Court judge).
- ▸ Frank.

Problem 27

a. Prosecutor. No reverse onus situation exists.

b. No.

c. In provincial court or at the police station in a JP's office.

d. Yes. The bail hearing must be conducted at the police station if the police officer is the prosecutor.

e. No. June must be present or may appear by any suitable telecommunication device, including a telephone, if the Justice deems it to be suitable and both the prosecutor and June agree.

f. Yes.

g. ▸ The Justice must release by means of an undertaking without conditions.
   ▸ No.

h. Prosecutor.

i. No. Hearsay evidence is admissible. The investigating officer may read witness statements during testimony. However, the prosecutor has the option of calling the actual witnesses.

j. ▸ Yes, to show a probability of conviction.
   ▸ Yes.
   ▸ Yes. It is relevant to primary and secondary grounds.
   ▸ Yes. It is relevant to primary and secondary grounds.

k. Yes.

l. No. June decides whether she will testify.

m. No. Not unless she testifies about the offence.

n. No.

o. No. The Information is laid before the bail hearing. Only the Crown attorney may withdraw an Information.

p. Yes.

q. Yes

r. The Justice must release June on an undertaking or recognizance, with or without conditions.

s. Unlimited. The Justice may impose any reasonable condition.

Problem 28

Eric. He has been charged with an indictable offence while awaiting trial for another indictable offence.

Problem 29

The prosecutor. Chris was arrested for an indictable offence while awaiting trial for another indictable offence. This does not constitute a reverse onus situation.

Problem 30

George. He was charged today with "fail to appear" while awaiting trial for a summary conviction offence. The same applies for "breach of undertaking."

Problem 31

Sam. He committed an indictable offence and does not live in Canada. If Sam had been charged with a summary conviction offence, the onus would have been on the prosecutor.

Problem 32

The prosecutor. This is not a reverse onus situation; the accused lives in Canada.

Problem 33

Walter.

Problem 34

a. Eleanor.
b. Eleanor must be held in custody.

CHAPTER 13

Problem 1

Yes. Any person, citizen, or police officer may lay an Information if the person has a belief based on reasonable grounds that a specific person has committed a criminal offence. Walter can prove reasonable grounds in this case. "Assault" is a dual procedure offence, which is temporarily classified as indictable at the time of offence. No time limit exists to charge.

Problem 2

No. The informant (applicant) must be named on the Information.

Problem 3

a. As soon as practicable afterward and before the court date specified on the promise to appear.
b. A Justice, defined as a Justice of the Peace (JP), or a provincial court judge. A JP is most commonly used.
c. Anywhere other than open court. An Information is usually laid in a JP's office at a police station.
d. You must swear under oath that the contents are true.
e. No.
f. Yes. An *ex parte* hearing is mandatory.
g. To prove reasonable grounds that Will committed "Fraud over $5,000.00" on the date(s) specified.
h. Yes. Hearsay evidence is allowed. However, the witnesses may be called to testify if the JP considers it necessary.
i. Yes. Unsworn evidence is not permitted.

j. No. The accused is absent from all *ex parte* hearings.

k. The JP will not sign the Information, and the promise to appear will be cancelled.

l. The JP will sign the Information, and will confirm the promise to appear.

m. When the JP signs the Information.

n. The Crown attorney.

o. No. An Information must be laid to commence the proceedings. A police officer cannot prefer an indictment; only a Crown attorney can.

Problem 4

Yes. An Information may be laid to charge an offender with any classification of offence. The Information commences proceedings regarding any criminal offence.

Problem 5

No. One wording must allege only one count. However, both counts may be joined on one Information.

Problem 6

a. No. The Crown would then have to prove that the offence occurred exactly at midnight, which is the time between those dates.

b. "Between March 22nd and March 25th"; the border dates must represent dates when the offence definitely did not occur. Consequently, the offence date may be March 23rd or March 24th.

c. No. Only the "city of Hamilton" must be included.

d. No. The informal short-form name of the offence does not constitute a valid wording because it does not contain all the facts-in-issue.

e. "did break and enter a certain place TO WIT: a dwelling-house situated at 1000 E. 200th St., and did commit the indictable offence of theft therein, contrary to s. 348(1)(b) *Criminal Code*."

f. No. An Information cannot be altered after it is signed by a Justice. Another Information must be laid to charge Eddie with the second break and enter.

Problem 7

a. Yes. However, the counts must be separated by using the phrase "and further" between the wordings.

b. Yes.

c. No. Jack and Eddie are co-accused persons by being joined on the same Information. Co-accused persons cannot be compelled by the Crown attorney to testify against each other.

d. They must be charged separately. If separate Informations are laid, they are not co-accused persons and may be compelled by the prosecution to testify against each other.

Problem 8

a. By laying an Information.

b. No. The hearing is mandatory.

c. No. A preliminary hearing is never conducted before a provincial court trial.

d. Yes.

e. Provincial court.

f. Yes.

g. To determine whether sufficient evidence exists for Will to stand trial.

h. The prosecutor.

i. No. The prosecutor may introduce only an amount of evidence that proves a prima facie case.

j. No.

k. Yes. The attorney general must first personally consent in writing.

l. Yes. The attorney general must first personally consent in writing.

m. It is sent to a clerk at the superior court of criminal jurisdiction. It will not be used at the trial.

n. A prosecutor completes one and signs it. It is not sworn before a Justice.

o. Yes. The prosecutor could have preferred an indictment with the attorney general's consent. Will could be caused to stand trial without the preliminary hearing being conducted.

CHAPTER 15

Problem 1

a. Yes. A motor vehicle is a place for the purpose of a search. This means that all the search and seizure laws must be followed relating to the search of the car. A motor vehicle is not a place in relation to break and enter offences only. This means that a person cannot be charged with a break and enter if the offender breaks into a car, but must instead be charged with an offence such as "Theft" or "Mischief."

b. Yes. There is no requirement to prove that reasonable grounds exist that the stolen property is in the car in order to ask for consent.

c. No. You must obtain consent only from one person who has lawful authority to give consent. Since Shane's father is the owner, and he is not present, obtain consent from the driver, Shane. The driver has control of the car and can regulate access into the car.

d. Yes. You must prove that he has knowledge of the specific act to be conducted and what the target of the search is. You must also distinguish what you want to search. In this case, there is one car and two people.

e. Yes. No law compels him to consent. Shane must know he has a choice. You may simply inform him, "you don't have to consent" or "you have a choice to let me search or not."

f. Yes. He must know that he may stop the search at any time.

g. No. Because he is not compelled to give consent, he is simply exercising his right to refuse. Refusing to do something that one is not legally obliged to do is not incriminating evidence and cannot be used against him.

h. No. There is no offence for refusing to consent.

i. No. Search of a person is an act separate from search of a vehicle; therefore, separate consent is needed. If there is more than one person, separate consent is needed for each person.

j. No. Shane can end the search at any time. However, you may try to obtain consent by using effective communication skills to regain consent. His refusal to open the trunk does not prevent you from trying to obtain his consent. A final alternative is to continue investigating and gather additional evidence that will allow you to obtain a search warrant to search the car.

k. No. Obtaining consent improperly constitutes a s. 8 Charter violation. The trial judge must then determine whether to admit or exclude the evidence, using the guidelines created by the Supreme Court of Canada, in the *Collins* case. The evidence in this case is physical items, and according to the guidelines, that type of evidence is usually admitted.

l. No. Both Shane and Tony are adults. No requirement exists for you to obtain consent in writing. You may obtain verbal consent, which should be recorded verbatim in your notebook. Alternatively, you may write a consent form on a statement or in your notebook and ask Shane to sign it.

Problem 2

No. The Supreme Court of Canada in *R. v. Edwards* (1996), agreed with the Ontario Court of Appeal, in *R. v. Pugliese* (1992), that the tenant alone may grant or refuse permission to enter the premises. Walter is not a lawful occupier of the apartment.

Problem 3

No. Eddie is not a lawful occupier as defined by the Supreme Court of Canada. He does not contribute to the household expenses, does not control the premises, and cannot regulate access. Tom, in the absence of his parents, is the lawful occupier because he has control of the premises. Additionally, Tom has a reasonable expectation of privacy whereas Eddie does not. Therefore, consent should be obtained from Tom if you intend to search without first obtaining a search warrant. Finally, it should be noted that if consent is improperly obtained, any evidence found will not be automatically inadmissible despite the commission of a s. 8 Charter violation. If the item seized is a physical item, it may be admissible.

CHAPTER 16

Problem 1

a. Yes. A s. 487 C.C. search warrant authorizes the search of a building, receptacle, or place. A motor vehicle is a place for this purpose.

b. Obtain valid consent.

Problem 2

Yes, it can be obtained to search for evidence that proves the commission of any classification of criminal offence.

Problem 3

a. Yes. Police are authorized to use a s. 487 C.C. search warrant to search for and seize any evidence that proves the whereabouts of a person who is believed to have committed any criminal offence.

b. No. You must obtain a Feeney warrant.

Problem 4

a. No. Section 487 C.C. does not have an exception that permits the police to search for this type of evidence without first obtaining a search warrant.

b. No. An Information To Obtain must always be completed before a search warrant may be issued. No circumstances allow you to bypass this step.

Problem 5

a. No. Only one specific place may be named on one Information to Obtain. Multiple places cannot be named.

b. No. If the items may be in any of three places, only mere suspicion exists that the items are in one of those places. Therefore, reasonable grounds do not exist that the items are in one of those places. The search warrants will likely be denied.

Problem 6

No. You must list specific items that will be evidence of that offence. Broad terms cannot be used because this prevents the recognition and identification of items that may be found. Each item must be described in detail, to allow you to positively recognize and identify items when they are found.

Problem 7

a. No. That description is general and prevents recognition and identification. Additional general information such as model, and make, if known, must be included. Afterward, specific descriptions that are unique features, such as serial number, damage, or any marks unique to that TV, must be added.

b. Yes. You cannot omit this information. You may name "Break, enter, and theft" as the offence. If you were not certain that Reg committed that offence, you could name "Possession of stolen property under $5,000.00." Do not use the short-form name. Use the formal wording that would be used on an Information.

c. Summarize the facts of the break and enter to prove that the offence actually occurred.

d. No. The warrant is directed to the place. If you know who the owner is, that fact will elevate the credibility of your reasonable grounds for belief. The important fact is to describe the place specifically on the Information to Obtain and on the Appendix B, which will explain your grounds for belief.

e. Yes. The option is yours to refer to Marg as an anonymous informant or to name her. The Supreme Court of Canada has recognized the need to protect the identity of informants. In this case, you should not divulge Marg's identity. Keep her anonymous because she has given you information in the past and is associated with known criminals, which indicates that she will probably be a long-term valuable informant. Additionally, the public may have access to the Information To Obtain if the items are found.

f. No. This simple conclusory statement is insufficient. The written grounds must include the basis for Marg's information. In this case, you should specify

- the time that Marg was at the house,
- the fact that she was in the livingroom,
- her exact observations about the TV (for example, the location of the TV and the fact that is was operating),
- a specific description of the TV,
- Reg's remarks about the TV, the break and enter, and his attempt to sell it,
- Marg's familiarity with Reg,
- all persons present, and
- Marg's past accuracy regarding information provided.

g. Yes, it should. She is an eyewitness regarding the possession of the stolen property and a recipient of a confession regarding the break and enter. Additionally, she has a degree of reliability based on past incidents.

h. Explain the connection between the TV and the offence named.

i. No. The JP must be a neutral, unbiased evaluator and cannot participate in the investigation. Advice from the JP would constitute a serious s. 8 Charter violation.

j. Anywhere but in open court. Usually, it would be the JP's office, but any place will suffice.

k. No. Advice from the JP would constitute a serious s. 8 Charter violation.

l. Present the Information To Obtain. The JP evaluates the written grounds and decides whether reasonable grounds exist. Avoid verbal, unsworn communication with the JP.

m. The JP does; you should not have possession of it.

n. You, the applying officer, must be named on the warrant. All other officers who will be executing the warrant with you do not have to be named. However, there is no requirement that you participate in the search. Your presence is desirable because it is likely that you will have more knowledge about the investigation.

o. No, the JP must specifically authorize night hours. The JP must write the authorized night hours on the warrant.

p. Any number of officers are authorized. You are not restricted to a certain number.

q. No, unless exigent circumstances exist.

r. Your decision depends on the reasonableness of the circumstances. The warrant does not stipulate that someone must be home; however, to prevent a s. 8 Charter violation, you must prove that you executed the warrant to prevent loss or destruction of the property.

s. Show him the warrant and let him read it. Do not give him a copy.

t. No. The search warrant does not authorize either the search or the arrest of persons.

u. No. The search is complete once all the named items are found.

v. No. You must re-apply for another warrant, and use Marg's new information as your grounds for belief.

w. Yes. You have reasonable grounds to arrest Reg without an arrest warrant. Marg was the recipient of a confession. This constitutes reasonable grounds.

Problem 8

A s. 487 C.C. search warrant only, which can be used to search any place for narcotics. A C.D.S.A. search warrant cannot be used to search a place that is not a dwelling-house.

Problem 9

a. A C.D.S.A. or a s. 487 C.C. search warrant.
b. No. The same rules apply.
c. At least one officer must be named on a C.D.S.A. search warrant to ensure that a specific officer is responsible for the control and conduct of the search. Naming two officers is acceptable, but not an entire drug unit.
d. Yes, and that officer must closely supervise the search.
e. Any number may participate, but seized evidence must be taken into the possession of the named officer.
f. Yes.

References

CASES

Barron v. Canada, [1993] 1 S.C.R. 416

Caccamo v. The Queen, 1975 CanLII 24 (S.C.C.)

Canada Post Corp. v. Canada (Attorney General) (1995), 95 C.C.C. (3d) 568 (Ont. Gen. Div.)

Chiau v. Canada (Minister of Citizenship and Immigration) (T.D.), [1998] 2 F.C. 642, 1998 CanLII 9042

Church of Scientology and the Queen (No. 6) (1987), 31 C.C.C. (3d) 449 (Ont. C.A.)

Cloutier v. Langlois (1990), 53 C.C.C. (3d) 257 (S.C.C.)

Eccles v. Bourque (1974), 19 C.C.C. (2d) 129 (S.C.C.)

Frey v. Fedoruk et al. (1950), 3 D.L.R. 527 (S.C.C.)

Hicks v. Faulkner (1878), 8 Q.B.D. 167 (D.C.)

Hill v. Hamilton-Wentworth Regional Police Services Board, 2007 SCC 41

Hunter et al. v. Southam Inc. (1984), 14 C.C.C. (3d) 97 (S.C.C.)

Mills v. The Queen (1986), 26 C.C.C. (3d) 481 (S.C.C.)

R. v. Abel & Corbett, 2008 BCCA 54

R. v. Akey (1990), 1 O.R. (3d) 693 (Gen. Div.)

R. v. Anderson (1984), 10 C.C.C. (3d) 204 (Ont. C.A.)

R. v. B.(G.) (1990), 56 C.C.C. (3d) 200 (S.C.C.)

R. v. Backhouse (2005), 127 C.R.R. (2d) 1 (Ont. C.A.)

R. v. Bartle (1994), 92 C.C.C. (3d) 289 (S.C.C.)

R. v. Beare (1988), 45 C.C.C. (3d) 57 (S.C.C.)

R. v. Beaudry (2007), 216 C.C.C. (3d) 353 (S.C.C.)

R. v. Belliveau (1985), 58 A.R. 334 (C.A.)

R. v. Belnavis (1996), 107 C.C.C. (3d) 195 (Ont. C.A.)

R. v. Belnavis (1997), 118 C.C.C. (3d) 405 (S.C.C.)

R. v. Bennett (1996), 108 C.C.C. (3d) 175 (Que. C.A.)

R. v. Black (1998), 50 C.C.C. (3d) 1 (S.C.C.)

R. v. Borden (1994), 92 C.C.C. (3d) 404 (S.C.C.)

R. v. Brydges (1990), 53 C.C.C. (3d) 380 (S.C.C.)

R. v. Burlingham (1995), 97 C.C.C. (3d) 385 (S.C.C.)

R. v. Burtasson (1982), 64 C.C.C. (2d) 268 (Ont. H.C.J.)

R. v. Bushman (1968), 4 C.R.N.S. (B.C.C.A.)

R. v. Caslake (1998), 121 C.C.C. (3d) 97 (S.C.C.)

R. v. Charlton, 1992 CanLII 367 (B.C.C.A.)

R. v. Clarkson (1986), 25 C.C.C. (3d) 207 (S.C.C.)

R. v. Clayton (2007), 220 C.C.C. (3d) 449 (S.C.C.)

R. v. Clement (1996), 107 C.C.C. (3d) 52 (S.C.C.)

R. v. Cline (1956), 115 C.C.C. 18 (Ont. C.A.)

R. v. Colarusso (1994), 87 C.C.C. (3d) 193 (S.C.C.)

R. v. Colgan (1987), 38 C.C.C. (3d) 576 (S.C.C.)

R. v. Collins (1987), 33 C.C.C. (3d) 1 (S.C.C.)

R. v. Cooper (2005), 195 C.C.C. (3d) 162 (N.S.C.A.)

R. v. Corcoran, 1995 CanLII 7085 (Ont. S.C.)

R. v. Cote (1977), 33 C.C.C. (2d) 353 (S.C.C.)

R. v. Cunningham and Ritchie (1979), 49 C.C.C. (2d) 390 (Man. Co. Ct.)

R. v. Daviault (1994), 93 C.C.C. (3d) 21 (S.C.C.)

R. v. Davidson, 2004 ABCA 337

R. v. Dean (1965), 3 C.C.C. 228 (Ont. C.A.)

R. v. Debot (1989), 52 C.C.C. (3d) 193 (S.C.C.)

R. v. Dedman (1985), 20 C.C.C. (3d) 97 (S.C.C.)

R. v. Duarte (1990), 53 C.C.C. (3d) 1 (S.C.C.)

R. v. Dyment (1988), 45 C.C.C. (3d) 207 (S.C.C.)

R. v. Edwards (1996), 104 C.C.C. (3d) 136 (S.C.C.)

R. v. Eng, 1995 CanLII 1794 (B.C.C.A.)

R. v. Evans (1991), 63 C.C.C. (3d) 289 (S.C.C.)

R. v. Evans (1996), 104 C.C.C. (3d) 23 (S.C.C.)

R. v. Feeney (1997), 115 C.C.C. (3d) 129 (S.C.C.)

R. v. Fegan (1993), 80 C.C.C. (3d) 356 (Ont. C.A.)

R. v. Ferris (1998), 126 C.C.C. (3d) 298 (B.C.C.A.)

R. v. Ferron (1989), 49 C.C.C. (3d) 432 (B.C.C.A.)

R. v. Fulton (1972), 10 C.C.C. (2d) 120 (Sask. Q.B.)

R. v. Genest (1989), 45 C.C.C. (3d) 385 (S.C.C.)

R. v. Gimson (1991), 69 C.C.C. (3d) 552 (S.C.C.)

R. v. Godoy (1999), 131 C.C.C. (3d) 129 (S.C.C.)

R. v. Golub (1997), 117 C.C.C. (3d) 193 (Ont. C.A.)

R. v. Grant (1991), 67 C.C.C. (3d) 268 (S.C.C.)

R. v. Grant (1993), 84 C.C.C. (3d) 173 (S.C.C.)

R. v. Gray (1993), 81 C.C.C. (3d) 174 (Man. C.A.)

R. v Grenier (1991), 65 C.C.C. (3d) 76 (Que. C.A.)

R. v. Guiboche (2004), 183 C.C.C. (3d) 361 (Man. C.A.)

R. v. Hall (2002), 167 C.C.C. (3d) 449 (S.C.C.)

R. v. Harrison, 2008 ABQB 81

R. v. Hebert (1990), 57 C.C.C. (3d) 1 (S.C.C.)

R. v. Hermanus (1993) (B.C. Prov. Ct.)

R. v. Hollis (1992), 76 C.C.C. (3d) 421 (B.C.C.A.)

R. v. Jackson (1993), 15 O.R. (3d) 709 (C.A.)

R. v. Jacques, [1996] 3 S.C.R. 312

R. v. J.E.B., 1989 CanLII 1495 (N.S.C.A.)

R. v. Jobin (1995), 97 C.C.C. (3d) 97 (S.C.C.)

R. v. Kalanj, [1989] 1 S.C.R. 1594

R. v. Knowlton (1973), 10 C.C.C. (2d) 377 (S.C.C.)

R. v. Kokesch (1990), 61 C.C.C. (3d) 207 (S.C.C.)

R. v. L. (M.C.), (2005) 196 C.C.C. (3d) 571 (Ont. C.J.).

R. v. Lal (1998), 130 C.C.C. (3d) 570 (B.C.C.A.)

R. v. Landry (1986), 25 C.C.C. (3d) 1 (S.C.C.)

R. v. Laramee (1972), 9 C.C.C. (2d) 433 (N.W.T. Mag. Ct.)

R. v. Latimer (1997), 112 C.C.C. (3d) 193 (S.C.C.)

R. v. LePage (1986), 32 C.C.C. (3d) 171 (N.S.C.A.)

R. v. Lerke (1986), 24 C.C.C. (3d) 129 (Alta. C.A.)

R. v. Lim (No. 2) (1990), 1 C.R.R. (2d) 136 (Ont. H.C.J.)

R. v. MacKenzie (1991), 64 C.C.C. (3d) 336 (N.S.C.A.)

R. v. Macooh (1993), 82 C.C.C. (3d) 481 (S.C.C.)

R. v. MacPherson, 1998 CanLII 6710 (B.C.S.C.)

R. v. Mann, [2004] 3 S.C.R. 59, 2004 SCC 52.

R. v. Manninen (1987), 34 C.C.C. (3d) 385 (S.C.C.)

R. v. McGregor (1985), 23 C.C.C. (3d) 266 (Man. Q.B.)

R. v. McKane (1987), 35 C.C.C. (3d) 481 (Ont. C.A.)

R. v. Mercer (1992), 70 C.C.C. (3d) 180 (Ont. C.A.)

R. v. Mitchell, 1997 CanLII 6321 (Ont. C.A.)

R. v. Moran (1987), 36 C.C.C. (3d) 225 (Ont. C.A.)

R. v. Neilsen (1988), 43 C.C.C. (3d) 548 (Sask. C.A.)

R. v. Nicholls (1986) (Ont. Dist. Ct.)

R. v. Nolan (1987), 34 C.C.C. (3d) 289 (S.C.C.)

R. v. Noseworthy (1995), 101 C.C.C. (3d) 447 (Ont. Gen. Div.)

R. v. O'Brien (1954), 110 C.C.C. 1 (S.C.C.)

R. v. Pavel (1989), 53 C.C.C. (3d) 296 (Ont. C.A.)

R. v. Pearson (1992), 77 C.C.C. (3d) 124 (S.C.C.)

R. v. Petri (2003), 171 C.C.C. (3d) 567 (Man. C.A.)

R. v. Pillay (2004), 119 C.R.R. (2d) 346 (Ont. S.C.)

R. v. Polashek (1999), 134 C.C.C. (3d) 187 (Ont. C.A.)

R. v. Primeau (1995), 97 C.C.C. (3d) 1 (S.C.C.)

R. v. Prosper (1994), 92 C.C.C. (3d) 353 (S.C.C.)

R. v. Pugliese (1992), 71 C.C.C. (3d) 295 (Ont. C.A.)

R. v. Purdy (1972), 8 C.C.C. (2d) 52 (N.B. S.C.)

R. v. Rao (1984), 12 C.C.C. (3d) 97 (Ont. C.A.)

R. v. Sandhu (1993), 82 C.C.C. (3d) 236 (B.C.C.A.)

R. v. Schmautz (1990), 53 C.C.C. (3d) 556 (S.C.C.)

R. v. Scott (1990), 61 C.C.C. (3d) 300 (S.C.C.)

R. v. Sharpe, 2002 BCSC 213

R. v. Shea (1982), 1 C.C.C. (3d) 316 (Ont. H.C.J.)

R. v. Siemens, 2000 BCSC 1015

R. v. Silveira (1995), 97 C.C.C. (3d) 450 (S.C.C.)

R. v. Simpson (1993), 79 C.C.C. (3d) 482 (Ont. C.A.)

R. v. Smellie (1994), 95 C.C.C. (3d) 9 (B.C.C.A.)

R. v. Smith (1989), 50 C.C.C. (3d) 308 (S.C.C.)

R. v. Smith (1992), 75 C.C.C. (3d) 257 (S.C.C.)

R. v. Speid (1991), 8 C.R.R. (2d) 383 (Ont. C.A.)

R. v. Spezzano (1977), 34 C.C.C. (2d) 87 (Ont. C.A.)

R. v. Stillman (1997), 113 C.C.C. (3d) 321 (S.C.C.)

R. v. Storrey (1990), 53 C.C.C. (3d) 316 (S.C.C.)

R. v. Strachan (1988), 46 C.C.C. (3d) 479 (S.C.C.)

R. v. T.(E.) (1993), 86 C.C.C. (3d) 289 (S.C.C.)

R. v. Tessling (2004), 189 C.C.C. (3d) 129 (S.C.C.)

R. v. Therens (1985), 18 C.C.C. (3d) 481 (S.C.C.)

R. v. Top (1989), 48 C.C.C. (3d) 493 (Alta. C.A.)

R. v. Tugnum, 2002 BCSC 1572

R. v. Waterfield (1964), 1 Q.B. 164 (C.C.A.)

R. v. West (1915), 25 C.C.C. 145 (S.C. App. Div.)

R. v. Whalen (1974), 17 C.C.C. (2d) 217 (Ont. Co. Ct.)

R. v. Whitfield (1969), 1 C.C.C. 129 (S.C.C.)

R. v. Wijesinha (1995), 100 C.C.C. (3d) 410 (S.C.C.)

R. v. Wills (1992), 70 C.C.C. (3d) 529 (Ont. C.A.)

R. v. Wise (1992), 70 C.C.C. (3d) 193 (S.C.C.)

R. v. Wong (1993), 60 C.C.C. (3d) 460 (S.C.C.)

R. v. Yamanaka (1998), 128 C.C.C. (3d) 570 (B.C.C.A.)

R. v. Zammit (1993), 81 C.C.C. (3d) 112 (Ont. C.A.)

Semayne's Case (1558–1774), All E.R. Rep. 63 (1604)

STATUTES

Bail Reform Act, S.C. 1970-71-72, c. 37

Canada Evidence Act, R.S.C. 1985, C-5

Canadian Charter of Rights and Freedoms, Part I of the *Constitution Act, 1982*, being Schedule B to the *Canada Act 1982* (U.K.), 1982, c. 11.

Controlled Drugs and Substances Act, S.C. 1996, c. 19

Criminal Code, R.S.C. 1985, c. C-46

Identification of Criminals Act, R.S.C. 1985, c. I-1

Interpretation Act, R.S.C. 1985, c. I-21

Narcotic Control Act, R.S.C. 1985, c. N-1

Police Services Act, R.S.O. 1990, c. P.15

Residential Tenancies Act, 2006, S.O. 2006, c. 17

Youth Criminal Justice Act, S.C. 2002, c. 1

BOOKS

Broughman, Lord H., *Historical Sketches of Statesman Who Flourished in the Time of George III* (1855)

Department of Justice, *Firearms Officer Desk Manual*, vol. 2 (1998).

Dukelow, Daphne A., and Betsy Nuse. *Pocket Dictionary of Canadian Law*. Toronto: Carswell, 1991.

Erhlich, Eugene, et al. *Oxford American Dictionary*. New York: Oxford University Press, 1980.

Greenspan, Edward L., Q.C., and Justice Marc Rosenberg. *Martin's Annual Criminal Code*. Aurora, ON: Canada Law Book.

Lawyer's Weekly, Feb. 12, 1993, vol. 12, no. 38. Toronto: Butterworths.

Lecture on "Powers of Arrest" at Ontario Police College, 1977.

Ministry of the Solicitor General of Ontario. *A Police Learning System for Ontario—Final Report and Recommendations*. Strategic Planning Committee on Police Training and Education, 1992.

Ministry of the Solicitor General of Ontario. *Powers of Arrest*. Ontario Police College, 1986.

Ministry of the Solicitor General of Ontario. *Statute Search Powers, Search Warrants*. Ontario Police College, 1986.

Québec, Ministère de la Sécurité publique, Direction générale des services correctionnels, *Evolution of Penal Policies and the Debate on Imprisonment in Canada and Québec: 1969 to 1999* (2000), http://www.msp.gouv.qc.ca/reinsertion/publicat/politiques_penales/politiques_penales_en.pdf.

Salhany, Roger E. *Canadian Criminal Procedure*, 5th ed. Aurora, ON: Canada Law Book, 1989.

Glossary

about to occur   An offence that has not been committed but for which a strong probability exists that it may be committed in the near future. *(Ch. 4)*

actual possession   Having an item on his or her person. *(Ch. 17)*

arbitrary—no belief   No justifiable reason at all to connect a person to an offence. *(Ch. 3)*

arrest   Defined in case law as actual restraint on a person's liberty without that person's consent; physical custody of a person with the intent to detain. *Arrest* and *detain* essentially have the same meaning. *(Ch. 1)*

arrest with a warrant   This lawful authority represents judicial authorization to arrest. The decision to arrest is made by a Justice and a police officer carries out the arrest. *(Ch. 1)*

arrest without a warrant   This lawful authority represents an arrest made without judicial authorization. A police officer makes the decision to arrest, not a Justice. *(Ch. 1)*

assault   The criminal offence of communicating a "threatening act or gesture"—for example, putting your hands on someone. *(Ch. 9)*

bail   Any form of release authorized by the *Criminal Code*. It may involve the deposit of money or valuable security as a condition of release. *(Ch. 11)*

belief   A level of certainty concerning a specific person's connection to a specific offence. *(Ch. 1)*

breach of the peace   The violation of the peace, quiet, and security to which one is legally entitled, as defined in the *Criminal Code*. *(Ch. 4)*

brief detention   An informal, short non-investigative custody for the specific purpose of identification. *(Ch. 4)*

building   A structure that is not used as a permanent residence, such as a business premises, an office, or a school. *(Ch. 17)*

caution   This relates to the arrested person's right to remain silent. It is not a statutory requirement in Canada; however, it is strongly recommended and can be a significant investigative benefit by helping to prove that an arrested person's statements were voluntarily made. *(Ch. 9)*

charge   An informal term for laying an Information. *(Ch. 11)*

circumstantial evidence   A set of circumstances that indirectly proves at least one fact-in-issue of an offence by means of inference or suggestion. The opposite of direct evidence, it includes any evidence that does not constitute eyewitness evidence or a full confession. *(Ch. 4)*

citizen   Not defined in the *Criminal Code*, but referred to as "any one" or "every one"; anyone who is not a peace officer—for example, security guards and private investigators. *(Ch. 17)*

classification of offence   The process by which a criminal offence is recognized as either summary conviction, indictable, or dual procedure (hybrid). The classification determines which authorities—for example, arrest and release—apply, and the maximum penalty incurred by the offence. *(Ch. 2)*

common-law exigent circumstances (CLEC)   A public safety emergency in which there is a risk to any person's life. *(Ch. 8)*

compel   To force; no choice allowed. In relation to a witness, it is the legal authority to demand that a witness appear in court to testify about an offence. *(Ch. 11)*

conclusory statement   A general conclusion or opinion offered with no explanation of its basis—for example, "An anonymous informant reports that the suspect has two stolen television sets in his house." *(Ch. 16)*

confession   A verbal or written inculpatory statement made by an offender to either a police officer or a citizen. A confession represents the best (strongest) type of reasonable grounds. *(Ch. 4)*

conscriptive evidence   Evidence by which an accused is compelled to incriminate himself or herself, by means of a statement, the use of the body, or the production of bodily samples, at the request of the state—for example, a confession made by an accused following a Charter violation, or the compelled taking and use of bodily substances, such as blood, which lead to self-incrimination. *(Ch. 9)*

consent   Defined in case law as a person's "voluntary and informed decision" to allow the police to search or question, or to permit the intrusion of the investigative process upon his constitutionally protected rights. *(Ch. 5)*

constructive possession   Having an item not on his or her person but in any place, whether or not he or she owns or occupies the place and has control or access to the item for his or her use or benefit. *(Ch. 17)*

count   The number of instances of an offence, stated on an Information—for example, three counts of "Assault." *(Ch. 13)*

criminal offence   A violation of a federal statute; the majority of offences are defined by the *Criminal Code*. *(Ch. 2)*

custody   Any extent of physical or psychological restraint of an individual without his or her consent. Defined by the Supreme Court of Canada as "the deprivation of liberty by physical constraint," the assumption of control over the movement of a person by demand or direction of a police officer, or a psychological compulsion existing within a person, or a perception that his or her freedom has been removed. *(Ch. 1)*

derivative evidence   A subset of conscriptive evidence, frequently described as conscripted real evidence; physical evidence that is discovered as the result of conscriptive evidence after a Charter violation has occurred—for example, a murder weapon that is discovered because of a suspect's confession obtained after a Charter violation. *(Ch. 9)*

detention   A shorter duration of custody exercised without judicial authorization. *Arrest* and *detention* are essentially the same concept. *(Ch. 1)*

disposition hearing   A hearing, convened on application by a police officer, to determine whether seized items will be restored to a person's possession or whether they will be disposed of. *(Ch. 17)*

distress call   Typically, a 911 call from within a dwelling-house. *(Ch. 17)*

dual procedure (hybrid) offence   A serious criminal offence such as "Theft under $5000" or "Sexual assault." For the purposes of arrest, a dual procedure offence is considered to be indictable. This means that, as with an indictable offence, an officer does not have to find committing to arrest an offender if the officer has reasonable grounds. A dual procedure offence about to be committed is also treated as indictable; an officer can arrest to prevent the commission of a dual procedure offence. *(Ch. 2)*

dwelling-house   The whole or any part of a building or structure that is kept or occupied as a permanent residence, including any building that is connected to the house by a doorway or covered and enclosed passageway (for example, an attached garage is a dwelling-house), and a unit that is designed to be mobile and to be used as a permanent or temporary residence, and that is being used as a residence. *(Ch. 17)*

election   An accused's choice about which level of court (superior or provincial) he or she will be tried in and whether the trial will be with or without a jury. *(Ch. 2)*

***ex parte* hearing**   A hearing conducted by a Justice, in the absence of the accused, before the Justice signs an Information. The hearing is mandatory regardless of whether the Information is laid before a summons/arrest warrant is issued or after the accused has been arrested and released. *(Ch. 13)*

exceptional circumstances   Situations "where the law enforcement interest is so compelling that it overrides the individual's right to privacy within the home." *(Ch. 17)*

exigent circumstances   A situation of emergency or importance; in relation to search, circumstances that may make it impossible or regrettable to wait to enter by means of a search warrant at that time. *(Ch. 8)*

expressed consent   Consent where no doubt exists that consent was given; the full case law informational component was communicated. *(Ch. 15)*

eyewitness   A person who saw an entire offence committed and is capable of recognizing the offender's face. *(Ch. 4)*

facts-in-issue   Elements of the offence that must be proven in order to convict an accused. *(Ch. 17)*

Feeney warrant   An informal term for a warrant that authorizes the police to enter a dwelling-house, for the specific purpose of arresting an offender, when reasonable grounds exist that the offender is in the dwelling-house. Searching for physical evidence is not the primary purpose. *(Ch. 8)*

Feeney warrant 1   Referred to as "Included Authorization," a warrant to enter a dwelling-house, obtained after the offender has been charged—that is, after an Information has been laid. *(Ch. 8)*

Feeney warrant 2   Referred to as a "Warrant to Enter," a warrant to enter a dwelling-house, obtained before the offender has been charged—that is, before an Information has been laid. This warrant is applied for when s. 495 C.C. authority to arrest without a warrant exists. *(Ch. 8)*

find committing   Derived from case law, the definition comprises two circumstances: (1) The commission of an offence in which the offender remains at the scene: seeing an offender actually commit the offence. This requires witnessing the offence completely, seeing all the elements of the offence (the facts-in-issue) and the person who committed the entire offence. Find committing does not include seeing a partial offence, or not seeing it occur but being told about it. (2) The commission of an offence in which the offender flees from the scene: seeing an offender actually commit an offence and pursuing the offender immediately and continuously until apprehension. *(Ch. 3)*

focus of search   A limitation placed on a search; it can be directed only at a person or a place. *(Ch. 14)*

forensic DNA analysis   In relation to an investigation, the analysis of a bodily substance and the comparison of the result with the results of the analysis of the bodily substance found at the crime scene, on or within the victim's body, or on or within the body of any person or thing associated with the commission of a criminal offence. *(Ch. 16)*

forensic DNA analysis warrant   A warrant authorizing forensic DNA analysis that may be obtained only in relation to certain designated offences, such as "Murder" or "Kidnapping." *(Ch. 17)*

forthwith   Immediately or as soon as practicable. *(Ch. 17)*

general warrant   Warrant used by police officers only to obtain information concerning the commission of an offence under any federal statute. The information may be obtained by any device, by any investigative technique or procedure, or by doing anything that would otherwise be an unreasonable search or seizure. *(Ch. 16)*

hearsay evidence   Observations that were not perceived by one's own senses—for example, a person witnesses a criminal act and tells a police officer. *(Ch. 11)*

hot pursuit   Defined in case law as "continuous pursuit conducted with reasonable diligence, such that pursuit and capture, along with commission of the offence, may be considered as forming part of a single transaction." *(Ch. 8)*

hunch   A baseless opinion premised on intuition gained through experience; unsubstantiated speculation, conjecture, rumour, or gossip. *(Ch. 3)*

immediate surroundings   The area in which a lawful arrest occurs, the size of which is governed by the s. 8 Charter requirement of reasonableness—that is, what is reasonable in the situation. *(Ch. 17)*

implied consent   A logical inference that consent was given—some doubt may exist. *(Ch. 15)*

inadvertent discovery   Finding unexpectedly, without prior knowledge; the plain-view doctrine provides the authority to lawfully search and seize a discovered item. *(Ch. 17)*

inculpatory statement   Words that incriminate or suggest one's guilt. *(Ch. 17)*

indictable offence   A major criminal offence such as "Murder" or "Robbery." A police officer does not have to find committing if reasonable grounds exist to arrest. There is no time limit to charge a person who commits an indictable offence. *(Ch. 2)*

indictment   A document that formally charges an offender. Its contents are the same as an Information, but it is written by a Crown attorney, not a police officer. *(Ch. 13)*

inducement   A threat or promise. *(Ch. 5, 15)*

informant   (1) A witness whom the police do not subpoena to court, in order to maintain confidentiality. The person may be known by name or may be anonymous and unknown to the officer. (2) The person (usually a police officer) who lays an Information. *(Ch. 4)*

Information   A formal document, sworn to under oath and signed by a Justice, that alleges a specific adult or young offender committed a specific offence, of any classification; Form 7 under s. 839 C.C. *(Ch. 13)*

Information to Obtain   An application made to a Justice, under oath, before a search warrant may be issued. *(Ch. 16)*

investigative detention   A brief removal of freedom, for investigative purposes, involving significant psychological restraint, without consent and without actually making an arrest. This custody authority applies to the level of belief, reasonable suspicion to detain. *(Ch. 1)*

joinder of counts   The procedure of listing more than one offence (committed by one person) on a single Information. The classification of offence must be the same for all—for example, three summary conviction offences. *(Ch. 13)*

joinder of parties   The procedure of naming more than one offender on a single Information. The named offenders are called co-accused persons and the prosecution cannot subpoena one co-accused to testify against another co-accused. *(Ch. 13)*

joint possession   Two or more persons having constructive possession of an item. *(Ch. 17)*

judicial authorization   Authority given by a Justice, who must be unbiased and neutral. *(Ch. 16)*

Justice   A provincial court judge or Justice of the Peace (JP) as defined in the *Criminal Code. (Ch. 4)*

justified use of force   Using as much force as is necessary when doing anything to enforce the law—for example, making a lawful arrest. *(Ch. 9)*

laying an Information   Completing a Form 7, bringing it before a Justice, and swearing its contents under oath; charging an offender. *(Ch. 13)*

legal justification   With respect to executing an investigative procedure or a police authority, to give concrete reasons for forming a belief. *(Ch. 4)*

Level 1 release   Refers to an analysis of release provisions (RICE), by the arresting officer, at the scene of the arrest; applies to the interval between the time of arrest and the time of arrival at the police station. *(Ch. 11)*

Level 2 release   Refers to Level 2 release considerations (RICE) that begin with the accused person's arrival at the police station. The OIC or any police officer is authorized to release at this level. *(Ch. 11)*

mens rea   Intent; guilty mind. *(Ch. 17)*

mere suspicion   Usually associated with an offence that is not in progress, it is based on logical but unsubstantiated theories that are supported only by very weak circumstantial evidence; a belief based on rumour, speculation, conjecture, or weak certainty. *(Ch. 1)*

non-conscriptive evidence   Evidence in whose creation the accused was not compelled to participate—for example, a murder weapon; physical items that do not emerge from the suspect. *(Ch. 9)*

number recorder (DNR)   Any device that can be used to record or identify a telephone number, or the location of the telephone from which a call originates or at which it is received or is intended to be received. *(Ch. 16)*

objective/subjective test   A two-pronged test, used by a Justice to determine whether a police officer's belief met the proper standard of reasonable grounds. In other words, the trial judge, who represents a reasonable person standing in the shoes of the arresting officer, must be convinced that reasonable grounds for a belief existed. The officer's own belief must pass the subjective test. Passing the objective test requires justifying the belief using concrete evidence. *(Ch. 17)*

offence recognition   Analyzing evidence—reported information, your own observations, and physical evidence—to determine whether an offence has occurred. *(Ch. 1)*

officer-in-charge (OIC)   The officer in command of the police force responsible for the lock-up or other place to which an accused is taken after arrest; a peace officer designated by the OIC; often the staff sergeant or sergeant who is the supervisor of the on-duty shift or platoon of officers. *(Ch. 11)*

oral consent   Conversation that is not written or signed in a statement form but recorded verbatim by the officer in a notebook and then signed by the consenting person. *(Ch. 15)*

paraphrasing   Condensing or summarizing a verbatim response into a general statement. *(Ch. 5, 17)*

perimeter   The privately owned property surrounding a dwelling-house; a place separate from the actual house. *(Ch. 8)*

place   In relation to search, a dwelling-house, the perimeter of a dwelling-house, a building, a receptacle, or a vehicle. *(Ch. 14)*

plain-view doctrine   A search-without-warrant authority found in case law authorizing a peace officer who is lawfully on any premises, whether pursuant to a warrant or otherwise, to seize any evidence that is in plain view and that is inadvertently found. *(Ch. 17)*

preliminary hearing   An opportunity for a Justice to determine whether sufficient evidence exists to conduct a trial and for the accused to analyze the prosecution's evidence before trial. The purpose is not to determine guilt or innocence. *(Ch. 13)*

***prima facie* case**   All facts-in-issue of the offence have been proved; sufficient evidence to convict. *(Ch. 17)*

primary grounds   With respect to release of an accused, concern about ensuring a court appearance. Having no primary grounds means having no concern that the accused will not attend court. *(Ch. 11)*

prior announcement   With respect to lawful entry into a dwelling-house, the act of making a proper announcement. *(Ch. 8)*

proper announcement   Communicating notice of presence (knocking on the door or ringing the bell), notice of authority (identifying as police officer), and notice of purpose (stating reason for entry). *(Ch. 17)*

real evidence   A physical item or any tangible item that exists as an independent entity. Blood and hair samples are often categorized as real evidence. *(Ch. 17)*

reasonable grounds (to arrest)   Formerly known as "reasonable and probable grounds." Though not defined by statute, the phrase is defined in case law as "a set of facts or circumstances which would cause a person of ordinary and prudent judgment to believe beyond a mere suspicion." This may be the most significant term in Canadian criminal law because it sets the mandatory standard needed to execute a number of police authorities, including arrest, charge, search, and seizure. *(Ch. 3)*

reasonable person   The average person in the community, but only when that community's current mood is reasonable. *(Ch. 17)*

reasonable suspicion to detain   A level of belief that is stronger than mere suspicion. It involves concrete circumstantial evidence, associated with a crime in progress, that connects a specific person to a specific offence. Formerly called articulable cause. The corresponding custody authority is investigative detention. *(Ch. 1)*

receptacle   A structure that is used to contain property, such as a shed or locker. *(Ch. 17)*

recognizance   A release condition or requirement—for example, a deposit from the accused of an amount not exceeding $500.00 if he or she lives inside the province or no more than 200 kilometres from the place of arrest and custody. *(Ch. 11)*

release   The termination of arrest, detention, and custody; restoring one's freedom. *(Ch. 11)*

return   The act of reporting back to a Justice after executing a search warrant and seizing items so that he or she can determine the disposition of the items by ordering their detention or release to the lawful owner; bringing the seized items, or a written report, to a Justice as soon as practicable after the seizure is made as the result of a search warrant. *(Ch. 16)*

RICE   An informal term, an acronym not found in the *Criminal Code*, representing four factors that must be considered in determining whether an arrested person must be released or whether continued detention and custody are necessary in the public interest. *(Ch. 11)*

search   Defined in case law as looking for things, including spoken words, to be used as evidence of an offence. *(Ch. 14, 17)*

search incident to arrest   The search of a person and the immediate surroundings after a lawful arrest. *(Ch. 5)*

search incident to investigative detention   A legal authority to conduct a partial search of a person, without consent, if an officer has reasonable grounds for believing that his or her own safety or the safety of others is at risk. This authority is not automatic when a lawful detention has occurred and it does not authorize a search for evidence. *(Ch. 5)*

search warrant   A written document that provides police with judicial authorization to enter and search a specific place for specific items, and to seize any items found that are evidence of a criminal offence. *(Ch. 16)*

secondary grounds   With respect to the release of an accused, concern about protecting the public—specifically, concern or risk that the accused, if released, will commit a criminal offence or interfere with the administration of justice. Determining that secondary grounds exist means that there are reasonable grounds for believing that the accused may commit a criminal offence and endanger the public. *(Ch. 11)*

section 487 C.C. search warrant   Commonly referred to as a *Criminal Code* search warrant, it is used to search any type of place for physical items that are evidence of an offence; the most basic kind of search warrant. *(Ch. 16)*

seizure Defined in case law as "the taking of a thing from a person, by a public authority, without that person's consent." *(Ch. 14)*

summary conviction offence A minor criminal offence such as "Cause a disturbance" or "Food fraud." An officer has authority to arrest only if he or she finds committing. Police officers have no authority to arrest on reasonable grounds, nor do they have authority to arrest to prevent a summary conviction offence from occurring. *(Ch. 2)*

tacit knowledge Experience-based expertise. *(Ch. 9)*

telewarrant A warrant obtained, out of necessity, by telephone or other means of telecommunications. *(Ch. 16)*

trace device A device used by a telecommunications company that can determine the source of a telephone call by identifying the address and name of the person to whom the phone circuit is registered. An investigative means of determining a suspect in a complaint of "Obscene phone calls" in order that a number recorder (DNR) can be installed to monitor the outgoing phone calls made by the suspect. *(Ch. 16)*

tracking device Any device that may help ascertain the location of any thing or person, by electronic or other means, when the device is installed in or on anything; a surveillance device. *(Ch. 16)*

tracking warrant A warrant that any citizen or police officer may obtain to authorize the installation, maintenance, and removal of a tracking device, in or on anything, including a thing carried, used, or worn by any person; and the monitoring of the installed tracking device. *(Ch. 17)*

unconditional release A warning or "break" given to the offender; the offender will not be required to attend court in answer to a charge. Considered an alternative means of solving a crime or resolving an incident. *(Ch. 11)*

undertaking A release document that may be issued at Level 2. *(Ch. 11)*

unreasonable search/seizure Unlawful search or seizure; conducted without any lawful authority. *(Ch. 14)*

valid consent *See* consent.

vehicles Cars, trucks, and other motor vehicles that are not designed to be used as a temporary or permanent residence and are not being used as a residence, whether being operated or parked and unoccupied. *(Ch. 17)*

verbatim Direct, word-for-word quotation including all questions, comments, and responses; the opposite of paraphrasing. *(Ch. 15)*

voluntary accompaniment Valid consent given by a person to a police officer to accompany the officer or remain with the officer for some law enforcement purpose—for example, questioning. It is neither an arrest nor detention and therefore the person may revoke the consent at any time. *(Ch. 4)*

warrantless search A search without judicial authorization and without consent; search without a warrant. *(Ch. 17)*

wording An informal term for a statement that alleges one count; a lengthy statement that includes each specific fact-in-issue that defines the offence and the legal name (not the short form) of the offence. *(Ch. 13)*

written consent Conversation that is written in a statement form by a police officer and then signed by a consenting person. *(Ch. 15)*

Index